Interest Groups in American Politics

Americans rail against so-called special interests, but at the same time many members of society are themselves represented in one form or another by organized groups trying to affect the policymaking process. This concise but thorough text demonstrates that interest groups are involved in the political system at all levels of government—federal, state, and local—and in all aspects of political activity, from election campaigns to agenda setting to lawmaking to policy implementation. Rather than an anomaly or distortion of the political system, it is a normal and healthy function of a pluralist society and democratic governance. Nonetheless, Nownes warns of the dangers of unwatched interest group activity, especially in the realms of the electoral process and issue advocacy.

Interest Groups in American Politics, Second Edition, is grounded by the role of information in interest group activity, a theme that runs through the entire book. This much anticipated revision of Nownes's text retains a student-friendly tone and thoroughly updates the references to interest group research, as well as adds a new chapter on the connections between interest groups and political parties. Numerous figures and tables throughout the book help students visualize important trends and information.

Anthony J. Nownes is a professor of political science at the University of Tennessee, Knoxville. He is the author of numerous works on interest group politics at the federal, state, and local level and is an award-winning teacher.

Interest Groups in American Politics

Pressure and Power

SECOND EDITION

ANTHONY J. NOWNES

Routledge
Taylor & Francis Group

NEW YORK AND LONDON

Second edition published 2013
by Routledge
711 Third Avenue, New York, NY 10017

Simultaneously published in the UK
by Routledge
2 Park Square, Milton Park, Abingdon, Oxon OX14 4RN

Routledge is an imprint of the Taylor & Francis Group, an informa business

© 2013 Taylor & Francis

First edition published by Houghton Mifflin 2001

Library of Congress Cataloging in Publication Data
Nownes, Anthony J.
   Interest groups in American politics : pressure and power /
   Anthony J. Nownes.
      p. cm.
   Includes bibliographical references and index.
   1. Pressure groups—United States. 2. Lobbying—United States. I. Title.
   JK1118.N68 2012
   322.4′30973—dc23   2012016780

ISBN: 978-0-415-89425-8 (hbk)
ISBN: 978-0-415-89426-5 (pbk)
ISBN: 978-0-203-80682-1 (ebk)

Typeset in Avenir and Dante
by Keystroke, Station Road, Codsall, Wolverhampton

Certified Sourcing
www.sfiprogram.org
SFI-00453

Printed and bound in the United States of America
by Edwards Brothers, Inc.

Contents

Preface

Famous Frenchman Alexis de Tocqueville remarked in 1834 that nowhere in the world were associations more ubiquitous and more important than they were in the United States. Over 175 years later, evidence that de Tocqueville's point still is incisive is everywhere. In Washington, DC, as well as in states, cities, counties, and everywhere else government decisions are made, interest groups are omnipresent. Their lobbyists roam the halls of government buildings, their advertisements fill the airwaves during election season, their membership pleas clutter our mailboxes, and their influence is blamed for everything from global warming and the financial crisis, to high gas prices and protracted war in the Middle East.

I have one very simple goal in writing this book—to provide an accessible, reasonably comprehensive overview of interest group politics in the United States to the reader with only a rudimentary knowledge of the subject. I do not assume that the reader knows *nothing* about American politics. Rather, I assume that the reader knows the very basics of the American governmental system—things such as how the American system of government is organized, what is in the Constitution, what powers the various branches and levels of government have, and how elections work. But I assume very little knowledge of interest groups. If you are a student reading this book, I assume you have taken a course or two in American politics. But I assume the courses you have taken touch only tangentially on interest group politics. If you are a curious layperson—in other words, not a student—I assume you know a little about American politics, but not a whole lot about interest groups.

Because I assume very little in the way of knowledge of interest group politics, I try to keep things straightforward here. My experiences teaching over the years have taught me that many people—even many intelligent people who know a lot about politics—simply do not know even the most basic facts about interest groups in American politics. This is not necessarily a terrible thing—it arguably is more important to learn about the president, and Congress, and the Supreme Court, and federalism, and the way your local government works than it is to learn about interest groups. But it means that a book like this needs to do something other than discuss the latest research on interest groups and wade into theoretical controversies; it must give readers the raw material they need to understand the *substance* of interest group politics. And that is what I do here—I provide a substantive overview of interest group politics in America. To be sure, along the way I will spend some time discussing theoretical issues and exploring theoretical developments. But my immediate goal is to provide you with the information you need to explore these issues and developments yourself, should you care to do so in the future.

There are not a huge number of books out there that cover the subject of interest group politics. But there are a few. What sets this book apart? First, and yes, this is a theme, this book is *accessible*. I want you to be able to read it, understand it, and use it. I like big words and expansive theories as much as the next person (maybe more). But this is not the place for these things. I think theories of interest group formation, and maintenance, and influence are fascinating and important. But I think you need to understand the basic stuff before you can understand and evaluate these theories. Second, this book is *comprehensive*. By this I mean that I try not to leave anything out. Many books on interest groups say a lot about interest groups in Washington, but little or nothing about interest groups in states and localities across the United States. From the very beginning of this book I make the point that interest groups operate everywhere in America, and I try to remind the reader of this fact as much as possible. You really cannot understand interest group politics in America by focusing narrowly on interest groups in Washington. This book also is comprehensive in that it examines *all the things* that interest groups do. Many books focus on lobbying but ignore the other things that interest groups do (such as fundraising, earning a profit, and monitoring government). To understand where interest groups fit into the American governmental system, you must understand all that they do. Third, this book is *topical*. I try, whenever possible, to reference current events and contemporary politics in my discussions of interest group politics. I try, for example, to use examples that are, as they say, "ripped from the headlines." This said, I want to acknowledge that the book is not weighed down with examples. If you are using this book as a textbook in a class, chances are that the class is not a standalone interest group class. Many courses that cover interest groups, for example, also cover political parties. Thus, I realize that I cannot write a 500-page tome and expect anybody to read it from start to finish. So I tried hard to keep this book on the brief side (while attempting maximum coverage, of course), and thus also to keep it on the inexpensive side.

Before I begin, I feel compelled to say a few things about what you will find in the pages that follow. First, I want to warn you that I use the word "I" a lot in the rest of this book. There are two reasons for this. One is that I do not like the passive voice. Another is that I study interest groups and I refer to my own studies several times in this book. I teach a course in interest group politics regularly, and I have found over the years that students like the stories I tell about my own experiences studying interest groups. I hope your students will like them as well. Second, a couple of pretty reprehensible groups show up on the pages of this book. One is NAMBLA—the North American Man/Boy Love Association. I do not include this group here for salacious or sensationalistic reasons. I do so because its existence makes an important point about interest group politics in the United States in a way that no other group can. Another questionable group you will encounter is the Westboro Baptist Church—the "religious" interest group that pickets the funerals of America's fallen heroes. Again, I include the group here because its existence makes an important point about interest group politics in America. Third, because most classes that cover interest groups cover political parties as well, I include a chapter on the relationships between political parties and interest groups (Chapter 8). The chapter is rather brief, but it tries to make a few general points about the differences between parties and interest groups, and about how political parties and interest groups interact. If you want to deal with definitional issues early on or wish to say something about political parties before getting to the end of this book, you can simply assign Chapter 8 after Chapter 1 or Chapter 2, or maybe even first. Fourth, some of the terminology I use here is my own, and is not widely accepted. For example, Chapter 6 is about what I call "electoral lobbying." Most other books on interest groups eschew this term, instead including chapters on "interest groups in elections" or "interest groups in campaigns." The term "electoral lobbying" is, in my opinion, very useful because it helps reinforce the point that interest groups use a large variety of methods to try to affect government decisions. I hope the term does not throw you off. Similarly, I use the term "indirect lobbying" for lobbying directed at the public rather than at government decision-makers. Many scholars and journalists use the term "grassroots lobbying" instead. I prefer my term for reasons I discuss in Chapter 7. There are a few other places in this book where I use my own term for something, but when I do this I am careful to define the term so you will know exactly what I am talking about.

Finally, I must give due thanks to the many people who have helped me over the years. First and foremost I wish to thank the hundreds of lobbyists and interest group personnel I have surveyed and interviewed since I started doing this. They have taught me a great deal about interest group politics, and I never fail to be amazed at how generous they are with their time and their insights. Second, I owe many thanks to my mentors, especially the amazing Allan J. Cigler ("faculty dad"), who has forgotten more about interest groups than I will ever know; and Paul E. Johnson (P.J.), one of the smartest people I have ever met. Third, I wish to thank my many co-authors and collaborators from across the years, including Robert M. Alexander, Mike Atkinson, Shari Garber Bax, William K. "Bubba" Cheek, David Elkins, Joseph Ellis, Patricia Freeland, Jim "Cook" Gilchrist, Colin Glennon, Darren Halpin, Sue Howerton, David J. Houston, Nathan Kelly, Daniel Lipinski, Jill MacMillan, Jana Morgan, Emil Nagengast, Cary Nailing, Grant Neeley, Adam Newmark, Mikel Norris, Elsa Nownes, Laura Nownes, Molly Nownes, Sara Nownes, William Nownes, and Marc Schwerdt. And yes, even Chris Cooper. And of course, I owe a great deal to the students who have taught me so much over the years, including Sina Bahadoran, Regis Boyle, Clint Cantrell, Townsend Collins, Brent Hall, and Garrett Johnson. All of these people deserve some of the credit if this is any good. But they deserve none of the blame for anything that is wrong.

Interest Groups in the United States

1

On April 20, 2010, *The Deepwater Horizon*, an offshore oil drilling rig, blew up. The rig, which was located approximately 400 miles off the Louisiana coast in the Gulf of Mexico, was drilling what is called an "exploratory well" almost one mile below the ocean's surface. Just before 10 a.m. on the 20th, highly pressurized methane gas burst out of the drill column and then caught fire. Most of the people who were working on the rig were rescued. But eleven people were never found. They are presumed dead. The fire raged for a day and a half, until on the morning of April 22nd, the crippled rig sank. On April 23rd, the company that leased the well, BP (formerly known as British Petroleum), reported that there was no oil leaking from either the sunken rig or the well. By the 24th, however, it was clear that BP was mistaken. No one knows for certain how many gallons of oil leaked from the wellhead before it was finally capped on July 15, 2010. But experts agree that the spill was the largest in U.S. history, far surpassing the *Exxon Valdez* spill that dominated headlines for a time in 1989. In all, hundreds of millions of gallons of oil spewed into the Gulf of Mexico. In the weeks and months after the explosion, the effects of the spill became obvious. Thousands of square miles of ocean were soiled with oil, endangering fish and other wildlife. In June, oil reached the Louisiana coast. By early July, oil had reached Alabama, Mississippi, and Texas.

The oil spill was disastrous for many people. It was most disastrous, of course, for the eleven workers who lost their lives. It was also disastrous for many of the people who live and work near the coastal areas of the Gulf states. But for some people the oil spill was a boon. Who? The answer is *lobbyists*. In the wake of the oil spill, BP, many environmental interest groups, and interest groups representing oil companies substantially ramped up their lobbying activities. Environmental groups hoped to use the spill as a justification for policies they had long championed—policies that would tighten regulations on oil drilling. Transocean Ltd., the company that owned the rig and leased it to BP, retained the services of a lobbying firm called Capitol Hill Consulting Group to help it stave off stricter federal regulations and to rehabilitate its image with the public and government decision-makers.[1] For its part, BP hired a slew of well-connected lobbyists in an effort to preempt punitive policies proposed by various Washington decision-makers intent on punishing the company for the spill.[2] The American Petroleum Institute, which represents energy producers including BP, stepped up its lobbying operations to make sure the federal government did not adopt new and onerous regulations that would add to the cost of doing business. Other organizations stepped up their lobbying efforts as well, including shallow water oil drilling companies that used the spill as an opportunity to tout their method of drilling as a safer and preferable alternative to the deep water drilling that led to the disaster.[3] In short, what was a disaster for many people was a boon to lobbyists.

The Paradox of Interest Groups

Oil spills do not happen every day. And a gigantic oil spill is a once-in-a-generation phenomenon. Thus, it is certainly *not* the case that the events that took place during the summer of 2010 represented "business as usual" in the nation's capital. Yet in one way the lobbying that took place *did* embody "business as usual"; for Washington, DC is a place where frenzied lobbying activity takes place almost all the time. For better or worse, in Washington as well as in cities, counties, towns, and states across America, interest groups and their lobbyists are everywhere government decisions are made.

The ubiquity of interest groups and their lobbyists worries many Americans. Lobbyists—the people who represent interest groups in front of government decision-makers—are not popular. Public opinion polls show that most Americans hold them in lower esteem even than auto mechanics, lawyers, and members of Congress. Americans believe that lobbyists are about as ethical and honest as car salespeople.[4] Interest groups themselves are similarly despised by the public. While the military, the police, and small businesses generally are well respected by most Americans, interest groups are scorned.[5]

Ordinary Americans are not the only ones who disdain interest groups. Politicians scorn them as well. Hardly a day passes without some high-ranking public official decrying the impact of "special interests" on government decisions. Presidents have proven especially contemptuous of interest groups. Every president since George Washington has taken time out from his busy schedule to castigate lobbyists and the organizations they represent. Even before the Constitution was adopted, for example, future president James Madison warned that interest groups posed a great danger to the republic because they worked to gain advantage for themselves at the expense of others.[6] Similarly, upon retiring from office, President Dwight Eisenhower warned of the pernicious influence of powerful organizations that were part of "the military-industrial complex." More recently, throughout the 1990s, President Clinton regularly denounced conservative groups that dredged up allegations of philandering. And President Barack Obama, frustrated by slow action on some of his signature initiatives, has repeatedly taken special interest groups to task.

Why all the fuss? What's *wrong* with interest groups attempting to influence government decisions? After all, most of us support *some* sort of interest group—be it conservative, liberal, moderate, or "none of the above." In fact, many of us actually *belong* to interest groups, and few of us can deny that there are at least some interest groups working to further our political goals. In the aftermath of the BP oil spill, for example, almost all possible viewpoints were represented by interest groups. As the vignette that opened this chapter attests, some interest groups lobbied for strict punishment of the people and companies responsible for the spill. And some groups lobbied for more regulations on oil drilling, while others lobbied for a more measured approach to punishment and less onerous regulations. This is the case in many political battles—there are groups on all sides of the issue.

The theme of this book is that there is something paradoxical about the way Americans view interest groups. On the one hand, all of us are sympathetic to *some* interest groups. On the other hand, most of us say we hate lobbyists and the interest groups they represent. Why the contradiction? What explains this paradox—a paradox I call "the paradox of interest groups"? The answer lies in the complicated nature of interest group politics in the United States. To explain this paradox, it is necessary to understand precisely what interest groups are, where they come from, how they operate, and the extent to which they influence government decisions.

My goal in writing this book is to provide readers with the information they need to explain the paradox of interest groups. In the remainder of this chapter I will provide the raw material necessary to deal with the information that appears in the chapters that follow. I begin, as they say, at the beginning—with the very meaning of the term "interest group." From here, I will define some other terms that will come in handy. Finally, I conclude with a brief tour of the universe of interest groups in America.

What is an Interest Group?

When most people think of an interest group, they think of an organization such as the American Civil Liberties Union (ACLU), the Christian Coalition, or the National Rifle Association (NRA)—that is, a politically active, mass membership organization. This narrow view of interest groups, however, overlooks the bulk of organizational activity that occurs in Washington and in states and localities across the country. Most important, it fails to acknowledge the vast numbers of *non*-membership organizations active in American politics. It excludes, for example, business firms, some of which are very active politically. In addition, this narrow view implies that politically active organizations consist of individuals. This is problematic because many political organizations in America do *not* consist of individuals. The members of the Chamber of Commerce of the United States, for example, a Washington, DC lobbying behemoth, are mostly small businesses.[7] Finally, this narrow view implies that a political group's members (if it has members) share goals. This, it turns out, is not always true. Research on why people join interest groups has found that in many organizations members do not share the goals of their fellow members or the group's leaders. Many people who join the AARP (formerly the American Association of Retired Persons), for example, join not because they share the goals of other members or the group's leaders, but because they value the hotel, insurance, and rental car discounts that come with membership.

So just what *is* an interest group? Here, the term "interest group" is defined as *any non-party organization that engages in political activity*. There are three components to this definition: non-party, organization, and political activity. To say an organization is a *non-party* organization is to say that it is not a formal part of a political party. I will say more about this below (and in Chapter 8). But for now, it shall suffice to say that to be an interest group an organization cannot be formally affiliated with a political party. To say a group is *organized* means that it has a budget, employees, and an office (if it can afford one). Groups that are not organized are not considered interest groups. Women as a group, for example, though they share several traits and may even share some ideas about government policies, do not constitute an interest group because not *all* women belong to the same organized group that engages in political activity. The National Organization for Women (NOW), in contrast, *is* an interest group. The crucial difference here is that while all women as a group are not organized, NOW is. The final component of my definition is *political activity*. This component is important because the main difference between interest groups and other types of organizations is that the former engage in political activity. What is *political activity*? The short answer is *lobbying*, which is defined as *attempting to influence government decisions*. As Chapters 5–7 will show, interest groups engage in a large variety of activities to influence government decisions. In this book, I consider all such activities lobbying. Unfortunately, determining if a group is politically active is sometimes not easy. Organizations such as the American Heart Association and the American Red Cross, for example, dedicate most of their time and energy to helping people, but nonetheless spend *some* of their time trying to influence government decisions. Are these organizations considered interest groups? My answer to this question is an emphatic yes. Again, an interest group is *any* organization that attempts to influence government decisions. And just because an organization's primary purpose is not political in nature, it does not mean it is not an interest group.

To help illustrate the differences between interest groups and other types of groups, I have created Table 1.1, which contains a sampling of groups that are not interest groups. The table contains both groups that are not organized and organized groups that do not engage in political activity. One particularly noteworthy entry in the table is "college students." Though you often hear people talk about college students as if they comprise an interest group, the reality is far different. Obviously, college students as a group are not organized—in other words, not all college students belong to one organized group. While some specific groups of college students are organized, the mass of college students throughout the United States is not.

Table 1.1   Selected Groups that are *Not* Interest Groups

Group	Reason that group is not an interest group	What is it then?
1. Association of Coffee Mill Enthusiasts	Does not engage in political activity	Hobby club
2. Beach Boys Fan Club	Does not engage in political activity	Fan club
3. The Chi Psi Fraternity	Does not engage in political activity	Fraternity
4. College Students	Is not organized	Unorganized group
5. Environmentalists	Is not organized	Unorganized group
6. Farmers	Is not organized	Unorganized group

Sources: Organizational websites at http://www.antiquecoffeegrinders.net/; http://www.beachboysfanclub.com/; http://www.chipsi.org/. All sites accessed on February 16, 2011.

The term "interest group" is the most important one in this book. Before going any further, however, I need to define a few other important terms. First, there is "political party." At first glance, political parties seem to fit the broad definition of interest group pretty well. After all, political parties *are* organized, and they engage in political activity. Yet it is important to recognize that political parties are not interest groups and interest groups are not political parties. What is it about political parties that make them different from interest groups? The answer is: political parties nominate candidates for election to public office. This is not to say that interest groups are not involved in election campaigns. As you will see subsequently, many are. But interest groups do not nominate candidates for office. Political parties do. Another important difference between political parties and interest groups is that political parties tend to have a much broader focus than most interest groups do. Both major parties in the United States, for example, take positions on literally hundreds of issues—everything from abortion to trade policy. In contrast, most interest groups have a relatively narrow focus and take positions on only one or a handful of issues.

Another important term used in this book is "interest." In the most general sense, an interest refers to any attitude, value, or preference.[8] It is important to note, however, that not all interests are of concern to people (like me) who study interest groups. Interest group scholars are only concerned with interests that have some relevance to government decisions. As political scientist Robert Salisbury puts it:

> it is the perceived or anticipated effects of policy—government action or inaction including all its symbolic forms as well as more tangible allocations—upon values that create politically relevant interests. Similarly, interested behavior expresses policy-related purpose, sometimes very broadly defined and sometimes highly specific and detailed.[9]

Following Salisbury's lead, I define the term "interest" as *an attitude, value, or preference with some relevance to government decisions.* I must point out two important things about interests. First, interests in this country may be represented by interest *groups* to varying degrees. In other words, some interests may have large, powerful, and perhaps multiple organizations working on their behalf, while others may have either very few or no organizations working on their behalf. Second, both individuals *and* institutions have interests. While most of us recognize that groups of individuals have interests, few of us stop to think that institutions also have interests. Here, an "institution" is defined as *a non-membership organization.* Business firms, colleges and universities, and governmental entities (such as counties or states) are institutions. Institutions are distinguished by the fact that they have interests separate from those of the individuals who comprise them. Businesses, for example, have political interests separate from those of the people who work for them. Likewise, colleges and universities have interests that are distinct from the interests of school administrators, faculty, staff, and students. I will have more to say about institutions later in this chapter.

One final useful term is "lobbyist." A lobbyist is *an individual who represents an interest group (or many different interest groups) before government.* In the broadest terms, every time you contact a government decision-maker to express your opinion you are lobbying. But this does not make you a lobbyist. The term "lobbyist" generally is reserved for an individual who represents an interest group when he/she contacts a government decision-maker. There are two types of lobbyists. *Professional lobbyists* lobby for a living, while *amateur lobbyists* lobby voluntarily. Many organizations use volunteer lobbyists because professional lobbyists can be expensive. Lobbyists—who they are and what they do—are the subjects of Chapters 4–7.

I will conclude this section with a term that will *not* come in handy in subsequent chapters. That term is "special interest." Any discussion of interest groups inevitably turns to the topic of so-called "special interests," which are sometimes referred to as "narrow special interests" or "selfish special interests." Generally, when people use the term "special interest," they use it pejoratively to imply that a certain interest group (or set of interest groups) has goals antithetical to the *public interest,* which is broadly defined as *an interest held in common by all members of society.*[10] For example, a supporter of gun control will decry the activities of the NRA, calling it a "special interest" group. Similarly, an opponent of gun control will disparage groups working for tighter regulations on gun ownership as "special interest" groups. There is a huge problem with the term "special interest." That problem is this: to call a specific interest group a "special interest" group is to imply that it has goals antithetical to the public interest. This is a problem because to say that an interest group has goals antithetical to the public interest is to imply that it has goals antithetical to the interests of *virtually everyone in this country.* Consider the following example. Each time labor unions push for a higher federal minimum wage they face opposition from business groups. Thus, they are not working for the public interest if by public interest we mean an interest held in common by all members of society. This is silly. Simply because labor unions face opposition does not mean that they are working against the interests of every man, woman, and child in the United States. It means only that they are active on an issue about which there is no public consensus. In America today there are many issues about which there is no public consensus. My point is this: the term "special interest" is fraught with baggage. It is not a term that is very useful for a serious discussion of interest groups. Rather, it is a term that is useful primarily to pundits, politicians, and interest group "spinmeisters" who wish to demonize their enemies. Consequently, I will eschew the use of this term for the remainder of this book.

The Universe of Interest Groups

The universe of interest groups consists of the myriad organizations that fit my definition of "interest group." No one knows for sure how many interest groups there are in the United States, but conservative estimates put the number at well over 200,000. What *are* all these groups and whom do they represent? In what follows, I will answer this question by examining the fifteen major types of interest groups active in the United States today. There may be some groups out there that do not fit into one of these categories, but most do.

For-Profit Business Firms

For-profit business firms are *enterprises that make, buy, or sell goods and/or services for profit*. Many for-profit business firms have an abiding interest in politics and government, and thus constitute interest groups.[11] The reason so many business firms take an interest in politics is that they are profoundly affected by government decisions. Every time the federal government raises the minimum wage, for example, businesses big and small across the United States are affected.

A business that wants to lobby can do its own lobbying, hire a lobbying firm to do its lobbying, or do both. Businesses that can afford to do so generally do their own lobbying and form separate Government Affairs, Government Relations, or Public Affairs divisions. Many *Fortune* 500 companies, for example, including Boeing, Ford Motor Company, IBM, and Procter & Gamble, have their own lobbyists.[12] Businesses that cannot afford or simply do not want to have large-scale public affairs divisions may hire lobbying firms to represent them.[13] Many foreign business firms also lobby in the United States. Companies such as Bayer (German), British Aerospace (British), and Nissan Motor Co. (Japanese), for example, have large American business operations and are quite active in American politics.

Non-Profit Business Firms

Non-profit business firms are *enterprises that make, buy, or sell goods and/or services, but do not do so for profit.* Non-profit business firms look and act a lot like for-profit business firms, but are different in that they do not distribute any surplus funds to owners or shareholders, but rather put these funds back into the business. Among the best-known types of non-profit businesses in the United States are hospital systems and medical centers (for example, the Kaiser Foundation Hospitals, the Mayo Clinic, and New York Presbyterian Hospital), health insurance companies (e.g., Blue Shield of California, Blue Cross/Blue Shield of Tennessee), and museums (e.g., Metropolitan Museum of Art, Museum of Fine Arts, Houston).

Like for-profit businesses, many non-profit businesses have an abiding interest in politics and government and thus constitute interest groups. Also like for-profit businesses, non-profit businesses are affected by government and politics, and this is why many of them lobby. A quick perusal of some state lobbyist registration lists shows that many non-profit businesses lobby. For example, in California, Blue Shield of California, the Museum of Latin American Art, and the Santa Barbara Museum of Natural History (among others) are all registered to lobby state government.[14] And in Texas, Baylor Health Care System, and FirstCare Health Plans (among others)[15] are registered to lobby state government. Non-profit businesses lobby at the local and federal level as well.

Trade Associations

Some business lobbying is conducted not by individual businesses, but by trade associations. A trade association is *an organized group of businesses.*[16] There are two basic types of trade associations. A *peak association* represents broad business interests, while a *single-industry trade association* represents businesses in a specific industry. Two of the biggest and best-known trade associations in the United States are the Chamber of Commerce of the United States and the National Association of Manufacturers (NAM), both of which are peak associations. Both NAM and the Chamber have massive memberships and work on issues that affect businesses of many kinds and sizes.

Single-industry trade associations are far more numerous than peak associations. Practically every industry you can think of has its own trade association. Petroleum asphalt producers, for example, belong to the Asphalt Institute. Similarly, pesticide manufacturers belong to CropLife America (formerly the

National Agricultural Chemicals Association), and businesses in the frozen food industry belong to the American Frozen Food Institute. Some single-industry trade groups have names that border on the comical. But while groups like the Association of the Nonwoven Fabrics Industry, the Beer Institute, and the Glutamate Association may have humorous names, they take their political activity quite seriously.

Few sectors of the American economy are home to more trade associations than the agricultural sector. One of the best-known and largest agriculture groups in the United States is the American Farm Bureau Federation (AFBF), a federated peak association with several million members. Other influential single-industry agricultural trade associations are the National Association of Wheat Growers, the National Corn Growers Association, and the National Cattlemen's Beef Association.[17]

Trade associations lobby government for the same reason that individual businesses do: because government activity affects business interests. Government activity is of such interest to corporate America, in fact, that many business firms lobby on their own *and* belong to trade associations.

Labor Unions

A labor union is *an organization of workers gathered together to secure better wages, benefits, and working conditions from employers.* Though labor unions are not organized primarily to influence government decisions, many are nonetheless heavily involved in politics. Traditionally, manufacturing industries like automobiles, rubber, and steel were the most heavily unionized in the United States. Today, most of the largest and most powerful labor unions represent public sector employees—people who work for the government. The National Education Association (and its state and local affiliates), for example, has over 3 million members and an annual budget of over $300 million.[18] Other prominent public sector unions represent postal workers, prison guards, and sanitation workers. None of this is to say that "old-line" unions are no longer powerful. The International Brotherhood of Teamsters, which represents over 1 million workers involved in transportation, is still very active and politically powerful.[19] Autoworkers, garment workers, and steelworkers also remain organized and politically active.

The best-known labor union in the United States is not really a labor union at all. The AFL-CIO (American Federation of Labor and Congress of Industrial Organizations), which is often called a labor union, is actually a federated *coalition* of labor unions (more about coalitions later).[20] The AFL-CIO uses some of the money it collects from member unions to engage in political activity on their behalf.

Professional Associations

A professional association is *an organization that represents the interests of people in a specific profession*. Unfortunately, there is no good definition of "profession," and the line between a "profession" and a "job" or an "occupation" is not at all clear. As a result, we are left to define "professional" by example. Generally, doctors, lawyers, nurses and other relatively highly paid, well-educated workers are considered professionals.

Two of the largest and most powerful professional associations in the United States are the American Medical Association (AMA, which represents doctors), and the American Bar Association (ABA, which represents lawyers). Each of these groups represents the broad interests of individuals in their profession, and provides goods and services to members. Though many professional associations are active in Washington, most concentrate their efforts at the state level. This is the case because the licensing of professionals is for the most part a state government responsibility.

Citizen Groups

A citizen group is *an interest group that is open to any citizen*. Citizen groups often refer to themselves as "public interest groups," but this term is so encumbered with meaning that interest group scholars tend to eschew it. The citizen group universe is incredibly varied, and contains groups representing children, consumers, the elderly, environmentalists, pro- and anti-abortion activists, pro- and anti-gun control activists, taxpayers, and myriad others. Citizen groups are what most people think of when they think of *interest groups*: many are explicitly political in nature, consist of individual members, and have meetings as well as rallies and social events.

The largest citizen group in the United States is the AARP. At first glance, it appears that the AARP does not fit my definition of citizen group because not anyone can join—you must be 50 years old to become a member. But because all of us (barring bad luck) will eventually reach age 50, the AARP is considered a citizen group. The AARP, which represents the interests of the elderly, is a massive organization. It has approximately 40 million members (that's over 10 percent of the American population),[21] dozens of lobbyists in Washington, offices in all 50 states, and an annual budget of almost $1.5 *billion*. The AARP spent over $20 million lobbying the federal government in 2010.[22] Other prominent citizen groups include the National Association for the Advancement of Colored People (NAACP), the NRA, the National Right to Life Association, the National Wildlife Federation (NWF), and the Sierra Club.

Think Tanks

A think tank is *an institution that conducts and disseminates research in an effort to affect government decisions.* In layperson's terms, a think tank is a group of politically motivated smart people organized to study things. Many think tanks have no members per se, but rather consist of "scholars" or "fellows" who conduct research, the goal of which is to affect government decisions. Among the best-known think tanks in the United States are the American Enterprise Institute, the Brookings Institution, and the Heritage Foundation. Most think tanks have an explicit ideology that is reflected in their work.[23] The American Enterprise Institute, for example, acknowledges its "free market conservative" ideology, and only publishes research that supports this ideology. Similarly, the liberal think tank Citizens for Tax Justice acknowledges that it is a "progressive" organization, and publishes research that supports its ideology.[24]

Domestic Governmental Entities

Domestic governmental entities are *interest groups that lobby one layer or part of American government on behalf of another.* Several thousand cities, counties, states, and townships lobby in Washington. All 50 states, for example, lobby in Washington, as do most major cities and many counties. In addition, many cities and counties lobby *state* governments. Governments lobby other governments because one level of government is often affected by the decisions of others. State governments, for example, take a keen interest in federal government policies on issues including environmental regulation, health care, and highway funding. Similarly, cities and counties are very interested in state government policies that affect the way they operate.

Churches and Church Organizations

A church is as *an organization of religious believers*. There are hundreds of thousands of churches scattered across the United States, and some of them engage in political activity. Many local Baptist churches throughout the country, for example, are active on issues such as abortion, civil rights, and religious expression. In addition, many of the largest religious denominations in the United States have their own ecclesiastical "governments" that make church policy, run church programs, and recruit members; many of these "church governments" also lobby. Catholics, Jews, Lutherans and several other major denominations, for example, have national organizations that engage in lobbying. The Catholic Church, for example, is active on issues including the death penalty, disaster relief, food stamps, and public housing. Other less hierarchical denominations also lobby.

Foreign Governmental Entities

Foreign governmental entities are *governmental bodies that lobby the American government on behalf of the government of another country*. Many foreign governments have lobbyists in the United States representing their interests. Not surprisingly, large countries are better represented than small ones. China, for example, retains several lobbyists in Washington, while Burkina Faso (a small African country) has little representation in the United States. Foreign countries have an interest in American politics because many decisions made here affect them. Trade pacts, for example, are negotiated with other countries, as are treaties. A number of other American domestic government decisions also affect foreign countries.

Universities and Colleges

Universities and colleges are *institutions of higher learning*. Colleges and universities exist to educate people. Nonetheless, because these institutions are affected by government decisions, many hire lobbyists. One political issue of great interest to colleges and universities is funding. Public colleges and universities receive some of their money from the government. Many, for example, are funded partially by state tax revenues. Moreover, virtually all are funded partially by student tuition, the level of which is set by state government decision-makers. Universities and colleges receive other forms of government support as well. The federal government, for example, through institutions such as the National Aeronautics and Space Administration (NASA), the National Endowment for the Humanities, and the National Science Foundation provides grants for university- and college-based research. Moreover, the federal government's student loan programs indirectly provide money to colleges and universities.

Coalitions

A coalition is *a loose collection of individuals and/or organizations "that cooperates to accomplish common objectives."*[25] There are two basic types of coalitions. First, there are temporary coalitions, which are fugacious entities that rise up to deal with a particular issue. For example, when Congress was debating President Obama's sweeping health care reforms in 2009 and 2010, a coalition of groups representing "health care professionals" who were not doctors gathered together into a coalition called Coalition for Patients' Rights.[26] Similarly, when the Clean Air Act of 1990 was being hammered out on Capitol Hill, environmental groups that supported the bill formed a coalition called the Clean Air Coalition, while industry groups formed their own opposition coalition called the Clean Air Working Group.[27] Most coalitions include interest groups of various types. The Clean Air Working Group, for example, consisted of both individual businesses and trade associations.

There are also longstanding coalitions, which are groups of individuals and/or interest groups that stay organized for a long time. The AFL-CIO, for example, has been around since 1955. Other examples of longstanding coalitions include: the National League of Cities (a group of cities and state municipal leagues, founded in 1924 to represent the interests of cities before the federal government); the Business and Labor Coalition of New York[28] (a state coalition of business firms, citizen groups, labor unions, professional associations, trade associations, and other types of groups that lobbies on economic development issues in the state of New York); the American Coalition for Ethanol[29] (a coalition of business firms, individuals, trade associations, and other types of groups that lobbies for continued government support of ethanol at the state and federal levels); and the North Carolina Coalition for Lobbying Reform (a coalition of charities, citizen groups, individuals, and other organizations that lobbies for stricter lobbying disclosure rules in North Carolina).[30]

Charities

A charity is defined as *an interest group engaged in the free assistance of the poor, the suffering, or the distressed.* Charities exist primarily to help people. Many, however, are also active politically. Among the best-known politically active charities in the United States are the American Heart Association, the American Lung Association, and the American Red Cross. Charities typically lobby on issues of social justice, and like churches, are often active in health care and disaster relief.

Political Action Committees

A political action committee (PAC) is *an organization set up to collect and spend money on electoral campaigns.* Federal laws, as well as laws in many states, forbid interest groups other than PACs from making direct monetary contributions to candidates for public office.[31] Thus, some types of interest groups (e.g., for-profit business firms, citizen groups, labor unions, professional associations, and trade associations) that wish to make such contributions must set up PACs. PACs that are set up (and subsequently run) by other interest groups are called "affiliated PACs." Many of America's largest business firms have affiliated PACs, as do many of the nation's largest citizen groups, labor unions, professional associations, and trade associations. "Unaffiliated PACs" are PACs that are not affiliated with other interest groups.[32] At the beginning of 2010, there were 4,618 federal PACs registered with the Federal Election Commission.[33] Approximately two-thirds of these PACs were affiliated PACs. In 2009, these PACs raised $555.7 million, and contributed $174.4 million to federal candidates (and remember, this was a non-election year).[34] Several thousand other PACs operate at the sub-national level. Chapter 6 says a great deal more about PACs.

Section 527 Political Organizations

Section 527 political organizations are *organizations that collect money and spend it on issue advocacy and voter mobilization campaigns, mostly in the months before an election.* Section 527 organizations are named after Section 527 of the Internal Revenue Code, which describes them and their activities. Section 527 organizations are designed primarily to help candidates win elections, and are most active during election season. Campaign finance laws in the United States are extremely complex, and I will discuss them in much more detail in Chapter 6.

For now, it must suffice to say that Section 527 organizations are a lot like PACs, except that instead of donating money directly to candidates, they spend money for (or against) candidates. Some 527 organizations are affiliated with other groups (especially citizen groups, labor unions, and coalitions), and some are unaffiliated.

What Type of Group is It?

Many of the politically active organizations you will encounter are easy to categorize. For example, Exxon Mobil is fairly obviously a for-profit business firm (a multi-national corporation to be exact), and the United Auto Workers (UAW) clearly is a labor union. However, some organizations are not so easy to classify, especially at first glance. For example, many people are surprised to learn that many (but not all) Blue Cross/Blue Shield companies are non-profit businesses rather than for-profit businesses. Similarly, many Americans falsely believe that the AFL-CIO is a labor union, when in reality it is a coalition of labor unions. There are many cases like these—cases of organizations that are not easy to classify. Then there are the cases of "hybrid" organizations— organizations that have features of more than one type of group. Consider, for example, AARP, which I classify above as a citizen group. While I stand by my classification, the reality of the situation is a bit more complicated. AARP, which many people think is a single organization, is actually several organizations under one umbrella. Aside from the AARP—the lobbying organization that most people are familiar with—the umbrella organization also comprises AARP Services Inc., a for-profit business firm affiliated with AARP. The company essentially sells AARP-branded products (produced/offered by other companies), and then takes a cut of the profits.[35] So is AARP a citizen group or a for-profit business? Since most people think of the citizen group AARP when they hear the name "AARP," it is generally classified as the former rather than the latter. More accurately it is both. Unfortunately, there simply is not enough space in this book to say a great deal about "hybrid" organizations and the various forms they take. For now, it must suffice to say that in the real world, many organizations are complex and multi-faceted entities.

The classification system here is not perfect (though it is useful in helping to categorize many if not most interest groups) and is not designed to be. Rather, it is designed to help you make sense of the universe of interest groups in America. More specifically, it is designed to help you understand two very important things: (1) the universe of interest groups in the United States is extraordinarily diverse, and (2) groups of many kinds—not just groups formed explicitly for political purposes—lobby government. In the end, we just have to accept that in the real world, unfortunately, it is not easy to categorize each and every politically active organization one encounters. But it is possible in most cases. The typology presented here is designed to help you make sense of a complex and variegated political world.

Box 1.1 What About Lobbying Firms?

In my typology of interest groups in this chapter, I did not include lobbying firms. A lobbying firm essentially is a for-profit business firm that represents clients—that is, interest groups such as business firms, charities, government entities, labor unions, professional associations, and trade associations—before government. In other words, lobbying firms lobby on behalf of the interest groups that hire them. I do not consider lobbying firms interest groups in their own right, because typically when they lobby they are lobbying on behalf of other interest groups, not themselves. Some lobbying firms essentially are divisions or subsidiaries of larger public relations firms or law firms. Some lobbying firms call themselves consulting or public relations or public affairs firms.

There are two basic types of lobbying firms. First, there are general lobbying firms—often large firms that offer a large variety of services to their clients. Many general firms offer various services to their clients that have nothing to do with lobbying. Patton Boggs, LLP, for example, which is one of the largest lobbying firms in Washington, DC, is an internationally active law firm that lobbies all three branches of the federal government, and also provides "strategic market research," state-specific litigation services, fundraising advice, and lots of other things that a client with some interest in government decisions would want. Second, there are boutique lobbying firms. The typical boutique lobbying firm is smaller in size than the typical general firm, and it specializes in something. For example, Congressional Strategies, LLC is a small Washington boutique firm that specializes in lobbying on defense issues. For example, it helps business firms that wish to sell things to the military get government contracts.

Lobbying firms are ubiquitous in Washington. They are also active in state capitals and in big cities. In short, wherever government decisions are made you will find lobbying firms. The whole idea of the lobbying firm is quite controversial with many Americans. Lobbying firms are controversial because of the way they tend to do business—they sell their wares to clients who pay them big bucks to help them get what they want from government. This, to many people, sounds a little like prostitution—a firm sells its wares to the highest bidder. Consider, for example, the clients that hired Patton Boggs to represent them in 2011. Among these clients were Air France-KLM, The Beer Institute, The Children's Tumor Foundation, The City of Mesa, Arizona, Microsoft Corporation, The United Way of America, Wal-Mart Stores, and Wayne State University. These clients appear to have little in common except for one thing—the ability to cut Patton Boggs a large check.

Lobbying firms are also controversial because they often have the deep pockets necessary to attract high-profile ex-government decision-makers to work for them after they leave government. The combination of these firms' ability to lure ex-government luminaries and their alleged willingness to go to work for the highest bidder, make lobbying firms the quintessential "bad guys" of American politics—"bad guys" that support the notion that American government is for sale to the highest bidder.

Sources: Firm websites at http://www.pattonboggs.com/, and http://www.congressionalstrategies.com/. Both accessed on March 27, 2012.

Why Do Groups Lobby?

Thus concludes my brief examination of the types of interest groups active in the United States. One thing to keep in mind as you read the rest of this book is that many organizations in the United States that fit into one of my fifteen categories of interest groups—for example, many for-profit business firms, non-profit business firms, charities, coalitions, government entities, and professional associations—do not lobby at all, and are thus not interest groups. So just because an organization fits into one of the categories here does *not* mean it is an interest group. To reiterate, my main points here are that there are lots of different types of interest groups in this country, and that lots of different types of organizations—not just the types of groups you think of when you hear the term "interest group" (for example, groups such as the AARP, the ACLU, or the NRA)—lobby government. But it is important to remember that it is not the case that *all* business firms or charities or government entities or other types of organizations are interest groups. There are many examples of local businesses (especially small ones) near you that do not lobby and thus are not interest groups. Similarly, there are undoubtedly many charities and churches near you that engage in no lobbying whatsoever, and focus only on their primary missions.

All of this begs the following question: Why do so many organizations lobby government? After all, no organization *has* to lobby. Business firms, for example, can simply go about their business trying to make money. Similarly, charities, churches, colleges, and other institutions can eschew lobbying and simply perform their primary functions. As for membership organizations, they too can eschew lobbying if they wish. Citizen groups, labor unions, professional associations, and trade associations, for example, can provide information to their members, hold meetings, and do other things, while ignoring politics altogether. Why then do so many interest groups lobby? The answer is quite simple: because what the government does affects them. In sum, government decisions affect interest groups, and that is why interest groups try to affect government decisions (i.e., lobby).

Three types of government decisions are of particular interest to interest groups. First, there are *public policy decisions*—government decisions (e.g., laws, rules, regulations, court decisions) made in response to societal demands for action on important issues of the day. For example, government decisions about high-profile issues such as abortion, business regulation, gay rights, immigration, Medicare, Social Security, taxes, trade, and war are public policy decisions. Most of the government decisions you hear about on television and read about on the Internet and in newspapers are public policy decisions. Public policy decisions are made at all levels of government, and they are made on a wide variety of issues. Second, there are *land-use decisions*. Land-use decisions are government decisions rendered in response to specific requests for permission to utilize land in a certain way. For example, when a city government decides whether or not to allow Wal-Mart to build a new store on a large piece of land within the city it is making a land-use decision. Most land-use decisions are made by local governments. Finally, there are *procurement decisions*. Procurement decisions are decisions concerning which specific goods and/or services the government will purchase. For example, when a local government decides which kind of school buses to buy, it is making a procurement decision. Similarly, when the federal government decides which company it will choose to manufacture its U.S. Army helmets, it is making a procurement decision. Procurement decisions are made by governments at all three levels, and they involve everything from very expensive military hardware to inexpensive goods such as trash cans and paperclips.[36] Governments make public policy, land-use, and procurement decisions every day. And almost invariably when they do, interest groups are there to try to affect them.

The Plan for *Interest Groups in American Politics*

My primary goal in this chapter has been to provide the raw material you need to deal with the information that appears in subsequent chapters. To this end, I defined a number of important terms, none more important than *interest group*. My definition bears repeating: an interest group is *any non-party organization that engages in political activity.* This definition is precise enough to differentiate between interest groups and other types of organizations, but broad enough to encompass the large range of interest groups active in American politics today. My secondary goal in this brief introductory chapter has been to illustrate that the universe of interest groups in the United States is quite varied. To help demonstrate this point, I have assembled Table 1.2, which contains a list of "interesting" interest groups. As you can see, the universe of interest groups in the United States is indeed quite diverse. In addition to Table 1.2, I have created Box 1.2. Box 1.2 contains information on one of the strangest interest groups in the United States—NAMBLA, the North American Man/Boy Love Association. If you ever doubt that interest representation in the United States is all-encompassing and broad, remember NAMBLA.

Table 1.2 Some Interesting Interest Groups

Adhesive and Sealant Council, Inc.
American Association of Grain Inspection and Weighing Agencies
American Massage Therapy Association
Carpet and Rug Institute
Chimney Safety Institute of America
Citizens against UFO Secrecy (possibly defunct)
Coalition for Non-violent Food
International Association of Heat and Frost Insulators and Allied Workers
Jews for the Preservation of Firearms Ownership
Marijuana Policy Project
National Black Republican Association
National Organization for the Reform of Marijuana Laws
Nude Beach Alliance (possibly defunct)
Pressure Sensitive Tape Council
Rubber Pavements Association

Sources: Organizational websites at http://www.ascouncil.org/; http://www.amtamassage. org/index.html; http://www.carpet-rug.org/; http://www.aagiwa.org/; http://www.csia. org/; http://www.v-j-enterprises.com/caus.html; http://www.insulators.org/pages/index. asp; http://jpfo.org/; http://www.mpp.org/; http://www.nbra.info/; http://norml.org/; http://www.nudebeachalliance.com/home.html; http://www.pstc.org/i4a/pages/index.cfm? pageid=1; http://www.rubberpavements.org/. All sites accessed on April 4, 2011.

Now that I have covered some of the basics, what is next? Here's the plan: Chapter 2 examines the evolution of interest groups in the United States. First, it documents the recent explosion in the number of politically active interest groups. Then it addresses two related questions: (1) Why are there so many interest groups in the United States? (2) Why are there so many *more* interest groups in the United States than there used to be? Chapter 3 addresses a question that has long puzzled scholars of interest groups: Why are some interests better represented by interest groups than others? This question deserves serious attention, as it speaks directly to the nature of American democracy. Chapters 4–7 examine what interest groups *actually do*. Throughout most of American history, the people who advocate for interest groups—lobbyists—have been portrayed as sleazy "fixers" who bribe government decision-makers, procure sexual companionship for political elites, and regularly lie, cheat, and steal to get what they want. These chapters point up the fact that lobbying is actually quite pedestrian. They show that lobbyists do many things, very few of which involve bribing, drinking, procuring, or lying. Chapter 8 examines interest groups and their relationships with political parties. While parties and interest groups are not the same, they share a number of characteristics and goals. Chapter 9 asks perhaps the most important question of all: How influential are interest groups in American politics? Through an examination of contemporary theories of interest group influence, the chapter illustrates the difficulties inherent in ascertaining the extent and nature of group influence. These difficulties notwithstanding, Chapter 9 concludes with a delineation of the circumstances under which interest groups are most likely to influence government decisions. The final chapter (Chapter 10) is a broad overview of the politics of interest groups in the United States. It attempts to resolve the paradox of interest groups.

Box 1.2 NAMBLA: The Most Controversial Interest Group in the United States?

If you watch *South Park* or *The Daily Show with John Stewart*, you probably have heard of NAMBLA—the North American Man/Boy Love Association.

NAMBLA is real. It is an actual interest group that operates in the United States. NAMBLA's mission, according to the group itself, is "to end the extreme oppression of men and boys in mutually consensual relationships." In short, NAMBLA wants to change age of consent laws so that men can have consensual sexual relationships with males who are now considered under age (and thus legally incapable of consenting to sex). Yes, that means that NAMBLA wants to make it legal for men to have sex with boys. NAMBLA also advocates for the release of men who are in jail due to consensual sexual contact with under-age males.

NAMBLA is the subject of many jokes, and many people think that the group does not exist. But it does. It is difficult to say how active the group is, as it does not appear to have many public meetings and its members tend to maintain a rather low profile.

The mere existence of NAMBLA, however, says a lot about interest group politics in the United States. Most importantly, it says that the United States is uncommonly tolerant of people who want to join or form interest groups. In short, if you want to form an interest group in the United States, you can probably do it, no matter how strange or unpopular your cause.

Source: Organizational website at http://www.nambla.org/.
Accessed on May 13, 2011.

Before proceeding to Chapter 2, it is worth noting that this book takes a holistic approach to the study of interest groups. In other words, whenever possible it examines interest groups *everywhere* they operate in America—in cities, counties, states, and towns as well as in Washington, DC. Unfortunately, there is a tendency in the media (and indeed in academia) to focus solely upon Washington group activity, despite the fact that interest groups operate at all levels of American government. This is the case mostly because academics know far less about interest groups in states and localities than they do about interest groups in Washington. Nonetheless, there is no doubt that interest groups are important players in state and local as well as national politics. Consequently such, throughout this book I try my best to give students a well-rounded picture of interest groups in the whole United States, not just in Washington.

Conclusion: Why Study Interest Groups?

It would be an exaggeration to say that interest groups are at the very center of American politics. In the end, the elected and appointed decision-makers who represent us in government are at the center of most political storms. And this is as it should be; for the founders of this country designed a democratic republic in which most authoritative decisions are left to government decision-makers. Yet government decision-makers are hardly the *only* players in the American political process. As the storm brewed over how to react to the BP oil spill, all sorts of interest groups got themselves involved. They met with government decision-makers, they mobilized citizens, they advertised on television and radio, they circulated petitions, and they held protests and rallies. What all these interest groups had in common is this: they participated in the American political process. And this is why we study interest groups—because they are important players in the American political process.

The Evolution of Interest Groups in the United States   **2**

No one knows for certain how many interest groups there are in the United States. But few experts deny that the number is enormous. In Washington alone, there are perhaps as many as 15–20,000 interest groups.[1] Outside of Washington, in states and localities across the country, the number of interest groups is probably over 200,000.[2] These numbers seem large because they are. There is a general consensus among interest group experts that there are more interest groups in the United States today than at any time in American history.[3] Moreover, though it is difficult to make comparisons (because we really do not know how many interest groups there are in other countries), it appears that the United States ranks in the top three (and probably is number one) worldwide in number of interest groups.[4]

Why does the United States have so many interest groups? Why are there so many more interest groups active today than ever before? These are the questions addressed in this chapter. I begin by placing the contemporary universe of interest groups in historical perspective by examining trends in interest group representation over time. Next, I examine how America's unique political system has fostered the proliferation of interest groups. Finally, I explain how social, economic, and political changes in this century have contributed to a tremendous explosion of interest groups over the past forty years.

The Twentieth Century: A Century of Interest Group Proliferation

From the very beginning, interest groups have been active in American politics. Labor unions, for example, are as old as the republic.[5] Moreover, throughout this country's earliest years, groups of all kinds pressed their demands upon government. In the 1820s, for example, temperance groups sprang up throughout the United States and urged government to ban the sale of alcohol.[6] Similarly, virtually from the moment the country was founded, abolitionist citizen groups appealed to lawmakers to end slavery.[7] And in the decades immediately following the Civil War, several interest group powerhouses including the National Rifle Association (NRA, 1871), the American Bankers Association (ABA, 1875), and the American Federation of Labor (AFL, 1886) were born.[8]

Nevertheless, while interest groups have always been part of the American political landscape, explosive interest group growth was largely a twentieth-century phenomenon. Numbers of interest groups began growing dramatically around the turn of the twentieth century.[9] Not only did existing organizations such as the NRA and the AFL gain in stature, but a number of new interest groups including such household names as the U.S. Chamber of Commerce (1912), the National Audubon Society (1905), the National Association for the Advancement of Colored People (1909), the National Association of Manufacturers (1895), and the Sierra Club (1892) came on the scene. By the 1920s, people who studied interest groups concluded that they had become major political players.[10] One historical study finds that the years 1900–1920—roughly the Progressive Era—were a period of explosive interest group growth, as the number of interest groups active in Washington politics rose from several hundred to several thousand.[11] Interest group proliferation continued unabated between 1920 and 1960, as more and more groups formed and pressed their demands on government.[12] Although data on sub-national interest groups are spotty, it seems clear that interest group proliferation took place at the state and local levels of government as well as at the national level.

Before going any further, it is important to note that people who study interest groups disagree among themselves about precisely how many groups there are in the United States now and how many there were in the past. Unfortunately, there is no master list of American interest groups and there never has been. Thus, we are left with estimates of interest group numbers—guesses based on archival and historical and survey research. The estimates presented here are designed to give you a general idea of interest group numbers rather than a highly specific enumeration. With this caveat in mind, I produced Figure 2.1, which is based on my own estimates (informed by the research of others, of course) of the number of interest groups active in Washington over time. Figure 2.1 graphically demonstrates what political scientists call "the advocacy explosion"—the expansive growth in the number of nationally active interest groups since 1900. It is fair to infer that a similar growth took place at the state and local levels as well. As Figure 2.1 shows, the number of interest groups active in Washington rose sharply from 1900 to 1920, grew steadily from 1921 to 1960, and rose again sharply after 1960.

It is hard to overstate the magnitude of group proliferation since 1960. Estimates suggest that in just the 20 years from 1960 to 1980, the number of nationally active interest groups more than tripled. And my own estimates suggest that there are roughly seven to eight times as many interest groups active in Washington today as there were in 1960. Again, while there are few good sources of data on the numbers of groups in states and localities, it is fair to say that explosive growth took place at the sub-national level as well after 1960.

A few examples help illustrate the true extent of interest group proliferation since 1960. First, the number of federal PACs has risen from 100 in the

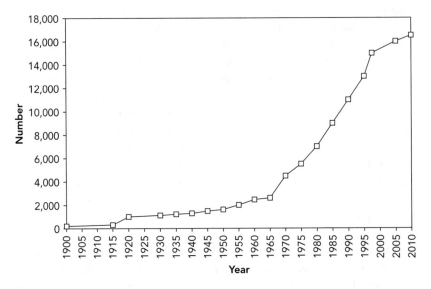

Figure 2.1 Trends in the Number of Washington-Based Interest Groups

Sources: These are my estimates based on several sources including: *Encyclopedia of Associations: National Organizations of the United States* (various editions); Petracca, "The Rediscovery of Interest Group Politics"; *National Directory of Trade and Professional Associations* (various editions); Tichenor and Harris, "The Development of Interest Group Politics in America"; Walker, *Mobilizing Interest Groups in America*, 1–3.

mid-1970s to approximately 4,600 today.[13] Second, the number of citizen groups active in Washington has grown from approximately 100 in the mid-1970s to several thousand today.[14] Third, one source notes that while before 1920 only one American business firm had a permanent office in Washington, DC, that number had risen to 175 in 1978 and more than 600 in 2004.[15] The true number of business firms active in Washington is actually much larger than 600, as many business firms that lobby do not have permanent Washington offices. Finally, the true vastness of interest group proliferation was illustrated to me a few years ago when I undertook a study of gay and lesbian advocacy in the United States since World War II. After extensive archival and historical research, I found that the number of nationally active gay and lesbian rights interest groups of all kinds (most but not all are/were citizen groups) in the United States grew from one in 1945, to more than 70 by the end of the 1980s.[16]

In sum, the available evidence, while not perfect, makes two things very clear. First, there are a lot of interest groups active in the United States. Second, there probably are more interest groups active in the United States than ever before.

The Diversification of Interest Groups

As the universe of interest groups has grown it has become much more diverse. For most of our history it appears that labor unions, professional associations, and trade associations constituted the bulk of the interest group universe.[17] My own estimates (again, based on a careful reading of available studies) suggest that before 1950, these three types of groups comprised perhaps as much as three-quarters of all interest groups active in American politics. This began to change around the turn of the twentieth century, as citizen groups became more prominent. In the decades after the Civil War, for example, several powerful veterans' groups formed and pressed Congress for more and better pension benefits.[18] Moreover, abolitionist groups were very active at the local, state, and federal levels. Nonetheless, pronounced diversification did not begin until the early 1960s. The degree of this diversification has been startling.

Political scientists Frank Baumgartner and Beth Leech recently concluded that the decades since the 1960s "have seen remarkable changes in the nature of the American interest-group system."[19] I have already noted the pronounced growth of PACs and business firms and citizen groups. The most important change, according to Baumgartner and Leech, has been the tremendous growth in the number of the latter.[20] To illustrate just how pronounced this growth has been, Baumgartner and Leech examine the growth of one type of citizen group—the nationally active environmental group. The number of environmental groups, they find, "almost tripled in the three decades from 1960 to 1990."[21] "Whereas the beginning of the 1960s saw 119 environmental groups with a combined staff of only 316 active at the national level," they note, "the beginning of the 1990s saw almost 3,000 staffers working for more than 300 groups."[22] The growth in environmental groups appears to have leveled off, but the number of such groups remains high. Although there are few studies of other specific types of citizen groups, overall citizen group numbers strongly suggest that anti-abortion and pro-choice, civil liberties, civil rights, consumer, elderly, gay and lesbian, religious, and taxpayer citizen groups also have proliferated since 1960.[23]

Along with business firms, citizen groups, and PACs, other types of interest groups have become more prominent in recent decades as well. The precise numbers are sketchy, but it appears that only a handful of the thousands of think tanks active across the United States today formed before 1960.[24] The figures on colleges and universities, coalitions, and domestic and foreign governmental entities also are sketchy, but there is evidence that they too have become much more prominent since 1960.

The results of the recent diversification are obvious in Figure 2.2, which illustrates the rough make-up of the contemporary Washington, DC interest group universe. Again, these numbers are estimates only; the figure is designed to give you a general idea of the make-up of the Washington interest group universe rather than a precise portrait. It shows that, as virtually always has been the case, labor unions, professional associations, and trade associations comprise a substantial proportion of this universe. However, Figure 2.2 shows that the Washington interest group universe is not dominated by any single type of organization, as there are numerous business firms, churches and church organizations, coalitions, and governmental entities competing for power alongside the interest group stalwarts. While Figure 2.2 contains data only on nationally active interest groups, studies suggest that state and local interest group communities are quite diverse today as well.[25]

The United States as Interest Group Incubator

Comparative studies show that the number of politically active interest groups in most countries (developed and underdeveloped alike) is relatively limited compared to that in the United States.[26] It is certainly not the case that interest groups are not active elsewhere in the world; clearly they are, and in some places they are quite numerous. All in all, however, it is safe to conclude that

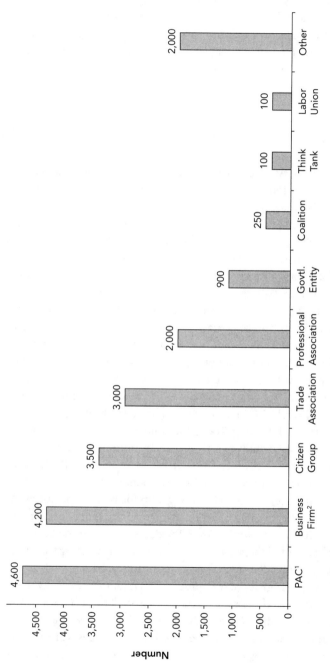

Figure 2.2 The Composition of the Washington, DC Interest Group Universe, 2011

Notes: 1. Approximately two-thirds of PACs are affiliated with other organizations, so they really do not count as separate interest groups. 2. Includes for-profit and non-profit businesses.

Sources: Estimates based on several sources including the following: Baumgartner and Leech, *Basic Interests*, 108; *Encyclopedia of Associations: National Organizations of the United States* (various editions); *National Directory of Trade and Professional Associations* (various editions); Petracca, "The Rediscovery of Interest Group Politics"; Tichenor and Harris, "The Development of Interest Group Politics in America"; Walker, *Mobilizing Interest Groups in America*, 1–3; Wright, *Interest Groups and Congress*, Chapter 2.

America is home to a larger number of interest groups than most other countries in the world. What is it about the United States that makes it such an ideal place for the formation and survival of interest groups? The answer is fourfold: *diversity, constitutional freedoms, federalism*, and the *separation of powers*. Each of these factors contributes to this country's unique status as an "interest group incubator."

Diversity

There is no question that America's diversity contributes to its favorable climate for interest group formation and survival. On virtually any dimension you can imagine, America is amazingly diverse. Take, for example, religion. There are several dozen different religious denominations in this country.[27] From Adventists and Baha'is, to Roman Catholics and Universalist Unitarians, virtually every religion on earth is practiced in this country. The United States is also ethnically and racially diverse. Though the majority of Americans (about 72 percent) are Caucasian (White), this country is home to a large number of Hispanics (16 percent), African Americans (13 percent), Asian Americans (5 percent), American Indians and Alaskan Natives (1 percent), and native Hawaiians and Pacific Islanders (0.2 percent).[28] Moreover, 3 percent of Americans say they are of more than one race.[29] Finally, the United States is economically diverse. Whereas some countries are dominated by one or a handful of essential industries, the United States produces everything from oil and coal to sorghum and sod. Just to give you an idea of how diverse our economy is, consider the following. Today, the United States ranks among the world's leaders in the production of artichokes (#8), automobiles (#3), corn (#1), copper (#2), movies (#2), onions (#3), steel (#5, if we count the EU as a country), and wheat (#5, if we count the EU as a country).[30]

How does diversity contribute to interest group formation and survival? Most important, diversity creates societal cleavages—differences of opinion about social, economic, and political matters. Political scientists Burdett Loomis and Allan Cigler have noted the importance of cleavages in creating a climate for interest group growth. "Substantial cleavages among citizens," they note, "are essential for interest group development."[31] Think of it this way: in a society where everyone is of the same racial or ethnic identity, has the same religious views, does the same thing for a living, has the same investments, and lives under the same conditions, the number of societal cleavages is likely to be small. In contrast, a society with lots of differences is likely to have many societal cleavages.

Constitutional Freedoms

Constitutional freedoms also make the United States an ideal place for interest group proliferation. As one study of interest group proliferation points out, "Guarantees of free speech, association, and the right to petition the government for redress of grievances are basic to group formation."[32] The First Amendment guarantees the right to free speech and assembly, as well as the right "to petition the Government for a redress of grievances." Though the Constitution does not explicitly mention the freedom of association, over the years the Supreme Court has consistently ruled that the Constitution protects this freedom. For example, the Court has ruled that the freedom to associate serves other essential rights such as the freedom of speech.[33] In addition, "general liberty as protected by the Fifth and Fourteenth Amendments," according to numerous Supreme Court decisions, often extends to the right to freely associate.[34] America is not unique in the freedoms it affords its citizens to join and participate in groups. But it is unusual. In most totalitarian systems, for example, lobbying and other forms of political participation are more or less prohibited. The Arab Spring of 2011, during which repressive regimes across the Middle East cracked down brutally on protestors and politically active citizens, demonstrates that not all the world's peoples have the right to express themselves politically. Even in many less repressive countries, relatively strict lobbying laws constrain the activities of interest groups.

Federalism

Federalism also contributes to America's favorable climate for interest groups. This country has close to 90,000 governments—1 national government, 50 state governments, over 3,000 county governments, over 35,000 municipal and town governments, and close to 50,000 school districts and special districts.[35] This is the case because the Constitution created a federal system of government—one in which power is divided among a central (national) government and numerous sub-national (state and local) governments. The opposite of a federal system is a unitary system—a system of government in which all power resides in a central government. What distinguishes a federal system from a unitary system is that in the former, a number of different and distinct governments make decisions that affect people's lives. All of this is important because federalism both allows and encourages interest group activity. It encourages interest group activity because it provides interest groups with numerous points of access to government. In my community, for example, if an interest group is dissatisfied with government policy, it has manifold outlets to vent its anger. One option is to contact an official in the federal government—the president, the vice-president, a senator, or a House member, or maybe a bureaucrat. Another is to contact someone in local government. The group could, for example, contact the city mayor, the county mayor, a member of the city council, or a county commissioner. In short, in a federal system like ours, interest groups have many options. This encourages interest group activity by making lobbying relatively easy and affordable. It is also worth restating that the very governmental entities created by federalism—the cities, states, and localities—act as interest groups themselves. This, then, is yet another way in which federalism acts to encourage interest group proliferation and activity.

Separation of Powers

Finally, the separation of powers helps make the United States an ideal place for interest group growth. In this country, numerous actors at each level of government share governmental power. At the national level, for example, power is shared by the executive branch (the president and the bureaucracy), Congress, and the judiciary. The fifty state governments have similar arrangements—the governor, state agencies, the state legislature, and state courts share power. Cities, counties, and towns also are characterized by a separation of powers. Much like federalism, the separation of powers increases the number of access points for interest groups. Consider, for example, what happens if you are a business lobbyist and you think that the president is an "anti-business liberal." Instead of "giving up," you can take your case to Congress, a federal agency, or a federal court. Loomis and Cigler point out that the separation of powers and federalism work together to encourage interest group development. "The decentralized political power structure in the United States," they note,

> allows important decisions to be made at the national, state, or local levels. Within each level of government there are multiple points of access. For example, business-related policies such as taxes are acted on at each level, and interest groups may affect these policies in the legislative, executive, or judicial arenas.[36]

On the whole, America's unique governmental system, together with constitutional freedoms and diversity, make it an ideal place for the proliferation of interest groups. Thus, not surprisingly, America has always been home to a great many interest groups.

Explaining Interest Group Proliferation

The United States always has provided a favorable climate for interest groups. Not until the twentieth century, however, did interest groups explode in number to the extent that they have. Why? What explains the massive proliferation of interest groups since 1900, and especially since 1960? Political scientists have identified two phenomena in particular as significant causes of massive interest group proliferation: *societal change* and *governmental growth*. This section takes a closer look at these two factors.

In a famous book called *The Governmental Process* (1951), political scientist David Truman explicated a general theory of interest group proliferation called "disturbance theory," a theory which holds that societal change is primarily responsible for interest group proliferation. According to the theory, as American society evolves and becomes more complex and differentiated, new interests emerge and multiply.[37] For example, *economic* change can lead to the creation of new economic interests. This is what happened, Truman notes, in the late nineteenth century as America evolved from a simple agrarian country to an urban industrial one, and new industries such as the automobile industry and the oil industry were born. According to Truman, new industries meant new interests. Similarly, *social* change can lead to the creation of new social interests. This is what happened, Truman notes, early in the twentieth century as the United States evolved from a relatively homogeneous country of white and African American Protestants and Catholics, to a multiracial, multireligious, heterogeneous one. Finally, *technological* change can make it easier for people to band together to form interest groups. Truman notes, for example, that early in the twentieth century, technological innovations such as the radio, the telephone, and the telegraph made it easier for people to communicate with one another and thus to identify other people who shared their interests.

Because Truman was writing in 1951, he did not examine the post-1960 proliferation of interest groups. Nonetheless, his disturbance theory helps explain this proliferation. The theory's logic implies that interest groups have proliferated since 1960 because of pronounced and substantial societal change. This is undoubtedly true. Clearly, part of the reason why interest groups have proliferated since 1960 is that American society has changed substantially since then. Three types of change in particular—economic change, social change, and technological change—have transformed America. First, there has been economic change. Specifically, since 1960, America has witnessed a post-industrial revolution that has reshaped the national economy. In the last few decades, new scientific and "hi-tech" industries have become prominent in the

American economy. This economic shift, much like earlier economic shifts identified by Truman, has given rise to new industries such as the computer industry and the wireless telecommunications industry, which have organized to protect their interests. In addition, this country has become much more affluent since World War II. Even after adjusting for inflation, the median income in the United States doubled between 1947 and 1972.[38] The rise of affluence has contributed to interest group proliferation in two ways. First of all, it has allowed many Americans to think about issues other than "bread and butter" economic issues for the first time. For example, as many Americans began to see themselves as economically secure, they became more interested in "quality of life" issues such as consumer safety, the environment, and women's rights, and moral issues such as abortion, euthanasia, and gay and lesbian rights.[39] In addition, affluence has made it easier and cheaper for Americans to join interest groups.[40] People with more money, the argument goes, have more money to spend on interest groups. Second, cultural, racial, and religious diversification has continued, as a new round of immigrants, especially Hispanics and Asians, have become part of the American "melting pot." Finally, further advances in communications technology—especially the rise of email and the Internet—have made it easier for organizations to form and survive as they have made it easier for people to communicate.

A crucial assumption in Truman's disturbance theory is that as new interests emerge they organize and press their demands upon government. New industries, for example, may organize and appeal to the federal government for protection from foreign competitors. Similarly, Truman's theory assumes that as more and more people become concerned about, for example, morality or the environment, they will band together and appeal to the government to pass laws concerning such things. According to Truman, the reason why new interests organize and appeal to government for help is simple: the government has the power to make and enforce societal rules.

There is a certain amount of logic in Truman's contention that when new interests emerge they organize and press their demands upon government. Truman underestimated, however, the extent to which the government itself could contribute to interest group proliferation. A number of studies show that *government growth* also has been an important cause of interest group proliferation in this country, especially since 1960. Before moving on to how government growth has contributed to interest group proliferation, it is important to acknowledge just how much government in the United States has grown since the 1920s. Again, the focus here primarily is on the federal government because figures on its growth are most accurate. But there is lots of evidence that state and local governments have grown tremendously as well.

So how much has the federal government grown? For the first hundred years of our history, the federal government did not do much—some people like to joke that it just delivered the mail and maintained the armed forces. Since about the turn of the twentieth century, however, the size and scope of the federal government have increased substantially. During the Progressive Era (the late 1800s and early 1900s), for example, the federal government began regulating railroads and "busting up" monopolies. Later, in the 1930s, New Deal Democrats took control of Washington and passed laws that regulated air travel, banking, broadcasting, and stock trading, among other things. During this period the federal government created the income security programs Social Security and "welfare" (Aid to Families with Dependent Children—AFDC). Government growth continued gradually throughout the 1940s and 1950s. In the 1960s, gradual growth gave way to truly massive growth. As part of Lyndon Johnson's Great Society (the label applied to a series of federal government programs adopted in the 1960s), the federal government levied substantially more regulations on businesses, and created some new income assistance programs and expanded some old ones. Specifically, under LBJ's leadership, the federal government began enforcing stricter federal environmental, occupational safety, and health regulations. In addition, the federal government created new programs in the areas of health care, education, housing, civil rights, and income security. Among the more important programs created by the Great Society were Medicare (a government health insurance program for the elderly), the Food Stamp program (which provides food assistance to the poor), and Medicaid (which provides medical assistance for the poor). And we must not forget that the American defense budget has grown enormously as well since the 1930s. Indeed, especially since World War II, we have spent more and more on national security, and today spend approximately three-quarters of a trillion dollars each year on defense and security.

To get an idea of how much the federal government has grown since 1960, consult Figure 2.3, which illustrates how federal budget outlays have exploded in the last fifty years. The rise in federal spending reflects the increase in the size and scope of the federal government. Figures on state and local government spending are less reliable than those on federal government spending, but research indicates that these governments have grown as well in recent decades.

Government growth has contributed to interest group proliferation in two principal ways. First of all, new government programs and initiatives, like disturbances, have created new interests. To use a simple example, consider the case of the National Alliance of State and Territorial AIDS Directors (NASTAD). NASTAD was founded in 1992, and is a professional association consisting of

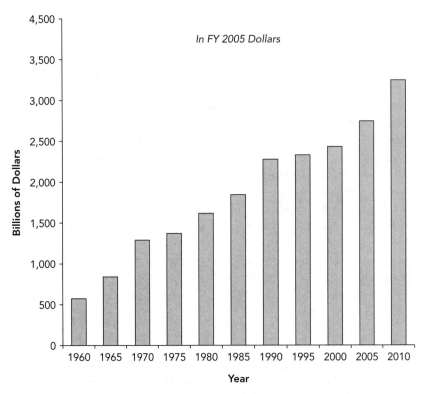

Figure 2.3 Annual Federal Outlays, 1960–2010

Source: Office of Management and Budget, Executive Office of the President of the United States, "Fiscal Year 2012, Historical Tables, Budget of the U.S. Government."

"the nation's chief state health agency staff who have programmatic responsibility for administering HIV/AIDS and viral hepatitis healthcare, prevention, education, and supportive service programs funded by state and federal governments." [41] In government, these are professionals who administer HIV/AIDS programs. NASTAD exists only because governments *have* HIV/AIDS programs. Without government HIV/AIDS initiatives NASTAD would not exist, because the profession of "government HIV/AIDS program administrator" would not exist.

Government growth has also contributed to interest group proliferation as interest groups have "mushroomed" around new policy initiatives.[42] This "mushrooming" occurs because government initiatives and programs entail costs and benefits for various groups in society, and thus provide incentives for groups to organize. An example can help illustrate this point. Slowly but surely since the Social Security program was created in 1935, the federal government has increased the benefits it provides to the elderly. Today, benefits to the elderly account for a large portion of federal government spending (approximately one-third). The most important way that government programs for the elderly have contributed to interest group proliferation is by providing powerful incentives for the recipients of these benefits (the elderly) to organize to protect these benefits. And organize they have! The main group concerned with protecting the interests of the elderly, the AARP, is the country's largest membership organization other than the Catholic Church. Government programs for the elderly have also contributed to interest group proliferation by providing incentives for service deliverers to organize to protect their interests. For example, the number of service deliverers that have organized around Medicare and other health care programs for the elderly is startling. One study notes that in the health care sector, service deliverers ranging "from professional associations of doctors and nurses to hospital groups to the insurance industry to suppliers of drugs and medical equipment" have organized to protect their interests.[43]

In sum, the massive proliferation of interest groups in the United States since 1960 can be attributed primarily to two factors: societal change and government growth. Since 1960, the American economy has changed and has created new economic interests and unprecedented affluence. In addition, cultural, religious, and social changes have accelerated since 1960, and technological changes have come fast and furious. Finally, the government has grown tremendously since 1960. Together, these factors help to account for the unprecedented interest group proliferation since 1960.

Conclusion: The Evolution of Interest Groups in the United States

The primary message of this chapter is as follows: *the United States is home to a huge number of interest groups*. No one knows precisely how many interest groups there are in the United States, but we know that there are hundreds of thousands of them. One of the reasons that America is home to so many interest groups is that it provides an ideal climate for interest group formation and survival. The combination of diversity, constitutional freedoms, federalism, and the separation of powers helps make the United States a virtual incubator for interest groups. While America has always been an ideal place for the proliferation of interest groups, only recently have interest groups proliferated massively. Two broad phenomena in particular have contributed to the massive interest group proliferation of the last 50–60 years: societal change and government growth.

At this point, it is tempting to ask: What has been the effect of this immense interest group proliferation on American politics? There are two schools of thought on this question. Some argue that interest group proliferation has been a good thing, because more viewpoints than ever before are now represented before government. Others argue that interest group proliferation has been a bad thing, because huge numbers of interest groups interfere with the government's ability to get things done and make it impossible for government decision-makers to serve the "public interest." Unfortunately, we are not yet in a position to answer this important question—because we do not yet know enough about what interest groups do and how much influence they exert over government decisions. If, on the one hand, we find that interest groups do very little and have little influence over government decisions, then we might conclude that interest group proliferation has had little or no effect on American politics. If, on the other hand, we find that interest groups do a great deal and have a great deal of influence over policy outcomes, then we might conclude that interest group proliferation has had a large impact on American politics. In short, we have much more to learn before we are in a position to "weigh in" on the effects of interest group proliferation.

What's Next

In the next chapter, I begin exploring the question of which interests are best represented before government. As you will see, despite the massive interest group proliferation and diversification, it turns out that some interests are better represented before government than others. For example, some interests have large and well-funded organizations working on their behalf, while others are represented by small "ragtag" operations. Furthermore, some widely shared interests are not represented by interest groups at all. Which interests are well represented by interest groups? Which are not so well represented? Why? These are the questions tackled in Chapter 3.

The Formation and Maintenance of Interest Groups

3

Polls show that approximately two-thirds of Americans support the death penalty for a "person convicted of murder."[1] Support for the death penalty has waxed and waned over the past thirty years, but since the early 1970s, a solid majority of Americans have said they support it. As for opposition to the death penalty, it is minimal. The Gallup Poll shows that no more than 30 percent of Americans have opposed the death penalty in any year since 1976.[2] In short, Americans want the government to put murderers to death. But if you favor the death penalty, finding an interest group working on your behalf is difficult. A quick Google search indicates that there are not very many interest groups in the United States working to increase the number of murderers put to death. A search for death penalty interest groups yields the names of scores of national groups including Campaign to End the Death Penalty, Catholics Against Capital Punishment, the National Coalition to Abolish the Death Penalty, and People of Faith Against the Death Penalty, as well as dozens of state groups including Coloradoans Against the Death Penalty, Delaware Citizens Against the Death Penalty, Illinois Coalition Against the Death Penalty, and Tennessee Coalition to Abolish State Killing. There is no group called the Campaign for More Death Sentences, or the National Coalition to Increase State Killing, or People of Faith for the Death Penalty. To be sure, there are some groups (including groups of police officers and crime victims) that support the death penalty. But even a cursory investigation indicates that death penalty opponents are much better represented by interest groups than death penalty supporters; and this despite the fact that the latter outnumber the former by a margin of approximately two to one.

A close look at the universe of interest groups uncovers numerous examples like this one—cases in which the composition of the universe of interest groups does not reflect the distribution of interests in society as a whole. There are many instances of bias in the system of interest group representation in the United States. In short, some interests are better represented by interest groups than others. This chapter asks: Why? In answering this question, I begin by delineating the barriers to interest group formation and survival. My purpose in doing so is to demonstrate that interest group formation and survival cannot be taken for granted. In other words, just because an *interest* exists does not mean that an *interest group* will form in its wake. From here, I explain how interest groups overcome the barriers to formation and survival. Finally, I examine how these barriers have manifested themselves in unequal interest group representation—the tendency for some interests to be better represented by interest groups than others. Ultimately, this chapter is designed to help explain unequal interest group representation wherever it exists.

Defining "Formation" and "Survival"

Before getting on with the main purpose of this chapter, it is essential to stipulate just what the terms "group formation" and "group survival" mean. While the terms seem straightforward, they're not. The term "formation," for example, means different things for different types of interest groups. For organizations that consist of individual members and are created with an explicit political purpose, "formation" means coming into existence. For example, Common Cause—a "good government" citizen group—was formed as an interest group in 1970 by a man named John Gardner. For some interest groups, however, formation is not synonymous with coming into existence. Many business firms, for example, do not become active in politics until many years after they come into existence. In cases like these, we say that the business firms were formed as interest groups when they became active in politics, not when they originally got up and running. The point here is this: when scholars speak of an interest group's formation, they are referring to *the point at which that organization becomes politically active*. For many organizations, this means the point at which they come into existence. For many others, however, it means the point at which they decide to try to affect government decisions.

As for "survival," it means *the ability to remain in business as an interest group*. Be careful, however, as the same warning that applied to the term "formation" also applies to the term "survival": it means different things for different types of interest groups. For interest groups that are initially formed for a political purpose—groups like Common Cause—survival means staying in business, period. For organizations that exist for non-political purposes yet still engage in political activity—businesses, for example—survival as an interest group means remaining politically active.

In sum, the terms "formation" and "survival" are not as straightforward as they seem. Both terms mean different things for different types of interest groups. It is important to keep this in mind.

The Barriers to Interest Group Formation and Survival

Now that we have a better idea of what formation and survival actually are, we can begin to examine the barriers to the formation and survival of interest groups. It is these barriers that help to explain why some interests are better represented by interest groups than others.

Disturbance theory, which we encountered in the last chapter, has a straightforward explanation for why some interests are better represented by interest groups than others. It posits that "elements of society possess common needs and share a group identity or consciousness, and that these are sufficient conditions for the formation of effective [interest groups]."[3] In other words, disturbance theory holds that as society evolves and new interests emerge, groups of individuals realize that they share interests and band together to protect these interests. This "cause and effect" logic implies that objective societal conditions determine which interests are best represented by interest groups, and thus explain why some interests are better represented by interest groups than others. Despite its considerable appeal, there are two major problems with this logic.

First, at numerous points in American history interest groups have not emerged when societal changes and disturbances would appear to have demanded it. For example, for most of our history, African Americans suffered horrendous treatment at the hands of the majority of (white) Americans. Enslavement, lynchings, and rampant discrimination throughout the eighteenth, nineteenth, and early twentieth centuries, for example, threatened the interests of millions of African Americans. Yet from 1789 to 1900, African Americans did not band together on a large scale to protect their shared interests. Similarly, throughout American history, homosexuals have been subject to all sorts of harassment and persecution. In addition to general societal disapproval, for most of our history homosexuals have faced prosecution under state and local sodomy laws. Yet not until the 1960s did homosexuals band together on a large scale to protect their shared interests.[4] Examples like these contradict the "cause and effect" logic of disturbance theory.

Second, even now—in a time of interest group ubiquity—interest group representation does *not* reflect the distribution of opinions and interests in American society. Consider, for example, the case that began this chapter. Recent polls show that a large majority of adult Americans support the death penalty. Despite this overwhelming support, *The Encyclopedia of Associations*— a directory of nationally active membership organizations in the United States—lists only *six* nationally active interest groups in its index under the key phrase *death penalty*.[5] The key phrase *capital punishment* yields a total of eleven groups.[6] Together, all of the groups listed under *death penalty* and *capital punishment* represent well under 1 million people (or less than 1 percent of death penalty supporters). Perhaps more shocking than this relative lack of interest group representation is the fact that *not one of these groups supports the death penalty*. To say the least, these numbers do not reflect the interests of the millions of Americans with opinions about the death penalty. Cases like this one, in which the composition of the universe of interest groups does not reflect the distribution of interests in society as a whole, augur against disturbance theory.[7]

In his landmark book *The Logic of Collective Action* (1965), economist Mancur Olson exposed the flaws in the "cause and effect" logic of disturbance theory.[8] Though he accepted the notion that increased societal complexity caused the emergence of new interests, he questioned the notion that the emergence of new interests necessarily leads to the creation of new *interest groups*. Olson concluded that shared interests alone are not sufficient to cause the formation of interest groups. In other words, according to Olson, just because a group of people shares an interest does not mean they will organize to protect that interest. Why? Olson answers: *because there are substantial barriers to interest group formation and survival*. According to Olson, two barriers in particular hinder the formation and survival of interest groups: *the "free-rider" problem* and *the political efficacy problem*.[9] Another has been identified by numerous scholars of interest groups—*cost*.

Cost

One reason why even individuals who share an interest may not band together to address their concerns is that doing so is costly. Simply sharing an interest does not pay the bills. Any unorganized group of people wishing to form an interest group must raise money to get the group "off the ground." Moreover, once an interest group successfully forms, it must continually raise money to stay in business. Money is not the only cost involved in forming and/or maintaining an interest group. Time and effort are also involved. Organizing meetings, recruiting members, and holding rallies, for example, require the time and effort of numerous people. These costs may not seem that important, but they are important when you consider that most people do not enjoy dedicating their free time to political activity—even if they feel strongly about a political issue. Most of us prefer to invest our extra time and effort in more personally rewarding activities such as earning more money, hanging out with family and friends, watching television, or going on vacation. In sum, one of the reasons why shared interests do not necessarily lead to the formation of interest groups is that forming and sustaining an interest group is costly.

The "Free-Rider" Problem

Another major barrier to interest group formation is the "free-rider" problem: *the tendency for individuals not to join interest groups that work on their behalf.* Why would an individual choose *not* to join an interest group that works on his/her behalf? Let's follow Olson's logic. First, Olson assumes that an individual will join an interest group when the benefits of doing so outweigh the costs. (It is important to reiterate here that not all membership interest groups consist of individual members. Trade associations, for example, consist of business firms. Olson's analysis applies to all types of membership organizations, not just those consisting of individuals.) Next, Olson notes that many interest groups lobby government for "collective benefits"—benefits that accrue to an interest group's members as well as to non-members. An example will help clarify what Olson means by collective benefits. Consider the case of the NRA. The group's primary political goal is the prevention of gun control legislation. This is a collective benefit: if it is achieved it accrues to all individuals in America who oppose gun control, not just members of the NRA. From here, Olson argues that individuals often choose not to join interest groups that work on their behalf because they can enjoy the collective benefits that these interest groups provide without joining. In the end, Olson concludes that most of us simply do not want to pay for something we can get for free.

To see the "free-rider" problem at work, assume for a moment that you hate gun control. As such, you support the NRA's political goals. You realize, however, that the NRA is working to achieve collective benefits. In other words, you know that if the NRA succeeds in preventing gun control, all people who hate gun control (including you) will benefit, not just NRA members. According to Olson, it is rational for you—although you share the NRA's interest in preventing gun control—not to join the group. Why? Because if the

NRA succeeds in preventing gun control, everyone who hates gun control—even people like you who decline to join—receive the benefits. In essence, you can get a "free-ride" by letting others join the NRA and pay for the collective benefits you value. Political scientists Burdett Loomis and Allan Cigler sum up Olson's "free-rider" logic like this: "'rational' individuals choose not to bear the participation costs (time, membership fees) because they can enjoy the group benefits (such as favorable legislation) without joining."[10]

The Political Efficacy Problem

The third major barrier to the formation and survival of interest groups is the political efficacy problem. The political efficacy problem flows from *the widespread tendency for people to think that "one person can't make a difference."* Who among us has not at some point looked inward and asked, "I would like to do something about that problem, but what can one person do?" Mancur Olson argues that this tendency manifests itself in the reluctance of individuals to join interest groups—even those that work on their behalf.

To see how the political efficacy problem works, let us again assume that you support the political goals of the NRA. The political efficacy problem means that though you support the group's political goals, you realize that neither its multi-million-dollar budget (the NRA has assets of over $200 million) nor its political efforts will substantially suffer if you decide not to join. Surely you realize that a group with millions of dollar and thousands of members, as well as a huge building on the outskirts of Washington, DC and thousands of staff people, does not really need your paltry annual membership fee. The political efficacy problem means that when confronted with the decision of whether or not to join the NRA (or any other interest group whose political goals you support), you ask yourself: "What difference can my contribution make?" You answer, "Not a whole heck of a lot." In the end, you decide not to join.

In sum, cost, the "free-rider" problem, and the political efficacy problem together represent substantial barriers to interest group formation and survival. These barriers help to explain why shared interests do not necessarily lead to the formation of interest groups. In summing up the significance of these barriers, political scientist Paul Johnson has written that their existence leads to two primary conclusions. "First," Johnson notes, "some large segments of the population [will remain] unorganized." Johnson cites the young, the homeless, and the poor as segments of society that largely have been unable to overcome the barriers to interest group formation. "Second," Johnson continues, "the interest groups that exist are not necessarily representative of the different interests that make up society."[11]

How Unorganized Constituencies Become Organized

Mancur Olson and other scholars who acknowledge that group formation and maintenance are difficult do not preclude the possibility that interest groups could form and survive. After all, the interest group I use to illustrate Olson's points about the barriers to formation and survival is the NRA—a group that has been in business for over 150 years and is very powerful. Scholars simply acknowledge that barriers must be overcome if a group of people is to form and/or maintain an interest group. To understand how interest groups form and survive, Olson and others argue, we must understand how they overcome these barriers. According to Olson, there are two primary ways that interest groups can overcome the barriers to formation and survival: *providing selective benefits* and *coercing people to join*. Writing after Olson, other political scientists identified another way that interest groups overcome the barriers to formation and survival: *procuring patron support*. Each of these methods deserves a closer look.

Providing Selective Benefits

One way an interest group can overcome the barriers to formation and survival is to provide selective benefits—*benefits that accrue only to an interest group's members*. Because many people will not join interest groups for collective benefits, Olson argues, they must be offered inducements they cannot receive unless they join. There are three basic types of selective benefits. *Material benefits* are benefits that have tangible economic value. Examples of material benefits include magazines, discounts, inexpensive insurance, hats, stickers, and newsletters. *Solidary benefits* are social rewards such as meetings, outings, and group gatherings. Finally, *expressive benefits* are intangible benefits derived from working for a cause.[12] One example of an expressive benefit is the good feeling you get when you work for a cause you believe in. Another is the avoidance of guilt for not having "done your part."[13]

To understand how selective benefits induce people to join interest groups, let us return to the case of the AARP—a massive organization that represents the interests of the elderly. The primary collective benefits sought by the AARP are programs and policies (e.g., Medicare and Social Security) that ensure financial and health security for older Americans. These benefits are collective because if they are obtained, they accrue to all elderly Americans—not just members of the AARP. Because the leaders of the AARP realize that collective benefits may not be enough to induce membership, they offer members a number of selective benefits. The range of benefits is astounding. For example, AARP members receive discounts on hotels such as Best Western, Hyatt, LaQuinta Inns and Suites, and Wyndham, among others; discounts on rental cars from major chains Alamo, Avis, Budget, Enterprise, Hertz, and National; and discounts on cruises from Norwegian Cruise Line, MSC Cruises, and Blount Small Ship Adventures. Members also receive America's largest circulation magazine, *AARP, The Magazine*. Members can also buy automobile, home, life, medical, mobile home, and motorcycle insurance from AARP partner companies. These are but a few of the material selective benefits the group offers members. The group also provides its members selective solidary benefits in the form of meetings, outings, and online chat rooms. Finally, the AARP provides its members with a sense of well-being associated with political activism. This constitutes a selective expressive benefit. The cost of an annual membership in the AARP is $16. Table 3.1 lists the collective and selective benefits offered by two citizen groups—the AARP and the NRA. As you can see from just these two groups, the variety of selective benefits that interest groups use to entice members is quite remarkable.

Providing selective benefits helps overcome all three barriers to interest group formation and survival. First, it overcomes the desire to "free-ride" by making some benefits unavailable to "free-riders." Second, it renders the political efficacy problem moot by delivering something tangible to members in return for their support. Third, it helps overcome the cost barrier by providing money for the organization by levying membership dues on people who wish to join.

Coercing People to Join

Another way interest groups overcome the barriers to formation and survival is by coercing people to join. Coercion is most common in labor unions. In some states, in some industries, labor unions are allowed under the law virtually to compel individuals to support them financially as a condition of employment. In 1935, the federal government passed the National Labor Relations Act (NLRA). Paul Johnson explains the effect of the NLRA: the NLRA "allowed labor unions to sign 'security agreements' with employers, stipulating that all employees had to pay union dues as a condition of employment."[14] In short, a business firm that operated under a security agreement with a specific labor

Table 3.1 Two Interest Groups and Some of Their Collective and Selective Benefits

Interest group	Collective benefit	Selective benefits[1]
AARP	Government policies that "protect Medicare and Social Security"	*Material*: Car rental, cell phone service, cruise, fitness club, home alarm system; hotel, movie theatre, restaurant, retail item, tour, and vacation package discounts Access to AARP-branded car, dental, home, mobile home, life, long-term care, "Medigap," and motorcycle insurance Monthly magazine: *AARP: The Magazine* Periodic publication: *AARP Bulletin* Career fair Tax preparation assistance Driver training programs *Solidary*: Local chapter meetings Annual convention *Expressive*: "Involvement in politics" "Feeling of doing your part"
NRA	Government policies that protect the "Constitutional right to keep and bear arms"	*Material*: Choice of one of the following monthly magazines: *American Rifleman, American Hunter, America's 1st Freedom* $5,000 death and dismemberment insurance $2,500 insurance coverage for covered firearms, air guns, bows and arrows Car rental, cell phone service, firearm training, hearing aid, hotel, and laser vision correction discounts Shooting clinics and competitions *Solidary*: Local chapter meetings Annual convention *Expressive*: "Having a voice in Washington" A good feeling from "pitching in"

Sources: This table is based upon a perusal of each group's website (aarp.org and nra.org, both accessed January 11, 2012), as well as a telephone conversation with a member of each group's staff. Words in "" are direct quotes from an interest group representative or the group's website.

Note: 1. This column describes only some of the benefits offered by each group, not all the benefits.

union agreed not to hire non-union employees. Thus, a person who wished to work for a business that had a security agreement with a specific union was, in essence, forced to join the labor union in order to do so. Security agreements were allowed in all states until 1947, when the Taft–Hartley Labor-Management Relations Act was passed. Taft–Hartley allowed states to adopt "right to work" laws that could forbid security agreements. Today, twenty-two states have right to work laws that make it very difficult for labor unions to coerce people to join. Yet twenty-eight states do not have right to work laws. In these twenty-eight states, under the NLRA, a person may be required to pay union dues as a condition of employment if the collective bargaining agreement between him/her and his/her employer contains a provision called a "union security clause" that requires all employees either to join the union or pay union dues. In short, there are still instances in which people are more or less coerced into joining labor unions as a condition of employment. Thus, coercion as a means of overcoming the barriers to interest group formation and survival is alive and well.

None of this is to say that unions have an easy time forming and/or surviving. Before a labor union wins the right to represent a group of workers for collective bargaining purposes it faces a serious barrier to formation—it must convince a majority of workers at a given site to affiliate with the union. To overcome this problem, labor unions generally emphasize the selective material benefits of labor union membership such as health insurance, life insurance, employment security, and seniority perquisites.[15] Nonetheless, coercion was instrumental in making labor unions strong in the late 1930s and early 1940s, and coercion continues to help some labor unions overcome the barriers to group formation and survival.

Some PACs also practice a form of coercion, though in a rather more subtle way than labor unions. Specifically, anecdotal evidence indicates that some business executives "strongly encourage" some of their employees to contribute to the corporate PAC. Over the years, many disgruntled corporate officers, division managers, and lawyers have reported that encouragement often is de facto coercion. Throughout American history many professional associations have used coercion as well, as it was all but impossible to engage in certain professions without being a member of a certain professional association. To this day, in thirty-two states and Washington DC one must be a member of the state (or DC) bar association to practice law.[16]

Coercion, like the provision of selective benefits, helps interest groups overcome all three barriers to formation and survival. First, it makes "free-riding" an impossibility. Second, it renders the political efficacy problem moot. Finally, it guarantees a steady flow of income for the interest group in question.

Relying Upon Patrons

Another way to overcome the barriers to formation and survival is to find a patron. A patron is defined as *an individual or institutional benefactor who/which contributes substantial resources to an interest group*. There are thousands of individuals and institutions out there that give away free money to interest groups. *Private foundations*, for example, are non-profit institutions that make grants to individuals and non-profit organizations. Private foundations get their money from wealthy individuals, groups of people, or families. Some private foundations then use this money to fund other organizations. Private foundations are important sources of income for some interest groups, especially citizen groups. For example, political scientist Benjamin Marquez highlights the importance of foundation support for high-profile Mexican American interest groups including the National Council of La Raza, the Mexican American Legal Defense Fund, and the Southwest Voter Registration Education Project. Over the years, these groups and many others received millions of dollars from private foundations, including the Ford Foundation, the Rockefeller Foundation, and the Charles Stewart Mott Foundation. Marquez goes so far as to suggest that these foundation patrons were so important to the groups they funded that they had some impact on the types of causes the groups supported and the types of activities they engaged in.[17] High-profile, politically engaged private foundation patrons include: the Ford Foundation (which has provided money to groups including California Latinas for Reproductive Justice, Planned Parenthood Federation of America, and the Urban Institute);[18] the John D. and Catherine T. MacArthur Foundation (which in the past few years has provided money to the Brookings Institution, Human Rights Watch, and Physicians for Human Rights);[19] and the Sarah Scaife Foundation (which has provided money to groups including the Cato Institute, the NRA, and the U.S. Chamber of Commerce).[20] In any given year, private foundations provide hundreds of millions of dollars to interest groups. The bulk of this money goes to citizen groups and think tanks. One study suggests that over 80 percent of all citizen groups received some type of private foundation support during their initial start-up.[21]

For-profit business firms are also important sources of patronage. Every year, corporate America donates billions of dollars to organizations across the country.[22] A great deal of this money goes to organizations that are not politically active, such as local United Way chapters and schools. However, some of each year's corporate support finds its way into the coffers of interest groups. This adds up to hundreds of millions of dollars per year. According to one study, think tanks and citizen groups are the types of interest groups that receive the bulk of corporate patronage.[23] The Sierra Club's annual report shows, for example, that the group receives a great deal of money from business firms. The environmental group's 2009 annual report shows that the group received matching gifts (that is, organizational contributions that matched individual gifts) from numerous businesses including American Express, Bank of America, Coca-Cola, Exxon Mobil, Nestle, Pfizer, and Sun Microsystems.[24] Think tanks —especially conservative think tanks—get lots of money from business firms as well. The Heritage Foundations, for example, lists the Boeing Corporation, Exxon Mobil, Lockheed Martin Corp., Northrup Grumman, and United Parcel Service (UPS) as corporate donors in its 2010 annual report.[25]

The government provides patron support as well. Government patronage usually comes in the form of contracts for services or grants. Many, many business firms, for example, get some of their money from government when they sell goods or services to the government. All the giant defense contracting companies in the United States, for example, including Boeing, General Dynamics, Lockheed Martin, Northrup Grumman, and Raytheon, get a great deal of money from the federal government each year. At the state and local levels, companies of various types also sell goods or services to government, and receive money in return. The government provides money to other types of groups as well. For example, the federal government and many state governments have provided millions of dollars over the years to Planned Parenthood and its state affiliates. Box 3.1, which describes recent battles over government support for Planned Parenthood, highlights some of the problems groups may face when they accept government patronage.

Box 3.1 The Costs and Benefits of Government Patronage: The Case of Planned Parenthood

Planned Parenthood Federation of America is a large, federal organization comprising eighty-five independent affiliates that together operate over 800 health centers across the United States. These health centers provide a number of reproductive health services (mostly for women) including cancer screening, pregnancy options counseling, and sex education. The organization also provides birth control, vasectomies, and abortions.

Ever since the 1970s, Planned Parenthood has received federal government patronage. Specifically, Planned Parenthood has received federal grants and contracts to provide services including sex education counseling, the provision of contraception, pelvic exams, and screening and treatment for sexually transmitted diseases (STDs). Planned Parenthood receives approximately $70 million per year from the federal government.

The benefits of federal government patronage are clear. The money provides Planned Parenthood with precious resources it can use to fulfill its mission. The costs, however, are not insignificant. Planned Parenthood has always had enemies (inside and out of government) because in addition to providing non-controversial services such as STD testing and health exams for poor women and men, Planned Parenthood performs abortions. This means that in addition to getting lots of government money every year, it gets lots of government *attention* as well. Most of this attention comes from anti-abortion members of Congress (most prominent among them is staunch abortion foe Mike Pence, a Republican from Indiana). Critics argue that though Planned Parenthood does some good things (such as provide HIV testing), it should not receive any government money because it does one thing (provides abortions) that many Americans abhor.

In 2011, the House of Representatives voted to cut off all federal funding for Planned Parenthood. The vote, however, was largely symbolic, as President Obama promised to veto the bill if it made it to his desk, and the Democratic-led Senate refused to pass it (at least at the time of writing).

The case of Planned Parenthood points up the pros and cons of government patronage. On the one hand, money is good—wherever it comes from. On the other hand, with government money comes scrutiny—mostly unwanted scrutiny. In the end, group leaders must decide for themselves if patronage is worth the trouble.

Sources: Groppe, "House Votes to Block Funds to Planned Parenthood"; Kliff, "Mike Pence's War on Planned Parenthood."

Interest groups other than for-profit business firms also often act as patrons. Many trade associations, for example, contribute money to think tanks and citizen groups. The Heritage Foundation, for example, which is cited above, lists the Pharmaceutical Research and Manufacturers of America (PhRMA, a trade association of pharmaceutical research and biotechnology companies) as one of its donors. Similarly, some labor unions support think tanks, coalitions, and citizen groups.

Finally, wealthy individuals sometimes pump large amounts of money into interest groups. The annual reports of most large citizen groups, for example, contain the names of individual patrons who have been especially generous. Perhaps the most famous wealthy individual patron in the United States is George Soros, the billionaire investor and financier.[26] Over the years, Soros has contributed millions of dollars to liberal (mostly citizen) interest groups including Center for American Progress, Democracy Alliance, and moveon.org. On the conservative side, the billionaire businessmen Koch brothers (Charles and David) have provided millions to interest groups including the Americans for Prosperity Foundation, Citizens for a Sound Economy, and the Cato Institute.[27]

Of course, locating a patron willing to donate large sums of money is not always easy. Some interest groups have an easier time attracting patron support than others. Few interest groups are totally dependent upon patronage. Nonetheless, patrons have been instrumental in the formation and survival of thousands of interest groups.

In sum, Mancur Olson, the preeminent analyst of interest group formation and survival, argues that interest groups must find a way to overcome substantial barriers if they are to form and survive. The reason some interests are better represented by interest groups than others, he argues, is that some interest groups have an easier time forming and surviving—that is, overcoming the barriers to formation and survival—than others. All this, of course, begs the following question: Which interest groups are in the best position to overcome the barriers to formation and survival? We have already established how interest groups can overcome these barriers. But we still have not looked at which types of interest groups are in the best position to use the solutions we have discussed. This is our next order of business.

Explaining Unequal Interest Group Representation

Let's summarize what we've learned thus far. First, some interests are better represented by interest groups than others. Second, the reason this is the case is that there are barriers to the formation and survival of interest groups, and some groups of people have an easier time overcoming these barriers than others. These two points are essential. But we're not done yet. In order to understand why some interests are better represented by interest groups than others, we must determine which types of interest groups have the easiest (and hardest) time forming and surviving. The remainder of this chapter is devoted to doing this. In what follows, I will move beyond the generic conclusion that "some interests are better represented than others by interest groups" and describe which types of interest groups are most plentiful and why.

Institutions

Institutions—non-membership interest groups including for-profit business firms, non-profit business firms, colleges and universities, and government entities—are ideally suited to overcoming the barriers to interest group formation and survival. Why? Because two of the barriers—the "free-rider" problem and the political efficacy problem—have virtually no relevance to them. Think of it this way: an interest group without members does not have to worry about either "free-riders" or individuals who do not feel politically efficacious. Institutions do, of course, face one major barrier: cost. Where do institutions get the resources they need to form and maintain interest groups? The answer to this question depends upon the type of institution we're talking about. Businesses—both for-profit and non-profit—get the money they need to form and maintain themselves as interest groups by selling products and/or services. Shoe giant Nike, for example, hires lobbyists and joins trade associations with some of the money it earns selling athletic equipment. Governmental entities and foreign countries use tax dollars to form interest groups. When the people of California, for example, pay their taxes, they are indirectly funding the state's lobbyist corps in Washington, DC. Similarly, when Chinese citizens pay taxes, they are indirectly supporting the country's lobbying efforts in Washington.

Institutions face a tremendous advantage over membership interest groups—they face neither the "free-rider" problem nor the political efficacy problem. The only significant barrier they face is *cost*. This is not an insubstantial barrier. But it turns out that many institutions have an advantage in overcoming this barrier as well—they have lots of resources at their disposal. Many business firms, for example, have huge sums of money in their treasuries. So do many colleges and universities and government entities. The reason why institutions often have money at their disposal is that most of them exist for some non-political purpose(s). For-profit businesses, for example, exist to make money. Similarly, universities exist to educate people, and local governments exist to deliver services to residents. The political activities of these institutions are secondary or tertiary to their main purposes. This is important because an interest group that exists for a non-political purpose has an advantage over explicitly political organizations in overcoming the cost barrier. This is the case because instead of asking or begging people or patrons for money, an institution can simply meet the costs of interest group formation and/or survival by diverting some of the resources it possesses as a result of its primary activities and investing these resources in political activity.

The ease with which institutions can form and maintain interest groups has manifested itself in "the dominance of institutions." The "dominance of institutions" is the phrase political scientist Robert Salisbury has used to denote the overwhelming presence of institutions in the universe of interest groups. In the biggest study to date of institutional representation before government, Salisbury concluded that despite the preoccupation of the public and the media with "traditional membership interest groups, it is institutions, especially those of business, which clearly dominate" interest representation in Washington.[28] In his detailed study of national agricultural policy, Salisbury concluded that only one-sixth of the interest groups active on agricultural issues were traditional "individual membership groups."[29] The bulk of active interest groups, he found, were business firms.

Figure 2.2 on p. 29 above buttresses Salisbury's claims. As you can see, institutions are much better represented by interest groups than individual citizens. This is the case in states and localities as well. Not surprisingly, the most prominent institutions are business firms. *Any way you slice it, business dominates the world of interest group representation.* As Figure 2.2 shows, of the approximately 20,000 interest groups active in Washington, about one-fifth are business firms and one-seventh are trade associations (which represent businesses). Moreover, more than 50 percent of federal PACs are affiliated with business firms or trade associations. Together, businesses and trade associations and business PACs comprise approximately half of all the interest groups in Washington. There is ample evidence that business is equally dominant in states and localities.[30]

Why are business groups dominant in the universe of interest groups? There are two answers. First, like other types of institutions, business firms face fewer barriers to interest group formation and survival than membership groups. To form an interest group (that is, to hire a lobbyist) or join a trade association, all a business firm has to do is divert some of the money it makes from selling things into a separate account for political activity. Second, many business firms have lots of money. Even many unprofitable business firms have money. And to many businesses, spending some money on political activity seems like a good investment.

So what are the implications of the "dominance of institutions"? In the most general sense this dominance means that in most policy battles the interests of institutions are much better represented by interest groups than the interests of individuals—even individuals who use or are affiliated with these institutions. The dominance of institutions means, for example, that in making higher education policy, state governments hear much more from interest groups representing the providers (colleges and universities) and funders of education (banks, savings and loans, government entities) than they do from interest groups representing individuals who receive education (students) or work for the institutions (faculty and staff). Similarly, it means that in political battles that affect business interests (which many do), there are likely to be many more interest groups representing businesses (producers) than there are representing consumers. In making health care policy, for example, the federal government hears much more from interest groups representing the health care industry than from interest groups representing patients. None of this means, of course, that institutions always get what they want from government. For one thing, not all institutions share the same interests. Business firms, for example, often disagree amongst themselves about what constitute good government decisions. In addition, the interests of groups of individuals are seldom completely ignored. Citizen groups, labor unions, professional associations, and other groups that represent the interests of individuals rather than institutions are still major players in interest group politics. In the end, however, the dominance of institutions means that in most major political battles, the interests of America's most prominent institutions are likely to be well represented by interest groups.

The Affluent and the Intense

For many institutions, organizing is simply a matter of desire. But what about groups of individuals? Why do some groups of individuals have large and powerful interest groups working on their behalf while others have either small "ragtag" operations or no interest group representation at all? Why, for example, are the bankrupt not represented by any interest groups? Why are death penalty opponents so much better represented by interest groups than death penalty supporters? Why are older people well represented by interest groups before government while younger people are not? We have already established that contrary to disturbance theory, the sheer number of people who share an interest does not determine to what extent groups of individuals are represented by interest groups. What then *does* determine the extent to which groups of individuals who share an interest are represented by interest groups? The short answer is this: *their ability to overcome the barriers to interest group formation and survival.* Groups of individuals that have the easiest time overcoming the barriers to interest group formation and survival are likely to be better represented by interest groups than groups of individuals that have a difficult time overcoming these barriers. Which groups of individuals have the easiest time overcoming the barriers to interest group formation and survival? There are two general answers to this question.

One answer is *groups of affluent individuals*. No matter what interest they may have in common, groups of affluent individuals have an easier time overcoming the barriers to interest group formation and survival than groups of non-affluent individuals. The reasons for this are numerous. First, the affluent have a relatively easy time paying the costs of interest group membership. Simply put, the affluent by definition have more money than the not-so-affluent. Second, affluent individuals are less susceptible to the political efficacy problem than the non-affluent.[31] Studies have shown that income is highly correlated with education,[32] and that education increases an individual's level of efficacy— the feeling that one person *can* make a difference. Third, affluent people are more likely to have effective leaders in their midst than non-affluent people. An effective leader essentially is someone who is capable of doing the things necessary both to get a group off the ground—raise money, design packages of selective benefits to attract members, organize meetings, hold rallies, etc.— and make sure it survives. The importance of effective leaders in overcoming the barriers to interest group formation and survival cannot be overestimated. Robert Salisbury has pointed out that virtually all interest groups—like business firms—require leadership, both at birth and throughout their existence.[33] Salisbury likens the people who start and run interest groups to business entrepreneurs. Research on leadership shows that interest group founders and leaders tend to be much more educated and affluent than the average American.[34] Thus, the affluent have more (and more skilled) potential leaders in their midst than the needy. Incidentally, it is worth mentioning that the crucial importance of leadership provides yet one more advantage to institutions: virtually all institutions have at least some capable leaders. Business firms, for example, are likely to have dozens of capable and effective leaders. These individuals—though they may not be political leaders—are likely to possess the skills necessary to get an interest group off the ground; which in this case means figuring out a way to divert some of the institution's resources into political activity.

The evidence that the affluent dominate individual membership interest group representation is overwhelming. First, studies show that upper-income individuals join membership groups at a much higher rate than lower-income Americans. One landmark study, for example, compared two income groups at the extremes—those with annual family incomes below $15,000 (which was the poverty line at the time of the study), and those with annual family incomes above $75,000—and found that 73 percent of people in the highest income bracket were affiliated with a political organization, compared to only 29 percent of people in the lowest income bracket.[35] In addition, data show that individuals in the highest income bracket are over twice as likely to belong to more than one political organization than individuals in the lowest income bracket.[36] Second, case studies show that membership groups, even those that claim to represent the "public at large," tend to draw their members from the upper circles of American society. A case study of the Sierra Club, for example, concluded that club members "are wealthier, better educated, and more likely to engage in political activity than average Americans."[37] In another noteworthy study, political scientist Andrew McFarland found that the median Common Cause member "had a family income of about $37,000 at a time when the national average family income was about $20,000 per year." Members were also hyper-educated. Close to 50 percent had earned graduate or professional degrees.[38] Similarly, a study of contributors to Christian Right political action committees found that 63 percent had incomes over $50,000 per year (at a time when the median was around $20,000), and 75 percent were college graduates. Finally, a number of studies show that when membership groups—especially citizen groups—recruit members, they focus most of their efforts on the affluent. Not surprisingly, their memberships are dominated by affluent Americans.[39]

The affluence advantage has several implications. First, and perhaps most important, it means that constituencies, no matter how large they are, which consist wholly or mostly of lower-income Americans—homeless people, illegal immigrants, the unemployed, farm workers, and welfare recipients, for example—are likely to be poorly represented by interest groups. Groups of individuals such as these simply do not have the same abilities to overcome the barriers to interest group formation and survival that more affluent people have. There are, of course, interest groups working on behalf of lower-income Americans. In Washington alone, for example, there are dozens of labor unions representing the interests of working people, as well as hundreds of citizen groups representing the interests of the homeless, the poor, the uneducated, and the indigent. Not surprisingly, however, these groups tend to have rather limited resources compared to interest groups representing upper- and middle-income Americans. Second, the affluence advantage means that even those interest groups that *do* represent the interests of lower-income Americans are likely to be formed and maintained by (that is, led by) upper- and middle-class Americans. Studies of group leadership have consistently found that with a few exceptions, interest groups working on behalf of America's most disadvantaged citizens tend to be formed and maintained by upper- and middle-class Americans.[40] Finally, the affluence advantage means that in any given political battle, the views of the affluent are likely to be well represented by interest groups. This is true if the affluent are united on a given issue—say, for example, if 80 percent of upper-income Americans believe that capital gains taxes should be lowered—or if they are divided—say, for example, if 50 percent of affluent Americans supported abortion rights and 50 percent opposed them. In the first case, the view that capital gains taxes should be decreased will most likely be better represented than the view that capital gains taxes should be increased. In the second case, which side is better represented by interest groups is likely to be determined by something other than how the opinions and views of affluent Americans are distributed.

In the end, of course, none of this means that the affluent always get what they want from government. For one thing, as you will see in Chapter 9, government decision-makers do not make all their decisions solely based on what interest groups want. Second, lower-income people do participate in politics in other ways—mainly, they vote (though at a much lower rate than higher-income people). And most government decision-makers who run for office know that they cannot simply ignore the views of lower-income Americans.

Another answer to the question of which groups of individuals have the easiest time overcoming the barriers to interest group formation and survival is *groups of intense individuals* (i.e., individuals who feel very intensely about an issue). Political scientists have found that no matter what interest they may have in common, groups of intense individuals have an easier time overcoming the barriers to interest group formation and survival than less intense individuals. The reason for this is simple: people who feel intensely about an issue are more willing to bear the costs of interest group membership than people who do not feel intensely. The intense are also more likely to see "pitching in" as their duty.

Intensity can mitigate the effects of the "free-rider" and political efficacy problems. The tendency of the intense to participate in collective endeavors explains why death penalty interest group representation is dominated by death penalty opponents. Those who oppose the death penalty do so with a zeal that is uncommon among death penalty proponents. Intensity also explains to some extent why the NRA has had so much success over the years. Polls consistently show that gun control supporters outnumber gun control opponents in the United States by a wide margin. Yet the NRA has thousands more members than virtually *all* nationally active anti-gun groups combined. Why? Because gun control opponents oppose gun control with almost revolutionary zeal.

Studies of individual political participation suggest that those who feel intensely about political issues—those who follow politics, who care about what happens, and care deeply about who wins and who loses—are more politically active than the less intense.[41] The same studies show that strong partisans—that is, people who most strongly identify with a political party—participate more in politics than weak partisans.[42] Furthermore, not surprisingly, studies of individual membership interest groups—especially citizen groups and other types of organizations open to all citizens—show that group members generally feel very strongly about the issues upon which they are politically active.[43]

The intensity advantage has several implications. First, it means that constituencies, no matter how large they are, which consist wholly or almost wholly of individuals who share an interest but do not feel very intensely about it, are likely to be poorly represented by interest groups. A second and closely related implication is that the interests of the intense—even if these interests are decidedly unpopular with the majority of Americans—are seldom ignored by government. In any given political battle, government decision-makers are likely to hear far more from the intense than they are from the rest of us. Again, none of this means that the most intense Americans always get their way on policy issues they care about. It does mean, however, that the views of the intense are taken into serious consideration by government decision-makers.

The Importance of Leadership

The importance of both affluence and intensity begs the following question: What explains the formation and survival of interest groups representing people who are neither affluent nor intense? One answer is *leadership*. Studies have found that effective leadership is capable of overcoming the barriers to interest group formation and survival—no matter how overwhelming these barriers seem. Perhaps nothing demonstrates the importance of leadership like the case of the United Farm Workers (UFW). Farm workers are (and always have been) some of the lowest-paid and marginal participants in the American economy. They earn little money. Many live and work amid squalor. Many are uneducated, and many are immigrants.[44] In short, as a group, farm workers seem unlikely candidates to overcome the barriers to interest group formation and survival. In fact, few constituencies in America seem less capable of overcoming the barriers to interest group formation and survival. Yet in the late 1960s, the UFW managed to mobilize. By the early 1970s, the union had over 100,000 members and contracts with over 300 growers. Though its membership dropped in the conservative 1980s, it remains in business to this day. The UFW not only mobilized, but succeeded in reaching collective bargaining agreements with hundreds of California growers. It also succeeded in obtaining legislation that safeguarded the rights of farm workers.

How did the UFW manage? Part of the answer is Cesar Chavez—the charismatic founder of the UFW. By many accounts, it was the late Chavez's sheer force of will that led to the creation of the UFW. By convincing farm workers of the need to organize, and enlisting powerful allies such as California Governor Jerry Brown, Chavez was able to form an unlikely interest group. The lesson of the UFW is this: virtually any constituency can overcome the barriers to interest group formation and survival with effective leadership. Leaders, it turns out, can use skill and charisma to overcome the barriers to interest group formation and survival. They may design attractive packages of benefits to attract members. They may successfully court patrons willing to subsidize their organizing efforts. Or they may convince individuals who share their interests that their participation is necessary and vital.

Leadership is not the only factor that explains the formation and survival of interest groups representing people who are neither affluent nor intense. Studies have found that *social pressure* can also help groups of poor, not-so-intense individuals overcome the barriers to interest group formation and survival. In a ground-breaking study of the civil rights movement, political scientist Dennis Chong showed that many individuals who might otherwise have eschewed joining interest groups were persuaded to join civil rights groups by their friends and neighbors. Chong states: "Many people participate in causes out of a sense of obligation to their families, friends, and associates; they go along to get along, to repeat a trite but true aphorism."[45] On a similar note, Chong concludes that many people joined civil rights groups—groups in which their friends and neighbors and family members were active—because they feared that not doing so might result in damage to their "reputation, ostracism, or repudiation from the community."[46]

In short, Chong concludes that groups active in the civil rights movement were able to survive by relying on social pressure to get people to "join up." This, of course, begs the question of how these groups got "off the ground" in the first place. In other words, Chong's ideas explain how civil rights groups were able to attract members once they got started, but they do not explain how these organizations got started in the first place. The key, according to Chong, was leadership. We have come full circle, back to leadership. In order to bring social pressure to bear, groups must get "up and running." And leaders are the ones who get groups up and running. This begs yet another question: What motivates leaders to start groups? In many cases, according to Chong, the answer is *altruism*. That is, sometimes people start groups simply because they feel that it is the "right thing to do." Mancur Olson, whom we encountered earlier, did not say much about altruism. But even he acknowledged that sometimes people are driven to act by altruism.

The ability of leadership (which is often accompanied by altruism) and social pressure to help groups of people overcome the substantial barriers to interest group formation and survival means that virtually any group of people have some chance of successfully forming an interest group, and thus being represented before government. This should not, however, cause you to lose sight of the larger message of this chapter: despite the fact that virtually any group of people can overcome the barriers to interest group formation and survival, some groups of people are better suited to doing so than others.

This has been a long section, so a summary is in order. The major point of this section has been this: some interests are better represented by interest groups than others because there are substantial barriers to interest group formation and survival and not all constituencies are equally capable of overcoming these barriers. The interests in American society that are most likely to be well represented by interest groups are those of America's preeminent (especially business) institutions. This is the case because institutions face far fewer barriers to interest group formation and survival than groups of individuals. Business firms in particular are in an excellent position to overcome these barriers. None of this means that the shared interests of groups of individuals go unrepresented by interest groups. As Chapters 1 and 2 attest, many groups of individuals are represented by interest groups. Not all groups of individuals with shared interests, however, are equally represented by interest groups. The reason for this is *not* simply that some constituencies are larger than others. Rather, which groups of individuals are best represented by interest groups partially is a function of which groups have the easiest time overcoming the barriers to interest group formation and survival. We have learned that groups of affluent individuals and groups of intense individuals are better represented by interest groups than other groups of individuals. Taken together, all of this means that interest group representation does not necessarily reflect objective societal conditions. In other words, you cannot determine the distribution of *interest groups* by looking at the distribution of *interests*.

The Effect of Disturbances and Societal Change on Interest Group Formation and Survival

All of this talk of costs and benefits and leadership and barriers inevitably leads to one question: Do disturbances—events or series of events that profoundly affect society—and/or societal change play any role in interest group formation and survival? A focus on costs and benefits and leadership, some argue, obscures the fact that societal change and disturbances actually *do* play a large role in interest group formation and survival. Take, for example, the spread of AIDS and HIV. The HIV was not even identified until the mid-1980s. Thus, not surprisingly, before the mid-1980s, there were no interest groups concerned with AIDS. By the mid-1990s, however, *The Encyclopedia of Associations* listed hundreds of nationally active interest groups concerned with AIDS.[47] Hundreds of AIDS groups are active to this day. Clearly, these groups formed partially as a result of a disturbance—the AIDS epidemic. Without the AIDS epidemic they would never have existed.

Societal change and disturbances often encourage the formation of interest groups by giving rise to new interests in society. Nonetheless, neither societal changes nor disturbances in and of themselves *cause* the formation of interest groups. In other words, while disturbances and societal changes may lead to the creation of new *interests*, they are not sufficient to create *interest groups*. Interest groups—actual organizations that engage in political activity— must be started by actual human beings, must be managed by actual human beings, and must be financed by actual human beings. This takes time and money and effort and tenacity and skills. And no disturbance is capable of either forcing an entrepreneur to form an interest group or forcing a person or patron to support an interest group. These decisions—decisions that are made by individuals and institutions every day—are made partially on the basis of costs and benefits, not just on the basis of objective societal conditions or shared interests.

Conclusion: Explaining Why Some Interests are Better Represented by Interest Groups than Others

This chapter began with the following observation: despite the incredible size and enormous diversity of the universe of interest groups in America, some interests are better represented by interest groups than others. The primary message of this chapter is: the reason why some interests are better represented by interest groups than others is that there are substantial barriers to the formation and survival of interest groups and not all constituencies are equally capable of overcoming these barriers. In other words, some interest groups have an easier time forming and surviving than others. The most important barriers to interest group formation and survival are cost, the "free-rider" problem, and the political efficacy problem.

Institutions have an easier time overcoming the barriers to formation and survival than groups of individuals. This is one reason why the universe of interest groups is dominated by institutions—especially business firms. All is not lost, however, for groups of individuals that wish to form and maintain interest groups. It is possible for such groups to overcome the barriers to interest group formation and survival. But it is not easy. It requires the provision of selective benefits, coercion, the procurement of patronage, or some combination of the three. Groups of affluent individuals seem to have an easier time forming and maintaining interest groups than groups of not so affluent individuals. Likewise, groups of intense individuals have an easier time forming and maintaining interest groups than groups of not so intense individuals. Nonetheless, it is possible for virtually any group of individuals to overcome the barriers to interest group formation and survival. One key is leadership.

What's Next

Now that we have some idea of where interest groups come from and how they survive, we can turn to matters that are (arguably) less recondite—what interest groups do and how much influence they wield. The rest of this book is devoted to these two topics. I turn first to the non-lobbying activities of interest groups. Then, I delve headlong into lobbying—attempts by interest groups to influence government decisions. Understanding how and why interest groups lobby is crucially important. For it is because interest groups lobby that political scientists (and media) pay them so much attention.

The Non-Lobbying Activities of Interest Groups

4

The primary reason why political scientists (and you) study interest groups is that interest groups lobby. Organizations that do not lobby—organizations such as business firms or charities that are not politically active, and fan clubs and social clubs—are not of much interest to scholars of politics. However, lobbying is not *all* that interest groups do. In fact, many (if not most) interest groups—or to be more precise, the people who work for them—spend far more time on non-lobbying activities than they do on lobbying. Most of the people who run and work for business firms, for example, spend far more time on the non-lobbying activities associated with designing, manufacturing, and selling things to consumers than they do on lobbying. Even lobbyists—the people who actually do a group's lobbying—spend a great deal of their time on non-lobbying activities. In short, a thorough understanding of interest group behavior requires a thorough understanding of the non-lobbying activities of interest groups.

This chapter takes a brief look at three of the most important non-lobbying activities in which groups engage: *organizational maintenance*, *monitoring*, and *self-governance*. Of course, this book devotes much more attention to lobbying than to non-lobbying activities. Indeed, Chapters 5–7 are fully devoted to the subject of lobbying, while only this chapter is devoted to non-lobbying activities. This uneven division of labor, however, should not cause you to overlook the fact that a full understanding of interest groups requires a full understanding of their non-lobbying activities.

Engaging in Organizational Maintenance

Political scientist James Q. Wilson has noted, "Whatever else organizations seek, they seek to survive."[1] To put it another way, survival is the preeminent goal of all interest groups. Why is survival so important? Because if an interest group ceases to exist it cannot possibly achieve any of its political goals. An analogy can help here. Assume for a second that you have two major goals in life: making a million dollars, and taking a trip to Borneo. If you die, the chances of you achieving either of these goals are nil. Interest groups are like you and me in this regard: they cannot achieve any of their other goals if they cannot survive. Thus, just as surviving on a day-to-day basis is a priority for most of us—this is why we continue to eat, breathe, protect our safety, and seek medical care when we feel bad—surviving on a day-to-day basis is a priority for interest groups.

In sum, to have any chance to achieve its political goals, an interest group must do what it takes to stay alive. Doing what it takes to stay alive is called engaging in "organizational maintenance." The cornerstone of organizational maintenance is *obtaining money*. Money is the key to organizational maintenance because money can be used to purchase or otherwise acquire the things that make an interest group powerful. Money can be used, for example, to hire lobbyists, to recruit members, to attract competent staff, to rent office space, and to pay the bills.

There are four basic ways that interest groups obtain money: performing a primary non-political function, procuring patron support, recruiting members and then asking them for money, and selling goods and/or services. As you read on, it is important to recognize that these four ways are not mutually exclusive—many interest groups use a combination of methods to obtain money.

Performing a Primary Non-Political Function

Many interest groups acquire money by performing their primary non-political function. Non-membership interest groups that exist primarily for non-political purposes (e.g., business firms, colleges and universities, and governmental entities), for example, obtain money by performing their primary functions. For instance, business firms obtain money by selling goods and/or services. Similarly, colleges and universities obtain money by charging students for educational services and acquiring grants for research and education. Table 4.1 lists several interest groups and describes the primary non-political function

Table 4.1 Some Interest Groups and the Things They Spend Most of Their Time On

Interest group	Primary non-political activity
BP Global	Producing and selling oil, gas, and other things
Boys and Girls Clubs of America	Administering programs to help young people
Government of China	Governing the country of China
Planned Parenthood Federation of America	Providing reproductive health and child care services
State of Minnesota	Designing and delivering governmental services to the people of Minnesota
University of California, Los Angeles	Educating students
Wal-Mart	Selling merchandise

Sources: Organizational websites: http://www.bp.com/bodycopyarticle.do?categoryId=1& contentId=7052055; http://www.bgca.org/Pages/index.aspx, http://www.gov.cn/english/; http://www.plannedparenthood.org/; http://www.state.mn.us/portal/mn/jsp/home.do? agency=NorthStar, http://www.ucla.edu/; http://www.walmart.com/?adid=777777779122 00165254&wmlspartner=PSBrand. All accessed July 5, 2011.

each group performs. All of the organizations in the table expend far more time on the function in question than they do on politics and lobbying. In short, for many interest groups politics is just one small part of what they do.

Procuring Patron Support

Some interest groups obtain money by acquiring patron support. (Recall the term "patron" was defined in Chapter 3.) Research has shown that three types of interest groups in particular rely heavily upon patrons for financial support: charities, citizen groups, and think tanks.[2]

The specific ways that interest groups go about procuring patron support vary. But in general, the process works something like this. First, an interest group conducts research to determine which patrons might be willing to support it. For example, an environmental citizen group will seek information on patrons who support environmental causes. Second, the interest group applies for patron support. The application process is straightforward: the applicant fills out some forms, discusses its qualifications, and spells out how granted funds will be used. In all, procuring patron support is analogous to applying for a scholarship. Just as a scholarship-seeking student does research to determine who might be willing to give him/her college money, a patronage-seeking interest group does research to determine who might be willing to give it money. Then, just as a student applies for the scholarships that he/she feels qualified for, an interest group applies for the patronage that it feels it qualifies for.

Of course, there is never any guarantee that an interest group that wants patronage will get patronage. Some interest groups simply cannot locate any patrons willing to support them. Others locate patrons that are open to support them, but nonetheless have their applications for patron support rejected. Today there is an extensive "funding infrastructure" that helps interest groups (especially charities and citizen groups) locate potential patrons and procure patron support. One important part of this infrastructure is an organization called the Foundation Center—a non-profit educational institution funded by private foundation and corporate patrons. The Foundation Center acts as a clearinghouse for information on how and where organizations can obtain patron support.[3] The Center has assets of over $20 million and maintains and prints a variety of databases, directories, guidebooks, and indices designed to connect interest groups (and non-politically active organizations as well) with potential foundation and corporate foundation patrons. The Center publishes *The Foundation Directory Online*, for example, an online directory of foundation patrons and grants that is updated weekly.[4] In the same vein, the Center publishes *Corporate Giving Online* (an online database of corporate funders and grants), and several print volumes, including *The Foundation Directory* (covering American private foundations), *National Directory of Corporate Giving* (corporate foundation and giving programs), and *Celebrity Foundation Directory* (foundations established by famous athletes, entertainers, and politicians). The Center also publishes a number of books designed to help organizations procure money once they have located patrons open to supporting them. It also maintains 450 document collections in locations across the country, and conducts fundraising and grant-writing seminars.[5]

The Foundation Center is not the only resource available to interest groups that seek patron support. There are many for-hire consultants that groups can hire to help them find patrons, and many other businesses and organizations publish volumes designed to help patronage-seeking groups as well. In addition, for interest groups that wish to secure federal government support, there are government publications including the *Catalog of Federal Domestic Assistance*[6] and websites such as *grants.gov*.

Recruiting Members

Many interest groups obtain money by recruiting members. For example, most membership interest groups—including charities, churches, citizen groups, labor unions, professional associations, and trade associations—spend some of their time and money recruiting members. Few people go out of their way looking for interest groups to join. In other words, many people who join interest groups must be asked to do so. There are several methods by which membership interest groups recruit new members. One way (probably the most common) is through *direct mail advertising*—member recruitment through the regular mail. Direct mail is so common among membership groups that a few more words about it are in order.

The direct mail advertising process starts with a mailing list—a list of names and addresses. Seldom do membership interest groups send direct mail "blindly"—that is, to a random bunch of people.[7] Instead, an interest group starts with a "prospect list"—a list of potential members who are likely to respond.[8] Gwyneth J. Lister, a direct mail expert, has given this advice to fundraisers within interest groups:

> I have asked many members of the public if they read the nonprofit [interest group] mail they receive. Most say, "Oh, no, I don't read those letters." But several have added, "Unless it is a cause I am interested in." It is a fact of life that not everyone will be interested in your cause. Your job is to find out who may be interested and why.[9]

A prospect list consists of the names of people who have joined similar groups in the past, or people who fit the basic demographic profile of a group's members, or people who seem to share the group's interests. A prospect mailing list for an environmental citizen group, for example, may consist of people who have supported other environmental groups in the past, or people who subscribe to magazines concerning backpacking or sailing or rock climbing. Interest groups either "rent" prospect lists from "list brokers" who specialize in putting together such lists, or rent them from or trade them with other interest groups with similar concerns.[10] Political scientists Grant Jordan and William A. Maloney have written, "A specialist niche industry creating and managing databases underpins many recruitment operations."[11]

In other words, interest groups can buy lists from people who compile them for a living.

The next step in the direct mail advertising process is to design the *direct mail package*—the parcel that contains an organization's direct mail advertisement. The typical direct mail package has three components: (1) an outside envelope, (2) an appeal letter, which is essentially a letter "describing the organization and its needs,"[12] and (3) a self-addressed stamped envelope that the recipient can use to respond. People who use and study direct mail have come up with a few "rules of thumb" for effective direct mail packages.

First, a direct mail package should be personal. This means that the outside envelope, as well as the appeal letter, should be directed to a specific person rather than "resident" or "addressee." It also means either handwriting the envelope and/or the letter, or if this is not possible (as it won't be in many cases), making the envelope and/or appeal letter *look* like they have been handwritten (often this is accomplished by using a cursive typeface).[13] In addition, it means using a pre-cancelled bulk mail stamp—that is, an actual stamp—rather than relying upon bulk mail indicia.[14] Finally, the appeal letter should mention the recipient by name. Kim Klein says that people are selfish and like to read about themselves, and thus an appeal letter "should refer to the reader at least twice as often and up to four times as often as it refers to the organization sending it."[15]

Second, a direct mail package should be simple but not too concise.[16] Interestingly, the conventional wisdom in the direct mail industry is that the ideal direct mail appeal letter is 3–4 pages long. A letter longer than one page, the argument goes, shows the recipient that the group has a certain gravitas and has a lot to say.[17] A long letter, however, need not be complex. Direct mail experts agree that appeal letters should eschew big words and long paragraphs.[18]

Third, a direct mail package must include an appeal for membership. This seems like a "no-brainer," but it is worth mentioning. For a direct mail package to work it needs to contain information about precisely what the group wants from the recipient; and what the group wants from the recipient is for him/her to join the group. Thus, the direct mail appeal letter should say something like, "We are writing you today to ask you to join our organization." As direct mail expert Gwyneth Lister has written, "Be sure to ask for financial support."[19]

Fourth, a direct mail appeal should contain some information about why a person should join the group. In many cases—the case of environmental citizen groups again comes to mind—a person who receives a direct mail letter knows that he/she has many choices if he/she wants to join an interest group. Why should he/she join *this* group instead of some other? The direct mail appeal needs to address this question. The type of information designed to appeal to donors might include information about the group's accomplishments ("We stopped Congress from passing that terrible law last year"), or its size and impressiveness (We are the biggest gun rights group in southeastern Jackson County, with over 1,000 members), or its history ("We have been around since 1975 and we will be here over the long haul").[20] Finally, and this too seems like a "no-brainer," a direct mail package must contain a way for the recipient to respond. This is why direct mail packages virtually always include a self-addressed stamped envelope.

For many years it was the conventional wisdom that there was one more thing that a direct mail package needed to have—negativity. Indeed, in a recent book on environmental citizen groups, Grant Jordan and William Maloney write: "groups have found that in many instances negative appeals have a greater pulling power than positive ones."[21] This is the case, they argue, because studies show that bad things, especially threats to a person's well-being, tend to increase a person's political efficacy, which in turn increases a person's willingness to join an interest group.[22] Negativity in direct mail appeals is manifested in exaggerating claims ("Things are so bad that if you do not act now the world is going to end"), and/or demonizing enemies ("Our opponents don't just disagree with us, they want to destroy America as we know it"). Political scientist R. Kenneth Godwin, who studied actual direct mail appeals from interest groups, concluded, "Propaganda techniques pervade direct mailings, tapping emotions designed to generate an immediate response, not to help think through a complex issue."[23] However, there is recent evidence that negativity may not be as widespread as previously thought. In a study of environmental citizen group communications, political scientist Melissa Merry recently has found that groups often use positive appeals, relying less on negative appeals than many people assume. In her study of environmental citizen groups—groups that are often criticized for relying heavily upon negative appeals and fear—she finds that direct mail from such groups contain many more positive messages than negative messages. Specifically, they say things along these lines: "Yes, there is a problem" (which is negative), "But we can fix it because we are a very effective group" (which is positive).[24]

Does direct mail work? On the one hand, everyone who studies direct mail acknowledges that the vast majority of direct mail that people receive, they throw away without even looking at. "Some marketing experts," direct mail expert Kim Klein writes, "estimate that up to 70 percent of [all] mail is thrown away unopened."[25] Even the most optimistic estimates suggest that a 2 percent response rate to direct mail solicitations is excellent, and a response rate of between 0.5 and 0.75 percent is acceptable.[26] At first sight, this hardly seems worth it. Consider that if your group sent out 5,000 pieces of direct mail and 1 percent of recipients responded, that would be a total of only 50 people. On the other hand, groups of all kinds—especially mass membership charities and citizen groups and unaffiliated PACs—rely heavily on direct mail to recruit members (or in the case of PACs, donors). Why? First, "direct mail remains the least expensive way to reach the most people with a message that they can hold in their hands and examine at their leisure."[27] The U.S. Postal Service gives bulk mailers—that is, organizations or people who send lots of pieces of mail at the same time—discounts; they do not pay the standard postage rate for a letter. Second, even a small response rate is enough to pay for a large mailing. This is the case because often after a group succeeds in recruiting a member once, that person or organization will remain in the group over the long haul. This means the person will continue to pay membership dues for a long time, and may even give money in excess of membership dues to the group.

In sum, membership groups continue to use direct mail to recruit members because though it costs money and direct mail packages are often tossed in the trash, it continues to be a cost-effective way to recruit new members. Charities and citizen groups and unaffiliated PACs appear to be the most prodigious users of direct mail recruiting, but it is also common in professional associations, trade associations, and labor unions. The Chamber of Commerce of the United States, for example, often sends direct mail solicitations to potential members—people who have recently started businesses or businesspeople who are not currently members.

Using Direct Mail to Tap Members for Donations

Membership interest groups use direct mail to recruit members, but they also use it to tap current members for donations in excess of membership dues. The process by which membership interest groups ask members for "special gifts" is similar to that by which they recruit members. They start with a list—except in this case it is a list of current members so no prospect list is necessary. Then a direct mail package is sent that typically makes a "special appeal." Usually a special appeal informs the member that the organization he / she belongs to needs "special help" at this time, either because there is some immediate dire threat to the group's goals (The recent oil spill has injured tens of thousands of birds. They need your help.) or because the group needs more money to fulfill its overall mission (The year is almost over and we need your money to meet our goal of raising $1,000,000 to help the environment).

The response rate for direct mail sent to current members tends to be higher than that for direct mail sent to non-members. In fact, response rates for these follow-up mailings average around 10 percent.[28] Moreover, once a person gives twice, he/she is very likely to give several more times. This is why direct mail professionals advise interest groups to send each of their members direct mail solicitations 2–4 times every year.[29] If you have ever joined an interest group you know that most interest groups follow this advice!

How important is tapping members for donations after they join up? We do not know for sure, but the evidence suggests it is extremely important. In a survey of donors to environmental citizen groups a few years ago, I learned that many of these donors give in excess of $1,000 a year to the group they belong to, and some give much, much more—sometimes millions. Moreover, some particularly rich and dedicated donors bequeath money and/or gifts to the groups they belong to. Essentially this means that a person writes a will in which he/she leaves some or all of the money or property he/she has to an interest group. Needless to say, such gifts are invaluable to interest groups, and often are worth hundreds of thousands or even millions of dollars.[30]

Other Ways to Recruit Members and Ask Members for Money

Direct mail advertising is not the only method by which interest groups recruit members and/or tap members for large donations. Several other methods exist as well. Perhaps most important among these other methods is *personally soliciting* money. This simply means recruiting members or asking current members for money via face-to-face interaction. Personal solicitations are particularly important for smaller groups (which may not be able to afford large-scale direct mail campaigns) and local groups (for example, neighborhood groups). In locally active small interest groups, for example, group leaders and/or board members may contact business associates, family members, and/or friends and ask them to either join the group or give the group money, or both. To start this process, a group may gather its staff together and ask them to brainstorm a list of names. From here, data are compiled about the people on the list, and a plan is hatched to contact them. After contact is made— perhaps by mail or telephone or electronic mail—a meeting is arranged and a pitch is made. Personally asking for money also is a very common way that groups—even large and nationally active groups—tap their current members for donations.[31] For larger groups, personal solicitation is generally used only to solicit large gifts from current donors.[32] The rules are basically the same, however—a list is compiled and contact is made. The list often is a list of current donors who seem like good "major gift" prospects based on their past giving and their profiles (information about their financial situation, for example). In the study I mentioned earlier (of large donors to environmental groups), several respondents reported that they were asked for large gifts quite often, and often had face-to-face contact with group leaders and staff.[33]

Another common way that interest groups recruit members and (especially) tap current members for donations face-to-face is by holding special events such as banquets, galas, house parties, or dinners.[34] A group can invite members or potential members to a special event, charge them "admission," and/or ask them for donations, and/or ask them to "purchase" a table. Special events are good venues for groups to raise money from current members because many donors like to be recognized, and dinners and galas are venues in which special thanks can be given to benefactors. A very quick Google search shows that many of the groups mentioned thus far in this book have special events on a regular basis. Many of the environmental groups mentioned here, for example, have local or state chapters that have annual "award" dinners. Many charities, of course, including local chapters of the American Heart Association, American Lung Association, and the American Red Cross, hold annual banquets or dinners to honor local luminaries and raise money. Similarly, many trade and professional associations—check out your local chamber of commerce chapter, for example—hold annual awards banquets or meetings to raise money.

Another way that interest groups recruit members and raise money is by *soliciting via email or the Internet.*[35] Not surprisingly, as the Internet has exploded in size and reach, Internet fundraising has done the same. Interest groups use the Internet and email in several ways to recruit members and get more money from current donors. First, groups place websites on the Internet. Indeed, virtually every interest group mentioned in this book has its own website. Even poor, small, and feckless groups have websites (because they are cheap). Studies show that a successful group website—that is, a website capable of attracting members and/or getting current members to join—contains information about the group's "mission, goals, objectives, and work" and information about how the group "uses donations and contributions."[36] Of course, it is also imperative that the group have a button on the website that makes it easy for website visitors to join and/or donate money to the group.[37] In addition to their own websites, more groups than ever have Facebook pages. Indeed, many of the groups mentioned in this book including the ABA, the AMA, the AFL-CIO, BP, the U.S. Chamber of Commerce, and the NRA have their own Facebook pages. Facebook pages need to have the same features as good websites to be effective.

In the past few years, more and more groups have turned to Twitter as well. Twitter is what computer gurus call a "micro-blogging tool." A Twitter account allows a group to send short messages (up to 140 characters) to subscribers. Many of the groups mentioned in this book have their own Twitter feeds. Yet another way that groups can use the Internet to recruit and tap members for money is by *blogging*. Blogging is simply writing on the Internet, and many groups have blogs connected to their websites or their Facebook pages. Blog entries are generally concise, readable, and (at least in theory) topical and interesting. Finally, groups can *send emails* to people.[38] Sending "cold" emails to people is uncommon, as such emails are generally considered "spam" (junk) and deleted or sequestered automatically. Thus, most groups that use email to recruit members send appeal emails only to people who have provided them with their email addresses (through, say, an online request for information). As for tapping members for donations, many members voluntarily provide their email addresses to the groups they belong to, and thus groups feel free to contact them regularly (in some cases, very regularly, perhaps as often as once per week) and ask them for money.

There are several other ways that groups can attract members and/or tap current members for donations. First, there is *direct telephone marketing*. Even in the age of "do not call lists" and cellphones, raising money by telephone remains surprisingly effective at bringing in money—especially for charities.[39] Direct telephone marketing is like direct mail advertising, except that it utilizes the telephone rather than the mail. Some studies suggest that direct telephone marketing is not very effective at recruiting new members, but *is* very effective in raising additional money from members.[40] Calling people is not particularly expensive these days, however, so some groups continue to use telephone marketing to recruit new members. Second, there is *advertising in the media* (in magazines, newspapers, television or radio). Some types of interest groups— especially charities and citizen groups—advertise in the media. One study suggests this is relatively common.[41] But many groups eschew this practice because it can be expensive and is not as efficient as other means of recruiting or tapping members for donations. Finally, groups can print and distribute *leaflets or pamphlets*. An interest group leaflet or pamphlet might look like a one-page mini-advertisement for the group, providing information about itself and how people can join or donate. One study suggests that leaflets are a relatively common way that groups attract members.[42] There is very little research on interest groups using this method to recruit members or ask people for money. Clearly, however, groups do this regularly. Indeed, interest group leaflets and pamphlets often pop up in numerous places. Usually such materials are strategically placed at locations most likely to connect with a specific audience. For example, at a recent visit to the county animal pound I encountered leaflets from the Humane Society of the United States. And on a visit to a local outdoor store I once encountered brochures from several environmental groups.

Finally, before leaving the topic of recruiting members and asking members for donations, it is worth noting that surprisingly large numbers of new members need not be recruited at all. In a recent study of a sample of interest groups in the UK, Grant Jordan and William Maloney report that a surprisingly large number of groups have members come to them "on their own initiative."[43] This is why "branding" is so important. A brand is defined as "a collection of perceptions about an organization, formed by its every communication, action, and interaction."[44] What this means in practice is that everything an interest group does sends a message to the public about what it is, what it wants, and how it works. So even things that interest groups do that are not designed primarily to attract members or donations build a group's brand and may (or may not) attract people to the group. People for the Ethical Treatment of Animals (PETA) is a good example of a group that has worked hard to build a unique brand. PETA is an animal rights group that is well known for doing outrageous things including sending naked or nearly naked people to public places to protest animal mistreatment, and printing advertisements of naked or nearly naked celebrities (for example, PETA has printed several advertisements in which celebrities including Steve-O from *Jackass* and actress and model Eva Mendes are naked under the words "I'd rather go naked than wear fur"). These advertisements are not designed to recruit members per se, but they publicize what PETA is all about and have succeeded in making PETA well known around the world. There is no doubt that these kinds of activities have made many people aware of the group and convinced some of them to join.

Selling Goods and/or Services

Many interest groups obtain money from selling goods and/or services. Of course, business firms rely heavily on the sales of goods and/or services to obtain money. But many non-business interest groups, including many charities, churches, citizen groups, labor unions, professional associations, and trade associations, obtain some of their money from the sales of goods and/or services.

Citizen groups are particularly noteworthy in the extent to which they obtain money from sales. The AARP came up earlier, but lots of other citizen groups make money from sales of goods and/or services as well. The Sierra Club, for example, sells books, calendars, clothing, coffee mugs, daypacks, greeting cards, notecards, and stuffed animals to members and non-members alike. In fact, sales are so important to the Sierra Club that it has its own bookstore (in Oakland, California), as well as an online store from which web surfers can purchase a huge variety of items.[45] In all, hundreds of citizen groups earn some income from sales.

But citizen groups are hardly alone in this regard. Almost all think tanks, for example, receive some money from the sales of books, research reports, and monographs. For example, the Heritage Foundation, a high-profile conservative think tank, has its own online bookstore that sells hundreds of books published by the Foundation's own press, with titles including *The Conservative Revolution*, *The Enduring Principles of the American Founding*, and *Why Obamacare is Wrong for America*.[46] Even trade associations and labor unions sometimes "get into the act." The United Farm Workers (UFW) labor union, for example, sells a number of items in its online store, including books (such as *Cesar Chavez: A Photographic Essay* and *Cesar E. Chavez: Pride of the People*) and UFW-labeled dog leashes, neon pencils, rulers, shot glasses, wall clocks, and water bottles.[47] Similarly, the Chamber of Commerce of the United States sells a number of business-related publications (with titles such as *2010 Analysis of Workers' Compensation Laws*, and *2008 Employee Benefits Study*).[48]

In sum, organizational maintenance is crucial to interest groups of all kinds. The key to organizational maintenance is obtaining money. Interest groups obtain money by performing a non-political function, and/or procuring patron support, and/or recruiting members, and/or selling goods and/or services.

Monitoring

Another non-lobbying activity that is crucially important to interest groups of all kinds is *monitoring*—keeping track of what government is up to. Monitoring is important for several reasons. First, interest groups that sell things to government—groups such as business firms—want to keep track of what the government is buying. If a local landscaping business wants to secure a government contract to landscape public buildings, it needs to know that the local government is interested in hiring a landscaping service. Only then can it lobby for the contract. Similarly, if a defense contractor wants to sell some sort of weapons system to the federal government, it needs to know what kinds of weapons systems the federal government is interested in buying. Local and state governments, as well as the federal government, often advertise in one way or another when they are looking for interest groups to buy goods or services from. Interest groups that wish to sell to government must be on the lookout for these advertisements if they are to be successful. In short, groups that sell to government need to monitor to know what government is buying and when.

Second, interest groups engage in monitoring because they need to be aware of potential government decisions that may affect them. For example, an environmental citizen group in your state will monitor the ongoing deliberations of the state legislature to be on the lookout for new policy proposals that may affect the environment. Similarly, a state professional association of physicians will keep track of what health care legislation the state legislature is considering because such legislation may affect the livelihood of its member doctors. The preeminent scholar of monitoring, political scientist Robert Salisbury, has written that "The great expansion in the scope of federal programs since World War II . . . has meant that many more elements of society are far more extensively affected by what the government does" than ever before.[49] A few years ago I interviewed a few dozen lobbyists about their monitoring activities, and one of them—a lobbyist in the state of Tennessee who was hired by different interest groups to represent their interests before state government—told me the following:

> They [the clients who hire me] want to know what's going down the pipe. They want to be plugged into the system. They want to be able to have a quick response as opposed to finding out too late. We read virtually every bill that is filed, [or] at least a synopsis of them.[50]

His clients, the lobbyist explained, wanted to be aware of any and all bills that came before the state legislature that might affect them. The lobbyist pointed out that for the typical interest group that hired him, almost *no* bills considered by the state legislature were relevant. However, monitoring was worth the cost, the groups told him, because when a bill came up that *was* relevant to their interests, they were ready for it.

Third, after an interest group monitors and discovers a potential government decision that may affect it, the group must then do *more* monitoring to decide what to do about it. Robert Salisbury calls this monitoring to determine a group's "true interests." He writes:

> In today's world of complex, interdependent interests and policies, it is often quite unclear what the "true interests" of a group . . . may be. The policy that will be maximally advantageous to an association often cannot

even be framed without prolonged and searching analysis involving extensive discussion among those who are knowledgeable about both the technical substance of the issue and the feasibilities of the relevant political situation.[51]

Another way to put it is like this: monitoring helps interest groups determine where they stand on specific things being considered by government. Before an interest group can advocate a particular policy, for example, it must find out what policy will best serve its interests.[52] A hypothetical example here is illustrative. Assume, for example, that Congress is considering federal legislation ostensibly designed to combat global warming. Now assume that you are a lobbyist for the National Association of Manufacturers, a massive trade association consisting of manufacturing companies. Before you do anything else— that is, before you take a stand on the legislation or begin lobbying—you must learn more about the legislation. What are its provisions? Will the law hurt or help your member companies? Are there alternative pieces of legislation being considered? How are the various pieces of legislation different? All these questions must be answered before an interest group undertakes political activity.

Fourth, interest groups spend a great deal of time monitoring because monitoring can provide important information about which lobbying strategies and tactics might be most effective. For example, if an interest group is thinking about approaching a particular government official (say, a legislator) about an issue, it may like to know where that government official stands on the issue. If an interest group finds, for example, that Republican legislators are completely unreceptive to its message, it may concentrate its effort on Democrats. Similarly, if an interest group learns that a certain policy proposal has no chance at the state level, it may shift its focus to the local level. Lobbying strategies are discussed more in the chapters that follow. For now, it must suffice to say that one of the reasons why interest groups monitor government is to gather information about what types of lobbying strategies are most likely to be effective.

Fifth, some interest groups monitor government to keep themselves and/or their members out of trouble. Political scientist Richard Harris notes that business firms, for example, spend a great deal of time and effort monitoring because government regulations and rules proscribe many aspects of their behavior.[53] Consider the cases of most manufacturing companies in America. There are literally hundreds of laws, rules, and regulations on the books that prohibit these companies from engaging in certain types of behavior (e.g., polluting, hiring undocumented workers, forcing people to work overtime for no pay). The costs of ignoring these laws, rules, and regulations can be high—fines can be imposed, executives can be punished, and profits can be threatened. Thus, it behooves the manufacturing companies to monitor government closely in order to keep current on new rules and regulations.

Several years ago, for a book called *Total Lobbying*, I interviewed lobbyists about what they did. Several told me that this type of monitoring was very important. One lobbyist gave me a great example. He was a Washington, DC lobbyist who worked on behalf of business firms in the health care industry, primarily insurance companies and health care providers. He told me that after the federal government adopted the Health Insurance Portability and Accountability Act of 1996 (HIPAA)—a sweeping law that reformed the privacy rights of patients—he spent a great deal of time counseling the companies that hired him about what they were and were not allowed to do with the information they collected from patients. He told me:

> You . . . try to give your client advice about how to comply and how to meet the expectations of the regulations. I [have] spent a lot of time in this area, particularly [with companies in] the clinical laboratory industry . . . One of my areas of specialty is helping them ascertain what they have to do to comply. [I have had] a lot of discussion with clinical labs on [this] issue. It's an area that . . . we haven't gotten a lot of [guidance] from the federal government, [and] there's still a lot of questions.[54]

Often, he told me, laws are written in arcane language and are difficult for business people to comprehend. Part of his job, he told me, was to help his business clients know precisely how to comply with the laws that pertained to them. About HIPAA, he continued:

> A lot of [what HIPAA requires] is not evident on the face of the [law]. [Understanding HIPAA] requires an understanding of the [health care] business and the regulations. They're asking you for advice [on how to comply with the law] and so you're giving them advice.[55]

Other types of interest groups that monitor to keep themselves out of trouble include governmental entities, professional associations, trade associations, and universities and colleges (which must keep abreast of government mandates).

Finally, many membership interest groups monitor government to gather information that can then be passed on to their members. Many abortion-related citizen groups, for example, keep abreast of governmental developments regarding abortion laws and regulations. They then pass this information on to their members who they know are keenly interested in abortion policy. Similarly, the AARP keeps a close watch on changes in Social Security and Medicare so that it can provide information to its elderly members who rely upon these programs. Political scientist Paul Johnson has noted that many interest groups use the information that they obtain from monitoring government as a selective benefit to attract and keep members.[56] The types of interest groups that monitor to gather information for their members include charities, churches, labor unions, professional associations, trade associations, and PACs.

Most interest groups have several staff people whose job it is to monitor government. In addition, most lobbyists spend a great deal of time monitoring.[57] Essentially, monitoring entails doing research—digging up reliable information on what government is up to. Where does this information come from? First, there are newspapers, magazines, and television and radio news broadcasts. Like the rest of us, interest groups rely to some extent on popular news publications and broadcasts. In fact, most studies of individual lobbyists suggest that most federal lobbyists start their days by reading the *New York Times* or the *Washington Post*, while most state or local lobbyists start with the state or local "paper of record."[58] Second, interest groups obtain information from government itself. As you will see in the chapters that follow, governmental bodies at all levels of government often have meetings, proceedings, hearings, etc. that are open to the public. City councils, for example, hold periodic public meetings. Similarly, state and federal legislative committees and executive agencies hold periodic public hearings. Public hearings and meetings offer a great deal of information about what government is up to. While most ordinary citizens ignore such public proceedings, lobbyists and other interest group personnel do not. Particularly when something of relevance to their interest group is at stake, interest group personnel attend public proceedings and pay attention to what happens there. In fact, it is no exaggeration to say that in many governmental public proceedings, interest group personnel outnumber ordinary citizens by a wide margin.

Interest groups also obtain information about what government is up to from specialized government publications. Governmental bodies at all levels issue publications that provide information about what they do. On the federal level, for example, the government publishes the daily *Federal Register*, which lists new and pending government regulations. Most state governments publish similar volumes. Similarly, Congress and most state legislatures publish the transcripts of legislative hearings, as well as copies of new and pending laws.

And at the local level, many cities and counties publish the minutes of public meetings. Finally, interest groups often obtain information from government decision-makers themselves. As you will see in the next few chapters, many lobbyists spend a great deal of time with government decision-makers and their staffs. Part of the reason they do so is to gather important information about what government is doing and/or planning to do.

In sum, monitoring is very important to interest groups of all kinds. Monitoring helps interest groups determine their true interests, and can also help interest groups plan their lobbying strategies. In addition, some interest groups monitor to keep themselves and/or their members out of trouble, and others monitor to keep their members abreast of government activities. Just how important is monitoring? A few years ago I sought to answer this question by surveying a sample of over 300 lobbyists in three states—Colorado, Ohio, and West Virginia. Lobbyists were asked how much of their work time they spent "actively lobbying" versus "monitoring government," "monitoring other interest groups and lobbyists," and "researching and analyzing government proposals." Table 4.2 contains the results of this analysis. The results were striking: the average lobbyist in my study reported spending 28 percent of his/her time "actively lobbying," and 40 percent on monitoring activities.[59] In other words, the typical lobbyist perhaps should be called a *monitorist* (which is not a real word) instead of a lobbyist.

Table 4.2   How State Lobbyists Spend Their Time

Activity	% time spent on	
	Mean	Median
1. Actively lobbying	28	25
2. Monitoring government	20	20
3. Interacting with clients or others within organization	14	10
4. Researching and analyzing government proposals	12	10
5. Other	10	0
6. Monitoring other interest groups and lobbyists	8	5
7. Doing administrative office work	8	5
	N = 318	

Source: Author's data.

Engaging in Self-Governance

The final non-lobbying activity considered here is engaging in *self-governance*—making decisions about how the organization goes about its business. All interest groups must make decisions about matters such as who to hire and fire, how to raise money; how, who, and where to lobby, and what issues to focus upon. Making these decisions is not easy. Even in small and simple organizations, there are many conflicting points of view to consider and many options available.

Structure

The vast majority of interest groups—even citizen groups that purport to represent people directly—organize themselves hierarchically to make self-governance easier and more efficient. Organizing hierarchically simply means giving some personnel—specifically, the people at the top of the organization—more power and authority over decisions than others. The hierarchical structure that an interest group chooses provides a basic framework in which organizational decisions are made. Unfortunately, there is an infinite variety of ways that interest groups organize themselves. Thus, it is impossible here to provide a definitive treatment of interest group self-governance. Fortunately, however, a few political scientists have studied self-governance, and have reached a number of general conclusions about how interest groups organize themselves for self-governance. What have they learned?

First, most interest groups have a *leader*. Leaders go by various titles including president, executive director, chairperson, chief operating officer, and chief executive. For interest groups that exist primarily for a political purpose—e.g., citizen groups, coalitions, and think tanks—the leader is probably the most important person in the organization. It is he or she who oversees the day-to-day operations of the organization and, perhaps with a small cadre of other top level personnel, sets the organization's political priorities and makes final decisions about many aspects of the group's work. For interest groups that exist primarily or partially for a non-political purpose—groups such as business firms and charities, for example—the leader is important, but less so when it comes to making decisions about organizational involvement in politics. For these types of interest groups, the leader generally delegates the responsibility for *political* decisions to others within the organization. In many business firms, colleges and universities, governmental entities, labor unions, professional associations, and trade associations, for example, the leader spends most of his/her time on non-political matters, and delegates responsibility for decisions about political activities to the leader of a separate public affairs or governmental affairs or governmental relations division. This is especially true in large business firms, colleges and universities, governmental entities, labor unions, professional associations, and trade associations. For example, the American Society of Mechanical Engineers has a Governmental Relations Division,[60] the City of Anaheim (California) has a Government Relations Division,[61] the National Association of Realtors has a Government Affairs Division,[62] and the United Auto Workers has a Governmental and International Affairs Department.[63] These specialized divisions within these large organizations are tasked with doing their groups' political work. The groups' primary leaders have little involvement in the day-to-day decisions of the divisions.

Second, most interest groups have a *board of directors*—a small group of people (say, a dozen or so) that is the ultimate source of formal authority for an organization.[64] Boards of directors vary greatly between types of interest groups. Highly paid business firm boards, for example, have very little in common with volunteer citizen group or charity boards. Nonetheless, there are some commonalties. First, most boards act more or less as oversight bodies—assemblies that meet periodically to evaluate how the organization is doing and to consider major changes that might be made if things are not going well. Second, most boards of directors have little say in the day-to-day activities of the organizations they oversee. Rather than micromanaging the organizations they oversee, boards of directors tend to set basic rules, policies, and priorities, and leave day-to-day decisions to leaders and staff people. Third, most boards have a large say in choosing their organization's leader. Because the leader of an interest group is usually a very influential person, choosing a leader is an important responsibility.

Third, most interest groups have *staff*—people who perform day-to-day organizational activities such as monitoring, organizational maintenance, and lobbying, and who are answerable to the organization's leader. In essence, an interest group's staff comprises the people who do the work of the organization. Most interest groups have two tiers of staff. On the top tier are executives and other "higher ups" who work closely with the leader and who have some independent authority to make decisions. Many interest groups have, for example, executives that report directly to the leader and have some control over important decisions. Below this top tier is a lower tier of staff that does the organization's quotidian tasks including filing, answering telephones, sending out mail, etc. Staff size varies greatly between organizations. Some of the country's biggest interest groups—groups such as the AARP and the Chamber of Commerce of the United States—have hundreds or thousands of staff members, while some interest groups that you have never heard of are run and staffed entirely by one or two people. Having a large staff—or even being a large group for that matter—is not necessary to have an impact. Box 4.1 tells the story of one organization—the Westboro Baptist Church—that has managed to have an impact disproportionate with its size.

Box 4.1 The Westboro Baptist Church: Not Big, but Big Enough to Make Noise

The Westboro Baptist Church (WBC) is a small independent Baptist Church located in Topeka, Kansas. The Church is well known throughout the world for its extreme anti-homosexual views and rhetoric. In its own words, the WBC:

> engages in daily peaceful sidewalk demonstrations opposing the homosexual lifestyle of soul-damning, nation-destroying filth. We display large, colorful signs containing Bible words and sentiments, including: GOD HATES FAGS, FAGS HATE GOD, AIDS CURES FAGS, THANK GOD FOR AIDS, FAGS BURN IN HELL, GOD IS NOT MOCKED, FAGS ARE NATURE FREAKS, GOD GAVE FAGS UP, NO SPECIAL LAWS FOR FAGS, FAGS DOOM NATIONS, THANK GOD FOR DEAD SOLDIERS, FAG TROOPS, GOD BLEW UP THE TROOPS, GOD HATES AMERICA, AMERICA IS DOOMED, THE WORLD IS DOOMED, etc. [emphasis in original]

The WBC is best known for picketing the funerals of soldiers who have died in Iraq and Afghanistan. The group does this, it says, to draw attention to the fact that (in its opinion) America has devolved into a sinful, godless society full of heathens. The Church has received worldwide media attention over the years. It is the subject of a 2007 BBC documentary entitled *The Most Hated Family in America*, has been publicly and roundly criticized by people from across the political spectrum (from Bill O'Reilly to Michael Moore), has been the subject of hundreds of media exposés, and attracts counter-protestors and local media in droves every time it shows up at a fallen serviceperson's funeral.

You can say whatever you want about the WBC, but you cannot say it is ineffectual; it has succeeded wildly in getting its message out. This is quite amazing in light of the fact that by all accounts the WBC has fewer than 100 members. In fact, it appears that the group essentially is one man—Fred Phelps—and his wife, children, and grandchildren. Fred and his progeny do virtually all of the group's work themselves, and they are amazingly peripatetic—they picket several funerals and venues each month.

The WBC proves that it does not take an army of staffers or followers to make an impact. The WBC—for better or worse—has managed to make an international name for itself despite virtually no paid staff and a minuscule budget. The WBC largely is one man's vision.

Source: Westboro Baptist Church, "God Hates Fags."

Oligarchy

Most interest groups have a leader, a board, and a staff. Beyond this, it is difficult to make any definitive statements about the ways that interest groups structure themselves for self-governance. This is not surprising given that the interest group universe features everything from giant multi-national business firms to local "mom and pop" citizen groups. There is, however, one other thing that political scientists have discovered about interest group self-governance. In the vast majority of cases—no matter what organizational structure is adopted—decision-making within interest groups tends *not* to be very democratic. As Paul Johnson has noted, "Most everyone who studies interest groups agrees that true internal democracy is rare among them."[65] It is not hard to see why. First of all, many types of organizations are inherently undemocratic. Institutional interest groups such as business firms, governmental entities, and colleges and universities, for example, cannot very well be democratic because they are not designed to represent the interests of people. A business firm, for example, has interests quite separate from the people who work for it. Second, even interest groups that *do* have members find it difficult, inefficient, and bothersome to include members in the decision-making process. Early in this century, political scientist Robert Michels formulated what is known as the "iron law of oligarchy," which basically holds that within virtually all organizations a relatively small group of professionals dominate decision-making.[66] Oligarchy is inevitable in most organizations, Michels argues, because running an organization—especially a large and complex organization—takes special expertise and skills that are not commonly held by rank-and-file organization members. In addition, allowing rank-and-file members to have input over decisions is inefficient. In the end, the evidence suggests that most interest groups are oligarchical.

None of this is to say, however, that members have *no* say over the decisions of the interest groups to which they belong. Some types of interest groups—especially many churches, citizen groups, labor unions, and trade associations—include members in the decision-making process. Most labor unions, for example, allow union members to choose their leaders in periodic elections, while many citizen groups allow rank-and-file members to elect some or all of their board members. In the National Education Association (NEA), for example, state- and local-level NEA members elect delegates to a national convention who then elect the group's leaders.[67] Similarly, the Sierra Club allows its members to elect its Board of Directors.[68] In addition, many interest groups allow rank-and-file members mechanisms to communicate their desires to group leaders. Many trade associations, for example, have advisory committees that consist of the heads of member firms. And many charities, citizen groups, labor unions, professional associations, and trade associations allow members to communicate their wishes to group leaders. Second, in most membership organizations, members have the option to leave. Economist Albert O. Hirschman has noted that members in any voluntary organization always have the option of exiting the organization if they are unhappy with its direction.[69] This provides an incentive for an organization's leaders to be at least somewhat responsive to members' needs and desires.

In sum, self-governance is an important task for interest groups of all kinds. Most interest groups organize themselves hierarchically. This means that they have a leader, a board of directors, and a staff. In most interest groups—even those committed to open and democratic government—important decisions are left to a handful of people, and members have limited input.

Conclusion: The Importance of Non-Lobbying Activities

It is easy to lose sight of the fact that in addition to lobbying, interest groups do several other things. This chapter has highlighted three of these things: engaging in organizational maintenance, monitoring, and engaging in self-governance. Without question, for most interest groups the most important non-lobbying activity is engaging in organizational maintenance. Organizational maintenance is crucially important because if an interest group does not survive it will not be able to influence government decisions. In short, survival must be the preeminent goal of any interest group. The key to organizational maintenance is obtaining money. Interest groups acquire money in several different ways. Some acquire money in the course of performing their primary non-political functions. Business firms, for example, acquire money by selling goods and/or services. Most other types obtain money from some combination of patrons, members, and sales.

Engaging in monitoring is also extremely important for interest groups of all kinds. Keeping track of what government is up to is important because it helps interest groups obtain the information they need to be effective advocates. It is also important because it allows interest groups to keep themselves and/or their members "out of trouble," and allows membership interest groups to keep their members abreast of what government is up to. In the end, monitoring is often little more than glorified "grunt work." As with most "grunt work," monitoring is more important than it is glamorous.

Finally, all interest groups engage in self-governance. The variety of organizational forms from which organizations can choose is virtually infinite. Therefore, it is hard to reach definitive conclusions about how interest groups organize themselves for self-governance. We can, however, make a few broad generalizations. First, most interest groups have a leader who is invested with great power. Second, most interest groups have a board of directors that oversees organizational activities. Third, most interest groups have staff people who perform the day-to-day tasks that keep an organization running smoothly. And finally, most interest groups are undemocratic in their decision-making processes. Even interest groups that presume to represent the "public" tend to be dominated by a small group of individuals.

It is safe to say that many if not most interest groups spend more time on non-lobbying activities than they do on lobbying activities. This is surely the case with interest groups such as business firms, charities, churches, governmental entities, and labor unions, which exist primarily for non-political purposes. Similarly, many types of interest groups that exist for a multitude of purposes—trade associations and professional associations come to mind—surely spend a great deal of time and money and energy on non-political activities. And even explicitly political groups such as citizen groups and think tanks must be preoccupied with survival, which forces them to spend vital resources on obtaining money rather than on engaging in political activity. In the end, it is important to remember that interest groups of all kinds are multifaceted organizations that perform multiple functions. No interest group lives by politics alone.

What's Next

This chapter has highlighted the non-political things that interest groups do. But of course the primary reason why we study interest groups is that they *lobby*—that is, they try to influence what government does. Thus, important as non-lobbying activities are to a full understanding of interest group politics in the United States, lobbying is even more important. It is so important, in fact, that it will be the subject of the next three chapters. We start our exploration of lobbying with two simple questions: What exactly is lobbying? And why do interest groups do it?

Direct Lobbying

5

The primary reason why political scientists (and you) study interest groups is that interest groups lobby. If that last sentence looks familiar to you, it should—it is the same sentence that began the last chapter. That chapter, however, was concerned with the non-lobbying activities of interest groups and their lobbyists. Now it is time to take a closer look at what interest groups and lobbyists do when they try to affect government decisions—that is, when they lobby. This chapter examines *direct lobbying*—lobbying that entails face to face contact with government decision-makers. Chapter 6 examines *electoral lobbying*—lobbying that is designed to affect the outcome of an election. And Chapter 7 examines *indirect lobbying*—lobbying that is aimed at citizens rather than government decision-makers, and is designed to mobilize citizens to contact government decision-makers and/or change their minds about a particular issue or set of issues.

In this chapter, I begin my examination of lobbying with a look at what appears to be the most common general type—*direct lobbying*. Specifically, the following question is addressed: Why do interest groups lobby? From here, I explore how lobbyists interact formally with government decision-makers in an attempt to influence what they do.

Why Lobby Government?

As Chapter 1 notes, many organizations in the United States that fit into one of my categories of interest groups do not lobby at all. This again begs the question: *Why* do so many organizations lobby government? After all, no organization is forced to lobby. A giant company such as General Electric, for example, could eschew lobbying altogether, content to sell its products and services and earn a tidy profit. Similarly, the AARP could help its elderly members get discount insurance, hotel rooms, and prescription drugs, and shun lobbying altogether. But these interest groups and lots of others *do* lobby. The question is, why?

Again, I want to reiterate: *interest groups lobby government because what the government does affects them.* The AARP, for example, has tens of millions of members, many of whom are retired. Most retirees in the United States receive federal government assistance in the form of Social Security benefits and/or Medicare insurance coverage. When the federal government tinkers with these programs—when, for example, it increases or decreases Medicare benefits, or considers privatizing some or all of Social Security—it affects the people who are beneficiaries of these programs. Thus, because the AARP's members are affected by government decisions, the group lobbies so it can have a say in what the government does. Similarly, the large oil company Exxon Mobil lobbies because its ability to make a profit depends partially on what the government does. The federal government regulates, among other things, where oil companies can drill for oil and what sorts of safety measures the companies must take to protect their employees and the environment. It is only natural that Exxon Mobil would work to affect the rules and regulations that govern how it conducts business. In sum, no organization in America *has* to lobby. But many organizations *choose* to lobby. They do so because what the government

Table 5.1   Top Interest Group Spenders on Lobbying, 2011

Interest group	Amount spent in 2011
U.S. Chamber of Commerce	$66,370,000
General Electric	$26,340,000
National Association of Realtors	$22,355,463
American Medical Association	$21,500,000
Blue Cross/Blue Shield	$20,985,802
ConocoPhillips	$20,557,043
American Hospital Association	$20,482,147
AT&T Inc.	$20,230,000
Comcast Corp.	$19,665,000
Pharmaceutical Research and Manufacturers of America	$18,910,000

Source: Center for Responsive Politics, "Top Spenders, 2011."

does affects them, and they would like to have some input regarding precisely what the government does. This point is so important that it deserves reiteration here.

How important is lobbying to interest groups? Table 5.1 provides a partial answer to this question. The table lists the ten biggest-spending interest groups in Washington in 2011. As you can see, the heaviest hitters in Washington lobbying spend tens of millions of dollars every year lobbying government.

Lobbying = The Provision of Information

In Chapter 1, the term "lobbying" was defined as *attempting to influence government decisions*. This definition is broad by design. It is broad because lobbying is an exceedingly variegated activity. This said, almost all of the lobbying techniques described in this chapter and the next (but not in Chapter 7) have something in common: they entail the provision of information. In other words, lobbying usually is about trying to affect government decisions by supplying information to government decision-makers. Here's an example to illustrate this point. Let's assume that Congress is considering a bill that would allow oil companies to drill for oil in the Arctic National Wildlife Refuge (ANWR), a federally protected part of northeastern Alaska where drilling is currently illegal. An oil company lobbyist whose company would gain the right to drill in ANWR if the law passed might provide information to members of Congress demonstrating that drilling would have all sorts of benefits. The lobbyist might, for example, provide information on the number of jobs that would be created if drilling was allowed. He/she might also provide information showing that more domestic oil production would reduce American dependence on foreign oil, and increase the supply of oil, which would decrease prices at the pump. A lobbyist for an environmental group opposed to drilling in ANWR would adopt a similar information-provision strategy. He/she might, for example, provide information to members of Congress demonstrating that drilling in ANWR would harm animal and human populations by increasing pollution. He/she might also present information to members of Congress showing that continued reliance on fossil fuels exacerbates global warming. Finally, he/she might provide information suggesting that the amount of oil in ANWR is not large enough to have a discernible impact on gas prices.

In short, lobbying generally is about providing information. While many people assume that lobbyists try to get their way by bribing, harassing, or even threatening government decision-makers, the truth is much more mundane.

Lobbyists, it turns out, generally try to persuade government decision-makers and/or the public to go along with what they want by providing them with information that supports their point of view. What kinds of information do lobbyists and interest groups use to try to get what they want? There are three basic answers to this question: policy analytical information, political information, and legal information.

Policy Analytical Information

Policy analytical information is *detailed and often technical information about the economic and/or social ramifications of a proposed government decision.*[1] Interest groups and their lobbyists often use policy analytical information to make their cases for or against certain government actions. To give you an idea of how lobbyists deploy this type of information, let us briefly examine a recent example. In 2010, California state Assemblywoman Julia Brownley (D–Santa Monica) introduced a bill that would have banned single-use plastic bags in grocery stores in the state.[2] Plastic bags, she and her supporters argued, cause considerable water (and land) pollution, and are nasty little things that blow around and make things ugly. Lobbyists on both sides of the issue used policy analytical information (among other arguments) to make their cases. Proponents of the ban (including environmental citizen groups, local governments, and some grocery stores and labor unions) presented government decision-makers (and the public) with scientific information showing that plastic bags take about 1,000 years to degrade, and thus are very difficult to get rid of. They also cited studies showing that plastic bags often end up in the ocean, where they kill or injure fish and other creatures. Finally, they presented studies showing that a ban was necessary because voluntary recycling programs designed to stop plastic bag pollution were not effective, as the vast majority of people in California did not recycle their plastic bags but just threw them away. On the other side of the issue was the American Chemistry Council (a trade association representing plastics and chemical companies) and its allies. The Council led the charge against the ban, using economic information showing that a plastic bag ban would lead bag manufacturers and chemical companies to fire workers, which would be bad for the state's already fragile economy. The Council also cited studies showing that a ban would increase costs for families, as they would be forced to buy paper or cloth bags, while plastic bags are provided free of charge. Finally, ban opponents presented information showing that recycling was working to decrease bag pollution, and that recycling programs were getting stronger every year and were capable of dealing with the problem. In the end, ban opponents won out, as the California Senate rejected the bill.

This example begs the following question: Isn't the policy analytical information provided by lobbyists on both side of the issue likely to be biased? Probably. Lobbyists tend to present policy analytical information that makes their side look good and bolsters their point of view (though it may not make the other side look bad). This, however, is not lying. In fact, generally speaking lobbyists cannot afford to lie—their credibility is an important asset. Because there are often good arguments on both side of an issue, lobbyists can usually find some credible policy analytical information that supports their point of view. Not surprisingly, they use it to try to get what they want.

Political Information

Another type of information a lobbyist may provide a government decision-maker is political information—*information about the political ramifications of a proposed government decision*. While most government decision-makers care about making good decisions, they care even more about keeping their jobs and/or remaining popular with their constituents. In other words, they care about their political futures. For legislators, chief executives, and other elected government decision-makers, political information entails information about how some proposed government decision or program will affect their re-election chances, the fortunes of their party, or perhaps their legacy. For bureaucrats and other appointed government decision-makers, political information may entail information about how a given proposal will affect an agency's budget or workload. Finally, for all types of government decision-makers, political information may entail information about the chance that a specific proposal has of being adopted. For a governor, for example, political information may entail information about the chances a given proposal has of being approved by the state legislature.

To understand how a lobbyist might use political information, let us consider the hypothetical example of a lobbyist for a citizen group that supports the death penalty. Now let's imagine that the governor of Texas has proposed a number of new crimes for which criminals are eligible for the death penalty. One of the things that the pro-death penalty lobbyist might want to provide state legislators is political information showing how popular the death penalty is in Texas. The message inherent in this information is obvious: "You should support the governor's proposal because your constituents support it. If you don't, your constituents may vote for someone else in the next election." In some cases, political information consists of poll or survey results. The pro-death penalty lobbyist might, for example, poll 2,000 people in a legislator's district (or cite poll results he/she obtained from another source) and—if the results show that the legislator's constituents support the death penalty—show the survey results to the legislator and say, "See, your constituents agree with me."

How might the pro- and anti-plastic bag ban lobbyists we encountered above use political information? Environmental groups supportive of the ban would (and did) make an argument like this: "Government decision-makers, you should support this ban because public opinion polls and the fact that we have hundreds of thousands of members illustrates that Californians are big believers in strict regulations that protect the environment." As for opponents, they might (and did) make an argument like this: "Government decision-makers, if there is one thing we know about Californians and Americans in general, it is that they do not like the government telling them what to do. People want choice when they go to the grocery store—they want to be able to choose which types of bags they will use to transport their groceries. They don't want the government telling them what they can and cannot do with their food." The political message inherent in both of these arguments is this: "You should do what our side wants you to do because if you do not your constituents might not like it and may vote for someone else in the next election."

Unfortunately, political information often conflicts with policy analytical information. Policy analytical information may show, for example, that the death penalty does not actually affect crime rates, while political information shows that the death penalty is massively popular. This can make a government decision-maker's job somewhat difficult.

Legal Information

Finally, lobbyists often provide government decision-makers with legal information—*information about the legal ramifications of a proposed government decision.* Laws, regulations, rules, and court rulings often raise difficult and complex legal questions. For example, every time a legislature considers passing a law, it must consider whether or not the law is constitutional, how it may affect other existing laws, and how difficult it will be to enforce. Thus, government decision-makers may look to lobbyists for legal information.

To understand how a lobbyist might use legal information, consider the hypothetical example of a lobbyist for a veterans' group that supports a federal law that bans flag burning. Members of Congress who support the law know that it raises difficult legal questions. Some people, members realize, feel that banning flag burning may violate people's First Amendment rights to free speech. Supportive members ask themselves: Will any law we pass get declared unconstitutional by the Supreme Court? Is there some way we can craft a law that does not violate the First Amendment? Should we draft a constitutional amendment instead of a law? All of these are legal questions that influence the decisions of government decision-makers. Realizing this, the veterans' group lobbyists may wish to give lawmakers legal advice on how to proceed with their flag-burning proposal.

Summary: Lobbying as Information Provision

No one knows for certain which of these three types of information lobbyists and interest groups provide to government decision-makers most. One reason why this is the case is that lobbyists may present different types of information to different branches, levels, and actors in government. Moreover, no two lobbyists are exactly alike, and some may specialize in one type of information while ignoring the others. But the best evidence we have suggests that policy analytical information is the type of information upon which lobbyists rely most when they lobby government decision-makers. In a recent giant study of congressional lobbying, political scientist Frank Baumgartner and his colleagues sought to discover what types of arguments congressional lobbyists used most.[3] Baumgartner and his colleagues use a more complex (yet similar) typology than the threefold one used here, but their results are translatable. After studying the types of arguments lobbyists make, the authors concluded that lobbyists rely most upon policy analytical information when they lobby. They find that arguments "that raise concerns or offer reassurance about the feasibility of policy options" are the most common types of arguments that lobbyists make.[4] The authors find that two other types of arguments are also very common. First, lobbyists rely heavily upon "argument[s] that the policy at hand promoted a widely shared goal or, alternatively, stood in the way of achieving some broad, appealing goal (e.g., public safety, improving the economy, improving rural health care)."[5] In addition, lobbyists rely heavily upon arguments involving "imposing or reducing costs on nongovernmental actors."[6] These three types of arguments all entail the provision of policy analytical information. Baumgartner and his colleagues do not conclude that lobbyists never provide either legal or political information. However, they do find that lobbyists rely much more upon policy analytical information when they lobby than other types of information.

Policy analytical information is valuable to government decision-makers because again, despite many Americans' low opinions of government, most government decision-makers truly are interested in making good decisions—that is, decisions that produce positive results and serve (what they perceive to be) the public good. Policy analytical information gives government decision-makers access to expert opinions and advice, and helps them sort out competing claims. It is important to remember that most government decision-makers face a daunting number of tasks each day. As such, many actually appreciate the fact that lobbyists provide them with information that may help them make decisions. Thus, though the conventional wisdom is that lobbyists often harass government decision-makers and buttonhole them to say their piece, the reality is that government decision-makers often value the information lobbyists provide. In its rawest form, lobbying amounts to this: a lobbyist telling a government decision-maker, "Please do what I want you to do." Lobbyists know that the best way to get government decision-makers to heed their advice is to provide them with information that shows that doing so is a good idea.

Lobbying the Legislature

Now that you have a better idea of what lobbying actually is, we can begin examining lobbying techniques—that is, the ways that interest groups and their lobbyists try to affect government decisions. I will begin by exploring how interest groups and their lobbyists lobby the legislature—because studies suggest that the legislature attracts more attention from lobbyists than any other branch of government. At both the federal and state levels, the legislature attracts far more attention from lobbyists than the other branches of government.[7]

There are two major reasons why the legislature attracts so much attention from lobbyists. First, in most policy areas, the legislature has a great deal of power. For example, at the federal level, the Constitution gives far more power to Congress than to either the president or the judiciary. To be sure, the other branches of the federal government are far from impotent. But Congress has a great deal of power to make things happen, and lobbyists and interest groups know this. As Article I of the Constitution states, Congress alone has the power to pass laws, tax, spend, declare war, and approve many presidential appointments. Likewise, in most states the legislature is very powerful. Second, the legislature attracts a great deal of attention because it is quite accessible to lobbyists. Legislatures provide a multitude of access points for lobbyists. First of all, legislatures have lots of members. Congress, for example, has 535 members, while the typical state legislature has between 100 and 200 members. In contrast, there is only one president, and every state has only one governor. Second, legislatures have lots of staff. The number of staff members working in the House of Representatives in 2009, for example, was close to 10,000, while the number working in the Senate was just over 6,000.[8] On average, a House member has 16 people working for him/her, while a Senator has 43. State legislators generally have much smaller staffs, but even in small states like South Dakota and Vermont, legislators have staff members to assist them. Finally, legislatures typically do their work in committees. This provides interest groups and their lobbyists yet more points of access to government decision-makers. Congress, for example, does almost all of its work in standing committees— semi-permanent subject matter committees in which bills are written. Currently, there are 23 standing committees in the House and 20 in the Senate. Beneath each standing committee are numerous subcommittees—smaller units within committees that get "first crack" at most legislation. State legislatures and some local legislatures also utilize standing committees. These provide yet more points of access. In short, legislatures tend to be accessible.

Lobbyists who lobby the legislature use two basic techniques. They *testify at legislative hearings*, and they *meet personally* with legislators and/or their staffs.

Testifying at Legislative Hearings

Most of the work done in legislatures is done in committees. Thus, a great deal of lobbying of the legislature is done in committees. Though most Americans, when they think of legislatures, think of "floor action"—debates and votes that take place on the floor of legislative bodies—most important legislative decisions are made in committees and subcommittees.

Studies show that most bills that are introduced into legislative bodies get dropped into the hopper, are assigned to a committee, and then are never seen or heard about again. In essence, the committee the bills are assigned to just ignores them and they go away.[9] One recent study of bills introduced in Congress, for example, showed that during the 110th Congress, just over 11,000 bills were introduced, but close to 10,000 of these were referred to a committee and "never saw any action, and died there."[10] Moreover, many of the bills that did not die immediately died after some discussion in committee. In all, the study concluded that only about 4 percent of bills introduced in Congress became law, and many of these bills were trivial in nature (that is, did things such as named post offices for dead people). If a committee decides that a bill is worth some serious consideration, it may (and does for many important bills) hold a legislative hearing for the bill. A legislative hearing, which may take place in a committee, a subcommittee, or both, is somewhat like a judicial hearing. Members of the committee sit at a table and listen to people speak for and against a particular proposal, often interjecting questions and comments. Legislators use committee hearings primarily to educate themselves about pending legislation.[11] Thus, committee hearings are an ideal place for lobbyists to provide all three forms of information to legislators. As political scientist John Wright puts it: "Hearings help legislators determine which options are most likely to achieve the desired policy objectives, which options are politically feasible, and which can be effectively implemented."[12]

There are two ways interest groups and their lobbyists can participate in a legislative committee hearing—they can testify in person, or testify *in absentia* by submitting a written statement. Committee hearings are an ideal place for interest groups and their lobbyists to lobby. Why? First of all, hearings allow lobbyists to present their views on pending government decisions directly to government decision-makers. Second, hearings, which may be attended by members of the media or even televised by C-SPAN, can bring publicity to an interest group's issue position. Third, testifying before a legislative committee is a good way for a group to get good publicity. Even groups that think they cannot actually affect the substance of a piece of legislation or the probability of a bill passing enjoy testifying at legislative hearings because it brings attention to the group. This attention may attract members or supporters, which, of course, groups like. Finally, testifying is not as costly as some other forms of lobbying. To be sure, testifying may require dozens of hours of a lobbyist's time. But because many lobbyists are stationed in the capital—be it Washington, Albany, Nashville, or wherever—testimony may require little travel and thus is often cheaper and easier than other forms of lobbying.

In order to testify at a congressional hearing, a lobbyist must be asked. This is often the case in state and local legislative committees as well. Being asked often is simply a question of asking someone associated with the committee— a legislator or a legislative staff member—to ask you. A legislator who supports a specific group's goals is often more than happy to ask a representative of the group to testify. For example, a "pro-life" member of Congress will happily invite a representative from the National Right to Life Committee or the Family Research Council (both conservative, anti-abortion citizen groups) to testify at a committee hearing on abortion. Similarly, a "pro-choice" member of Congress will be pleased to offer representatives from the American Civil Liberties Union and NARAL Pro-Choice America (both liberal, abortion rights citizen groups) the chance to testify.

Table 5.2 The Use of Direct Lobbying Techniques: Proportion of State Lobbyists Reporting that They Use Each Lobbying Technique (N = 376)

Lobbying technique	% reporting they use technique regularly or occasionally (as opposed to never)
1. Meeting personally with state legislators	98
2. Meeting personally with state legislative staff	93
3. Helping to draft legislation	92
4. Meeting personally with executive agency personnel	91
5. Testifying at legislative committee hearings	89
6. Meeting personally with members of the governor's staff	88
7. Submitting written testimony to legislative committees	78
8. Submitting written comments on proposed rules and regulations	76
9. Helping to draft regulations, rules, or guidelines	76
10. Interacting with liaison offices within the governor's office	73
11. Engaging in informal contacts with state legislators	71
12. Engaging in informal contacts with state legislative staff	68
13. Meeting personally with the governor	65
14. Serving on advisory committees and/or boards	62
15. Testifying at executive agency hearings	61
16. Taking part in regulatory negotiations	56
17. Doing favors for legislators	54
18. Engaging in informal contacts with members of the governor's staff	50
19. Doing favors for legislative staff	44
20. Filing suit or otherwise engaging in litigation	35
21. Engaging in informal contacts with the governor	23
22. Doing favors for members of the governor's staff	20
23. Giving gifts to state legislators	19
24. Doing favors for executive agency personnel	15
25. Doing favors for the governor	14
26. Giving gifts to state legislative staff	10
27. Giving gifts to members of the governor's staff	5
28. Providing travel for state legislators	3
29. Providing travel for state legislative staff	3

Table 5.2   continued

Lobbying technique	% reporting they use technique regularly or occasionally (as opposed to never)
30. Giving gifts to the governor	2
31. Providing travel for members of the governor's staff	2

Source: Nownes and DeAlejandro, "Lobbying in the New Millennium," 435–36.

Notes: Each respondent was given a list of advocacy techniques and asked to indicate how often he/she used it—never, occasionally, or regularly. The number represents the proportion of respondents who reported using the technique occasionally or regularly.

How common is testifying at legislative hearings? Table 5.2, which contains information on the use of several direct lobbying techniques, shows that 89 percent of state lobbyists report engaging in this activity. Table 5.3, which contains information on the use of direct lobbying techniques by Washington lobbyists, shows that 100 percent of Washington lobbyists engage in this activity.[13] Numerous studies suggest that testifying at legislative hearings is one of the most common lobbying techniques used by lobbyists at all levels of government.

Meeting with Legislators and Legislative Staff

Another way that lobbyists lobby the legislature is by meeting personally with legislators and/or legislative staff. This allows lobbyists personally to "make their cases." Like legislative hearings, personal meetings are ideal places for lobbyists to present both policy analytical information and political information. Meeting personally with legislators and/or legislative staff is a particularly good way to present political analysis. Sometimes, legislators even allow lobbyists to help draft legislation (as Table 5.2 shows). Meeting personally with legislators and/or their staff is consistently cited by lobbyists as a most effective way to influence legislation.[14]

What happens at these personal meetings? My interviews with lobbyists over the years suggest that what happens is that lobbyists present information

Table 5.3   The Use of Direct Lobbying Techniques: Proportion of Washington Lobbyists Reporting that They Use Each Lobbying Technique (N = 50)

Lobbying technique	% reporting they use technique regularly or occasionally (as opposed to never)
1. Contacting Congress personally	100
2. Testifying in Congress	100
3. Contacting [executive] agency personnel	100
4. Testifying at [executive] agency hearings	88
5. Serving on public advisory boards	79
6. Participating in litigation over policy	73

Source: Kollman, *Outside Lobbying*, 35.

Notes: Each respondent was given a list of advocacy techniques and asked to indicate how often he/she used it—never, occasionally, or regularly. The number represents the proportion of respondents who reported using the technique occasionally or regularly.

to government decision-makers that make their side look good. In some cases, they also use these meeting to present information that makes the other side look bad. It is important also to realize that in many cases (though certainly not all), lobbyists meet with legislators or staff members who already agree with them.[15] In these cases, they still try to make their side look good (to shore up their support). But they also meet to offer their services to their allied government decision-makers. They offer, for example, policy analytical information that an agreeable decision-maker can use to lobby other government decision-makers. Or they may offer an ally political information about what other government decision-makers intend to do when a bill is being considered. Finally, a lobbyist may offer an ally labor.

Surveys show that a large proportion of lobbyists say they actually draft bills for legislators. A legislator may allow a lobbyist for a group he/she supports to draft a bill so he/she can spend his/her time doing something else. Legislators, after all, are quite busy. This exchange between a lobbyist and friendly legislator is good for both parties. The legislator gets free labor (so he/she will not have to do the "dirty work" of drafting a bill and can instead concentrate on something else such as fundraising or talking with constituents), while the lobbyist (obviously) benefits from uncommonly effective input into government decisions.

It is hard to emphasize enough how important and effective meeting personally with legislators and/or their staffers is for lobbyists. Studies going back a century show that meeting personally is one of the (if not *the*) most effective things a lobbyist can do to get what he/she wants from government. Unfortunately, getting personal meetings with legislators or their staff members is not always easy. Many legislators are very busy. This is why they have so many staff people in the first place. But even staff members tend to be overworked and harried. Thus, lobbyists consistently report that developing a relationship with a legislator and his/her staff is the key to getting personal meetings with legislators and/or their staffers. The ability to get meetings is often called "having access." Because face-to-face encounters are such an important and effective lobbying tool, lobbyists value access above all else. The question of how lobbyists *gain* access is discussed further in the chapters to come.

As Tables 5.2 and 5.3 show, almost all Washington and state lobbyists have some face-to-face contact with legislators and/or their aides.

Lobbying the Executive

In the American system of separated powers, few government decisions are handled solely by the legislature. One actor who has some power (exactly how much power depends upon which chief executive we are talking about) over government decisions is the chief executive. The president, for example, has the power to veto bills passed by Congress, appoint federal judges, and appoint many bureaucrats. Moreover, the president is arguably more powerful than Congress in policy areas such as defense and foreign affairs. State governors have veto power as well (though they differ in some ways across states), and some have line-item veto power as well.[16] Governors also have appointment powers (though they vary across states), budgetary powers (such as the power to write and submit a budget), and the power to write and submit legislation. Finally, some local chief executives (including some mayors) have budgetary powers, veto powers, and appointment powers as well. In short, because American government at all levels divides power between actors, some lobbyists lobby chief executives.

Lobbyists who lobby the chief executive use two basic techniques: *meeting with the chief executive and/or his/her staff*, and *interacting with special liaison officers*.

Meeting with the Chief Executive and/or His/Her Staff

The "ultimate" for any lobbyist is to meet personally with the chief executive him/herself. Meeting personally with the president or the governor or the mayor, however, is not always easy. After all, while there are many legislators (no matter what legislative body we are talking about), there is only one chief executive. And chief executives are busy people. We do not have great data about how often lobbyists meet with chief executives. Data on state lobbyists (which are presented in Table 5.2), however, suggest that many lobbyists do indeed lobby the governor at some point. The data on presidential lobbying are sparse, but one recent study suggests that on a typical issue, approximately 10 percent of involved lobbyists end up lobbying the White House, and this includes White House aides as well as the president.[17] In short, meeting personally with the president is not a commonly used lobbying technique.

As you might expect, however, meeting personally with chief executive aides and advisors is easier than meeting personally with the chief executive him/herself. Like legislators, chief executives typically have staff people helping them do their jobs. The president, for example, has a whole slew of advisors helping him out. First, there is what presidential scholar Paul Light has called the "inner circle"—the dozen or so advisors closest to the president. The inner circle generally consists of a handful of White House staffers in whom the president has the most trust, the vice-president, a few particularly loyal and/or important department heads, the First Lady, and even a few personal friends with special White House passes. Each of these people is a tad more accessible than the president (though not particularly accessible), and some, including the vice-president and the First Lady, even have their own staffs. Second, there are the many people who work within the White House Office—advisors who do a number of things including help the president with the day-to-day details of his job. Currently many entities including the Domestic Policy Council, and the Office of the White House Counsel exist within the White House Office. White House staffers who work within these entities often have titles such as "counsel," "special assistant," "assistant to the president," and so on. Many of these staffers also have their own staffs. Most governors and local chief executives do not have staffs as large as the president's, but many have extensive staffs nonetheless. The governor of a large state such as California or Texas or New York, for example, might have a triple-digit number of advisors, while the governor of a smaller state might have a dozen or so advisors. The chief executive of a small locality might have only a handful of staff members.

In a recent study of the White House, lobbying and presidential expert Joseph A. Pika notes that many White House staff people assume liaison responsibilities for interest groups that are important election constituents for the president and his party.[18] Some White House staffers, for example, have close ties to certain business firms, and may meet with representatives from these firms on a regular basis. Similarly, a staff member might have close professional relationships with specific labor unions, and might meet with representatives from these unions occasionally to get policy advice and feedback.

Interacting with Special Liaison Offices

Chief executives, like legislators, realize that interest groups and their lobbyists can be important sources of information. In fact, most of our recent presidents have viewed lobbyists and the interest groups they represent as important allies that can help them achieve their goals. This is why the White House now has an "Office of Public Liaison" (OPL)—an official White House entity that maintains contact with interest groups. The OPL was created (though under a different name) in 1970 by Richard Nixon, who designed it to "reach out" to constituencies he felt were important to his re-election. Since 1970, the OPL has been a permanent feature in the White House. The idea behind the OPL is simple: to provide interest groups a "place to go" if they wish to lobby the White House.

The OPL is staffed by people who maintain constant contact with "friendly" interest groups. For Democratic presidents, this generally means labor unions, civil rights citizen groups, environmental citizen groups, and women's rights citizen groups. It also includes business groups, though many such groups feel more comfortable with Republicans. For Republican presidents, it generally means business firms, trade associations, religious conservative citizen groups, and conservative think tanks. The OPL also provides a place where "unfriendly" interest groups can communicate their desires to the president. However, "enemies" generally receive far less attention from OPL staffers than friendly groups. Many state governors have some formal body akin to the OPL, as do some local chief executives.

Presidents use the OPL to gather advice on specific policy matters, to see how interest groups (especially supportive interest groups) feel about what the president is planning to do, to inform interest groups of what the president is doing, and in some cases even to get interest groups to whip up support for the president and his proposals. President George W. Bush, for example, used the OPL to foster relationships with trade associations including the National Association of Manufacturers, the National Federation of Independent

Business, and the U.S. Chamber of Commerce. These groups then lobbied Congress and advertised on television and radio to support specific presidential initiatives.[19]

The OPL is not the only special liaison office between the White House and lobbyists. The Intergovernmental Affairs Office (IAO), for example, keeps in contact with state and local governments. Needless to say, this is an important place for lobbyists who work for domestic governmental entities to communicate with the White House. Furthermore, many chief executives form short-term specialized liaison entities to interact with interest groups. When George H.W. Bush was president, for example, he formed something called the Quayle Council on Competitiveness (named after vice-president Dan Quayle, who chaired the committee), which served as a special liaison between the White House and certain hand-picked business interest groups. The Council held periodic meetings at which Quayle and other White House aides listened to the wishes of business organizations.[20] The interest groups invited to these meetings were grateful for the opportunity to interact personally with the vice-president and other executive branch heavyweights. Similarly, while formulating his ill-fated health care reform package in 1992 and 1993, President Clinton formed a special task force headed by his wife, First Lady Hillary Rodham Clinton. In a series of private meetings, the task force solicited advice from a number of interest groups including labor unions, business firms, and trade associations. Specialized entities such as the Quayle Council on Competitiveness and Clinton's health care task force are not very common on the state level, but they are not unheard of.

Many governors have offices akin to the OPL and the IAO. The governor of Pennsylvania, for example, has an Office of Public Liaison, as well as an Advisory Council on Rural Affairs, a Green Government Council, and an Advisory Council for Hunting, Fishing, and Conservation (among other offices).[21] Similarly, the governor of Arizona has an office of Constituent Services as well as several other entities within her office.[22] These offices and others like them within the governor's office give interest groups a place to meet with governors' aides and staffers. Finally, many local government chief executives have outreach offices as well. Most big and medium-sized city chief executives, for example, have an outreach office that deals with neighborhood associations (local citizen groups that deal with neighborhood issues) that is called something like "Office of Neighborhoods."

Table 5.2 shows that substantial majorities of state lobbyists meet personally with the governor and interact with special liaison offices within the governor's office. Moreover, one study reports that 76 percent of state lobbyists consider the chief executive a "very important" target of lobbying attention.[23]

Unfortunately, surveys of national and local lobbyists have tended not to ask respondents about their lobbying directed at the chief executive's office. But there is good reason to believe that a large number of lobbyists at the national and local levels interact in some way with personnel within the chief executive's office.

Lobbying the Bureaucracy

The chief executive is only one part of the executive branch. The other part is the executive bureaucracy. The bureaucracy is broadly defined as *the set of agencies and bureaus that implement public policy*. The federal government and all 50 states have large bureaucracies. Many local governments also have large bureaucracies. The federal bureaucracy, for example, consists of over 2,000 separate agencies, commissions, and departments, and currently employs over 2 million people.[24] There are tens of thousands more agencies, bureaus, commissions, and departments at the state and local levels of government. To give you an idea of how big the bureaucracy is, consider this: together, state and local governments employ about 18 million people, or about one-tenth of the American workforce.

The primary job of the bureaucracy is to implement public policy decisions made by other branches. For example, the Internal Revenue Service enforces and implements tax laws made by Congress and the president, the Environmental Protection Agency enforces environmental laws, and your local Department of Motor Vehicles office implements car registration and driver's licensing laws made by your state government. Over the years, however, bureaucratic agencies have obtained the power virtually to make public policy decisions on their own. This is the case because elected officials at all levels of government delegate some of their policy-making responsibilities to bureaucratic agencies.[25] For example, Congress has granted the Federal Communications Commission broad powers to issue regulations regarding radio and television broadcasts. Likewise, Congress has given the Food and Drug Administration (FDA) leeway to issue new regulations regarding food and drug safety.

An example will help illustrate what actual regulations look like. The federal United States Fish and Wildlife Service, which is a bureau of the Department of the Interior, was created by Congress in 1871, and is charged with implementing laws and policies regarding fish and wildlife and their habitats. The Service engages in a number of activities, including issuing duck stamps, finding and helping to prosecute people who violate the Endangered Species

Act, and working to protect wetlands. Like many federal agencies, the Service also issues regulations, which are public policy decisions. For example, in 1974 (the regulation has been amended since), the bureau issued a regulation designed to protect migratory birds. The regulation concerned taxidermy (that is, obtaining and then stuffing animals). The regulation essentially says that if you want to engage in some taxidermy with migratory birds (or their parts, nests, or eggs) you need to get a permit from the government. The regulation reads in part:

> 21.24 – Taxidermist permits.
> (a) Permit requirement. A taxidermist permit is required before any person may perform taxidermy services on migratory birds or their parts, nests, or eggs for any person other than himself. [26]

The regulation then goes on to explain how you can get a permit. In part, the regulation reads:

> (b) Application procedures. Submit application for taxidermist permits to the appropriate Regional Director (Attention: Migratory bird permit office). You can find addresses for the Regional Directors in 50 CFR 2.2. Each application must contain the general information and certification required in § 13.12(a) of this subchapter . . .[27]

Many people do not give too much thought to regulations, especially regulations like this one that apply to a fairly small number of people. But make no mistake about it—regulations are very, very important; they have the force of law, and affect interest groups (not to mention citizens) just like laws passed by the legislature and chief executive. For example, if you are a taxidermist who wishes to use migratory birds in your work, you need to know about and abide by this regulation. It is the law, and if you break it you can find yourself in some trouble. In short, because bureaucratic agencies often have the power to adopt regulations and rules—policy mandates that have the force of law—they are important players in American politics. In fact, for many interest groups, rules and regulations made by bureaucratic agencies are more important than laws passed by legislatures and the chief executive, because agencies tend to issue lots of rules and regulations, while legislatures pass relatively few laws.

Bureaucratic agencies and the people who work for them also make important procurement and land-use decisions. For example, at all levels of government, when a government agency or entity wishes to buy something, it is primarily bureaucrats who collect information from prospective vendors (that is, people and business firms that want to sell to the government) and then choose who gets the government contract. Government contracts are worth lots of money, so interest groups that sell to government spend a lot of time and effort trying to influence bureaucrats. Similarly, at the local level of government, land-use decisions are profoundly affected by bureaucrats—people who work for local government agencies. The decisions of these bureaucrats have the force of law, and interest groups that wish to affect land-use decisions spend a great deal of time and effort trying to affect them.

In short, at all levels of government, bureaucrats—people who staff the bureaucracy—make important decisions. As such, they attract the attention and effort of lobbyists. Lobbyists who lobby the bureaucracy use several specific techniques including the following: meeting personally with bureaucrats, submitting comments on proposed regulations, serving on advisory committees, attempting to influence bureaucratic appointments, testifying before agencies, and taking part in regulatory negotiations.

Meeting Personally with Bureaucrats, and Submitting Comments

Bureaucratic agencies write and adopt regulations through a process known as "administrative rule-making." Rule-making comprises three main stages.[28] First, a proposed regulation is drafted by agency personnel. Second, the proposed regulation is published so that anyone who wants to read it can do so. In Washington, proposed regulations are published (on paper and online) in something called the *Federal Register*, which comes out every business day. In states and some localities, they are published in similar periodic publications (and often online as well). Third, the agency decides whether or not to adopt the regulation. If the agency decides to adopt the regulation, it has the force of law (like the taxidermy regulation mentioned above).

Interest groups and their lobbyists can participate in both of the first two stages. In Stage 1, lobbyists can help bureaucrats craft rules and regulations by *meeting personally* with bureaucrats. In fact, the evidence suggests that lobbyists really like this form of bureaucratic lobbying and find it very effective, as it allows them not just to react to new government regulations, but to craft them in the first place.[29] In Stage 2, lobbyists lobby executive agencies by *submitting "comments"* for or against a proposed regulation. In fact, this is the whole idea behind Stage 2—to give affected parties a chance to comment about proposed rules and regulations. The federal government requires agencies that wish to adopt new regulations to publish these regulations and then allow interested parties (usually lobbyists, but sometimes ordinary citizens) to submit comments on them.[30] Many states and localities have a "notice and comment" process as well. Evidence suggests that comments submitted by lobbyists (and sometimes citizens) do tend to affect the final regulations adopted by agencies, and unfavorable comments can even stop regulations before they are adopted.[31]

Today, commenting on proposed regulations is easier than ever before. This is the case due to "e-rulemaking" (or electronic rulemaking). Most federal rulemaking agencies and many state and local rulemaking agencies now allow lobbyists and citizens to submit comments on proposed regulations via electronic mail or to input comments directly through a web portal. More and more local, state, and federal agencies are using the Internet to publish proposed (and final) rules as well, and some even allow unsolicited advice to agency personnel.

While most of the research on the lobbying of bureaucrats has examined lobbying to affect regulations, lobbyists often meet with bureaucrats to affect their procurement and land-use decisions as well. When lobbyists attempt to affect these types of decisions (as opposed to public policy decisions), they almost always use the first bureaucratic lobbying technique mentioned above—they meet personally with bureaucrats.

How common are these two forms of bureaucratic lobbying? As Tables 5.2 and 5.3 indicate, the answer is *very common*. Large majorities of lobbyists in the states and in Washington report lobbying executive agencies using one or both of these techniques. For example, over 90 percent of state lobbyists and virtually all Washington lobbyists report meeting personally with executive agency personnel, and 76 percent of state lobbyists report helping to draft rules, regulations, or guidelines (which they do while meeting with bureaucrats).[32] As for submitting comments, the data indicate that 76 percent of state lobbyists engage in this activity.

Serving on Advisory Committees

Some federal and state and local agencies have special advisory committees that advise agency personnel who write rules and regulations and make other types of decisions.[33] These advisory committees often serve three purposes. First, they provide technical information to bureaucrats. This information is useful for bureaucrats who write regulations or make land-use or procurement decisions. For example, many regulations are arcane, technical, and complex, and some agencies feel the need to call on "experts" for technical information. So if an agency is writing, for example, new regulations about how much mercury can be emitted from cement kilns when they burn stuff, it might want to have some scientists and mercury experts around to help determine precisely what level of mercury emissions make scientific and/or economic sense. This is where advisory committees come in. Second, the committees "serve as sounding boards for testing agency proposals."[34] In other words, executive agency personnel use advisory committees to discuss their plans with lobbyists and other interested parties. They can run proposed regulations by members of the advisory committee before publishing them, or they can ask for advisory committee input about how to craft them. This activity is akin to the first, but tends to be more informal. Finally, advisory committees can help set an agency's agenda. "Setting the agenda" is simply determining what an agency will do. Advisory committees often advise agencies about what issues they should be dealing with. If members of an advisory committee for the Fish and Wildlife Service learn that taxidermists are a problem, for example, members of the advisory board might say to the agency's personnel, "Hey, you might want to write a regulation about how taxidermists use migratory birds in their work." Of course, this example is completely fictional.

Not everyone who serves on an advisory committee is a lobbyist. But some members of these committees are lobbyists or other types of group representatives. Advisory committees allow lobbyists access to the people who write regulations and make other types of important decisions. This gives lobbyists yet more opportunities to affect the decisions of bureaucrats. Studies have shown that access to executive agency personnel is highly prized by lobbyists. As Tables 5.2 and 5.3 show, membership on advisory boards and commissions is not uncommon: 62 percent of state lobbyists and 79 percent of Washington lobbyists report having some presence on such boards.

Attempting to Influence Bureaucratic Appointments

Interest groups also lobby the bureaucracy by attempting to influence bureaucratic appointments. Technically when interest groups and their lobbyists attempt to influence bureaucratic appointments they are not really lobbying the bureaucracy at all. Rather, they are lobbying the individuals—usually the chief executive and his/her aides—who make the appointments, and/or the individuals who confirm bureaucratic appointments (usually, legislators). But because bureaucratic appointments are so important to so many groups, many interest group scholars consider efforts to affect these appointments bureaucratic lobbying efforts.

The vast majority of bureaucrats at all levels of government (e.g., bus drivers, CIA agents, firefighters, NSA agents, parole officers, police officers, postal workers, and transportation workers) get their jobs through the civil service system. That is, they are hired based on merit or expertise just like employees in the private sector. At all three levels of government, however, some high-level bureaucrats (e.g., agency heads and directors) obtain their jobs through appointment. For example, the heads of all fifteen federal cabinet departments are appointed to their positions. Moreover, over 4,000 other federal bureaucrats obtain their jobs via appointment.[35] The heads of many state and local executive branch agencies are also appointed. Because they control the general direction of the bureaucratic agencies they lead, high-level bureaucrats can have a profound impact on government decisions. This is why interest groups are active in the bureaucratic appointment process.

Most bureaucrats who obtain their jobs through appointment are appointed by the chief executive. Some appointees can assume their positions as soon as the chief executive appoints them. For example, in most states and in Washington, a chief executive's personal staffers can begin work as soon as they are appointed. However, a large number of bureaucratic appointees—including many who hold high-level positions in executive agencies and departments—must be *confirmed* before they can assume their positions. At the federal level, the Senate confirms presidential bureaucratic appointments. Though the confirmation process varies from state to state and from locality to locality, in many places, some part of the legislature confirms bureaucratic appointees selected by the chief executive.

Interest groups are active at both stages of the appointment process. During the first stage, an interest group may try to convince the chief executive (or whomever does the appointing) that he/she should or should not appoint a certain person to a certain position. In cases for which confirmation is not required, this stage is obviously all-important. But even in those cases for which confirmation is required, the initial appointment stage is extremely important. This is the case because almost all bureaucratic appointees who require confirmation are eventually confirmed.[36] Interest groups get involved in this stage of the appointment process by making suggestions to chief executives and their staffs about who they would like to have appointed to various bureaucratic positions. During the Reagan and George H.W. Bush administrations, for example, conservative interest groups such as the Christian Coalition and the Heritage Foundation were not shy about pushing candidates for high-level bureaucratic positions. They pushed their preferred candidates by meeting with the president and his staff. They also engaged in the tried and true method of sending résumés to the president. Subsequent presidents have received similar numbers of résumés from ambitious office-seekers. When Barack Obama took office, for example, labor unions, environmental groups, and other traditional liberal interest groups not so subtly suggested various appointees to the president. In short, presidents are inevitably bombarded with résumés and interest group suggestions shortly after taking office.

Some interest groups are active at the second stage of the appointment process as well. At this stage, an interest group may try to convince the legislators who will vote on an appointee's confirmation that the appointee should or should not be confirmed. Again, as is noted above, almost all bureaucratic appointees sail through the confirmation process easily, as legislators defer to the chief executive's wishes. However, some bureaucratic appointees are quite controversial, and thus are not assured of being confirmed. Interest groups that wish to lobby for or against a particular bureaucratic appointee have a number of options. First, they can lobby legislators and their staffs personally. Second, they can "go public," sending letters to voters, appearing on television on radio, or buying advertising, in an attempt to turn public opinion toward or against a nominee. Third, they can testify at legislative confirmation hearings—hearings at which legislators gather information about bureaucratic appointees before they vote on them. An example illustrates how groups try to derail appointees they do not like. In 1997, President Bill Clinton appointed James Hormel, a University of Chicago law graduate and subsequent Dean of Students, ambassador to Luxembourg. Normally senators—the people who have to confirm ambassadors appointed by the president—do not pay too much attention to the ambassador to Luxembourg. But Hormel is openly gay. Thus, after his nomination, a number of conservative citizen groups including the Family Research Council and the Traditional Values Coalition lobbied senators to reject Hormel. Conservative senators agreed with the conservative groups, and refused to allow the Hormel nomination to come up for a full Senate vote, hoping it would die. But President Clinton essentially did an end run around the Senate, giving him the job as ambassador during a congressional recess period (yes, this is legal), and thus allowing Hormel to take the job. Hormel served as our ambassador to Luxembourg for two years.

How common is lobbying to affect bureaucratic appointments? Unfortunately, the surveys used to construct Tables 5.2 and 5.3 did not contain questions on attempting to affect bureaucratic appointments. One survey of Washington lobbyists conducted in the 1980s, however, contained an item on how often lobbyists "attempted to influence appointment to public office." In all, 53 percent of Washington lobbyists reported that they attempted to influence appointments to public office.[37] However, this question is generic, so it applies to both lobbyists who attempt to influence appointments to the judiciary and lobbyists who attempt to influence appointments to the bureaucracy. Thus, we have no clear picture of precisely what proportion of interest groups attempt to influence bureaucratic appointments.

Other Methods of Bureaucratic Lobbying

In his excellent study of participation in rulemaking, political scientist Cornelius Kerwin notes that there are other ways that lobbyists lobby the bureaucracy. One fairly common way is *testifying at executive agency hearings*. As political scientist Scott Furlong has noted, "some agencies conduct public hearings in which organizations and people can offer oral comments" on proposed regulations.[38] This is the case at all three levels of government. Interest groups and their lobbyists are also asked (or ask) to testify at these hearings, and they do so hoping to affect the final regulation adopted by the agency holding the hearing. Public hearings about proposed executive branch decisions are particularly common at the local level of government.

Another way that interest groups and their lobbyists can lobby the bureaucracy is by *taking part in negotiated rulemaking*. Some federal and state and local executive agencies engage in what is known as "negotiated rulemaking." In the 1980s, scholars and politicians alike began to think that the rulemaking process, especially at the federal level, was badly broken. It produced, according to numerous studies, regulations that were costly, inefficient, burdensome, and very unpopular. As a result, the interest groups and individuals subject to regulations were often resentful, upset, and in some cases noncompliant. Some scholars came up with an idea. Instead of having regulations proffered in the traditional fashion, why not bring parties interested in proposed regulations into a room, have them sit down together with regulators, and basically talk until they could come to some sort of consensus (or near consensus) on the shape of the final regulation? The free flow of information would increase the quality of regulations, affected interest groups and citizens would feel better about regulations because even if they lost they would feel they had a stake in the process, and bargaining might produce regulations that, while not perfect, had something to make everyone happy. Well, that was the ideal (and clearly, this is simplifying things a bit). In short, some agencies, when they propose regulations (especially big and important ones) rely on negotiated rulemaking in which the regulators sit down with interested parties and hammer out new regulations. In many cases, an agency that uses negotiated rulemaking chooses who is involved in the negotiation. If you are a lobbyist interested in a matter being negotiated, clearly you would like to be involved in the negotiated rulemaking. The survey of state lobbyists used to create

Table 5.2 indicates that over half of state lobbyists have testified at executive agency hearings.

Lobbying the Courts

There is one federal court system in the United States, as well as fifty-one state court systems. The judiciary exists primarily to resolve civil and criminal disputes. Courts also, however, have broad powers to make public policy decisions (and in some arcane cases, land-use and procurement decisions). Courts have the power, for example, to interpret laws. Many legislative scholars have noted that seldom do laws cover each eventuality that may occur during implementation. Thus, courts are often called upon to clarify what laws passed by the legislature "really mean." Courts also have the power to declare both laws and acts of the executive branch unconstitutional. The Supreme Court of the United States, for example, can review state and federal laws and declare them invalid if they violate the Constitution. Similarly, many state supreme courts (or "courts of last resort") can declare state and local laws unconstitutional. Courts have similar powers to declare the actions of executive branch personnel (be they chief executives or bureaucrats) unconstitutional. Obviously, if an individual in the executive branch is determined to have acted unconstitutionally he/she must stop his/her unconstitutional behavior.

Lobbyists who lobby the judiciary use three basic techniques. They *litigate*, they *file amicus curiae briefs*, and they *attempt to influence judicial appointments*.

Litigating

The most direct way for interest groups to lobby the courts is through litigating—bringing a suit or a series of suits before the courts to obtain court rulings that favor the litigating group. Generally, the purpose of litigation is to force some sort of change in government behavior (that is, to get the government to stop doing something it is doing or start doing something it is not doing). No interest group in history has used litigation more effectively than the NAACP. A brief summary of its litigation activities illustrates how interest groups use litigation.

The Fourteenth Amendment to the Constitution (passed in 1868) guarantees "equal protection of the law." From 1868 to 1964, however, many state and local governments actively circumvented the Fourteenth Amendment by mandating "separate but equal" policies designed to keep black Americans from achieving true equality. In one of the most famous case in all of American law, the NAACP sponsored litigation challenging the "separate but equal" doctrine. The case they chose to litigate involved a girl in Topeka, Kansas named Linda Brown. Brown lived less than a block from a white public school but was nonetheless forced to attend a school far from her home. This, according to the NAACP, was an unconstitutional violation of Brown's Fourteenth Amendment rights to equal protection of the law. The idea behind the lawsuit was simple: the NAACP wanted "separate but equal" policies declared unconstitutional by the federal judiciary. If this took place, state and local governments would have no choice but to scrap such policies. In 1952, the group filed suit on behalf of Brown.[39] The suit alleged that Brown's rights were violated by "separate but equal" policies. The case went all the way to the United States Supreme Court, and the Court ruled (in *Brown vs. Board of Education*) unanimously that Brown's rights had indeed been violated. The Court also declared that policies such as the one that mandated Brown's attendance at an all-black school were unconstitutional and thus must be scrapped.[40]

Needless to say, the NAACP considered its litigation a success. It resulted in a court ruling—which essentially had the force of law—which served the public policy goals of the group. Of course, *Brown* did not occur in a vacuum. The NAACP and other civil rights groups had been lobbying Congress, the president, and state and local governments for decades before they filed the *Brown* case. In addition, the NAACP had filed numerous other court cases designed to challenge the constitutionality of the "separate but equal" doctrine and discriminatory Jim Crow laws. *Brown* is a glaring example of a successful case of interest group litigation.

Most cases of interest group litigation are similar in a broad sense to this case: they involve interest groups essentially "suing" (that is not exactly what they are doing, which is why the term is in quotes) some level or branch or part of government to get it to start or stop acting in a certain way. Since the *Brown* decision, interest group litigation has become more common. Not just any interest group, however, can litigate. Federal and state laws strictly proscribe who can and cannot litigate. For the courts to consider a case for review, the party bringing the suit must have something called "standing." In order for an interest group to have standing, it must prove to the courts that it has some direct interest or stake in the litigation in question. For example, the Sierra Club, an environmental group, probably would not have standing in a case that involves the age at which alcohol can be drunk or the rights of homosexuals to marry. It may have standing, however, in a case that involved new emission standards for motor vehicles. Since the 1960s, the rules of standing—which are far too complex to discuss in any great detail here—have been relaxed in both state and federal courts. Today, interest groups have wide latitude to participate in litigation if they can show that the individual or institutional interests they represent are affected by the law or policy in question.[41]

Filing Amicus Briefs

Another way that interest groups can lobby the courts is through the filing of *amicus curiae* briefs. The term *amicus curiae* means "friend of the court" in Latin. Amicus briefs (as they are called for short) are short memos in which information is presented on behalf of one party or the other in a court case. The idea behind an amicus brief is to provide additional "ammunition" for one side or the other in a court case in hopes of influencing a court's final decision (opinion). Each time the Supreme Court considers the constitutionality of an abortion restriction adopted by a state government, for example, both pro- and anti-abortion interest groups file amicus briefs that explain their opposition to, and support of, respectively, the pending law. In order for an interest group to file an amicus brief, it must obtain the permission of either the litigants or the court itself. Generally, such requests are granted.

Attempting to Influence Judicial Appointments

Interest groups also lobby the judiciary by attempting to influence judicial appointments. Technically, when interest groups attempt to influence judicial appointments they actually aim their efforts at the executive branch, the legislature, or the public. So it is a bit of a misnomer to characterize attempting to influence judicial appointments as judicial lobbying. However, because the ultimate goal of such lobbying efforts is to affect the composition and direction of the judiciary, all attempts to affect judicial appointments are considered "judicial lobbying."

At the federal level, all judges are appointed by the president and must be confirmed by the Senate. At the state level, the process by which judges get their jobs varies considerably from state to state. But many states have a process somewhat similar to that operative in Washington—that is, the chief executive appoints judges and one house of the state legislature or some other body (such as a commission on judicial appointments) decides on confirmation. Interest groups that wish to affect judicial appointments generally lobby either the chief executive, the legislators who vote on confirmation, or both. In some states judges face election at some point in their careers. Interest groups in some cases try to affect the outcomes of these elections much as they try to affect the outcomes of other elections.

To illustrate how interest groups lobby to affect judicial appointments, let us consider the classic case of Justice Clarence Thomas. In 1991, shortly after liberal Supreme Court justice Thurgood Marshall retired from the Supreme Court, President George H. W. Bush chose Clarence Thomas to take his place. At the time, Thomas was a fairly obscure federal appellate court judge with strong conservative credentials. After Thomas was nominated, the Senate Judiciary Committee held a confirmation hearing at which members heard a great deal of testimony for and against Thomas. The hearings became a public spectacle due to the testimony of University of Oklahoma law professor Anita Hill, who testified that Thomas sexually harassed her (allegedly by, for example, directing her to look at his can of Coca-Cola and saying, "Who has put pubic hair on my Coke?") while she worked for him at the Equal Employment Opportunity Employment Commission.[42] Hill's accusations began a titanic battle over Thomas's appointment. After several days of televised hearings, the Senate eventually voted 52–48 to confirm Thomas.

Interest groups were involved in the Thomas appointment every step of the way. Early on in the process, a number of conservative citizen groups lobbied President Bush and his staff to appoint a "true-blue" conservative to fill Marshall's seat on the court. In fact, conservative organizations had been pressuring Bush for years to appoint conservatives to the bench. After Bush chose Thomas, interest groups stepped up their activities. They aimed their lobbying efforts at two targets: senators and the public. Not surprisingly, interest groups on both sides of the struggle made entreaties to the senators who were to decide Thomas's fate. Lobbyists met personally with senators and their staffers, and many provided testimony at Thomas's confirmation hearings. Interest groups also targeted the public. For example, the Christian Coalition spent more than $1 million on a public advertising campaign designed to convince Americans that Thomas would make a great Supreme Court justice and should be confirmed.[43] Similarly, the conservative Family Research Council spent $500,000 on television and print advertisements in support of Thomas's nomination. Thomas's opponents also lobbied the public. For example, a coalition of liberal interest groups that included the National Organization for Women, the Leadership Council on Civil Rights, and People for the American Way, contacted liberal activists and asked them to contact their senators and express opposition to Thomas's confirmation.[44]

Very few justices get the "Thomas treatment." But even non-controversial justices named to the Supreme Court tend to engender some interest group activity. As Tables 5.2 and 5.3 show, the judiciary attracts less attention than either the executive branch or the legislature. The surveys used to create these tables show that 73 percent of Washington lobbyists and 35 percent of state interest groups engage in judicial lobbying. One reason why judicial lobbying is less common in the states is that the rules of standing are more strict than in the federal courts.

Direct Informal Lobbying

For many years the conventional wisdom was that lobbying was all about giving government decision-makers free stuff and, to put it bluntly, "sucking up" to them. Lobbying was viewed by scholars and the media alike primarily as a personal business that involved favors and corruption rather than information. Today the conventional wisdom is quite the opposite. Lobbying, most scholars agree, is mostly about providing accurate and timely information to government decision-makers. "Sucking up" does not get you anywhere if you don't know what you're talking about. Nevertheless, there is no question that wining and dining, doing favors, and just "hanging out" are staples of the lobbying business. How common are such practices? What forms do they take? How often do they mutate into unethical and illegal practices? These are the questions addressed in this section.

Scandalous Practices: Lobbying and Corruption

Throughout American history interest groups and their lobbyists have sometimes resorted to questionable practices to achieve their goals. As political scientists Larry J. Sabato and Glenn R. Simpson have pointed out, political corruption "is truly a staple of our Republic's existence."[45] Among the most common questionable lobbying practices are bribery, and the use of sex and/or alcohol to gain favorable treatment from government decision-makers.

Bribing government decision-makers is not a common lobbying technique. Nonetheless, the use of bribery by lobbyists is not unheard of. Perhaps the most outrageous example of lobbyist bribery in our history took place in the early 1920s, in an incident known as the "Teapot Dome Affair." Shortly after his election in 1920, President Warren G. Harding began to distinguish himself as one of the nation's worst presidents. He was particularly notorious for his disastrous political appointments. His worst appointment was Interior Secretary Albert B. Fall of New Mexico. Fall, who left the Senate to join Harding's cabinet, was financially strapped when he took over the Interior Department. In short order, however, Fall began buying huge and expensive chunks of land around his modest ranch in New Mexico. These purchases raised some eyebrows at the time, in light of his $12,000 annual salary. The money, it turns out, came from oil companies that wanted favors from Fall. In late 1921, Fall asked the president to transfer control of some naval petroleum reserves from the Department of the Navy to the Department of the Interior. Fall then turned around and sold the drilling rights to two millionaire oilmen. The oilmen received immensely valuable land at a fraction of its value, and Fall received over $400,000 for his work on their behalf. Eventually Fall was tried and convicted of graft. He was the first cabinet officer in history to go to prison.[46]

Unfortunately, this is not the only example of lobbyist bribery in our history. Fifty years before Teapot Dome, a company called Credit Mobilier, which was hired to construct America's first transcontinental railroad, staved off congressional inquiries about questionable billing practices by illegally distributing stock and cash to members of Congress.[47] Ultimately a congressional investigation uncovered evidence that Vice-President Schuyler Colfax, Speaker of the House James G. Blaine, and others had received payoffs from the company. More recently, in the midst of his Watergate troubles, Richard Nixon asked for and received massive and illegal cash contributions from business lobbyists. In the last few decades, state legislators in Arizona, California, Kentucky, and South Carolina have been convicted of receiving bribes from lobbyists. And the last decade has been one of spectacular lobbying scandals. For example, in 2005, former Member of Congress Bob Ney (R–Ohio) pleaded guilty to corruption charges involving bribes from lobbyists. His Republican colleague, Randall Cunningham (R–California), is currently serving out a prison term for accepting millions of dollars in bribes from defense contractors. And of course there is Jack Abramoff, the Republican über-lobbyist who spent time in prison for a variety of charges including tax evasion, fraud, and corruption.

Sex and alcohol have also featured prominently in some lobbying scandals. Though lobbyists understandably often decline to discuss the role of either in public, periodic scandals show that both can be used as lobbying tools. For example, in one of the more bizarre political scandals ever, lobbyist Paula Parkinson reported that she regularly traded sex for votes in Congress in the late 1970s and early 1980s. Parkinson, a contract lobbyist and political consultant, admitted to wining, dining, and servicing several Republican members of Congress in exchange for their votes on legislation. Parkinson claims that one member paid for her 1980 abortion. No legislators have ever acknowledged having sex with Parkinson.[48] As for alcohol, it has always been in ample supply in locales where government decisions are made. The relationship between alcohol and lobbying was particularly apparent in a 1986 episode in Tallahassee, Florida. It was there that after a night of carousing and drinking a state legislator and a lobbyist were involved in a hit and run accident. When the police caught up with the duo, the lobbyist quickly confessed that he was driving the car. The legislator lately admitted that he had been driving the car. When asked about the incident, the lobbyist replied, "You know, I am a lobbyist, and you have to take the fall when you work for a legislator."[49] More recently, reports indicate that disgraced lobbyist Jack Abramoff regularly entertained government decision-makers at his own restaurant (called Signatures), and alcohol was regularly served.

Despite the examples cited in this section, interest group scholars agree that bribery, sexual and substance-related misconduct, and illegal lobbying activities are not common. The public perception that lobbyists are sleazy, disreputable characters who regularly violate the law is mistaken. Like all professions, the lobbying profession has its "bad apples." These bad apples have occasionally engaged in behavior that has brought the worst aspects of the lobbying business to light. But virtually every scholarly study of lobbying ever conducted has concluded that most lobbyists abide by the law and conduct themselves in a thoroughly professional manner. Why, then, does the lobbying profession have such a bad reputation? There are two answers to this question.

First, media tend to focus on the bad apples rather than the "good eggs." Most of the time news media ignore lobbying. Covering lobbying extensively would be difficult and boring. There is nothing particularly noteworthy about professional lobbyists testifying before legislative committees, filing lawsuits, or commenting on proposed federal regulations. However, lobbying becomes newsworthy and interesting when illegal behavior is involved. Bribery, sexual peccadilloes, and other unsavory practices—even if they occur infrequently—make the news. Thus, when the public at large hears about lobbying, it tends to hear things that make lobbying seem much dirtier than it is. Second, lobbying has a bad reputation because sometimes it takes place "behind the scenes." In other words, lobbyists sometimes meet with government decision-makers in informal settings outside of the halls of government. Many Americans seem to think that this shows a disregard for the law and democratic process. As we shall see, however, most informal contacts between lobbyists and government decision-makers are quite harmless. In fact, they generally entail the exchange of information and little more. However, the widespread use of informal lobbying techniques does raise legitimate questions about democracy, representative government, and the role of lobbyists in politics.

The Techniques of Direct Informal Lobbying

Occasional scandal is the inevitable result of a political system that allows lobbyists such high levels of access to government decision-makers. For better or worse, government decision-makers in the United States generally develop close relationships with lobbyists. These relationships generally develop from extensive informal contacts between lobbyists and government decision-makers. Both parties to the exchange of information between a lobbyist and a government official benefit from this closeness. For their part, government decision-makers obtain valuable information that helps them make decisions. As for lobbyists, closeness allows them access to the people who make the decisions that affect them and their clients.

One form of direct informal lobbying entails drinking, schmoozing, going out for lunch or dinner, playing golf, and otherwise hanging out with government decision-makers. These types of interactions are undeniable parts of lobbying. As Table 5.2 shows, large majorities of state lobbyists report engaging in these sorts of informal contacts with government decision-makers. Studies of Washington lobbyists suggest that engaging in informal contacts with government decision-makers is quite common among Washington lobbyists as well. Informal contacts often take place in bars and restaurants. Most state capitals have well-known watering holes, pubs, and grills at which lobbyists and government decision-makers mingle. In Washington, restaurants and bars along the "K Street corridor" serve as meeting places for government decision-makers, lobbyists, journalists, and others involved in Washington politics.

What happens at informal meetings between lobbyists and government decision-makers? First of all, lobbyists provide information. In other words, informal get-togethers, meetings, and encounters are forums at which lobbyists pass on policy analytical, political, and/or legal information to government decision-makers. In other words, informal meetings over food, coffee, or liquor are yet other avenues through which lobbyists provide information to government decision-makers. Second, lobbyists *receive* information from government decision-makers. In their roles as monitors, lobbyists often use informal meetings to gather information about political happenings. A lobbyist may, for example, inquire about the status of a given piece of legislation. Or he/she might ask a legislative staffer when a certain piece of legislation is "going to the floor" for a vote. Alan Rosenthal, the preeminent scholar of state lobbying, has noted that lobbying often "comes down to basic human relationships."[50] He concludes: "Whatever the political system or culture, the lobbyist's goal is to make connections and develop close relationships" with as many government decision-makers as possible.[51] According to Rosenthal, building relationships allows lobbyists to prove their credibility, honesty, and reliability. He concludes that lobbyists try to develop relationships "that allow them to demonstrate the worthy attributes they themselves possess, which is prerequisite for promoting their client's wares."[52] Developing relationships is also important because it leads to increased access to government decision-makers. For example, if a lobbyist strikes up a friendship with a legislator, it may translate into more invitations to congressional hearings or greater input during the markup of a bill.

Drinking and eating are not the only ways lobbyists informally lobby government decision-makers. There is also *providing gifts* and *doing favors* for government decision-makers. As Table 5.2 shows, 54 percent of state lobbyists say that they do favors for legislators. Again, studies of Washington lobbyists suggest that a similar proportion of Washington lobbyists engage in this sort of behavior.[53] More specific survey items aimed at state government decision-makers show that 15 percent do favors for executive agency personnel and 14 percent do favors for the governor. As for gifts, we do not have good data on how often Washington lobbyists provide them to government decision-makers, but the results of the state lobbyist survey summarized in Table 5.2 show that 19 percent of state lobbyists report giving gifts to legislators, while only 2 percent report giving gifts to the governor. As for specific gifts, studies show that lobbyists provide everything from perishables such as flowers, candy, cigars, and peanuts, to free babysitting, tickets to athletic events, and rides to work.[54]

While most gifts and favors are small and apolitical, lobbyists agree that they help build relationships. Gifts and small favors help government decision-makers see a lobbyist's clients in a favorable light. One of the most popular gifts is the "junket," which is a free trip. Junkets are generally provided to legislators and their aides, as many other government decision-makers are barred from accepting them. Junkets can take many forms. Until 1995, when Congress adopted a law that banned some types of junkets, the typical federal junket consisted of an all-expenses-paid trip to a "conference" or "forum." Expenses included airfare, luxury hotel accommodations, meals, drinks, and incidentals. Interest groups that could afford to, usually held these conferences or forums at well-equipped hotels and resorts in Hawaii, the Virgin Islands, Las Vegas, San Diego, or Florida. Members of Congress defended such junkets, of course, saying that they provided them the opportunity to listen to their constituents and learn about important issues. Though Congress banned some types of junkets for its members in 1995, they are alive and well in the form of trips for "fact-finding missions" and "conferences" at which legislators serve as panelists or speakers. Junkets are also common in the states. While some states and localities have laws that essentially prohibit junkets, many others have laws that allow them. Moreover, even in places where junkets are banned, some government decision-makers, especially legislators and their aides, find ways to go on trips with lobbyists. To learn more about what types of trips are allowed in your state or hometown, you should contact your state or local government. As Table 5.2 shows, while providing travel to government decision-makers is not common, it is not unheard of either.

In sum, informal lobbying techniques—wining, dining, schmoozing, gift-giving, and providing travel—are alive and well wherever lobbying takes place. Surveys suggest that chatting with government decision-makers over food or coffee is the most common form of informal lobbying. Giving gifts, doing favors, and providing travel are not unheard of. However, it is important to realize that despite the disproportionate media attention given to these types of lobbyist–government-decision-maker interactions, they are quite uncommon compared to other techniques of lobbying. While informal interaction is common, it is arguably less common than the kind of formal interaction that takes place in the actual halls of government. It is important to keep this in mind as we evaluate the worth and appropriateness of informal lobbying.

Is There Anything Wrong with Direct Informal Lobbying?

Critics of informal lobbying say that it is corrupt and wrong. It is unfair, they say, because it allows lobbyists to "buy" government decision-makers. Critics may have a point. Obviously close relationships between government decision-makers and lobbyists raise the dismaying possibility that the former make decisions based not upon what they or their constituents think is best, but rather upon what the most profligate lobbyists think is best. Moreover, informal contacts and munificent lobbyists may be bad for the political system because they increase public cynicism by fostering the notion that everyone in public life is "for sale." Finally, gifts and favors may distort representation by privileging the views of the richest among us—those who can afford to pay for such things. In short, critics believe that informal lobbying is likely to amplify the voices of affluent institutions and individuals, and squelch the voices of everyone else.

At the federal level, Congress itself acknowledged some of the problems with informal lobbying when it passed the Lobbying Disclosure Act of 1995—the most comprehensive piece of federal lobbying legislation ever passed, and then later amended and strengthened it with the Honest Leadership and Open Government Act of 2007 (HLOGA)—another important piece of legislation designed to regulate lobbying. Before turning to lobbying laws, it is important to note that the most egregious types of corrupt and unethical lobbying behavior, including bribery, blackmail, and threatening with bodily harm, generally are forbidden under criminal statutes unrelated to lobbying. Thus, though heinous practices such as these are not explicitly banned in lobbying legislation, they are nonetheless against the law.

The Lobbying Disclosure Act of 1995 and its HLOGA amendments together contain two main provisions. The first requires lobbyists to register with the federal government and disclose their activities. The Act goes into some detail about who must register and who does not have to register. For our purposes, it should suffice to say that a person who lobbies on behalf of an interest group and spends more than 20 percent of the time that he/she works on behalf of that interest group on lobbying activities is required to register with the federal government. The same applies to lobbying firms. In practice, this means that most people and lobbying firms (though certainly not all) who spend a substantial amount of time and money lobbying must register with the federal government (specifically, the House and the Senate).[55] The law defines the term "lobbying" quite broadly as virtually any direct attempt to influence the decisions of government decision-makers including the president, the vice-president, and members of Congress, congressional staffers, and high-ranking bureaucrats.[56] Registration, political scientist Ronald G. Shaiko has noted, "is a two-step" process."[57] First, "Within forty-five days of an initial lobbying contact, lobbyists are required to register with the clerk of the House and the secretary of the Senate."[58] Initial registration entails "providing pertinent information regarding the lobbyist, his or her clients, the issues, the activities, and the governmental institutions associated with the lobbying efforts."[59] The second step in the registration process is the filing of periodic reports of lobbying activities.[60] These reports include information on how much lobbyists spend, what they do to try to influence policy, and how much they are paid by the interest groups that employ them. The idea behind the lobbyist registration provision is that if lobbyists are forced to make their activities public, they are less likely to engage in corrupt, unethical, or illegal practices. Any citizen can go online and see these lobbyist registration reports.

The second set of provisions of the Act restricts certain kinds of informal lobbying activities. Specifically, the Act bars lobbyists from providing gifts, meals, and travel to members of Congress and people who work for/in Congress, as well as executive branch personnel. In short, the law holds that lobbyists may not provide anything of value to anyone in government. However, there are lots of exceptions to these rules, especially for members of Congress. For example, there is a "personal friendship" exemption that allows lobbyists with longstanding personal ties to a specific government decision-maker to give gifts to him or her. In addition, lobbyists can provide "nominal food" that is "not part of a meal" to government decision-makers, and can also provide gifts of nominal value such as T-shirts, coffee mugs, or baseball caps. As for travel, the gift ban provisions forbid all members of Congress and their aides, as well as executive branch personnel, from accepting all-expenses-paid trips from lobbyists. However, there are exceptions here as well, as organizations that do not employ or use lobbyists can still provide such trips, and even organizations that do employ or use lobbyists can provide such trips as long as they are for "official purposes" and the trip-taker does not have extensive contact with a lobbyist during the trip.[61]

The idea behind registration requirements is that citizens have the right to know precisely which lobbyists are asking for what from whom, and what these lobbyists are doing to try to get what they want. As for gift ban provisions, they are based on the notion that lobbyists should not be allowed to buy access to government decision-makers with expensive trips, meals, and gifts. The proponents of gift ban provisions contend that lobbyist "freebies" corrupt the integrity of the federal government and increase the probability that legislators will respond to lobbyists rather than their constituents.

Currently all fifty states and thousands of local governments have regulations that require lobbyists to register and report their activities. Moreover, many states and localities have gift bans similar to the federal gift ban. Unfortunately, because each state and locality is different, it is impossible to generalize about the nature and extent of state and local lobbying laws. Some states and localities have strict lobbying laws that require virtually all active lobbyists and interest groups to register, while others have lax laws that force only the most active and well-heeled lobbyists and interest groups to register. Similarly, many states and localities have lobbying laws that forbid all sorts of informal contacts and gifts, while others have lax laws that allow lobbyists to do almost anything (e.g., provide gifts, take on trips) short of bribery.

To summarize, no matter where they operate, most lobbyists and interest groups are subject to some regulations. First of all, most active federal lobbyists and interest groups, as well as many state and local lobbyists and interest groups, are required to register with the government they lobby. This allows government decision-makers and the public to keep abreast of what lobbyists are doing. In addition, virtually all lobbyists are barred from doing certain things. Bribery, blackmail, assault, and other heavy-handed tactics are, of course, unlawful for lobbyists just as they are for the rest of us. Furthermore, federal lobbyists and many state and local lobbyists are barred from providing government decision-makers with expensive gifts, meals, and trips.

At this point, the obvious question is: How well do lobbying laws work? Scholars who have addressed this question have concluded that the evidence is mixed. On the one hand, registration laws appear to be quite successful. Most lobbyists at all levels of government appear to abide by registration laws, and dutifully report who they are, what they do, how much they spend, and who they lobby. On the other hand, the record of gift ban provisions is decidedly mixed. For example, despite seemingly tough federal laws, lobbyists have proven quite adept at sidestepping some of their major provisions over the years. For example, though the Act prohibits lobbyists from providing all-expenses-paid trips to members of Congress, lobbyists still manage to pay for expensive junkets. A website called legistorm.com compiles data on trips taken by members of Congress that are paid for by non-governmental entities (such as interest groups), and their data are telling. Randomly clicking on the name of Representative Don Payne (D–New Jersey) tells us that in 2008 he took privately funded trips to St. Maarten (for the "13th Annual Caribbean Multi-National Business Conference") and Paris (to attend a conference put on by the Aspen Institute). On the Republican side, House Speaker John Boehner took a privately funded trip to Palm Beach, Florida in 2010, while staffers from his office took trips to Monterrey, California, and Perth, Australia in 2011. Of course, these trips were perfectly legal, and when asked, members of Congress, their staffers, and executive branch personnel tend to say that such trips are for "fact-finding" purposes. But make no mistake about it—these sorts of trips can be useful for lobbyists. As for the ban on expensive gifts and meals, federal rules have several loopholes, some of which are mentioned above. One of the more ingenious ways that lobbyists get around these rules these days is by providing meals for members of Congress at fundraising events—events that are not subject to lobbying rules! Thus, if a lobbyist wants to provide an expensive meal for a member of Congress, all he / she has to do is hold a fundraiser for the member.[62] State and local lobbying laws also have loopholes that lobbyists have freely exploited. In the end, though gift bans have had some effect on the way lobbyists do business, it is safe to say that lobbyists still provide some travel, some gifts, and some food for government decision-makers—especially legislators.

In the end, nothing is likely to stop gift giving, junkets, and other forms of direct informal lobbying that many Americans find objectionable. Lobbying remains a "people business." As is pointed out repeatedly in this chapter, lobbying is often about one person supplying information to another. As long as this is the case, lobbyists and government decision-makers are bound to grow close in some instances, lobbyists will try to exploit and use personal relationships to their clients' advantage, and government decision-makers are bound to trust and like some lobbyists better than others.

For lobbyists, the value of informal lobbying is obvious. First, it allows close and often protracted opportunities for lobbyists to make their cases. Second, doing favors for government decision-makers or giving them free stuff may tip the scales in a lobbyist's favor. Finally, and perhaps most importantly, informal lobbying may allow a lobbyist to build a close relationship with government decision-makers and thus may improve a lobbyist's access to government decision-makers in the formal settings. Many lobbyists, in fact, believe that building relationships with government decision-makers may increase the chances that their telephone calls will be returned, that they will be able to set up personal meetings with government decision-makers, that they will be invited to testify at legislative or executive branch hearings, or that they will be asked for their input during the drafting of a bill or regulation.

The Lobbyists: Who They Are and Where They Come From

Like the interest groups they represent, lobbyists are ubiquitous in the United States. Figure 5.1 shows that there were approximately 13,000 active, registered lobbyists working in Washington in 2010. The number has been in the 10–15,000 range for the past fifteen years. Because some lobbyists are not required to register, there are probably closer to 25,000 professional lobbyists working in Washington. There are tens of thousands of additional lobbyists operating in states and localities across the country. For example, in 2010, over 1,500 lobbyists were registered to lobby in Texas,[63] over 800 were registered in Montana,[64] and over 500 were registered in Iowa.[65] And most big cities and counties have hundreds of lobbyists, and even small cities and counties have dozens (and in some cases hundreds).

The term "lobbyist" evolved from the term "lobby agent," which was first used in the early 1800s to describe association representatives active in New York state politics. Popular mythology has it that lobby agents were deemed so because they waited in the corridors of power to buttonhole legislators. The term was subsequently shortened to "lobbyist." Political scientists generally distinguish between two basic types of lobbyists: *association lobbyists* and *contract lobbyists*. An association lobbyist is *one who works for, and is employed by, a single interest group*. In contrast, a contract lobbyist is *a lobbyist who has a number of clients and works for whomever hires him/her*. Newspaper and magazine stories on lobbyists tend to focus on powerful contract lobbyists. Yet while these "super lobbyists" make for fascinating copy, they are the exceptions rather than the rule in national, state, and local politics. Studies show that between 75 and

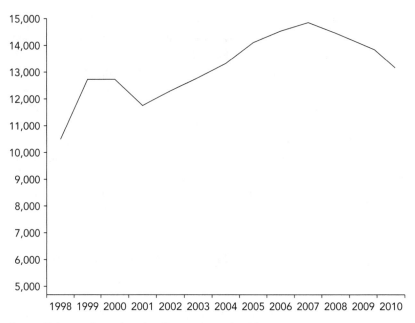

Figure 5.1 Number of Federally Registered Lobbyists, 1998–2010

Source: Center for Responsive Politics, "Lobbying Database."

80 percent of lobbyists are association lobbyists.[66] It is important to note, however, that many interest groups have their own lobbyists *and* "hire out" for special lobbying services. Thus, though association lobbyists outnumber contract lobbyists, the latter are used at one time or another by many interest groups.

One reason why the media focus on contract lobbyists is that their numbers have increased in recent decades. The recent proliferation has produced a new player in interest group politics: the *lobbying law firm*, which is a law firm that employs a number of contract lobbyists. The number of lobbying law firms is on the rise in Washington and state capitals and big cities. A lobbying law firm provides "one-stop shopping" for its clients. Today's all-purpose lobbying law firm provides a wide variety of services to interest groups including public relations, fundraising, direct lobbying, indirect lobbying, media services, and political consulting. The trend toward all-purpose lobbying shops has seemingly accelerated as lobbying has become increasingly technological.

As for the question of who lobbyists actually are, over 40 years ago political scientist Lester Milbrath found that the typical lobbyist was a well-educated, upper- or middle-class, 40–60-year-old white male.[67] Virtually every subsequent study of lobbyists has painted a similar picture.[68] There is some evidence, however, that the lobbying community is becoming more diverse, as women and ethnic and racial minorities invade previously inaccessible "good ol' boy" lobbying networks.[69]

Many lobbyists make a pretty good living. One recent study found that the average lobbyist makes a little over $98,000 annually.[70] It is not unusual for a high-profile Washington lobbyist to make between $500,000 and $1 million per year, while some particularly well-connected lobbyists (especially former members of Congress) make well over $1 million.[71] Many state lobbyists are similarly well paid. Some of the top lobbyists in big states such as California and Texas, for example, make over $1 million annually.[72] Moreover, even in smaller states such as Colorado and Arkansas a number of lobbyists make six-figure salaries, while the average lobbyist makes approximately $50,000.[73]

Though lobbying is an elite occupation, few children grow up aspiring to lobby for a living. Most people who become lobbyists do so via other jobs. Government is the primary training ground for Washington, state, and local lobbyists. Studies suggest that over half of all Washington lobbyists and a similar proportion of state lobbyists have some sort of government experience.[74] Among the most common government positions previously held by lobbyists are legislator, legislative aide, chief executive aide, and executive agency official. Not all lobbyists come from government. Many association lobbyists, for example, serve their employers in other capacities before they become lobbyists. Excluding public service, the two occupations that produce the most lobbyists are law and business. All told, lobbying is an elite profession. Many of its practitioners are well educated, well off, well paid, and well traveled. There's a reason for this: lobbying is not a job for slackers—as the communications theory of lobbying implies, it requires expertise. Policy analytical information, for example, often requires substantive knowledge about the "ins and outs" of a specific policy area. Similarly, most political analysis requires an intimate understanding of the powers, roles, and motives of government decision-makers, as well as the intricacies of the government decision-making process. Finally, legal analysis requires legal expertise—familiarity with the law and the legal process. Where does one get expertise? The career paths of lobbyists tell the story. Both policy and political expertise come from a combination of education and government experience. Not surprisingly, legal expertise often comes from going to law school and subsequently practicing law.

Expertise is essential if a lobbyist is to make his/her case. But valuable as expertise is, it may be less valuable than *access*—having the opportunity to present your case to government decision-makers. Access is the ability to put your expertise to work for you. Virtually all forms of direct lobbying require some level of access. And, of course, access is critical if a lobbyist wishes to have face-to-face contact with any government decision-maker. The importance of access explains why most lobbyists have government experience. As the previous section notes, having a close relationship with government decision-makers is important to lobbyists. And building a relationship with government decision-makers is not necessary if you already have a relationship with government decision-makers.

Interest groups, realizing the importance of access and closeness, often go out of their way to hire ex-government decision-makers as lobbyists.[75] One recent study showed that "in the past 10 years" alone, "Nearly 5,400 former congressional staffers have left Capitol Hill to become federal lobbyists."[76] Another study showed that "Of the 352 members of Congress who . . . left office" between 1998 and 2011, a whopping 79 percent became lobbyists.[77] In fact, all manner of high-profile erstwhile government decision-makers are the subject of bidding wars by lobbying firms and interest groups wishing to cash in on their connections. Some of the most influential and important government decision-makers of the past twenty-five years are working as lobbyists. For example, former Senator Chris Dodd (D–Connecticut) now works for the Motion Picture Association of America; former House Majority Leader Dick Armey (R–Texas) works for an interest group called FreedomWorks; former Attorney General of the United States John Ashcroft has his own lobbying law firm called the Ashcroft Group; and former Senator Tom Daschle (D–South Dakota) works for the lobbying law firm DLA Piper.[78] Wherever lobbying takes place, lobbying firms and interest groups pay big bucks to land ex-government decision-makers. The reason they do this is clear—they believe that erstwhile government decision-makers have the connections and/or expertise that make them more effective lobbyists.

The prevalence of "in and outers"—government decision-makers who become lobbyists after they quit or are removed from government—has raised eyebrows among critics who fear that this "revolving door" may harm the integrity of government. The revolving door issue raises a number of ethical questions. First, like informal lobbying, junkets, and gifts, it may bias interest group representation in favor of the few. Because ex-government decision-makers are very expensive to hire, the richest interest groups are generally the ones that can afford to hire them. Second, many critics believe that the revolving door may make government decision-makers, while they are in office, more responsive to potential future employers than to their constituents. For example, a member of Congress who plans to retire before the next election may make decisions while in office that are designed to make him/her attractive to certain interest groups that may hire him/her after the election. Similarly, a bureaucrat at the Department of Defense may do what he/she can while employed by the agency to curry the favor of weapons manufacturing companies in hopes of receiving a lucrative job offer after he/she quits. Finally, the revolving door raises questions about the propriety of selfishly parlaying a government job into a lucrative lobbying career. Political analyst Pat Choate once imagined the following scenario.[79] An individual is working for the Department of Commerce on trade issues. He/she is doing so at the taxpayers' expense. While working for the U.S. government, he/she receives invaluable experience in matters of international trade. After a few years on the job, the government employee quits. He/she is then quickly hired at a salary several times higher than that he/she received at the Department of Commerce by a foreign business firm. As the head lobbyist for the company, this person works hard to help the firm compete more effectively against American companies. The scenario, says Choate, is played out on a daily basis in Washington. Choate asks: Why should taxpayers subsidize interest groups by training their future employees, especially when these employees often work against the interests of vast numbers of Americans?

Over the years, a number of government decision-makers have paid lip-service to ending the revolving door. When he first took office, for example, President Clinton issued new rules that forbade former presidential appointees from lobbying their former employers for five years after they left government. These rules, like most others designed to thwart the revolving door, proved ineffective. One of Clinton's first appointees, deputy chief of staff Roy Neel, left the White House in late 1993 to take a job with the United States Telephone Association—a trade association. Technically Neel was not a lobbyist and did not directly contact the White House. He did, however, begin immediately to supervise lobbyists who regularly contacted the White House. More recently, when President Barack Obama took office, he announced that he would make all of his top political appointees sign a pledge saying that if they left the White House to become lobbyists they would not lobby the White House at all while Obama was in office. However, since Obama took office many of his aides have left government to become lobbyists, avoiding running afoul of the pledge they signed by lobbying other parts of the government (e.g., Congress) instead of the White House, and "supervising" other lobbyists who *do* lobby the White House. In short, the revolving door continues to spin unabated. The real reason the revolving door continues to operate is that government decision-makers like it. Ex-government decision-makers believe they should be able to do what-ever they want with their lives when they leave government. Moreover, many government decision-makers enjoy politics and become lobbyists to remain

Table 5.4   A Few Former Members of Congress and Their Current Employers, 2012

Name	Former position	Current employer
John H. Adler	Representative (D–New Jersey)	Greenberg Traurig, LLP (lobbying firm)
Evan Bayh	Senator (D–Indiana)	McGuireWoods, LLP (lobbying firm)
Robert F. Bennett	Senator (R–Utah)	Arent Fox, LLP (lobbying firm)
Michael N. Castle	Representative (R–Delaware)	DLA Piper (lobbying firm)
Chris Dodd	Senator (D–Connecticut)	Motion Picture Assoc. of America
Blanche Lincoln	Senator (D–Arkansas)	Alston and Bird, LLP (lobbying firm)
Walt Minnick	Representative (D–Idaho)	The Majority Group (lobbying firm)
Zachary Space	Representative (D–Ohio)	Vorys, Sater (lobbying firm)
Bart Stupak	Representative (D–Michigan)	Venable LLP (lobbying firm)
John Tanner	Representative (D–Tennessee)	Prime Policy Group (lobbying firm)
Zach Wamp	Representative (R–Tennessee)	Zach Wamp Consulting (consulting firm)

Source: Center for Responsive Politics, "Revolving Door: Former Members of the 111th Congress."

involved and active. Table 5.4 contains the names of a handful of members of Congress who left in 2011. The table contains the names of some former heavyweights, all of whom went on to become lobbyists for prestigious Washington lobbying firms.

What Makes a Successful Lobbyist?

What separates the successful lobbyist from the failure? Unfortunately, there is no easy answer to this question. In any given political battle, several factors determine the outcome. Most of these factors are beyond the lobbyist's control. For example, in the battle over President Obama's sweeping health care reform legislation in 2009 and 2010, the legislators deciding on various aspects of the plan were influenced by ideology, party affiliation, public opinion, their opinion of the president, the opinions of their constituents, and many other factors. In short, lobbyists were just one small element in a huge variety of factors that determined how legislators voted. Because many factors appear to affect government decisions and many are out of the lobbyist's control, lobbying is seldom determinative. Thus, it is impossible to identify the factor or factors that *ensure* lobbying success. The best we can do is identify factors that, all other things being equal, maximize a lobbyist's chances of getting what he/she wants.

For a look at what makes an effective lobbyist, I will look primarily to two recent works on the subject of lobbying—a book called *Lobbying and Policy Change: Who Wins, Who Loses, and Why*, by political scientists Frank Baumgartner, Jeffrey Berry, Marie Hojnacki, David Kimball, and Beth Leech;[80] and a recent article called "The Ideal Lobbyist: Personal Characteristics of Effective Lobbyists," by interest group expert Dr. Conor McGrath.[81]

The Six Characteristics of the Effective Lobbyist

Conor McGrath set out to determine what makes an effective lobbyist by interviewing sixty lobbyists—some in Washington, some in Brussels (where the European Union is headquartered), and some in London—and asking them which skills they thought were most important. Even though some of the lobbyists McGrath studied were foreign, his findings are consistent with studies of U.S. lobbyists, and thus are worth a closer look. McGrath reached a number of conclusions. First, he concluded that the effective lobbyist is *a good listener*. His interviewees told him that listening was important for a variety of reasons. For one thing, lobbyists can gather important political information from government decision-makers when they listen. In addition, listening to what government decision-makers want can help lobbyists determine what types of arguments to make when they lobby.

Second, McGrath concluded that the effective lobbyist is *observant*. McGrath relates the story of a lobbyist who noticed that a member of Congress he was lobbying was a baseball card fan. He then proceeded to give the member a set of baseball cards as a gift. As it turns out, the gift had to be returned as it was too valuable for the member to accept. But McGrath's point is that being observant paid off for this lobbyist—it allowed him to find a way to connect with the member on a personal level. This connection, McGrath implies, made the member more receptive to the lobbyist's message. In more general terms, being observant—watching government decision-makers—may help lobbyists determine which types of arguments they will make when they lobby government decision-makers. If, for example, a government decision-maker likes baseball, a lobbyist can use a baseball metaphor. Or if a government decision-maker is a devout Catholic, a lobbyist might make religion-tinged arguments. Listening and observing are closely related. McGrath makes the point that both are valuable because they allow lobbyists to see how their message is being received. An observant and thoughtful listener, one of McGrath's respondents notes, does better than a chatterbox because he/she can gauge how he/she is doing. If he/she is doing badly—that is, the message he/she is sending is not working—the lobbyist can change course and try a different approach or a different argument.

Third, McGrath finds that the effective lobbyist is *courteous*. This seems like a "no-brainer," but it is worth mentioning. It is worth mentioning because lobbyists often encounter government decision-makers with whom they disagree. A liberal environmental lobbyist, for example, might have to interact regularly with a very conservative member of Congress who wants to eliminate the Environmental Protection Agency. While a lobbyist might be tempted to be nasty to the member, there are good reasons not to be. "Burning bridges"— that is, upsetting a government decision-maker so much that he/she never wants to deal with you again—is a bad idea. Even if a lobbyist disagrees with a government decision-maker 99 percent of the time or even hates the person, he/she might end up working with the person at some point in the future. Maintaining cordial relationships is important if a lobbyist is to maintain access to government decision-makers. Moreover, government decision-makers are only human. It is only natural for them to be, all other things being equal, more receptive to courteous and cordial lobbyists than to nasty and mean lobbyists.

Fourth, McGrath notes that the effective lobbyist has *good relationship skills*. Another way to put this is that effective lobbyists tend to be "people people"— people who enjoy socializing and talking with other people. Every in-depth empirical study of lobbying ever conducted indicates that lobbying, no matter what else it is, is a people business—it is about people trying to convince other people to do (or not to do) things. Thus, people skills are important. What kind of people skills? My own interviews suggest that lobbyists should be good at "small talk," should be comfortable with introductions, should be gregarious and personable, and should genuinely enjoy human contact. All of us know a person like this—one who lights up a room when she enters, who always has a good joke or funny story to tell, and whom people genuinely enjoy being around because of her effusive personality and appealing manner. This type of person makes a good lobbyist. To convince yourself of this, let's picture the opposite—a person who enjoys spending lots of time alone in dark rooms playing World of Warcraft or watching YouTube videos, is terrible at making "small talk," and would rather be alone than with other people. Even if this person is a policy expert, his demeanor and personality make him a poor candidate for a lobbyist position.

Fifth, McGrath notes that an effective lobbyist is *honest*. This may surprise some people—that is, people who think that all lobbyists are liars and manipulators. But most lobbying studies show that honesty is crucial to effective lobbying. One reason why telling the truth is so important is that lobbyists tend to deal with the same government decision-makers over and over again over time. If a lobbyist is caught lying even once, most lobbyists agree, he/she will be shunned. Thus, telling the truth is crucial. McGrath quotes one lobbyist as saying, "If you don't tell the truth, you are finished, and will never be listened to or trusted again."[82] Another puts it this way: "If you ever mislead an . . . official—even once—you are basically out of business."[83] Another reason why being honest is important is that it creates a dependency. If a lobbyist becomes invaluable to a government decision-maker—that is, he/she becomes a trusted source of good information—the government decision-maker will become dependent upon that lobbyist for information. And this is what all lobbyists want.

Sixth, McGrath concludes that the successful lobbyist is *ethical*. This may sound strange given the low esteem in which lobbyists are held by many Americans. But McGrath points out that lobbying studies and interviews with government decision-makers consistently show that effective lobbyists are ethical. Being ethical means telling the truth, being trustworthy, behaving with integrity, and abiding by high moral standards. One reason why being ethical is important is that government decision-makers fear being linked with unethical lobbyists, should these ever be "outed" as sleazebags. After disgraced lobbyist Jack Abramoff was thrown in jail, for example, all sorts of members of Congress tried to distance themselves from him. Government decision-makers fear being linked with unethical lobbyists, so most lobbyists behave themselves.

Getting to Yes

In their magisterial study of lobbying and lobbyists called *Lobbying and Policy Change: Who Wins, Who Loses, and Why*, Frank Baumgartner, Jeffrey Berry, Marie Hojnacki, David Kimball, and Beth Leech also offer some insights into what makes a successful lobbyist. They do not study this issue per se, but their results provide insights into what makes some lobbyists more successful than others.

First and most important, the effective lobbyist is *a subject-matter expert*.[84] Baumgartner and his colleagues point out that lobbyists most often rely upon policy analytical information when they lobby. In order to use this type of information—remember, this is detailed and often technical information about the economic and/or social effects of a proposed or existing policy or program—a lobbyist must know an awful lot about the thing that he/she is lobbying about. A lobbyist for a trade association representing corn growers, for example, needs to know a lot about corn, the farm economy, and all things related to corn. At the local level, for example, if a lobbyist for Wal-Mart is lobbying a local government so the company can build a new superstore in a specific location, he/she had better be well versed in local land-use laws and rules. And he/she had better have a good understanding of the costs and benefits of Wal-Mart's presence in the community. In short, because lobbying is about information, an effective lobbyist needs to have good information.

Second, the effective lobbyist *stays the course*.[85] Baumgartner and his colleagues show that many political battles—especially public policy battles—last months, years, or even decades. As such, one key to success simply is staying with it. There are two aspects to "staying the course." The first simply is continuing to work—that is, not giving up. Few battles are won in a day. The second aspect to "staying the course" is sticking to one argument. Baumgartner and his colleagues point out that effective lobbyists tend to pick an argument and stick to it. If an environmental group lobbyist, for example, argues that protecting a specific piece of land from development is good for the environment, he/she should probably stick with this story over the long haul. If he/she does not, and begins to argue, for example, that protecting the land would actually be good for the economy because it would attract tourists to the area, this might raise suspicions among government decision-makers. They might ask: Why is the lobbyist changing his/her story? Was he/she lying the first time around? Did he/she change his/her mind about the environmental value of that land? The old saying, "that's my story, and I'm sticking to it," seems to have some worth in the lobbying profession.

Finally, *experience helps*. Baumgartner and his colleagues note throughout their book that lobbyists become valuable to government decision-makers only to the extent that they have information that decision-makers want. Over time, effective lobbyists develop reputations for having good information, and this makes them valuable to decision-makers. The key word here is *time*. Time allows lobbyists to develop reputations, and this is why experience is so important. The longer a (good) lobbyist is at it, the more experience he/she has (obviously) and the more widely known he/she becomes. In another major study of Washington lobbying, political scientist Robert Salisbury and his colleagues concluded that experience is valuable because it produces increased knowledge about policy issues, as well as contacts and familiarity with the policy process, all three of which increase a lobbyist's chances of success.[86]

Conclusion: Direct Lobbying and the Provision of Information

Interest groups lobby because what the government does affects them—often profoundly. Contrary to many people's opinions, lobbying is seldom sleazy and/or slimy. At its core, most lobbying consists of providing information to government decision-makers. Specifically, lobbyists provide policy analytical, political, and legal information. Lobbyists often provide information directly to government decision-makers in a type of lobbying called *direct formal lobbying*. Such lobbying takes place in the legislature, the executive, and the judiciary. Though the legislature attracts the most attention from lobbyists, the other two branches of government attract a great deal of lobbyist attention as well. Lobbyists also engage in *direct informal lobbying*. While many people are uncomfortable with the idea of lobbyists cavorting with and socializing with government decision-makers, it happens all the time. And this sort of lobbying raises many questions about the nature and functioning of American democracy. These questions have led many governments to regulate lobbying to one extent or another.

Research suggests that some lobbyists are more effective than others. In general, being honest, ethical, and upright increase a lobbyist's effectiveness. In general, experience and expertise also help.

Despite my "one at a time" approach to covering lobbying techniques, it is important to note that in practice lobbying is seldom an "either/or" type of activity. In other words, lobbying one branch of government or one specific government decision-maker does not preclude lobbying another branch or decision-maker. In fact, in a recent study of state lobbyists I found that the typical lobbyist lobbies all three branches of government and utilizes a dozen different lobbying techniques.[87] Studies suggest that many lobbyists try hard to lobby whenever and wherever they can. This means deploying a wide variety of techniques and contacting government decision-makers across branches of government, and developing relationships with as many government decision-makers as possible. In short, lobbyists try hard to "spread themselves thin." How thin often depends upon the resources an interest group has at its disposal.

What's Next

So far, we have learned a little bit about what lobbyists do. However, we have more or less ignored the role of *money* in lobbying. It is time to remedy this exclusion. The next chapter examines a form of lobbying that does *not* entail the provision of information to government decision-makers—electoral lobbying. Though few government decision-makers bear strong resemblance to Albert Fall, many are the recipients of large amounts of money from interest groups and lobbyists. Most of this cash is legal. Our campaign finance system allows interest groups to contribute large sums of money to some government decision-makers. Electoral lobbying is a common, important, and extremely controversial form of lobbying. It is the focus of the next chapter.

Electoral Lobbying   **6**

Election campaigns in the United States are expensive. The figures, as they say, speak for themselves. During the 2008 presidential election campaign, candidates raised almost $1.7 billion.[1] In all, in 2008, candidates, political parties, and interest groups spent approximately $5.3 billion attempting to affect the outcome of federal elections.[2] In the 2010 House races, candidates spent $1.08 billion, while Senate candidates spent $745 million.[3] The average winner of a House election spent $1.439 million, while the average Senate winner spent $9.78 million.[4] To put these numbers in perspective, consider that a House member serves a two-year term, and a Senator serves a six-year term. If a House member wanted to raise $1.439 million to assure him/herself a good chance of winning, he/she would have to raise approximately $1,971 per day, every day (including holidays and weekends) for the entire two-year period. A senator would have to raise approximately $4,465 per day, every day for six years to reach the average winning figure of $9.78 million.

No one knows precisely how much state and local candidates spent in 2009 or 2010, as there is no central source for information on the thousands of subnational elections that take place in the United States each year. The evidence suggests, however, that like those at the federal level, state and local election campaigns can be quite costly. A number of recent races indicate just how costly. For example, in the 2009 New York City mayoral race, "shoe-in" incumbent candidate Mike Bloomberg spent over $100 million.[5] In California, gubernatorial candidate Meg Whitman spent $178.5 million on her 2010 election loss.[6] And it's not just in big states such as New York and California that candidates spend copiously. Candidates for the Iowa state legislature, for example, spent a combined $18 million in 2010.[7] And in 2011, just to use one example of local spending, Robert Reichert spent approximately $175,000 to become mayor of Macon, Georgia.[8] After researching the topic, my best estimate is that candidates, parties, and interest groups will spend well over $6 billion (and probably closer to $7 billion) during the 2012 election season.

In short, winning elective office in the United States can be expensive. This does not mean, of course, that money assures victory. No one knows this better than failed candidate Meg Whitman, who spent $144 million of her own money (the rest came from donors) only to lose to former governor Jerry Brown. And who can forget third party candidate Ross Perot, who spent $70 million—over $63 million of his own money—in his failed 1992 presidential campaign? He spent almost $40 million to get crushed in 1996.[9] History is filled with other high-profile, free-spending losers including California Senate candidate Michael Huffington, who spent $27.9 million of his own money in a failed 1994 attempt to unseat Senator Dianne Feinstein, and Steve Forbes, Jr., who spent $42 million in the 1996 Republican presidential primaries. Nonetheless, though money does not guarantee success, most candidates for office know that to win an election you have to spend some serious money.

What do candidates buy with all this money? There are four basic answers to this question. First, they buy advertising.[10] Candidates advertise everywhere they can afford to, including on television and radio, and in newspapers and magazines. Many also distribute yard signs, pass out bumper stickers, and knock on doors. One of the reasons why many campaigns are so expensive these days is that television advertisements can be expensive. As much as 80 percent of campaign expenditures in competitive elections goes on television advertisements, and my best estimate is that the typical candidate at any level spends well over half of his/her campaign money on television advertising.[11] Second, candidates buy goods and services associated with advertising. The most obvious such costs are copying and mailing costs. Third, candidates buy campaign help. Few candidates run their campaigns by themselves. Most candidates for statewide and national positions, as well as many for local positions, employ high-paid assistants who have titles such as campaign manager, media consultant, or pollster, as well as clerical staff. Finally, candidates spend money on travel. Many candidates for public office travel a great deal while campaigning, especially to meet and greet voters. No matter what form of transportation a candidate uses to get around, travel can be costly.

Where Does the Money Come From? Campaign Finance in the United States

There are five main sources of campaign money: individuals, interest groups, political parties, the government, and candidates themselves. Research suggests that more money comes from individuals than any other source. President Obama, for example, got close to 90 percent of the $745 million he raised for his 2008 election campaign from individual donors,[12] while Senator John McCain received 54 percent of his $368 million from individuals.[13] Evidence indicates that individuals account for the majority of campaign money contributed in other election campaigns as well.[14]

Unfortunately, it is beyond the scope of this book to examine the entire American system of campaign finance. Nonetheless, to understand how interest groups engage in electoral lobbying, we must first understand the part of the campaign finance system that pertains to interest groups. Today, interest groups are important sources of money for electoral campaigns at all levels of government. This has not always been the case. For most of the twentieth century, political parties accounted for a large portion of campaign spending.[15] Evidence suggests that campaigns were much cheaper before 1960, primarily because parties relied heavily upon volunteer labor to do campaign "leg work." Moreover, television was not nearly as ubiquitous. In a system known as the "patronage system," parties rewarded loyal party workers with favors, jobs, gifts, and improved public services for their support on election day. As for the money that parties did spend, they got it primarily from two sources: the candidates themselves (who were chosen partially on the basis of how much money they were willing to spend on their own campaigns) and "fat cats"—wealthy individuals willing to underwrite party activities.[16] The party-dominated system of campaign finance was relatively simple. Parties nominated candidates and provided most or all of the money for their campaigns. Things began to change in the late 1950s and early 1960s. As Americans increasingly turned to television for news and entertainment, candidates came to rely more and more on televised advertisements to get their messages out. This produced an explosion in campaign spending. As Figure 6.1 indicates, spending in all American electoral campaigns rose from approximately $140 million in 1954 to $200 million in 1964; and then to $425 million in 1972. Spiraling campaign costs forced candidates to locate new sources of support. One place they looked was ordinary people. For example, a number of presidential candidates, including Barry Goldwater in 1964, George Wallace in 1968, and George McGovern in 1972, looked to small individual contributors to bolster their chances. Candidates also came to rely more and more upon their own "fat cats," circumventing parties in the process. Richard Nixon, for example, found a *really* "fat cat" in 1968: he received a campaign gift of $2.8 million from insurance tycoon W. Clement Stone. This was a lot of money.

As candidates scoured the landscape for new sources of money, they came to rely less and less on party money. They also came to rely less and less on other forms of party support. Increasingly, candidates began to hire their own

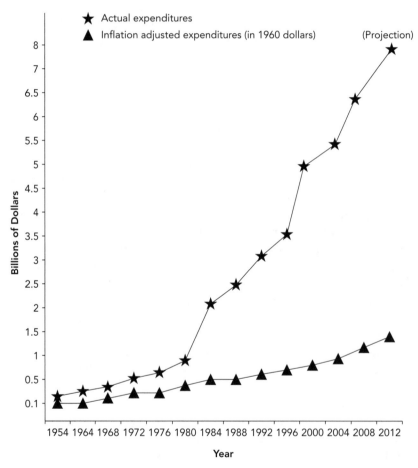

Figure 6.1 Estimated Campaign Costs, 1954–2012

Notes: Figures are total expenditures for the nomination and election of public officials at all levels of government.

Sources: Keefe, *Parties, Politics, and Public Policy in America,* 152; Sorauf, *Inside Campaign Finance,* Chapters 1 and 2; "Political Campaign Media Spend to Reach All-Time High of $4.5 Billion in '08"; Sailer, "The Five Billion Dollar Election."

staffs, raise their own money, and "call their own shots." As campaign expert Frank Sorauf has written, "Whereas the people and events of the old campaigning had pivoted around the political party, the new configuration centered on the candidate."[17] By the late 1960s, national electoral campaigns had become "free for alls" in which candidates desperately sought ever-increasing sums of money needed to win office.

Responding to public concern about the deleterious effects of "big money" on elections, Congress passed the Federal Election Campaign Act of 1971 (FECA 1971). Just as FECA 1971 took effect, the Watergate scandal convinced Congress and the public that further reforms were needed. Shortly after Richard Nixon resigned from the presidency, Congress passed the Federal Election Campaign Act Amendments of 1974 (FECA 1974). FECA 1974 essentially elaborated on FECA 1971. FECA was amended twice more in the 1970s—once in 1976 and once in 1979. Henceforth FECA 1971 and all of its amendments will be referred to simply as "FECA."

FECA mandated five major changes in federal campaign finance law. First, it established contribution limits—that is, limits on how much individuals, parties, and PACs were allowed to contribute to federal candidates. For example, individuals were limited to giving $1,000 per candidate per election (a primary and a general election count as two separate elections), up to a total of $25,000 per calendar year to all candidates and political action committees. In addition, PACs (which will receive more attention later in this chapter) were limited to giving $5,000 per candidate per election, with no aggregate limit. Second, FECA instituted a disclosure regime. Specifically, FECA required all candidates for federal office to file itemized reports of all contributions and expenditures over $200. Third, FECA created the Federal Election Commission (FEC), the federal agency charged with enforcing federal campaign finance law. Fourth, FECA created a system of public financing for presidential election campaigns. This system is extremely complex, but its basic contours are as follows. During the presidential primaries, the federal government provides matching funds for small donations to viable presidential candidates. During the general election, presidential candidates are eligible to receive full public financing for their campaigns. The money used for matching funds and public financing comes from the voluntary check-off on your tax return. In return for public money, presidential candidates in both the primaries and the general election agree to limit their spending. In the general election, the recipients of federal funds agree not to raise or spend money from other sources. Fifth, FECA instituted spending limits for congressional candidates. These limits, however, were subsequently ruled unconstitutional by the Supreme Court in *Buckley v. Valeo*.[18] Finally, FECA clarified the role of interest groups in campaign finance. Specifically, FECA banned all direct contributions to federal candidates and political parties from all interest groups other than PACs.

Before going too much further, it is important to note that the rules of FECA do *not* apply to state and local elections. In other words, if a candidate is running for governor or the state legislature or mayor or county commissioner, FECA does not apply to him/her. However, if a person runs for state and/or local office, state and/or local campaign finance laws *do* apply to him/her. Unfortunately, it is difficult to generalize about campaign finance laws and rules across the country because they differ from place to place. Moreover, these laws change occasionally as sub-national governments tweak their laws and rules. This said, it is important to realize that starting in the 1970s, many states and localities passed rules akin to FECA. For example, many states have laws that are very much like FECA: they limit contributions, mandate disclosure, and empower an agency to keep track of disclosure reports and punish wrongdoers. As such, if you understand the basics of FECA, you may also understand the basics of campaign finance laws where you live. But remember, *specific* campaign finance laws and rules vary from state to state and locality to locality, so fully to understand how campaign finance applies to state and local elections where you live, you will have to do your own research.

Electoral Lobbying: Lobbying with Campaign Money

The people who wrote FECA (as well as their state and local analogs) were concerned about the role of interest groups in election campaigns. They worried that candidates for public office would increasingly look to interest groups for the large sums of money they needed to be competitive. This was a problem, many reformers thought, because it raised the specter of government decision-makers being beholden to rich and powerful interest groups as opposed to ordinary citizens. The reformers knew that there were already rules on the books. But they viewed these rules as antiquated and ineffective. They noted, for example, that the outright federal ban on direct contributions from business firms, which had been in place since 1907, did not stop President Nixon from essentially blackmailing business firms and their executives for campaign contributions. They also acknowledged that a similar federal ban on direct labor union contributions, which had been on the books since 1943, did not stop unions from forming special affiliated organizations to collect voluntary contributions from members, to be passed along to candidates for federal office. In short, the people who wrote FECA and laws like it were concerned that the rules governing interest group involvement in federal election campaigns were neither clear nor effective.

One of the goals of the FECA-era reformers was to clarify and strengthen extant campaign finance laws. To this end, Congress included a provision in FECA that outlawed all direct contributions from interest groups other than PACs. In essence, FECA banned all types of interest groups except for one from contributing money to federal electoral campaigns. Nonetheless, today thousands of interest groups are active in election campaigns across the country. How is this possible? This is the question that is addressed in the remainder of this section. Specifically, this section examines how interest groups lobby electorally with campaign money. More specifically, it examines seven specific techniques by which interest groups lobby with campaign money: making PAC contributions to federal candidates; making PAC contributions to state and local candidates; making direct contributions to candidates; spending independently on behalf of or in opposition to candidates; "bundling"; making in-kind contributions to candidates; and making contributions to "Super PACs."

Making PAC Contributions

The most important way that interest groups lobby electorally with campaign money despite FECA's ban on direct contributions to federal candidates is by making PAC contributions to federal candidates. To understand how, I must delve deeper into what PACs are and how they operate. Before doing this, however, it is important to note that, at all levels of government, giving money directly to candidates for public office for their personal use to influence their decisions is against the law. This, of course, is bribery. However, as you will see subsequently, contributing money to a candidate's *electoral campaign* is not against the law. The fact that direct contributions to all government decision-makers for their personal use are illegal, while contributions to electoral campaigns are not, has two important implications that you should keep in mind as you proceed with this chapter. First, it means that when any person or organization contributes money to a candidate, this does not actually contribute money to the candidate him/herself. Rather, the money is contributed to the candidate's electoral campaign. An example will help clarify how the system works. If you wish to give $1,000 to Senator Bob Corker (R–Tennessee), you cannot simply hand Bob Corker a check for $1,000—that is, a check that says "Pay To The Order Of Mr. Bob Corker"—for him to deposit in his personal bank account. Rather, you must write a check to Corker's campaign committee—a separate organizational entity that exists solely to help Bob Corker win elections. This committee is not allowed to pass any money along to Corker himself for personal use. It can only spend money on Corker's behalf in electoral campaigns. The fact that direct contributions to candidates are illegal while contributions to electoral campaigns are not has one other important implication. The vast majority (over 99 percent) of government decision-makers at all levels of government are ineligible to receive monetary contributions of any kind for any purpose. Since most government decision-makers, including legislative staffers, bureaucrats of all stripes, federal judges, and chief executive aides, do not run for office, they are ineligible to receive monetary contributions from any source. In sum, it is important for you to recognize that when interest groups, individuals, PACs, or parties contribute money to candidates, they are *not* contributing money to the candidates themselves. Rather, they are contributing money to the candidates' campaign committees.

Now, let's get back to precisely how interest groups lobby with campaign money. I will first consider how interest groups lobby electorally through their PACs at the federal level. Though FECA does not allow interest groups other than PACs to contribute money to candidates for federal office, it does allow some[19] business firms and citizen groups and coalitions, as well as labor unions, professional associations, and trade associations, to create affiliated PACs to do so. Specifically, FECA states that certain types of interest groups (the vast majority are either for-profit business firms, citizen groups, coalitions, professional associations, and trade associations) may make monetary contributions to federal candidates by setting up "separate segregated funds" called PACs. A "separate segregated fund" is defined by FECA as one that does not contain "membership dues or other money as a condition of employment or membership or any money obtained through a commercial transaction."[20] This language in the law exposes an important catch for interest groups that wish to set up PACs—the money that flows to an interest group's federal PAC does not come from the treasury of that interest group, but rather comes from individuals and (less commonly) other PACs, political parties, and candidate campaign committees. The amount a single individual, PAC, campaign committee, or national party committee can give to a federal PAC currently is limited to $5,000 per calendar year.[21] FECA also states that an affiliated PAC—a PAC connected to another interest group—can solicit contributions *only* from individuals associated with its parent organization. A labor union PAC, for example, can solicit contributions only from the union's members. Interestingly, however, though affiliated PACs can *solicit* contributions only from certain people, they may *receive* contributions from any adult American citizen.[22]

In their entirety, the rules that govern interest groups and their federal PACs are complicated and difficult to fathom. To give you a basic idea of how FECA's rules on federal PACs work in practice, let us consider the hypothetical case of an oil company called Exoff. Exoff's executives have decided that the company wants to make a contribution to an oil-friendly senator from Texas—a hypothetical man we will call Senator Stone Rockman. FECA does not allow Exoff to take money from its treasury—money it obtains from selling petroleum products—and contribute it to Senator Rockman. However, FECA does allow Exoff to set up a separate affiliated organization—let's call it Exoff PAC—to contribute money to Senator Rockman. Exoff PAC can solicit money from Exoff executives and shareholders and some other employees. As per FECA's contribution limits, Exoff PAC can then contribute up to $5,000 per election to the senator.

Our hypothetical scenario begs the following question: Can't Exoff simply create a PAC, transfer money from its corporate treasury to the PAC, and have the PAC pass money on to the senator? The answer to this question is no—FECA forbids interest groups from funding their affiliated federal PACs in this manner. Nonetheless, the relationship between a parent organization and its PAC can be a close one. In 1975, a business firm called Sun Oil Company went to the FEC and asked if it was allowed to pay for the administrative and fundraising costs of operating its affiliated PAC. The FEC, which was given by Congress the power to interpret FECA, answered yes. Thus, though interest groups are not allowed to contribute money directly to their affiliated federal PACs, they *are* allowed to pay some expenses incurred by their affiliated PACs. This "administration loophole" blurs the line between a PAC and its parent organization. Nonetheless, the line still exists, and is drawn most obviously at the point at which a PAC can contribute money to candidates while a parent organization cannot.

PACs operate in states and localities as well as in Washington. And the FECA rules discussed above do not apply to PACs operating in state and local elections. Thus, another way that interest groups lobby electorally with campaign money despite FECA's rules is by making PAC contributions to state and/or local candidates. Campaign finance laws vary from place to place. But one thing that virtually all states and localities have in common is that they allow some types of interest groups, either directly or through political action committees, to give money to candidates for elective office. In places that allow direct contributions to candidates, the eligible interest groups simply donate money from their treasuries to candidates they support. I will say more about this in a moment. In places that have laws like FECA, eligible interest groups establish PACs that behave much like federal PACs. It is difficult to make any definitive statements here about either which individuals and entities are allowed to contribute to state and local PACs, or about contribution limits. This is the case because laws and regulations stipulating who may contribute and how much they may contribute vary widely from place to place, and there are lots of places in the United States. To learn more about rules affecting PAC giving where you live, consult your state and local governments' websites.

Unfortunately, definitive data on the number of interest groups active in state and/or local elections are not available. However, it is clear that the number of sub-national PACs has increased dramatically since the early 1970s. One study found that in most states PAC numbers rose between 200 and 800 percent between the mid-1970s and mid-1980s.[23] Another study from the early 1990s estimated that there are well over 12,000 active sub-national PACs.[24] Surely there are many more today. For example, in Nevada alone there were 620 PACs registered in 2010,[25] and there were 295 registered PACs in Maryland as of mid-2011.[26] In Texas a whopping 1,302 active PACs reported expenditures in the state's 2010 elections.[27]

Thus far, I have discussed only *affiliated PACs*—PACs that are affiliated with other interest groups. I pay more attention to affiliated PACs because they are the major PAC players in politics. As Table 6.1 shows, most of the top ten federal PACs are affiliated PACs. It is important to note, however, that FECA also allows the creation of *non-affiliated PACs*—PACs that have no parent organizations. A non-affiliated PAC essentially is a citizen group that collects money and spends it on election campaigns. One big difference between affiliated federal PACs and non-affiliated federal PACs is that the latter can solicit money from virtually any American adult. Non-affiliated PACs constitute only about a quarter of all federal PACs. One specific type of non-affiliated PAC deserves special mention here—the *leadership PAC*. A leadership PAC is a PAC set up by a current, former, or prospective government official—usually a legislator. Dozens of leadership PACs are active at the federal level, and hundreds more are active in state and local elections. To get an idea of how a leadership PAC works, let's take a look at one—the Every Republican Is Crucial PAC, the leadership PAC of current House Majority Leader, Representative Eric Cantor. The PAC operates like other non-affiliated PACs. Specifically, it collects money from individuals and (to a lesser extent) the Republican Party and other PACs, and then contributes the money to other Republican candidates. During the 2010 congressional elections, for example, the PAC contributed $45,000 to eight Republican Senate candidates, and $1.6 million to 232 House candidates.[28] Leadership PACs are a very good way for politicians to raise their public profile, help candidates they like, and curry favor with other politicians. Virtually every national politician of any stature has his/her own leadership PAC. For example, all the party

Table 6.1   The Top Ten Federal PACs, by Distributed Funds, January 1, 2009–December 31, 2010 (2010 Election Cycle)

Name	Type of PAC	Amount
1. ActBlue	Unaffiliated	$59,627,472
2. SEIU COPE (Service Employees International Union, Committee on Political Education)	Labor union	$36,741,535
3. MoveOn.org	Unaffiliated	$29,049,996
4. EMILY's List	Unaffiliated	$22,943,125
5. AFSCME (American Federation of State, County, and Municipal Employees)	Labor union	$18,348,503
6. DRIVE (Democrat Republican Independent Voter Education, Teamsters)	Labor union	$14,134,388
7. Voter Education PAC for the NRA (National Rifle Association)	Citizen group	$13,965,233
8. Victory Fund 1199 of the SEIU	Labor union	$12,904,002
9. Action Fund, American Federation of Teachers	Labor union	$11,612,207
10. National Association of Realtors PAC	Professional assoc.	$11,468,369

Source: Federal Election Commission, "Table 9, Top 50 PACs By Disbursements January 1, 2009–December 31, 2010."

leaders in Congress have their own leadership PACs, as do all the major presidential candidates. Many state and local luminaries have leadership PACs as well.

FECA's rules governing federal PACs opened the door to far-reaching interest group involvement in federal election campaigns. As Figure 6.2 attests, the number of PACs active in federal elections increased almost exponentially between 1970 and 1984. In 1972, there were only 113 PACs registered with the FEC. By the end of 1974, there were five times that many (608). By the end of 1984, there were 4,009. That's an increase of 3,500 percent in 12 years. Between 1984 and 2004 the number of PACs stayed steady, but has risen a bit of late. As of early 2011, there were 4,859 PACs registered with the FEC.[29] As the number of PACs has grown, so has the level of PAC involvement in federal electoral campaigns. During the 2007–2008 election cycle, "PAC contributions to federal candidates . . . totaled $412.8 million, up 11 percent over 2005–2006."[30] Early indications are that the 2012 elections will set new records for PAC contributions.[31]

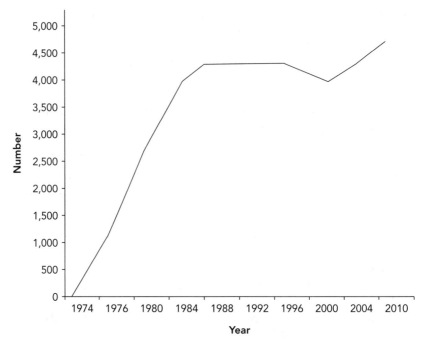

Figure 6.2 The Number of Federally Registered PACs, 1974–2010

Source: Federal Election Commission, "PAC Count, 1974 to Present."

How important are PACs in federal elections? First of all, they are not as important as individuals. And the numbers actually suggest they are of relatively minimal significance. For example, of the over $1.68 billion raised by 2008 presidential election candidates, over $1.3 billion came from individuals, while only a little over $5 million came from PACs.[32] PACs are much more active in congressional elections, but they are still far from the most important sources of campaign money. In the 2009–2010 House elections, for example, contributions from PACs accounted for 38 percent of total receipts, while in the Senate the total was only 15 percent.[33]

As for the importance of PACs in state and local elections, again there are no definitive figures showing precisely how much PACs spend. But evidence from many quarters suggests that the total is in the tens of millions of dollars. In Massachusetts, for example, PACs contributed $2.75 million to state and county government candidates in 2010, an all-time record.[34] And in Texas, PACs spent over $130 million on state elections in 2010.[35] In all, the evidence suggests that PACs are fast becoming major sources of campaign money in sub-national elections. In many states, PACs regularly account for over 30 percent of

Table 6.2   Federal PACs with Humorous Names

Name	Description
Bake PAC	Independent Bakers' Association PAC
Cubist PAC	Cubist Pharmaceuticals Inc. PAC
Egg PAC	United Egg Association PAC
Fish PAC	National Fisheries Institute PAC
Fresh PAC	United Fruit and Vegetable Association PAC
Lol PAC	Land O' Lakes Inc./Agrialliance LLC PAC
Pork PAC	National Pork Producers PAC
Pump PAC	American Concrete Pumping Association PAC
Snack PAC	Snack Food Association PAC

Source: Federal Election Commission, "Pacronyms."

contributions to legislative candidates. And in several states, PACs regularly account for over half of all contributions to incumbent legislators.

To help you remember that PACs are important players in electoral politics, Table 6.2 provides the names of a few funny-sounding PACs compiled from the FEC's list of "pacronyms." While their names are funny, their missions are not.

Making Direct Contributions to Candidates

It is very difficult to generalize about campaign finance laws in states and localities. Different places have different rules. However, one thing that almost all states and localities have in common is that they allow interest groups, either directly or through political action committees, to give money to candidates for elective office. As I say above, interest groups in some states and localities must form PACs to contribute money to candidates. Some places (including thirty-five states[36]), however, allow direct contributions to candidates from some types of interest groups. Thus, another way that interest groups lobby electorally with campaign money is by making direct contributions to candidates. In places where direct contributions from interest groups are allowed, the eligible interest groups simply donate money from their treasuries to the candidates they support.

Many campaign finance reformers (including those at "good government" groups such as Common Cause) believe that laws allowing direct contributions from interest groups to candidates encourage corruption and are akin to bribery. Some types of interest groups, they argue, especially for-profit business firms, have lots of money and can use it essentially to "buy" government decisions. I will have more to say about this later.

Spending Independently on Behalf of or in Opposition to Candidates

Another way that interest groups lobby electorally with campaign money despite FECA's ban on direct contributions to federal candidates is by spending independently on behalf of or in opposition to candidates. There are two basic ways that interest groups do this: (1) they engage in PAC independent spending; and (2) they engage in direct independent spending.

First, I will take a closer look at *PAC independent spending*. FECA stipulates that interest groups, through their federal PACs, may conduct independent spending campaigns on behalf of or in opposition to candidates for federal office. Many states and localities allow PACs to spend independently as well. In general, PACs that spend independently on behalf of or in opposition to candidates do so on pro- or anti-candidate advertisements, usually on television. The appeal of independent spending at the federal level is that a PAC may spend as much as it wants for or against a candidate—there is no $5,000 limit as there is with contributions to candidates. FECA stipulates, however, that independent spending must be truly independent. That is, a PAC that spends independently on a candidate's behalf must refrain from coordinating its efforts with that candidate. States and localities have different rules on precisely how "independent" this independent spending must be. To learn more about your state or local government's rules about independent PAC spending, consult your state and local governments' websites.

At the federal level, PAC independent spending became newly visible in the 1980 congressional elections, during which the pioneering National Conservative Political Action Committee (NCPAC) spent over $3 million.[37] NCPAC targeted six liberal Democratic senators, four of whom lost. Despite NCPAC's apparent success, independent expenditures typically account for a small portion of all PAC spending in both federal and sub-national campaigns in a typical election year (though the amount appears to be increasing). In the 2009–2010 election cycle, for example, PAC independent spending in federal elections totaled approximately $68.5 million, while direct PAC contributions to candidates and political parties totaled close to $500 million.[38] There are no definitive data on how much independent PAC spending goes on in state and local elections, but evidence suggests that direct PAC contributions are far more common than independent expenditures. There are two reasons why PAC independent spending is uncommon. First, many PACs—especially those affiliated with business firms, trade associations, and professional associations—do not wish to alienate candidates with whom they may have to deal subsequently. If a PAC takes a strong and public and expensive stand in favor of one candidate over another in a particular election, it runs the risk of supporting the loser and alienating the person with whom its affiliated interest group will eventually have to deal. Many interest groups (though certainly not all) like to have good relationships with all the government decision-makers with which they deal—not just those who share their views. Second, independent spending is expensive. Television advertisements in particular are very costly.

A second way that interest groups can lobby electorally with campaign money is by engaging in *direct independent spending*. In its 2010 decision *Citizens United vs. Federal Election Commission*, the United States Supreme Court—which was considering the constitutionality of the Bipartisan Campaign Reform Act (2002)—ruled that certain types of interest groups could not be stopped by the government from spending money directly from their treasuries independently on behalf of or in opposition to candidates for office at any level of government. It also ruled that certain citizen groups that spent independently did not have to reveal their donors (some of which were interest groups themselves) to the government, and could accept donations of any size. The decision is complicated (like campaign finance in general), and its implications could fill an entire chapter. But for our purposes the important thing to know is that in essence, it means that under current law, certain types of interest groups—for example, some for-profit business firms, citizen groups, coalitions, labor unions, professional associations, and trade associations—can spend as much money as they want from their treasuries directly on behalf of or in opposition to candidates for office at all levels of government. This is called direct independent spending. Because both the tax code and campaign finance regulations are complex, it is difficult here to list definitively which interest groups can spend independently directly from their treasuries and which cannot. For now, it must suffice to say that if an interest group can form a PAC, it probably can spend independently. If you identify a particular interest group and wonder if it can spend independently, you can email the FEC or do a quick bit of Internet research to find out if it can do so legally.

While many observers have concluded that this decision will radically change interest group involvement in American elections, the fact is that in the decade before *Citizens United*, interest groups of various kinds (especially citizen groups) engaged in something similar to this type of direct independent spending quite often—either by forming special kinds of interest groups called "527 organizations" (so-called because of the section of the tax code that deals with them), or by using a certain type of citizen group (called a "501 (c) (4) organization") that was not subject to regulation by the FEC. The real change here is that business firms, which in the past generally did not advertise directly for or against candidates (but could and did contribute money to other types of groups that did these things), are now free to use money from their treasuries to run their own election advertisements. How common is such direct independent spending? The truth is that we do not yet know because the *Citizens United* decision is relatively fresh. In the years to come we will learn more about who engages in this sort of activity and how much they spend.

Bundling

Some interest groups lobby electorally with campaign money by "bundling"— collecting a bunch of checks from individual contributors and then turning them over to a candidate or candidates. Bundling takes place at the federal level as well as the state and local levels. A lot of bundling is done by PACs, but some other types of interest groups bundle as well. Here is how bundling works. A PAC or interest group collects a large number of checks from individuals. Each individual check, however, is addressed not to the PAC or the group, but rather to the candidate who will eventually receive the money. The PAC or group then "bundles" each candidate's checks together and passes them along to him/her. Thus, when a PAC or other group bundles, it is not technically the source of the money, but rather acts as a conduit or "middle man/woman." The reason PACs and other groups bundle is that it allows them to circumvent the limits or ban on contributions. Thus, instead of giving a one-time only PAC contribution of $5,000 to a candidate for federal office, a PAC may bundle a bunch of individual checks together and contribute much more than $5,000.

An example will help illustrate how bundling works in practice. The most prolific and successful PAC bundler in history is a feminist citizen group called "EMILY's List." EMILY is an acronym for "early money is like yeast." It is like yeast, the founder of EMILY's List likes to say, because "it makes the dough rise." EMILY's List was founded in 1986 by political veteran Ellen Malcolm, who designed it as a vehicle to support pro-choice, Democratic, female congressional candidates.[39] EMILY's List relies heavily on bundling to support candidates. To join EMILY's List, a contributor must make a contribution to the PAC itself, and must also pledge to contribute to candidates endorsed by EMILY's List. The direct contribution goes to cover the PAC's fundraising and administrative costs. The contributions to the candidates are sent not to the candidates themselves, but rather to EMILY's List to be bundled with other contributions and then passed on to candidates.[40] Individuals are still subject to individual contribution limits spelled out in FECA and state and local laws. However, EMILY's List is not limited in how much bundled money it can give to any specific candidate. EMILY's List, which is widely recognized as one of the pioneers of bundling, has demonstrated to other PACs that bundling can work. In recent years a number of state and local PACs have begun bundling.[41] Nonetheless, despite the success of EMILY's List, bundling remains the purview primarily of a few non-affiliated, ideologically driven PACs. For reasons discussed later, most PACs would rather contribute money directly to candidates than bundle.

Making In-Kind Contributions to Candidates

Interest groups also lobby with campaign money by making in-kind campaign contributions. An in-kind campaign contribution is a *gift other than money that is given by a PAC or interest group to a candidate*. The most common types of in-kind gifts are services with monetary value. One of the most famous users of in-kind contributions is a PAC called the National Committee for an Effective Congress (NCEC). The case of NCEC nicely illustrates how PACs make in-kind campaign contributions. NCEC is one of the oldest PACs in the United States, and was founded by Eleanor Roosevelt in 1948 to support "progressive" candidates for Congress. Though like most PACs it contributes money to candidates, it spends most of its money on in-kind campaign contributions. Specifically, NCEC provides services designed to help candidates get elected. For example, it provides "progressive" candidates with expert advice on how to mobilize liberal voters. In addition, it provides polling services and advertising advice. The NCEC changed its name to NCEC Services Inc. in 2010, and appears to have fallen upon hard times. However, the way it used in-kind campaign contributions is illustrative of how other PACs use in-kind contributions. EMILY's List, mentioned above, also provides in-kind contributions to candidates. In addition to money, a candidate backed by EMILY's List can expect campaign consulting services, voter mobilization help, and fundraising assistance. In-kind contributions are not nearly as common as monetary contributions. But there is some evidence that they are becoming more common. At the federal level and in states and localities, in-kind contributions from interest groups (be they direct or through PACs) generally are treated like monetary contributions for legal purposes. Thus, where direct contributions are limited, so are in-kind contributions.

Making Contributions to "Super PACs"

Finally, one way that interest groups lobby electorally with campaign money is by contributing money to "Super PACs." Current federal campaign finance law, as well as the law in some states and localities, allows some interest groups to make direct contributions to special organizations called "Super PACs" that can then be used by these PACs to campaign for or against candidates. Super PACs are labeled "super" because they are allowed under the law (again, at the federal level and in some states and localities) to collect contributions from individuals and some types of interest groups (for example, some business firms, citizen groups, and coalitions, as well as labor unions, professional associations, and trade associations) and then spend this money to help candidates. At the federal level, the difference between a Super PAC and a regular PAC is that Super PACs are "independent expenditure only" PACs, which means that the only thing they do is advertise for or against candidates; they do not contribute money to candidates, as other PACs can.

The advantages of giving to a Super PAC are twofold. First, an interest group—say a large for-profit business firm—can contribute money to a Super PAC that helps the group's preferred candidates without having to do the "dirty work" itself. So, for example, if an oil company hates a liberal Democrat running for Congress, rather than running advertisements against the candidate (that is, spending independently) itself, it can contribute money to a Super PAC which then runs advertisements against the candidate. This way the company has plausible deniability—it can say, "We did not run those ads, we just gave money to a PAC." If this company runs its own advertisements (that is, spends independently) in opposition to this candidate, it has to disclose its identity in the advertisements. This means if it ran a commercial, the commercial would have to acknowledge that it was paid for by the company. The Super PAC has to disclose its identity in its commercial too, but it does not have to disclose the fact that the company in question gave it money.[42]

The second advantage of giving to a Super PAC is that the amount an interest group can give is unlimited (at least at the federal level; limitations vary across states and localities). If you recall, an interest group cannot contribute money directly to its own PAC, nor can it contribute money to other PACs. It can, however, contribute money to a Super PAC, and the amount it can contribute is unlimited. Super PACs are a relatively new phenomenon, at least at the federal level. This is the case because until the *Citizens United* ruling (which is referenced above), campaign finance laws forbade unlimited contributions from any source to PACs. It is hard to say how important Super PACs will be in upcoming elections, but preliminary indications are that they will become more plentiful and active in the years to come.[43]

Other Ways Interest Groups Try to Affect Election Outcomes

Thus far, I have discussed only how interest groups lobby electorally by contributing money and advertising on behalf of candidates. But interest groups engage in other forms of electoral lobbying as well. This section will examine some of these other ways that interest groups engage in electoral lobbying. They include distributing voter guides, endorsing candidates for office, and mounting voter mobilization drives.

Distributing Voter Guides

Another way that interest groups engage in electoral lobbying is by distributing "voter guides." A voter guide is *a brief tract that presents candidates' positions on issues of concern to interest groups and their supporters.* An example will help illustrate how interest groups use voter guides. The Christian Coalition, a conservative citizen group, is a prodigious user of voter guides. For each of the last several presidential elections, the group has issued a voter guide comparing presidential candidates. The group also issues voter guides for some other races as well. In 2008, the voter guide showed where the two major party presidential candidates stood on a series of issues, including off-shore oil drilling, gay marriage, and abortion.[44] The Christian Coalition distributed these voter guides to voters it believed were sympathetic to their causes—that is, evangelical Christians. They sent some voter guides through the mail to voters, and hand-delivered them to others. The Christian Coalition's 2008 voter guide stopped short of explicitly endorsing John McCain. The guide made it very clear, however, how a person should vote. For example, the voter guide says, "Life begins at conception," and under a picture of John McCain it says SUPPORT, while under a picture of Barack Obama it says OPPOSE. The voter guide also says "Resume off-shore oil drilling," and under a picture of McCain it says SUPPORT, while under a picture of Obama it says OPPOSE. In short, the Christian Coalition's voter guides were designed to get conservative Christian voters to show up on election day and vote for John McCain.

In many cases voter guides do not explicitly urge the election or defeat of a specific candidate. This is the case because as long as voter guides do not explicitly urge the defeat or election of a candidate, they may be issued even by interest groups (such as charities) that are not allowed to form PACs and are not allowed to engage in direct or independent election spending. In short, voter guides are a way for interest groups at all levels that cannot utilize other modes of electoral lobbying to engage in electoral lobbying. It is difficult to say how widespread distributing voter guides is, and scholars have seldom studied them. Thus, we just do not know for sure how often groups engage in this form of electoral lobbying.

Endorsing Candidates

Interest groups can also lobby electorally by endorsing candidates. For an interest group, endorsing a candidate entails simply acknowledging officially and publicly that it supports the election of a certain candidate. Many types of interest groups endorse candidates (and the law in many places dictates that some types of interest groups, including charities and churches, may not endorse candidates), but the evidence suggests that citizen groups and labor unions are the most prodigious users of candidate endorsements. For example, the National Rifle Association endorsed candidates in two-thirds of all congressional races in 2010.[45] Many other interest groups, including some of the nation's leading labor unions, and trade associations such as the National Federation of Independent Business and local Chambers of Commerce, endorse candidates. Scholars have spent relatively little time studying candidate endorsements, so we really do not know how widespread this practice is. But during election time—no matter what the election is for—chances are that at least some interest groups are engaging in this activity.

Mounting Voter Mobilization Drives

Finally, many interest groups lobby electorally by mounting voter mobilization drives. A voter mobilization drive simply is *an attempt to get people to show up at the polls on election day.* Interest group experts Matthew Burbank, Ronald Hrebenar, and Robert Benedict note that there are two basic kinds of voter mobilization drives.[46] First, there are nonpartisan efforts designed to get anyone and everyone to vote. These sorts of drives are undertaken by civic groups such as the League of Women Voters. Second, there are partisan or ideological efforts designed to mobilize only certain types of voters. Most interest groups prefer the second kind of voter mobilization drive. Labor unions and gay rights citizen groups and environmental citizen groups, for example, don't just want people to vote, they want people to vote for the candidates (mostly Democrats) they agree with. Thus, they focus on mobilizing people who they have reason to believe support them. Likewise, anti-abortion groups and the National Rifle Association don't just want everyone to vote, they want conservatives to vote.

Interest groups use a variety of methods to encourage people to vote. Specifically, they go door to door to register voters and encourage them to vote, call people on the telephone and urge them to register and/or vote, send direct mail urging people to register and/or vote, and set up booths or displays in public places that allow people to register and/or encourage them to turn out on election day. No one has ever studied group voter mobilization drives in great detail, but evidence from many quarters suggests that this practice is widespread in federal, state, and local elections. Interest groups including the AFL-CIO and Association of Community Organizations for Reform Now (ACORN) played an important role in mobilizing voters to vote for Barack Obama in 2008.[47]

How Often Do Interest Groups Engage in Electoral Lobbying?

Studies show that well over half of all interest groups active in the states and in Washington engage in some form of lobbying with campaign money.[48] Unfortunately, I have no way of knowing how often each technique described here is used by interest groups. We have data (albeit old) about two techniques in particular—making monetary contributions to candidates, and endorsing candidates, and Table 6.3 shows how often interest groups report doing these two things.

What Does Campaign Money Buy?

Few things invite cynicism and suspicion like electoral lobbying by interest groups, particularly interest groups donating money (either directly or through their PACs) to candidates for office. The reason for this is simple: contributing money smacks of bribery. Many people feel that monetary contributions make elected officials beholden to interest groups. Other sorts of interest group assistance may make government decision-makers beholden to groups as well. Veteran political reporter Brooks Jackson concluded over 20 years ago that interest group contributions to candidates "twist the behavior of ordinary"

Table 6.3   The Use of Electoral Lobbying Techniques

Lobbying technique	% reporting they use technique	
	States	Washington
1. Making monetary contributions to candidates	45	58
2. Endorsing candidates	24	22

Source: The state data come from Nownes and Freeman, "Interest Group Activity in the States," 92; The Washington data come from Schlozman and Tierney, "More of the Same—Washington Pressure Group Activity in a Decade of Change," 357.

Notes: Each respondent was given a list of advocacy techniques and asked to indicate how often he/she used them—never, occasionally, or regularly. The number represents the proportion of respondents who reported using a technique occasionally or regularly.

government decision-makers by rewarding "those who cater to well-funded interests" and punishing those who do not.[49] Is Jackson right? Does interest group campaign money skew government decisions toward the interests of big money donors and away from those of ordinary citizens?

Overall, the weight of the evidence seems to suggest that the answer is "probably not."[50] In short, scholars simply have been unable to prove that money buys votes. Most (but not all) academic studies indicate that in most cases, campaign contributions and other forms of campaign help do not substantially influence government decision-makers' behavior. There are two reasons why this is the case. First, there are simply too many factors other than money that influence government decision-makers' decisions. Factors such as political party, ideology, and constituent opinion, for example, are far more influential than money. Second, most interest group contributions are simply not that large. Though interest groups and their PACs give tens of millions of dollars to candidates and parties each year, most campaign contributions are very small. In one study, the authors found that the average federal PAC donation is only $1,700. This is nowhere close to the maximum allowable donation of $10,000 ($5,000 for the primary and $5,000 for the general election).[51] Interest group contributions to state and local government decision-makers generally are even smaller. Few elected officials are willing to "sell out" for a thousand bucks or so. If money doesn't substantially alter the policy decisions of government decision-makers, or even if groups are unsure that money affects government decisions, why do so many interest groups give so much of it away? The answer lies in what money *can* buy: access, effort, and a government more to your liking.

There is considerable evidence that campaign money and campaign help can buy interest groups access—*the ability to see and speak with government decision-makers.*[52] The most compelling evidence we have that lobbying can buy an interest group access to an elected official comes from elected officials (and their staffers) themselves. For his book entitled *The Art of Lobbying*, political scientist Bertram J. Levine conducted extensive interviews with sixty-five former and current federal government decision-makers (i.e., members of Congress or congressional staffers), and he writes that his "interview subjects tended to agree . . . that money does purchase access."[53] One of his respondents reports, "It is indisputable that for a certain segment of members—probably by far and away the majority of members—money translates into access."

Table 6.1 contains a list of the ten most active federal PACs in the 2010 election. The table shows that seven of them are affiliated with parent organizations. This is important because all seven parent organizations engage in a wide range of lobbying activities. The point here is this: for many interest groups, lobbying with campaign money is just one small part of a larger strategy that encompasses many lobbying techniques. Thus, for many interest groups, contributions are designed primarily to complement other lobbying techniques. Lobbyists know that their primary weapon is not money, but information—information that might persuade government decision-makers to "vote their way." They also know that information is useless if they don't get to deliver it to government decision-makers. One way to increase the probability that a government decision-maker will receive a lobbyist's information and pay it some attention is to contribute money to his/her campaign. Money may not "win a government decision-maker over," but at least it gets a lobbyist's "foot in the door." Lobbyists and interest groups realize that most elected officials are very busy and thus do not have time to meet with everyone who asks for their attention. Thus, lobbyists try to ensure access by contributing money. As political scientist Alan Rosenthal reports in his study of state lobbying, lobbyists consistently report that campaign contributions buy "the assurance that [a lobbyist's] issues will get a fair hearing."[54] One lobbyist that Rosenthal interviewed put it like this: "Money gets you in the front door." Another noted that contributions "buy access . . . and an ability to speak one's case."[55]

The desire of some PACs to buy access is best demonstrated by their propensity to contribute money primarily to incumbents—government decision-makers with whom they deal on a regular basis. Some interest groups are less reluctant to support challengers than others. Citizen groups and labor unions, for example, regularly support challengers. Nonetheless, they too tend to concentrate their efforts on incumbents. Table 6.4 contains information on the allocation of PAC contributions to members of Congress over the past seven election cycles. As you can see, the vast majority of PAC contributions to federal recipients accrued to incumbents. The tendency for interest groups to support incumbents is visible at all levels of government.[56] This means that even when interest groups prefer the challenger to the incumbent—which is often the case—they tend to contribute to the incumbent in order to improve their relationship with a sitting government decision-maker. This tendency for interest groups to support incumbents is quite frustrating to challengers. Throughout the last two decades, for example, Republicans in Congress expressed frustration at the fact that many PACs associated with business firms and trade associations, their ostensible political allies, contributed heavily to Democratic incumbents. Republicans felt that by doing so, corporate PACs were "shooting themselves in the foot." Corporate PACs, however, felt differently. They maintained that because Democrats were in charge, they had to support them or their interests would go unrepresented. The desire to ensure access is also demonstrated by the tendency of PACs to contribute most of their money to the most powerful government decision-makers. Within the House and Senate, for example, PACs support party leaders (e.g., the Speaker of the House, the Senate Majority Leader) and people on the most powerful committees (e.g., those who write tax laws and make appropriations) much more than "rank and file" legislators.

Campaign money and/or help can also help an interest group "obtain" a government it likes. Interest groups that lobby with campaign money may be pragmatic, but they're not stupid. This means that they seldom support government decision-makers who are openly hostile to them. You won't see

Table 6.4 PAC Contributions to Candidates for Federal Office by Candidate Status, 1998–2008

	Incumbents	Challengers	Open seats
1997–98	$170,900,000 (78%)	$ 22,100,000 (10%)	$ 27,000,000 (12%)
1999–00	$195,400,000 (75%)	$ 27,500,000 (11%)	$ 36,900,000 (14%)
2001–02	$213,400,000 (76%)	$ 28,500,000 (10%)	$ 40,200,000 (14%)
2003–04	$246,800,000 (80%)	$ 22,300,000 (7%)	$ 41,300,000 (13%)
2005–06	$279,300,000 (80%)	$ 36,300,000 (11%)	$ 32,400,000 (9%)
2007–08	$304,700,000 (79%)	$ 48,800,000 (13%)	$ 32,400,000 (8%)

Sources: Federal Election Commission, "Growth in PAC Financial Activity Slows."

Note: Numbers were rounded by FEC.

many labor unions, for example, supporting arch-conservatives such as Speaker of the House John Boehner (R–Ohio) just because he's a powerful incumbent. And few business PACs (except maybe Ben and Jerry's PAC) are going to give socialist Senator Bernie Sanders (I–Vermont) a big wad of cash. Thus, while interest groups are likely to support incumbents and "power brokers," they are not likely to support incumbents and power brokers who have a consistent record of bashing them.

What to do then, if the make-up of the government is not to your liking? Do you continue to buy access to government decision-makers who you know will never "come around to your way of thinking"? Some interest groups do. But others do not. One option for the interest group that is not happy with the current make-up of the government is to support candidates in open seat elections—elections that have no incumbent. The value of an open seat contribution is that it does not offend a powerful incumbent, yet allows an interest group to support a candidate who shares its political views. As you can see from Table 6.4, open seat contributions are a tad more common than contributions to challengers. Studies have shown that campaign contributions can significantly influence a non-incumbent's chances of being elected. Thus, PAC contributions to candidates in open seat elections can have a large impact on election outcomes.[57]

Finally, there is some evidence that campaign money and/or help can buy interest groups *effort*. A campaign contribution may not change a government decision-maker's overall point of view, but it may cause him/her to insert a short amendment into a large piece of legislation, push harder for a specific proposal than he/she otherwise might have, or "put in a good word" for a contributing interest group. These things do not represent huge changes in behavior. But in the end, they can mightily benefit an interest group.[58]

Campaign Money: Is There Need for Reform?

The purpose of FECA and other similar laws at the state and local levels was to limit the influence of interest groups in elections. The idea behind these types of laws is that elections should be sacrosanct. The basic argument is that because only individual U.S. citizens have the right to vote, only individual U.S. citizens should be involved in elections. This chapter should convince you that campaign finance laws notwithstanding, interest groups are major players in election campaigns. Critics in politics, the media, and the public alike continue to express distrust and disdain for the practice of electoral lobbying, especially contributing money to candidates. Why? On what basis do critics object to electoral lobbying? Are the critics' objections off-base? Or do they have merit? Before concluding this chapter, I will briefly examine the moral and ethical implications of lobbying with money by addressing these questions.

Critics have raised four major concerns about interest group campaign contributions and other forms of electoral lobbying. First, many critics feel that campaign money may skew representation toward moneyed interests by affecting which candidates can run for, and ultimately win, elected office. The argument goes like this. If money is absolutely critical to being elected (which it is in many cases), it is possible that candidates who do not appeal to "big money" donors might never run for office regardless of their other qualifications. If this occurs, our government decision-makers will increasingly come to represent not the entirety of their constituencies, but rather those portions of their constituencies that are able to provide them with the money they need to win elections. This criticism is particularly troubling when you consider that the many interest groups that engage in electoral lobbying are business-related interest groups—interest groups that already have a considerable advantage in interest group representation. Currently, for example, 38 percent of all federal PACs are affiliated with individual business firms.[59] Only 6 percent of federal PACs are affiliated with labor unions. In all, business firm and trade association PACs account for approximately two-thirds of all PAC contributions to federal candidates in the typical election year.

A second and closely related objection to interest group campaign contributions is that they make some people and interests—specifically, those with lots of money to spend on electoral campaigns—more influential in elections than others. This seems to violate the "one person one vote" principle that is the bedrock of American democracy. In essence, this argument goes, people and interests with lots of money have more influence over election outcomes than people and interests without lots of money. And since elections are the primary ways that ordinary citizens express their political preferences, this is a bad thing.

Third, despite academic studies to the contrary, many critics believe that campaign contributions *do* influence the way government decision-makers behave. Some analysts have argued that though contributions may not buy votes, they may buy less noticeable but nonetheless important favors for "big money" donors. Congressional scholar Richard Hall, for example, has observed that monetary contributions and other forms of campaign assistance may be effective "at the margins" of government decision-makers' behavior. Campaign money may, for example, convince a legislator to withhold an amendment in a committee markup, provide a lobbyist with important information on legislative procedures, or do other things that are seemingly minor but nonetheless important to interest groups.[60]

Finally, some critics believe that massive interest group contributions to electoral campaigns increase public cynicism by convincing people that all politicians are "for sale."[61] Money, it seems, is at the center of most lobbying scandals. Jack Abramoff, who was convicted of tax evasion, fraud, and corruption, became a successful lobbyist and then a criminal primarily because he had a lot of money to spread around. Abramoff infiltrated the highest circles of national government and got prime access to government decision-makers partially because he had a lot of money to give. The Center for Responsive Politics, an independent watchdog organization that researches campaign finance and lobbying in America, reported the following about Abramoff:

> during the time that Jack Abramoff was their lobbyist his clients contributed at least $5 million to members of Congress and their political action committees, to candidates for federal office and to political parties. More than 300 members of the 109th Congress received campaign contributions from a client of Jack Abramoff while he was their lobbyist— 81 Senators and 227 members of the House of Representatives, the Center found. On average, each recipient got about $16,000.[62]

Abramoff's arrest and conviction convinced many people that Washington politicians were for sale to the highest bidder and that politics is all about money.

In sum, electoral lobbying is controversial because it raises the specter of bribery. While Americans have always been suspicious of "big money" in politics, there is evidence that they are more cynical today than ever before— partially due to the enormous amounts of campaign cash flowing to candidates from both major parties from interest groups. In recent years, concerns about the deleterious effects of "big money" in politics have led to numerous reform proposals. Some reformers argue that the government should finance elections, thus taking interest groups and big money donors out of the picture. Indeed, several states including Arizona, Connecticut, and Maine have some form of public financing of elections. The idea behind public financing of elections is that if candidates get money only or mostly from one source—the government—they will not be beholden to individual or group big money donors and will be more responsive to the needs of regular citizens. Reformers, however, are facing an uphill battle. The Supreme Court in its *Citizens United* ruling (which is referenced above) demonstrated that it has a dim view of campaign finance restrictions. Moreover, many states are moving *away* from stricter regulations on campaign finance and are making laws that make it easier for interest groups to spend and give more. In the short term at least, it appears that interest groups will be less restricted in what they can do in elections rather than more restricted.

How do interest groups and their defenders answer their critics? Defenders of the current system offer several rebuttals. One argument that government decision-makers often make is that lobbying with money is not a big deal because they would never—*never!*—allow themselves to "be bought." Government decision-makers' denials to this effect are generally offered with a healthy dose of righteous indignation. Any time a government official is confronted with evidence that he/she did something in return for a campaign contribution, he/she responds that he/she is not for sale and would never sell him/herself for money.

Another common response to critics' barbs—one that is regularly offered by interest groups—is that contributing money to government decision-makers, far from being an extreme evil, is an important and unfairly maligned form of political participation. In short, interest groups are quick to say that contributing money is a form of legitimate political participation. Another common defense of the current system is that things are not really as bad as critics say they are. One of the best-known purveyors of this point of view is conservative columnist George Will. Essentially, he argues that though campaign spending may seem to be out of control, it really is not. Will wrote just before the 2000 presidential election:

> Total spending, by all parties, campaigns and issue-advocacy groups, concerning every office from county clerks to U.S. senators, may reach a record $4.2 billion in this two-year cycle. That is about what Americans spend in one year on yogurt, but less than they spend on candy in two Halloween seasons. Procter & Gamble spent $8.6 billion on advertising in its most recent fiscal year.[63]

Along the same lines, some analysts have pointed out that PACs—the most controversial types of interest groups—are not really all that important in the big scheme of things. For one thing, PACs are not the main sources of money for electoral campaigns. Presidential candidates tend to get the vast majority of their money from individuals. Legislative candidates rely more on individuals than PACs as well. Defenders of the current system also note that though PACs are numerous, many are puny "shoestring operations" that exist in name only. During the 2009–2010 election cycle, for example, fully 26 percent of all federally registered PACs spent less than $5,000 total, and 59 percent spent less than $50,000.[64] PACs are even less active in state and local elections.

Perhaps the most common defense of campaign contributions is the one offered by the most prominent defender of the current system, Senator Mitch McConnell (R–Kentucky). McConnell, who speaks for many other Republicans in Congress, argues that though the system is not perfect, the proposed solutions would actually make things worse. McConnell and his supporters are fond of saying, for example, that public financing of federal elections, a remedy favored by Ralph Nader and other liberal activists, is nothing more than an unfair tax on ordinary citizens. Similarly, McConnell often points out that contribution bans and spending limits violate people's First Amendment rights.[65]

There are good reasons to be suspicious of monetary contributions. As the case of Jack Abramoff suggests, money sometimes makes people do things that they otherwise might not do. However, it is possible to "go overboard" in attacking campaign spending. Academic studies have consistently shown that campaign contributions by themselves seldom influence the behavior of government decision-makers. Moreover, the case of the tobacco industry suggests that lobbying with campaign money can only take you so far. Despite massive donations to candidates of both parties and the parties themselves over the past three decades, the tobacco industry was unable to avoid an historic settlement that forced them to pay state governments $368 billion in return for some protection against lawsuits. Nonetheless, there is reason to believe that campaign contributions, especially in conjunction with other lobbying efforts, may reap rewards for the interest groups that can afford to make them.

Conclusion: Electoral Lobbying

Giving money directly to government decision-makers in an attempt to influence their decisions is against the law everywhere. This is called bribery. Nonetheless, interest groups lobby with campaign money to an astounding degree. They do so in seven major ways: making PAC contributions to federal candidates; making PAC contributions to state and local candidates; making direct contributions to candidates; spending independently on behalf of or in opposition to candidates; bundling; making in-kind contributions to candidates; and making contributions to Super PACs. By far the most common way that interest groups lobby with campaign money is by contributing money to candidates for public office. Campaign contributions generally (but not always) flow through PACs—special types of interest groups that are set up solely to collect money from individuals and spend it on electoral campaigns. PACs are now an important, though far from dominant, source of campaign money. PACs are perhaps the most controversial types of interest groups in the United

States. The specter of moneyed interests bankrolling campaigns and spending millions to affect government decisions rightly frightens and worries many Americans. Only time will tell if the current system of campaign finance—a system that allows interest groups great latitude to lobby with campaign money—will survive in the end. For now, however, it is safe to say that interest groups will continue to be an important source of campaign money.

Interest groups attempt to affect election outcomes in other ways as well. For example, they distribute voter guides, endorse candidates for office, and mount voter mobilization drives. Interest groups are not the driving forces behind most campaigns (individual candidates and their campaign organizations are), but there is evidence that they are becoming more and more important.

What's Next

We're not quite through with our look at how interest groups attempt to influence government decisions. Though media tend to focus upon direct lobbying and electoral lobbying, interest groups have become quite adept at another type of lobbying: *indirect lobbying*. This is where we're headed next.

Indirect Lobbying

7

It makes sense to assume that interest groups lobby only government decision-makers. After all, government decision-makers are the people who make government decisions. Who else *would* interest groups lobby? The answer, it turns out, is *you and me*. Numerous studies of lobbying show that interest groups often lobby ordinary citizens who have little or no power directly to make government decisions. This sort of lobbying, lobbying that is aimed at ordinary people rather than government decision-makers, is called "indirect lobbying," and is the subject of this chapter.

I begin by exploring what indirect lobbying is. As you will see, indirect lobbying has one hugely important thing in common with direct lobbying—its goal is to influence government decisions. Next, I ask: Why do interest groups engage in indirect lobbying? The answer to this question lies in the very nature of our representative democracy. From here, I examine the techniques by which interest groups lobby citizens. As with direct lobbying, interest groups have a number of distinct techniques at their disposal. I conclude with a look at recent trends in indirect lobbying. Though indirect lobbying has been around for a long time, it is more common now than ever before.

What is Indirect Lobbying?

Indirect lobbying is defined as *lobbying that is aimed at citizens rather than government decision-makers*. It is important to note that some people refer to indirect lobbying as "grassroots lobbying," which is defined as *lobbying aimed at ordinary citizens which is designed to mobilize them to contact legislators and/or other decision-makers.* In addition, some people call indirect lobbying "outside lobbying." The term "indirect lobbying" is preferable for two reasons. First of all, not all lobbying that is aimed at citizens is designed to mobilize them to contact legislators and other government decision-makers. Some is designed to shape people's attitudes and opinions. Thus, the general definition of grass-roots lobbying is simply too narrow to encompass all the forms of lobbying examined in this chapter. Second, the word "indirect" is much more accessible than the word "grassroots." The term "indirect lobbying" provides a nice contrast to the term "direct lobbying."

The very definition of indirect lobbying begs the following question: Why would an interest group lobby citizens rather than government decision-makers? The answer is simple: Because interest groups know that ordinary citizens profoundly affect what the government does. In fact, one of the bedrock principles of American democracy is that ordinary citizens—people like you and me—are the ultimate sources of government authority. Ordinary citizens influence government decisions in three particularly important ways. First, *they choose* many (but not all) government decision-makers. The founders of this country created a government of representatives. In this system, ordinary citizens do not have a chance to vote on most political issues directly. (I say "most" because there are some instances in which citizens directly make authoritative government decisions. I will talk more about this below.) Rather, they vote on the people who make government decisions directly. They also exert control over how government decision-makers behave once they are in positions of powers. The mechanism by which voters choose some government decision-makers—elections—provides them with a means by which to either induce government decision-makers to be responsive or punish them for failing to respond.

Second, citizens *pressure* government decision-makers to do or not to do certain things. As Chapter 2 pointed out, the Constitution guarantees American citizens the right to make their opinions known to government decision-makers. In practice, this means that by participating in political parties, contacting government decision-makers, attending rallies and protests, and joining interest groups, citizens have the opportunity to affect the decisions of government decision-makers. Although government decision-makers do not always respond to citizen pressure, generally they consider ordinary citizens' opinions when they make decisions—mostly because they know that their jobs may depend upon it.[1]

Finally, citizens sometimes make government decisions directly by *voting in initiative or referendum campaigns.* An initiative is a "proposal of a new law or constitutional amendment that is placed on the ballot by petition, that is, by collecting signatures of a certain number of citizens."[2] There is no federal initiative process, but currently twenty-four states have some form of initiative.[3] The number of signatures required to place a law or constitutional amendment on the state ballot varies across states. A referendum is "a proposal to repeal a law that was previously enacted by the legislature, and that is placed on the ballot by citizen petition."[4] Twenty-four states have a referendum process.[5] Thousands of local governments, including many counties, cities, and towns, allow initiatives and referendums as well. In fact, nearly 90 percent of cities in the United States "report having some form of referendum procedure," and many have the initiative process.[6] Initiatives and referendums are not all that common, but they are becoming more so. In 2006 there were 64 initiatives on state ballots (35 of which were approved), and in 2008 there were 68 (26 of which were approved).[7] Over the years, Oregon, California, and Colorado have been the states in which the initiative is used the most.[8]

In sum, indirect lobbying is lobbying that is aimed at citizens rather than government decision-makers. Interest groups lobby citizens because they know that citizens often have a profound impact on government decisions. Though ordinary citizens do not often make decisions directly, they often indirectly influence the direction of government decisions.

Influencing Government Decisions through Indirect Lobbying: Changing Attitudes, Changing Behavior

It is important to remember that the ultimate goal of all indirect lobbying is the same: *to affect government decisions.* The more immediate goal of indirect lobbying, however, is to do one or both of the following: (1) *Influence* people's opinions; (2) *Encourage* people to contact government decision-makers and make their opinions known. If an indirect lobbying effort successfully does either or both of these things, it has the potential to affect government decisions.

Lobbying for Values

Some indirect lobbying efforts attempt to shape people's attitudes and opinions about an issue or series of issues. This type of indirect lobbying is called "lobbying for values."[9] The basic premise of lobbying for values is simple. Because people's attitudes and opinions are eventually translated into government decisions, it makes sense to try to affect them. A great deal of political science research shows that people's attitudes and opinions about political issues and candidates affect how they vote, how often they vote, and to what extent they participate in other political activities such as contacting government decision-makers, engaging in protest, joining interest groups, and contributing money to candidates for public office.[10] In short, to shape people's opinions about political issues is to shape—albeit indirectly—government decisions.

An example will help illustrate how lobbying for values works in practice. Mobil Oil (now Exxon Mobil), one of the nation's leading petroleum companies, has engaged in lobbying for values for decades. The company regularly has placed advertisements in the *New York Times* and other national newspapers that are designed to shape people's attitudes and opinions. The advertisements look much like standard editorials, and generally appear in the "opinion" section of newspapers. The advertisements are different from their regular consumer advertisements in that they do not say, "Buy Exxon Mobil gasoline." Rather, they contain the company's thoughts and ideas about energy policy in the United States. One recent advertisement sings the praises of "New drilling technologies combined with a time-tested process called hydraulic fracturing" that are "unlocking vast amounts of cleaner-burning natural gas from shale rock—and providing economic benefits for communities across the country."[11] In general, Exxon Mobil hopes that its advertisements will affect people's opinions on energy-related manners. In this particular case, Exxon Mobil wants to convince you and me that hydraulic fracturing—a method of energy production that many environmentalists say is dangerous and harmful to the environment—is perfectly safe. In addition, the advertisement wants to convince you and me that this method of natural gas production is good for the economy. In the end, the company hopes that *its* opinion on this issue of hydraulic fracturing will eventually affect *your* opinion on the issue of hydraulic fracturing (which many environmentalists want to regulate more stringently), and might convince you to engage in political activity favorable to the company such as voting for a candidate who shares Exxon Mobil's view or opposing a bill that Exxon Mobil opposes.

Of course, in order for lobbying for values to work citizens must be receptive and responsive to the information they receive from interest groups. Are they? Because myriad factors determine each individual's political attitudes and opinions, it is impossible to say for certain. But there are two good reasons to believe that citizens may be receptive and responsive to the information they receive from interest groups.[12] First of all, research on advertising indicates that most people are willing to consider information from outside sources when making up their minds about particular things.[13] In fact, the whole premise of advertising is that people are open to the messages they receive from outside sources. Second, it appears that campaign advertisements—advertisements that have a lot in common with advocacy advertisements—shape the attitudes, opinions, and behavior of some voters.[14] There is even some direct evidence that interest group advertisements can shape people's opinions.[15] While many people ignore campaign advertisements and interest group advertisements, some Americans actually respond to them. In sum, research on advertising and campaigning suggests that "lobbying for values" has some chance of success.

Lobbying for Contact

Not all indirect lobbying efforts are aimed at changing people's attitudes and opinions. Some are intended to encourage citizens to make their opinions known to government decision-makers. This form of indirect lobbying is called "lobbying for contact." Lobbying for contact involves getting ordinary citizens to pressure government decision-makers to support an interest group's agenda.[16] The premise of this type of indirect lobbying is simple. Because government decision-makers—especially elected officials—want to keep their jobs, they will respond to the desires of ordinary people.[17]

Lobbying for contact was on display in a big way during the political battle over President Obama's health care reform plan in 2009 and 2010. The AARP, which supported Obama's plan, was particularly active. Political scientists Richard L. Hall and Richard Anderson recently wrote:

> one 2009 AARP ad urged viewers to "tell Congress not to let myths get in the way of fixing what's broken with health care." The ad then directed them to the group's Web site [sic], where they would find links to congressional Web sites [sic].[18]

An opposing, more conservative citizen group called "The 60 Plus Association" ran television advertisements that said, "Tell Congress: Don't Pay for Health Care Reform On the Backs of Our Seniors."[19] Hall and Anderson explain that "The final frame displayed a phone number. The viewers who called it were patched through to their own representatives' offices."[20]

Lobbying efforts like these which are designed to convince people to make their views known to government decision-makers rest upon the assumption that citizens *are willing* to make their views known to government decision-makers. Are they? The answer is an emphatic "Yes." Each year, almost one-third of all adult Americans—over 50 million people—contact a government decision-maker about a policy issue. In fact, as Figure 7.1 shows,

Percentage of Americans who, in a typical year:

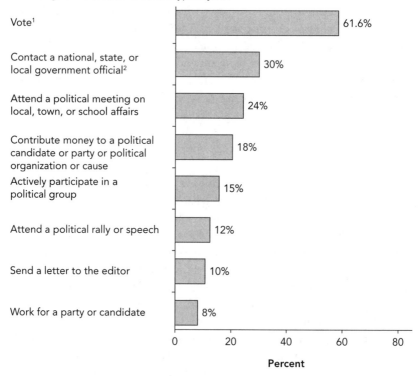

Figure 7.1 The Political Activities of Ordinary Citizens

Sources: 1. This is the percent of eligible voters who voted in the 2008 presidential election. From McDonald, "2008 General Election Turnout Rates"; 2. For all other activities, see: Smith et al., *The Internet and Civic Engagement*, 16.

contacting government decision-makers is surprisingly common in the United States. It is one of the most common forms of political activity among adult Americans. It is important to note that citizens do not limit their contact to elected officials. It is not unheard of for citizens to contact bureaucrats and even judges.

Perhaps even more important than the fact that citizens are willing to contact government decision-makers is the fact that they are *more* willing to do so if they are asked to do so.[21] Stories of indirect lobbying campaigns successfully mobilizing people to contact government decision-makers are legion. During the battle over President Clinton's health care reform proposal in 1992–1993, for example, the National Federation of Independent Businesses (NFIB) managed to generate 500,000 letters to members of Congress.[22] Also in the 1990s, in an epic battle over gun control legislation, the National Rifle Association managed to produce 3 million pro-gun telegrams to members of Congress in three days.[23] And then there is the case of the American Bankers Association, which in one indirect lobbying campaign "orchestrated an estimated 22 million postcards, letters, and mailgrams to force Congress to cancel a requirement that banks and other financial institutions withhold income taxes on interest and dividends."[24] More recently, a "pro-immigrant" citizen group called We Belong Together managed to get close to 5,000 letters from children urging President Obama and Congress to stop detaining or deporting the parents of legal immigrant children.[25] If groups can get children to sit down and write letters, certainly they can get adults to do so. Stories such as these leave no doubt that indirect lobbying campaigns can be successful in generating public pressure on government decision-makers. Whether or not this public pressure influences the behavior of government decision-makers and thus the direction of government decisions is, of course, an entirely different question. It is explored in some detail in Chapter 9.

There are several ways that citizens can make their views known to government decision-makers. First of all, they can write *letters*, place *telephone calls*, send *emails*, or send *faxes*. Many elected government decision-makers in this country, as well as some unelected government decision-makers, have an office at which they can receive mail, telephone calls, and fax messages. Today, many of these same government decision-makers also have *email* accounts. Moreover, most high-ranking government decision-makers at all levels of government— for example, members of Congress, governors, mayors, and state legislators— have their own websites. No one knows for certain how many letters, telephone calls, and faxes government decision-makers receive each year. But the number is surely in the hundreds of millions. One report from the mid-2000s found that "Congress received 200,388,993 communications in 2004."[26] The report goes on to state: "the House received 10,400,000 communications by post and 99,053,399 via the internet; the Senate received 7,935,594 by post and 83,000,000 via the internet." One recent report states that the president receives "about 65,000 paper letters every week and about 100,000 emails, 1,000 faxes and 2,500 to 3,500 phone calls per day."[27] State and local government decision-makers receive hundreds of millions more communications each year. Of course, many government decision-makers do not open their own mail, look at their own emails, answer their own telephones, or fetch their own faxes. That's what staffers are for. But make no mistake: government decision-makers—especially elected officials—pay attention to messages they receive from their constituents.

Citizens can also make their views known by *meeting with* government decision-makers face to face. How easy is it to set up a meeting with a government decision-maker? It depends. For influential constituents—corporate "big wigs," small business owners, and community leaders, for example—it may be fairly easy.[28] For ordinary citizens, depending on the government decision-maker, it may be easy or it may be difficult. Though few government decision-makers meet with every person who calls and says, "I want to meet with you," many government decision-makers are willing to meet with particularly vocal and perseverant citizens.[29] Elected officials, for example, regularly meet with constituents at public forums and meetings. In addition, government decision-makers of all stripes attend interest-group-orchestrated "lobby days." Most of the interest group leaders and lobbyists I have spoken to over the years believe that personal meetings are the most effective ways for citizens (or lobbyists) to communicate their opinions and beliefs to government decision-makers. The advantages of personal meetings are manifold. First, they allow a citizen to establish a relationship with a government decision-maker which may lead to consistent access. Second, they allow a citizen to "make his/her case" forcefully and emotionally. Letters and faxes and telephone calls are not effective media for the transmission of emotion and passion. Third, they allow a citizen to put a "human face" on an issue. It's one thing for a legislator to get 1,000 telephone calls from teachers. But it's quite another for a legislator to walk outside of his/her office and see 1,000 teachers and their children milling about the Capitol steps.

Another way that citizens can make their views known to government decision-makers is by engaging in *protest*. A protest is an event at which citizens gather together and "make their case" by creating a public spectacle. Protest was the method of choice for civil rights and anti-war activists in the 1960s, many of whom felt that their letters, telephone calls, and personal entreaties to government decision-makers were being ignored. In the past 20–30 years, the most prodigious users of protest have been anti-abortion activists and their opponents. For example, every year on January 23, which is the anniversary of the controversial *Roe v. Wade* Supreme Court decision which effectively legalized abortion in this country, interest groups on both sides of the abortion debate stage massive demonstrations in Washington, DC.[30] The years 2009–2011 were marked by extensive protests across the United States. First, there were dozens of conservative "Tea Party" protests and demonstrations. The Tea Partiers largely are conservative, anti-tax, anti-big government protestors who want Congress and the president to cut spending and lower taxes. Some of the largest Tea Party protests took place on April 15, 2009 (tax day) in cities across the nation. The largest protest—in Atlanta, Georgia—attracted 5–10,000 protestors.[31] Another Tea Party protest later in 2009 in Washington, DC attracted over 50,000 protestors.[32] Tea Party protests of various sizes continued throughout 2009 and 2010. Then there were protests in Madison, Wisconsin, orchestrated by labor unions and their liberal interest group allies. The protests were a response to Republican Governor Scott Walker's plan to strip public unions of their collective bargaining rights. There were numerous protests throughout 2011, the largest of which drew 50–60,000 protestors.[33] Then, throughout 2011, there were "Occupy" protests across the nation. The "Occupy" protests were mostly liberal in tone, decrying increasing income inequality in the United States, and urging the federal government to do something about it. Some of the largest Occupy protests occurred in New York, where Occupy Wall Street protestors swelled to around 15,000 in number in October.[34]

Citizens can also make their opinions known by engaging in *dramatics*. Dramatics are similar to protest, but generally are more carefully orchestrated and more provocative. The best way to define dramatics is by example. Interest groups active in the battle over abortion produce the best examples. Throughout the 1980s, anti-abortion activists regularly showed up at protests with child-sized coffins draped in velvet, and trashcans filled with doll parts covered with red paint. Their desire was to shock people, as well as attract media attention. Their histrionics did both.[35] More recently, anti-abortion groups, especially a group called the Center for Bio-Ethical Reform, have conducted protests across the nation in which they show large graphic posters of bloody aborted fetuses.[36] The Westboro Baptist Church, which we encountered in Chapter 1, has taken histrionics to a whole new level. The group regularly demonstrates at soldiers' funerals, holding signs that read "God Hates Fags," "God Hates America," "Thanks God for IEDs," "Thank God for Dead Soldiers," and "USA=Fag Nation."[37] We do not know for certain if these histrionics work, but they certainly draw media and public attention to the people who engage in these sorts of things.

Finally, citizens may make their opinions known by presenting *petitions* to government decision-makers. The typical petition contains a brief statement followed by lots of places where people can sign to indicate their support for the statement. Typically, a group organizes a petition drive, then collects signed petitions and delivers them to one or more government decision-makers. To illustrate how groups use petition drives, consider a recent example. In 2011, local affiliates of the American Postal Workers Union launched petition drives in several locations across the country to urge Congress not to cut the Postal Service's budget and thus shut down many local post offices. For example, when postal workers in Kokomo, Indiana were told that congressional plans would lead to the laying off of twenty-one people, the union started a petition drive and gathered 500–600 signatures from local residents. The petition basically urged Congress to reconsider the cuts, and was delivered to the office of Republican House member Dan Burton.[38] Petition drives are particularly common in local politics. Recently, for example, I was asked to sign a petition— one written up by a local citizen group—saying that I opposed the building of a new cellular phone tower in my neighborhood. A representative of the group knocked on my door and asked me to sign the petition, and he told me that the petition would be delivered to members of the local planning commission, the city mayor, and members of the City Council. I am not sure if there was a relationship between the petition and the final outcome, but a company's proposal to build the cellphone tower in my neighborhood eventually was rejected by my local government. So maybe the petition worked.

Before moving on, it is important to note that some indirect lobbying efforts are designed *both* to encourage citizens to make their views known to government decision-makers and to shape people's attitudes and opinions. In the case of a "two for one" advertisement, a group will tell its side of the story *and* ask people to contact their representatives in Congress, the state legislature, or elsewhere. In other words, not every interest group advertisement either lobbies for values or lobbies for contact; some advertisements do both.

The Informational Basis of Indirect Lobbying

All indirect lobbying efforts—just like all direct lobbying efforts—entail the provision of information. However, unlike direct lobbying, indirect lobbying entails the provision of information to citizens, not government decision-makers. In many cases, this information is policy analytical information, which was defined in Chapter 5. The policy analytical information that interest groups provide to citizens is considerably less complex and technical than the policy analysis they provide to government decision-makers. For example, when I was asked to sign the petition against the cellphone tower, I was told, "Cellphone towers are ugly. And they lower property values." This is pretty unsophisticated information; but it is policy analytical information nonetheless. Similarly, the spate of health care reform advertisements mentioned above generally contained very simple information. Opponents of reform, for example, told citizens something akin to: "This is bad policy because it means more government control over your health care choices and more bureaucracy and higher costs." As for supporters, they presented information in this vein: "Health care reform will provide coverage for people who don't have it, and will help control costs." Again, this is unsophisticated information, but it is policy analytical information nonetheless. In short, no matter what information groups provide to citizens when they lobby indirectly, the goal is the same: to "win people over" to the interest group's way of thinking or to get them to contact government decision-makers. Of course, if indirect lobbying is successful—that is, if it either convinces people of the rightness of an interest group's cause or convinces people to contact government decision-makers—it also provides information to government decision-makers. Indirect lobbying efforts that produce citizen pressure on government decision-makers, for example, provide important political information to government decision-makers about how people are likely to vote in the next election.[39] Similarly, indirect lobbying efforts that successfully affect people's opinions and attitudes eventually produce political activity that provides political information to government decision-makers.

Any time an interest group decides to engage in indirect lobbying it must decide exactly whom it is going to lobby. That is, to whom it is going to provide information. An interest group that engages in indirect lobbying essentially has three options. First, it can lobby the *mass public*—that is, as many people as possible. Second, it can lobby the *attentive public*—some subsection of the larger population that is concerned with a particular issue or series of issues. Finally, it can lobby only *members, activists, and sympathizers*. Some people call this "narrowcasting"—focusing narrowly rather than broadly. Several factors determine to which audience an interest group directs its indirect lobbying efforts. One is *cost*. Not surprisingly, the more people an interest group wishes to reach, the more expensive it is. Many interest groups that would like to reach the mass public simply cannot do so because it is too expensive. Another factor that determines which audience an interest group targets in an indirect lobbying campaign is the *immediate goal* of the campaign. When interest groups wish to change the attitudes and opinions of large numbers of people, they generally focus broadly. In contrast, when interest groups "lobby for contact," they generally focus more narrowly—usually on members and sympathizers who they have reason to believe will respond positively to their appeals. Focusing more broadly runs the risk of mobilizing opponents as well as supporters. Finally, which audience an interest group targets is determined to some extent by the *level of success of its direct lobbying efforts*. Interest groups that are not successful in their *direct* lobbying efforts have an incentive to "broaden the scope of conflict" by getting more people involved.[40] One way to get more people involved is to lobby citizens.

Finally, before beginning our discussion of precisely how interest groups lobby indirectly, it is important to note that because the goal of indirect lobbying is to reach citizens, interest groups often seek media attention for their indirect lobbying efforts.[41] Media attention can increase the number of people an interest group reaches. There are three ways that interest groups can attract media attention. One way is *to notify news outlets* of their activities. Another way is *to give interviews* on radio and/or television. A third way is to *do something outrageous*—such as showing up at a demonstration with a sign that reads "God Hates Fags"—that is certain to attract media attention. The publicity that comes from media coverage can attract new supporters (or opponents) to an interest group's cause, generate enthusiasm among current supporters, and cause government decision-makers to take notice. The value of media coverage was particularly apparent during the civil rights movement of the 1960s. The citizen groups at the forefront of the movement successfully mobilized tens of thousands of citizens to make their views known to government decision-makers (mostly via protest). In doing so, they also attracted media attention. The media attention galvanized public support for the civil rights movement.

Techniques of Indirect Lobbying: The Classics

Indirect lobbying has been around forever. In his 1951 book, *The Governmental Process*, political scientist David Truman noted that "A primary concern of all organized political interest groups in the United States is the character of the opinions existing in the community."[42] As such, Truman continued, interest groups of all kinds engage in "program[s] of propaganda, though rarely so labeled, designed to affect opinions concerning the interests" of the organization.[43] Truman also concluded that interest groups "frequently urge members to participate" in the political process by making their views known to government decision-makers.[44] Sound familiar? It should. Truman is basically saying what I said in the last section: interest groups often try to influence government decisions by lobbying for values or lobbying for contact.[45]

In Truman's time, there were relatively few ways for interest groups to reach citizens. Today there are dozens of ways. This section briefly examines the techniques of indirect lobbying that are considered the "classics"—techniques that have been around for a long time. The most common of these techniques are: contacting people directly; distributing brochures and pamphlets; advertising in newspapers and/or magazines; and sending direct mail.

Contacting People Directly

One of the most time-honored indirect lobbying techniques is contacting people directly. Throughout most of American history, interest groups have used personal encounters to lobby citizens. Civil rights groups in the 1950s and 1960s, for example, relied heavily upon personal encounters to convince people of the rightness of their cause and to mobilize people to march, boycott, and "sit in."[46] In fact, peer pressure played an important role in getting many people to participate in civil rights demonstrations and protests. Of course, throughout most of the eighteenth and nineteenth centuries, contacting people directly was one of the only ways for interest groups to lobby citizens. In the absence of telephones, televisions, computers, and fax machines, interest groups simply did not have very many options.

Contacting people directly remains an important way for interest groups to lobby citizens. Many local interest groups, especially citizen groups, rely on door-to-door contact with citizens. One of the most prodigious users of direct citizen contact over the years has been the environmental citizen group Greenpeace. The group goes from door to door to raise money and recruit members, but it also regularly sends volunteers and staffers to people's homes to ask them to sign petitions and contact government decision-makers and attend meetings and demonstrations.[47]

Distributing Brochures and Pamphlets

Another seasoned indirect lobbying technique is distributing brochures and pamphlets. Throughout the last century interest groups used brochures and pamphlets both to "make their case" to the public and to encourage citizen participation. In the late 1940s, for example, the American Medical Association (AMA) distributed brochures and pamphlets in opposition to President Harry Truman's compulsory federal health insurance plan. One AMA tract, entitled "The Voluntary Way is the American Way," tried to convince citizens that Truman's plan was wrongheaded. The pamphlet read: "If the doctors lose their freedom today—if their patients are regimented tomorrow who will be next? YOU WILL BE NEXT!"[48] The tendentious brochure explained that the "socialization" of health care could lead to the socialization of the entire American economy. It also argued that the "socialization" of medicine in Germany eventually led to horrific Nazi medical experiments. The AMA's brochure clearly was designed to mold people's attitudes and opinions about health care issues. It also explicitly encouraged citizens to contact their representatives in Congress.

Most brochures and pamphlets bear a striking resemblance to the AMA's early prototype. They use inflammatory language and appeal to widely accepted values like "freedom," "liberty," and "fairness." Nothing is more popular in pamphlets and brochures, however, than fear-mongering. The idea behind fear-mongering is to convince people that they must act in order to stave off impending doom. Fear-mongering was in abundance during (and after) the debate over President Obama's health care reform bill, which he signed in 2010. A number of right-leaning interest groups, including some anti-abortion citizen groups and conservative Christian citizen groups, warned the public that the reform would lead to government "death panels" that would decide who lives and who dies, and would be akin to National Socialism (that is, Nazism) in its disregard for the elderly, infirm, and mentally challenged.[49] The goal of such fear-mongering is clear—to convince people that a particular government decision is good or bad.

One interest group that uses brochures often to lobby indirectly is PETA (People for the Ethical Treatment of Animals). The group prints large numbers of pamphlets and brochures, with titles including "Kentucky Fried Cruelty" (a leaflet that describes the way KFC treats chickens), "Being Boiled Hurts" (a brochure that suggests it is cruel to drop live lobsters into boiling water), and "McCruelty: I'm Hatin' It" (a brochure about some McDonald's corporate practices that PETA thinks are wrong).[50] These brochures are striking, inflammatory, and informative. Whether or not they work is an open question, but they are one way that the group attempts to get its message across to citizens.

Advertising in Newspapers and/or Magazines

Another venerable indirect lobbying technique is advertising in newspapers and/or magazines. Print advertisements have been around for many decades.[51] Stylistically and substantively, print advertisements are very similar to brochures and pamphlets. For example, most print advertisements appeal to widely accepted norms and values, and use fear as a motivator. One of the largest ever print advertising campaigns took place during the battle over the North American Free Trade Agreement (NAFTA) in 1993. NAFTA, which was designed to improve trilateral trade between Mexico, Canada, and the United States, was opposed vigorously by environmental citizen groups and labor unions. In the midst of the congressional debate over NAFTA, a short-term coalition of environmental citizen groups mounted a multi-million-dollar print advertising campaign. The cornerstone of this campaign was a series of advertisements that appeared in national newspapers such as the *New York Times* and the *Washington Post*. One such advertisement—which took up a full page in the *New York Times*—began as most print advertisements do: with a warning. At the top of the advertisement in big letters was the following:

ENVIRONMENTAL CATASTROPHE, CANADA TO MEXICO.
8 Fatal Flaws of NAFTA.[52]

The text of the advertisement was full of disquieting and fear-inducing words and phrases. For example, the advertisement stated that NAFTA would create a "toxic hell" in Texas border towns. It also warned that the inevitable result of NAFTA would be "environmental devastation and joblessness." The advertisement concluded with the following instructions: *"As currently written, NAFTA is not fixable and will cause disaster*. Help us fight against it. Use the coupons below. Thank you. [italics in original]" The coupons were three "cut along the dotted line" boxes that could be removed from the advertisement and sent directly to government decision-makers. Each of the removable coupons contained a brief statement of opposition to NAFTA, and a place for the name and address of the sender. One coupon was addressed to then House Majority Leader Richard Gephardt, one was addressed to then President Clinton's Director of Public Affairs, and the other allowed the sender to write in the name of his/her House member.

More recently, during the battle over President Obama's health care reform bill, interest groups of all kinds ran print advertisements. For example, one citizen group, an upstart organization called Conservatives for Patients' Rights, ran an advertisement called "An Open Letter to President Obama," in which the president of the group (a former health care company executive) says he has grave doubts about the president's plan because, "Many Americans are leery about allowing the government to have a more significant role in making private health care decisions."[53] On the pro-reform side, the AARP ran print advertisements in a variety of publications. One advertisement read, "These days, far too many Americans have the same health care plan, Don't get sick."[54] Another of the group's pro-reform advertisements read, "Discharge, readmit, discharge, readmit. It's time to break this unhealthy pattern."[55]

Sending Direct Mail

Another common indirect lobbying technique is sending direct mail. Though direct mail has not been around as long as brochures and print advertisements, it has been used extensively by interest groups for at least thirty-five years. As Chapter 4 mentions, a number of interest groups use direct mail to recruit members and raise money. Many, however, also use direct mail to lobby indirectly.

As with direct mail campaigns designed to recruit members, indirect lobbying direct mail campaigns begin with a "mailing list." Some (probably most) of the time the mailing list has only the names of group members. Sometimes, however, the mailing list consists of members and also people who are sympathetic to the interest group's cause. Very seldom do interest groups send out direct mail blindly to random citizens. Next, each person on the mailing list is sent a letter. An indirect lobbying letter generally consists of two parts. The first part describes the problem at hand. The second part is a "call to action" that suggests what specific action can and should be taken to solve the problem. Direct mail expert R. Kenneth Godwin has discovered that most direct mail lobbying letters share two important traits.[56] First, like many print advertisements and brochures, they use fear and guilt to motivate recipients, and emphasize "the darker side of politics, portraying the opposition with strong negative descriptors such as 'bureaucrats,' 'left-wing hippies,' 'destroyers,' and 'so-called minorities.'"[57] Second, direct mail letters demand that people act immediately.[58]

Techniques of Indirect Lobbying: Newer Modes of Reaching Citizens

Though indirect lobbying has been around for long time, a number of prevalent indirect lobbying techniques are relatively new. Among these new techniques are: advertising on television; running television programs; appearing on television programs; advertising on radio; running radio programs; appearing on radio programs; calling people on the telephone; sending "new" direct mail; using the Internet; and publishing research reports. As you will see, most of these new techniques were born of changes in telecommunications technology.

Using the Television: Advertising, Programming, and Talking

There are several ways that interest groups use television to lobby citizens. One way is *advertising* on television. Interest group television advertising really came into its own in 1993 during the battle over President Bill Clinton's ill-fated health care reform package. Shortly after the president released his ambitious plan, a trade association called the Health Insurance Association of America (HIAA) began televising advertisements featuring "Harry and Louise," a fictional white, middle-aged couple who despaired at the prospect of Clinton's reforms. In the commercials, the all-American couple sat in their kitchen in a not too distant future in which the federal government had taken over health care. In this hellish future, Louise says, "Having choices we don't like is no choice at all." Harry responds, "If they choose . . ." Louise then finishes the sentence, ". . . we lose." ("They" is the federal government by the way.) The HIAA spent over $14 million on the advertisements, and Harry and Louise were credited with helping to sink President Clinton's health care plan.[59] In terms of content, television advertisements tend to resemble print advertisements: they use fear as a motivator and appeal to widely accepted values. Stylistically, however, television advertisements are unique in that they allow interest groups to make use of striking visual images.

The more recent battle over President Obama's health care plan also featured television advertisements (and lots of them). For example, Harry and Louise returned in 2009, but this time on the other side of the health care debate. This time they performed in television advertisements produced by Families USA and the Pharmaceutical Researchers and Manufacturers of America, in which they urged government decision-makers to work together to reform health care along the lines proposed by the president. In the same kitchen they sat in the 1990s (but at a newer table), Louise says to her husband, "A little more cooperation, a little less politics and we can get the job done this time."[60] Dozens of other interest groups got into the act during the battle over President Obama's health care plan. For example, the AARP ran a famous advertisement in which an ambulance with sirens blaring, presumably speeding to the hospital, is intercepted and kept from getting there by a set of ominous-looking black SUVs. The voiceover suggests that the ambulance (the good guy) represents health care reform trying to achieve worthy goals, while the black SUVs (the bad guys) are "special interests" looking to derail reform. In an advertisement opposing health care reform run by Conservatives for Patients' Rights, a young woman sits in a doctor's office consulting with her doctor, seemingly considering what to do about some health problem, when after a few seconds of discussion out pops a nerdy-looking man (complete with thick black glasses) with a clipboard gaudily labeled "FEDERAL HEALTH POLICE." The voiceover narration tells us that if the president's public option plan is adopted, the federal government will get between people and their doctors.[61]

Some interest groups also lobby citizens by *running* television programs. No force in American politics has had more success with television programming than the Christian Right. Throughout the 1970s and 1980s, Jerry Falwell used his nationally syndicated television show *Old Time Gospel Hour* to lobby citizens on a wide variety of "Christian" issues. Today, the dominant force in television lobbying is Pat Robertson. For several years, Robertson has used his *700 Club* to preach on everything from school prayer and abortion to income taxes and campaign finance reform. Recently, interest groups have taken to the airwaves by running "infomercials," much like the ones you see on late-night television for the ShamWow, Walk-fit orthotics for your feet, and the George Forman Grill. In a recent example, the United States Chamber of Commerce bankrolled a "documentary" called *InJustice* that "exposed" America's class-action lawsuit system and argued that it was terrible for businesses, as it cost them millions of dollars.[62] The show was aired on the ReelzChannel. A number of other interest groups including the National Rifle Association and the Humane Society of the United States have run infomercials as well. As the proliferation of channels on television continues, there is reason to believe that infomercials will become more common.

Another way that interest groups use television to lobby citizens is by *appearing* on television programs. Television has become an important medium for political debate.[63] A lot of the debate (if you really want to call it that) takes place on political talk shows such as *The O'Reilly Factor* and *Hannity* on Fox News, and *Hardball* and the *Rachel Maddow Show* on MSNBC. When these types of shows first appeared, they tended to rely on a limited stable of pundits including George Will, Morton Kondracke, and Michael Kinsley, who made their living endlessly editorializing about political issues. Today, however, representatives from interest groups often appear on such programs. Over the years, for example, hundreds of group personnel for conservative causes have appeared on *Hannity* and *O'Reilly*, and hundreds of group personnel for liberal causes have appeared on the *Rachel Maddow Show* and *Countdown with Keith Olbermann*. Occasionally group personnel appear on more regular news programs such as CNN's *The Situation Room* or Fox News's *Fox Report with Shepard Smith*. The way this works is that the host of a program, Wolf Blitzer, for example, may want a couple of people to talk about global warming, so he calls a staff scientist from the Sierra Club (a citizen group that favors stronger environmental regulations) and an economic analyst from the Chamber of Commerce (a trade association that opposes many environmental regulations). Interest groups consider television talk shows important avenues for reaching citizens, and often put talk show hosts "on notice" that they are willing to appear on their shows.[64] At the state and local levels, interest groups may try to get their personnel to appear on cable access shows, or locally broadcast public affairs programs, or even the five or six o'clock local news.

Using the Radio: Advertising, Programming, and Talking

Interest groups use radio much like they use television. One way groups use this medium is by *advertising* on radio. During the battle over health care reform, for example, some of the same groups that ran television advertisements also advertised on radio. The groups' radio advertisements were much like their television advertisements (without the pictures, of course). Interest groups also use radio by *running* radio programs. For example, the conservative Christian organization Focus on the Family sponsors radio programs on Christian-oriented radio stations throughout the country. Finally, interest groups use the radio by *appearing* on radio programs. Many conservative interest groups, for example, try to convince Rush Limbaugh, Sean Hannity, and other conservative talk show hosts to put their personnel "on the air."

Calling People on the Telephone

Interest groups also lobby indirectly by calling people on the telephone. The telephone, of course, has been around for a very long time. Its use as an indirect lobbying tool, however, is a relatively recent phenomenon. In the past two decades, as long-distance rates have fallen, interest groups have come to rely more and more on the telephone to lobby citizens. Telephone lobbying is similar to telephone selling. Telephone indirect lobbying is easier than it used to be. Today, special computer programs allow interest groups to call large numbers of people at a relatively low cost. One such program automatically selects names and telephone numbers from a massive CD-ROM database according to specifications dictated by the user. The program also dials numbers automatically, delivers a recorded message to whomever answers the phone, and even connects the call's recipient directly to the office of his/her member of Congress.

Sending the "New" Direct Mail

Advances in communications technology have not only given rise to new forms of indirect lobbying, but have also changed the face of an old form of indirect lobbying—sending direct mail. First of all, computers have made direct mail more personalized. Before computers, interest groups sent identical form letters to the people they wanted to reach. Today, interest groups send different letters to different people. By using large databases, interest groups can find out what issues interest you, and emphasize those issues in their mailings. In addition, interest groups can use powerful computers to personalize a letter's salutation. Second, today's direct mailings are more sophisticated. For example, they contain more graphics and color. Moreover, because computers can put real stamps on envelopes and print addresses in cursive typefaces, they *look* more like actual mail than junk mail. The increased sophistication and personalization of direct mail increase the probability that an individual will open a direct mailing rather than throw it away unopened.

Using the Internet

One of the newest indirect lobbying techniques is using the Internet. The Internet consists of thousands of hugely powerful mainframe computers all over the world that are linked together in a "web." This web is easily accessible at libraries, schools, businesses, colleges and universities, and increasingly, private homes. Interest groups use the web primarily by managing *their own websites*. A website is essentially an electronic document that exists in cyberspace and contains information about the individual or organization that maintains it.

Tens of thousands of interest groups now have their own websites. To see how interest groups use their websites for indirect lobbying purposes, let's take a look at an example. Recently I accessed the Christian Coalition of America's website.[65] At the top of the first screen of text was the title "Welcome to the Christian Coalition of America" next to the Coalition's logo. Below the title were buttons labeled, "Home," "About Us," "Get Informed," "Get Involved," "Take Action," "Blogs," "News," and "Church." In a box below these buttons was the headline, "Pray and Vote: Join Our Campaign to Help Educate Voters for the 2012 Elections!" This headline changed periodically to "Congressional Scorecard," "Get Involved," and "Energy Campaign." Like most interest group websites, the Coalition's site contains something akin to a table of contents that guides visitors. There are several ways that the Christian Coalition uses its website to lobby citizens. For example, it includes on its site a permanent section entitled "Take Action," which tells visitors how to contact members of Congress and other government decision-makers. If the visitor clicks on the "Contact Elected Officials" button, he/she is taken to a screen that details how he/she can contact any member of Congress by mail, telephone, or in person. In addition, the Coalition has another button on its front page called "Campaigns" which lists some of the group's current advocacy campaigns. When I visited the site, for example, one of its campaigns was entitled "Stand with Israel." When I clicked the "Stand with Israel" button, I was taken to a page on which I could sign an online petition (meant to be delivered to government decision-makers) saying that I stood with Israel. An "action alert" message is essentially an "online" print advertisement that urges viewers to take action on a specific policy proposal. Finally, the site contains a treasure trove of information for visitors. Much of the information explains where the group stands on various issues. This sort of information is meant for both supporters and curious visitors, and clearly is a form of "lobbying for values."

Virtually every interest group mentioned in this book has its own website. Websites are very inexpensive, and they are easy to change. Moreover, they are valuable and wonderful ways for groups to reach lots of people. Virtually all the (well-designed) sites are like the Christian Coalition's site: they feature information on what the group stands for and does, how the group operates, how a person can join the group, how a person can donate to the group, how a person can lobby government decision-makers on the group's behalf, and how a person can contact the group.

Another way that interest groups use the Internet to lobby indirectly is by sending *email*. Today, many interest groups have special "listserves" that enable them to send electronic mailings to large numbers of people simultaneously. In general, interest groups use electronic mail much like they use regular mail—they send letters to raise money or goad people into action, or both. These days when you join an interest group, it will generally ask you for your email address as well as your home address. Email represents yet one more way for interest groups to lobby citizens. Though email indirect lobbying is in its infancy, there are good reasons to believe that it will become increasingly prevalent in years to come. First, email is easy. Listserves allow interest groups to send letters to untold numbers of people at the press of a button. Second, email is inexpensive. In fact, it is virtually free. Finally, email allows an interest group to react to things immediately. A direct mail, telephone, or door-to-door indirect lobbying campaign may take days or weeks to "get off the ground." In contrast, an email indirect lobbying campaign can be devised and carried out in a few hours.

Interest groups also increasingly have turned to using *Facebook*. Many of the interest groups mentioned in this book, in fact, have their own Facebook pages. For example, the Chamber of Commerce of the U.S. has its own Facebook page, and on its "wall" it periodically places information of interest to members and the general public. This information generally concerns the group and its political views and activities and goals. One recent "wall post" read: "The EPA is at it again, proposing unreasonable rules that will have negative economic impacts."[66] I visited the Facebook page of PETA recently, and in addition to posting information on the group's history and activities, as well as instructions on how to join the group, contribute money to the group, or buy PETA-themed items from the group, PETA used its page to sing the praises of Israel, which recently had outlawed declawing cats. Like many other groups, PETA also uses its Facebook page to announce rallies and activities, goad people into action, try to get people to sign petitions, and generally publicize the group. It is important to note that interest groups use Facebook not just to engage in indirect lobbying, but also to recruit members, raise money, and sell merchandise.

More and more interest groups are placing *videos* on the Internet as well, using sites such as YouTube. If you go to YouTube and enter the terms "National Rifle Association," or "Natural Resources Defense Council," or "Chamber of Commerce of the United States," you will find videos made by these interest groups. You will also find, however, videos made by opponents of these groups. Again, interest groups use YouTube and other video-hosting sites not just to lobby indirectly, but also to raise money and recruit members.

Finally—though it is not really part of the Internet—*Twitter* is worth mentioning. Many interest groups engage in indirect lobbying by sending Twitter messages to people. As Chapter 4 mentions, Twitter is a "micro-blogging tool" that allows a group to send short messages (up to 140 characters) to subscribers. Again as Chapter 4 mentions, more and more interest groups have their own Twitter feeds. Groups use their Twitter feeds for a variety of purposes, among them indirect lobbying. Regular group users send several Twitter messages per week to subscribers, informing them of the group's activities and priorities, and (briefly) giving the group's point of view on issues. Groups also regularly use Twitter to lobby for contact, alerting respondents during political battles to contact government decision-makers in some way. No one has ever studied Twitter use by interest groups extensively, so we do not know how many groups use Twitter or precisely how they use it. But my own experience with Twitter suggests that virtually all major national interest groups use Twitter, and large numbers of smaller, as well as state and local organizations also use Twitter.

Publishing Research Reports

Finally, interest groups lobby indirectly by publishing research reports. Research reports are similar to pamphlets and brochures, but are generally longer and more sophisticated. Research reports generally contain policy analytical information. They became especially prominent in the 1970s, as the federal government began dealing with highly complex and technical policy issues more often. Think tanks are more likely than other types of interest groups to lobby through the publication of research reports, but recently other types of interest groups have taken up publishing research reports as well.

To understand how groups use research reports, let us revisit some of the information presented in Chapter 4. In that chapter, I noted that many think tanks publish research reports, books, and monographs to make money. I mentioned, for example, the Heritage Foundation, a high-profile conservative think tank, which has its own online bookstore that sells hundreds of books published by the Foundation's own press. Among the titles published by the group are books called *The Enduring Principles of the American Founding*, and *Why Obamacare is Wrong for America*.[67] These publications are polemics designed to convince readers that the Heritage Foundation's conservative views are the correct views. Of course, most of the people who read reports like these probably already agree with the group. But at the very least the publications can reinforce readers' conservative views, and perhaps even goad them into doing something such as contact government decision-makers.

My discussion in this section has shown that interest groups can reach citizens in a number of ways. This, of course, begs the following question: What factors determine which indirect lobbying technique an interest group uses? Two factors in particular seem to be important. First, of course, there is *cost*. If an interest group does not have much money it most likely will eschew expensive techniques such as running television advertisements, and rely instead upon contacting people directly or distributing brochures. Another important factor is the *number of people* an interest group wishes to reach. If an interest group wishes to reach millions of people, its best bet probably is to advertise on television. In contrast, if an interest group wishes to reach only a few hundred people, direct mail, telephone calls, emails, or faxes are better bets.

Trends in Indirect Lobbying

The future of indirect lobbying is impossible to predict. Nonetheless, several developments are already apparent. First of all, indirect lobbying is more common than ever before. Second, the rise of indirect lobbying has given rise to an indirect lobbying industry. Finally, indirect lobbying has become very controversial. Before exiting this chapter, it is worthwhile briefly to examine each of these trends.

One of the reasons I have devoted an entire chapter to indirect lobbying is that it is *more prevalent than ever before*.[68] Tables 7.1 and 7.2 show the proportion of state and Washington lobbyists, respectively, who report utilizing several indirect lobbying techniques. Table 7.1 clearly shows that the vast majority of state lobbyists use indirect lobbying techniques, while Table 7.2 shows that almost all Washington lobbyists report using indirect lobbying techniques. The numbers reported in the two tables indicate a huge expansion of indirect lobbying since the 1940s, 1950s, and 1960s.[69] Why have interest groups increasingly turned to indirect lobbying? The answer is twofold. First, interest groups have come to realize that indirect lobbying works. In the 1960s and 1970s, interest groups of all kinds began to realize that indirect lobbying could produce results. They saw, for example, that by "taking to the streets," civil rights groups were able to force the revocation of discriminatory laws and policies. This success led many interest groups that previously had eschewed indirect lobbying—especially businesses and trade associations that believed they were being hurt by stricter government regulations—to give it a try. Another reason interest groups have turned to indirect lobbying is that advances in communications and computer technology have made indirect lobbying easier. Today, with the press of a button, an interest group can call, write, fax, tweet, or email almost anybody in the United States. And websites are inexpensive to set up and maintain. In the "old days," if an interest group wanted to contact a person directly, it had to look in the telephone book and either call, write, or "drop

Table 7.1 The Use of Seven Indirect Lobbying Techniques in the States: Proportion of Respondents Reporting that They Engage in Each Lobbying Technique (N = 376)

Technique	% using
1. Inspiring letter-writing, telephone, or email campaigns to state legislators	80
2. Inspiring letter-writing, telephone, or email campaigns to the governor	63
3. Inspiring letter-writing, telephone, or email campaigns to executive agencies	45
4. Appearing on radio programs	42
5. Appearing on television programs	38
6. Running advertisements in the media	31
7. Engaging in protests and/or demonstrations	18

Source: Nownes and DeAlejandro, "Lobbying in the New Millennium," 435–6.

Note: Each respondent was given a list of advocacy techniques and asked to indicate how often he/she used it—never, occasionally, or regularly. The number represents the proportion of respondents who reported using the technique occasionally or regularly.

by." Today, interest groups have access to huge databases that allow them to contact people at home or at work with relative ease. Moreover, interest groups now have a plethora of tools with which to reach people. Sixty years ago, interest groups could not and did not reach citizens by cellphone, fax, computer, or television. Finally, technology has made many forms of indirect lobbying less expensive. For example, telephoning people is less expensive than ever before.

Not surprisingly, the rise of indirect lobbying has led to the rise of indirect lobbying firms. In Washington, as well as in states and cities across the country, an adjuvant industry has arisen to meet the needs of interest groups that wish to mount indirect lobbying campaigns. To give you an idea of how these firms operate and what they do, I will borrow an example presented by interest group experts Burdett Loomis and Allan Cigler. They use the example of a firm called the Clinton Group, which sells numerous services to interest groups of all kinds. The example is a bit old (they wrote about it over ten years ago), and the Clinton Group has since changed its name to American Directions Group.[70] But the example nicely illustrates how lobbying firms help interest groups lobby indirectly. Loomis and Cigler describe how the Clinton Group might help a liberal citizen group such as the National Organization for Women (NOW) that opposes a Supreme Court nominee because of his/her opposition to abortion rights:

> The Clinton Group will take the membership rolls of the group and match names to phone numbers. It might also use its computer to cross-reference magazine subscriptions, data on personal purchasing habits, and precincts with particular voting and income profiles to come up with a bigger list of sympathetic people.
>
> At the company's phone bank in Louisville, Kentucky, a computer dials the numbers. When someone answers, an operator comes on the line and explains NOW's position, offering to transfer the caller, at no charge, to the White House switchboard or local member of Congress.[71]

Though American Directions Group works primarily for left-leaning and moderate interest groups, conservatives need not worry. Washington is also home to the powerful Bonner and Associates, an indirect lobbying firm that works mostly for business firms and trade associations pushing conservative positions. Bonner and Associates is now a multi-million-dollar firm that offers a wide range of indirect lobbying services to interest groups. The ubiquity of indirect lobbying firms makes it easier than ever for interest groups to lobby citizens.

Table 7.2   The Use of Six Indirect Lobbying Techniques in Washington, DC: Proportion of Respondents Reporting that They Engage in Each Lobbying Technique (N = 50)

Technique	% using
1. Talking to the press	98
2. Mobilizing group members	94
3. Organizing letter-writing campaigns	90
4. Holding press conferences	79
5. Advertising policy positions	52
6. Protesting	32

Source: Kollman, Outside Lobbying, 35.

Notes: Each respondent was given a list of advocacy techniques and asked to indicate how often he/she used it—never, occasionally, or regularly. The number represents the proportion of respondents who reported using the technique occasionally or regularly.

In recent years, indirect lobbying has generated a great deal of controversy. Controversy has arisen because of the ease with which interest groups can mount "phony" indirect lobbying campaigns. To give you an idea of what "phony" means, consider the following case, one of the first in which indirect lobbying raised eyebrows. In 1995, with the help of Washington lobbyist Bob Beckel, a trade association called the "Competitive Long Distance Coalition," which consisted of MCI, Sprint, and AT&T, mounted a massive indirect lobbying campaign aimed at stopping legislation designed to make it easier for local telephone companies to offer long distance service. Here's how the campaign worked: the Coalition telephoned MCI, Sprint and AT&T customers, asked them if they favored "competition" in the long distance telephone industry, and then sent up to four telegrams to members of Congress on behalf of each person who answered "yes."[72] The Coalition succeeded in generating over 500,000 telegrams. About half of the telegrams were fake. Many contained bogus names and signatures. Some were "signed" by people who were dead. This case is not an isolated one. Every year since 1995, some interest groups somewhere have mounted indirect lobbying campaigns that produce fake "grassroots" communications from citizens. Such indirect lobbying efforts are often referred to as "astroturf" lobbying campaigns (astroturf = phony grass; get it?).

More recently, none other than the aforementioned Bonner and Associates was implicated in an astroturf lobbying scam. In 2008, when Congress was considering some environmental legislation, some members of Congress received letters urging them to oppose the legislation on the grounds that it would increase energy costs. One of the letters to members of Congress read as follows:

> You are about to vote on important environmental legislation (the Waxman–Markey bill). We support making the environment cleaner, but the reason we are writing is that we are concerned about our electric bills. Many seniors, as you know, are on low fixed incomes. The cost to heat and cool our homes, run hot water and use other appliances is very important to those on a budget.
>
> Our state gets 56% of its electricity from coal. We urge you to pass legislation that reduces greenhouse gases but at the same time protects consumers from unaffordable increases in the basic necessity of electricity.
>
> We ask you to use your important position to help protect seniors and other consumers in your district from higher electricity bills. Please don't vote to force cost increases on us, especially in this volatile economy. We urge you to make pro-consumer changes in the Waxman–Markey bill to protect seniors and all of your constituents from unaffordable energy cost increases.[73]

This letter was allegedly from an ordinary person who worked for a senior center in Virginia. Other similar letters were signed by individuals affiliated with a Charlottesville, Virginia NAACP chapter, a group called Jefferson Area Board on Aging, and the American Association of University Women.[74] The problem was that these letters were all fakes—they were actually written by someone who worked at Bonner and Associates.

Bogus indirect lobby campaigns raise some troubling questions. Generally speaking, it is easy for a government decision-maker to check up on a lobbyist who contacts him/her directly. First of all, in most places lobbyists are required to register—i.e., to disclose for whom they work and how they can be reached. Thus, if a lobbyist calls a legislator and says, "My name is Tom Jones and I work for Amalgamated Controls Inc.," the legislator can easily find out if there is such a company, and if there is, if Mr. Jones actually works for it. Second, it is often relatively easy for a government decision-maker to verify the information lobbyists provide. For example, if Mr. Jones tells a legislator that his company has four plants in the legislator's district, the legislator can ask friends, confidants, and even other lobbyists if this is true. In sum, it is easy for government decision-makers to check up on the people who lobby them directly. In contrast, it is difficult for government decision-makers to check up on the ordinary citizens who contact them during indirect lobbying campaigns. First of all, a successful indirect lobbying campaign might produce tens or even hundreds of thousands of telephone calls, letters, faxes, or emails. It would be impractical and impossible for a government decision-maker to determine if each and every one of these communications was genuine. Another reason it is difficult for government decision-makers to check up on the people who lobby them indirectly is that the information citizens provide to government decision-makers during indirect lobbying campaigns is not generally factual in nature. Rather, it is opinion. Thus, it is impossible to verify in any objective sense. In short, government decision-makers have to take it for granted that people actually mean what they say.

The point here is this: while it is difficult to mount phony direct lobbying efforts, it is easy to mount phony *indirect* lobbying efforts. Not only does computer technology make it easier than ever for an interest group to simulate the effects of a real indirect lobbying campaign, government decision-makers seldom have the resources to check out the thousands of letters, telegrams, phone calls, and faxes they receive each day.

All of this said, recently government decision-makers have become savvier at distinguishing between real and phony indirect lobbying efforts. They have come to recognize, for example, the telltale signs of bogus indirect lobbying campaigns. One such sign is sudden and overwhelming public outcry about a particular issue. Another is multiple letters, faxes, phone calls, or emails from the same source. Nonetheless, fraudulent indirect lobbying remains a problem.

Conclusion: Indirect Lobbying and the Provision of Information

Indirect lobbying is defined as *lobbying that is aimed at citizens rather than government decision-makers*. There are two general types of indirect lobbying: "lobbying for values" and "lobbying for contact." The former is designed to influence people's attitudes and opinions. The latter is designed to encourage people to contact government decision-makers and make their opinions known. Both types of indirect lobbying have the same ultimate goal: to affect government decisions.

Indirect lobbying, like direct lobbying, entails the provision of information. However, when they lobby indirectly, interest groups provide information to citizens rather than government decision-makers. The information that interest groups provide to citizens is generally policy analytical information. This policy analytical information, however, generally is considerably less complex and technical than that which interest groups provide to government decision-makers. If indirect lobbying is successful—that is, if it either convinces people of the rightness of an interest group's cause or convinces people to contact government decision-makers—it also provides information to government decision-makers. Generally, it is political information about how people are likely to vote in the next election.

Interest groups lobby citizens in a number of ways. Among the classic techniques are meeting with people face to face, distributing brochures and pamphlets, running print advertisements, and sending direct mail. Among the more contemporary techniques are advertising on television, advertising on radio, running programs on television, running programs on radio, appearing on television talk shows, appearing on radio talk shows, using the Internet, and publishing research reports.

In the last 20–30 years, indirect lobbying has changed significantly. First, it has become more common. Second, it has given rise to an indirect lobbying industry. Third, it has created a great deal of controversy. These trends are likely to continue. One of the reasons that indirect lobbying has become more common is that it works. Box 7.1 examines the issue of abortion and how anti-abortion citizen groups have managed to use indirect lobbying successfully. The example shows that indirect lobbying is an important and effective tool in the lobbyist's tool kit.

Box 7.1 Did Anti-Abortion Indirect Lobbying Work?

Abortion has long been a contentious issue in American politics. As such, there has been an inordinate amount of interest group lobbying on the abortion issue over the years. On one side are "pro-life" citizen groups including the National Right to Life Committee, which has chapters in all fifty states and several hundred thousand members. On the other side are "pro-choice" citizen groups including NARAL Pro-Choice America, (NARAL is an acronym for National Abortion Rights Action League), which also has hundreds of thousands of members.

Groups on both sides of the issue have used a variety of tactics and techniques over the years. But both sides have been prodigious users of indirect lobbying techniques in particular. In fact, both sides have used many of the techniques mentioned in this chapter, including contacting people directly, distributing pamphlets and brochures, advertising in newspapers and magazines, sending direct mail, and organizing protests and demonstrations. One of the main strategies of groups on the "pro-life" side has been to convince people that abortion is wrong. It is wrong, these groups argue, because it is akin to taking a life. To prove this, some groups (the more aggressive ones) show gruesome photographs of aborted fetuses, while others (the more mainstream ones) show sonograms. The intention here is clear—to convince citizens that fetuses are people and that they deserve the same legal protection as everyone else. "Pro-choice" groups, of course, have done their best to counter these claims, arguing that at least in the earliest stages of pregnancy an abortion essentially eliminates a clump of cells rather than a person, and that women should be free to do what they choose with their bodies rather than be proscribed by government.

There is some evidence that the "pro-life" groups have been successful in their attempts to "lobby for values." Since 1995, the American public has moved gradually toward the "pro-life" view of abortion. In 1994, the percentage of Americans who said that abortion should be "illegal in all circumstances" was 13 percent. By 2005 the proportion was 22 percent, and in 2011 it was 20 percent. Moreover, in 1994 the percentage of Americans who said that abortion should be "legal under any circumstances" was 33 percent. In 2005 it was 26 percent, and it was 26 percent in 2011. This is not a huge movement in the "pro-life" direction, but it is noticeable and significant.

In short, the public views abortion differently today than it did in the mid-1970s. There is some evidence that this is due to "pro-life" groups' success at convincing ordinary citizens that abortion is wrong. "Pro-life" groups have spent millions over the years on indirect lobbying, and scholars who study abortion acknowledge that the changes in public opinion on abortion have been due at least in part to these indirect lobbying efforts. In sum, "pro-life" groups have been better than "pro-choice" groups at convincing people that their view of the issue is the correct one.

Sources: Gallup Poll, "Abortion"; Maxwell, *Pro-Life Activists in America*; Doan, *Opposition and Intimidation*; Rose, *Safe, Legal, and Unavailable?*.

What's Next

Thus far, this book has said very little about political parties—the organizations in American politics that are most closely related to, and most similar to, interest groups. I am about to remedy this oversight. In the next chapter I examine political parties and their relationships with interest groups. These relationships, as you will see, are complicated and multifarious.

Interest Groups and Political Parties

8

In Chapter 1, "interest group" was defined as *any non-party organization that engages in political activity*. Initially, I thought the best definition was *any organization that engages in political activity*. This definition, however, would have included political parties, which makes it problematic. Political parties are *not* interest groups. But they often work with interest groups, and they do lots of the same things (e.g., raise money for candidates) that interest groups do. Because of the similarities between political parties and interest groups, and because political parties sometimes work with interest groups, this chapter will say a few words about political parties and their relationships with interest groups. It will begin with a few words about political parties—what they are and what they do.

What is a Political Party?

In her seminal book on political parties entitled *Party Politics in America*, Marjorie Randon Hershey defines a political party as "a group organized to nominate candidates, to try to win political power through elections, and to promote ideas about public policies [emphasis removed]."[1] There are lots of definitions of the term "political party" floating around out there, but in my opinion this is the best one. This definition is clear, concise, and comprehensive. This definition has three parts, and each part is crucial. Let's look at them one at a time. The first part of the definition is probably the most important, because nominating candidates is about the only thing that political parties do that interest groups do not do. To *nominate* a candidate is to place his or her name on the ballot for election to an office as an official representative of the party. A lot of things that political parties do, interest groups do as well. But interest groups do *not* nominate candidates for office. You will never see, for example, the National Rifle Association or the Chamber of Commerce of the United States place a person's name on a ballot for election under the group's banner. There are Republican and Democratic and Libertarian and Green Party candidates out there running for office, but there are not Chamber of Commerce or NRA candidates doing this. This is not to say that interest groups are not involved in elections; as we learned in Chapter 6, they are. But interest groups do not nominate candidates for office, only political parties do.

The second part of Dr. Hershey's definition of political party states that political parties try "to win political power through elections." Essentially, what this means is that parties are first and foremost about winning elections. For many interest groups, engaging in electoral activity (what is called "electoral lobbying") is just one small part of what they do. Moreover, many interest groups do not engage in electoral activity at all. But engaging in electoral activity—recruiting candidates, nominating candidates, and helping candidates win—is what political parties are all about. Electoral activity is at the very core of a political party's mission. Finally, Dr. Hershey's definition states that political parties "promote ideas about public policies." This means, essentially, that parties do more than just nominate candidates and engage in other forms of electoral activity. They also take public stands on policy issues (such as abortion, gay marriage, government spending, immigration, and taxes) and promote them. Interestingly, these final two parts of Dr. Hershey's definition of political party do not help us much in distinguishing political parties from interest groups. This is the case because many interest groups engage in electoral activity, and many also promote policies. So in distinguishing political parties from interest groups, it is important to remember that nominating candidates is the one thing that political parties do that interest groups do not.

The three-part definition of political party reproduced above should convince you that the concept of political party is not a straightforward one. To further convince you of this, consider that a single political party actually has what Dr. Hershey called "three interacting parts."[2] The three parts are:

> the **party organization**, which includes party leaders and the many activists who work for party causes and candidates; the **party in government**, composed of the men and women who run for public office on the party's label and who hold public office; and the **party in the electorate**, or those citizens who express an attachment to the party [emphasis in original].[3]

In short, when we say "political party," we are actually talking about government decision-makers *and* people who work for the party and get paid to do so *and* regular people like you and me. Thus, when we talk about the Republican Party, for example, we are not just talking about the Speaker of the House John Boehner, or the head of the Republican National Committee, or even retired president George W. Bush; we are talking about all of these people as well as the millions of Americans who call themselves Republicans.

American Political Parties

In this country there are two major political parties—the Democratic Party and the Republican Party. Some countries have more than two major parties, but in the U.S. we have only two (for reasons that are too difficult to explain here). There are, however, other parties in this country. While the vast majority of elected and appointed government decision-makers, as well as citizens, identify with either the Democratic or Republican Party, there are other parties in the U.S. The largest of these other parties are the Constitution Party, the Green Party, the Libertarian Party, the Peace and Freedom Party, and the Reform Party. Keep this in mind as you read this chapter; while most people think only of the two major ones when they think of political parties, it is important to remember there are others.

What Does It Mean to Be a Member of a Party?

Table 8.1 shows the distribution of party identification in the United States, as of 2008. As the table shows, most Americans identify with one of the two major political parties. The reason we say that people "identify with" political parties rather than "belong to" political parties is that the concept of "party membership" is quite ambiguous. Many membership groups, including many citizen groups, labor unions, professional associations, and trade associations, have members in the true sense of the word. That is, the people and/or organizations that belong to them pay dues, are on a membership list somewhere, get certain benefits (e.g., magazines, newsletters), and may even get a membership card. Political parties are different. Basically, all you have to do to be a member of a political party is say, "I am a member of this political party." And all you have to do to quit a political party is say, "I am no longer a member of this political party." To be sure, political parties try to keep track of their "members." They do this so they can ask members for money, try to get them to help

Table 8.1   Partisan Identification in the United States, 2008

Strong Republican	13%
Not very strong Republican	13%
Independent who leans toward the Republican Party	12%
True Independent	11%
Independent who leans toward the Democratic Party	17%
Not very strong Democrat	15%
Strong Democrat	19%

Source: National Election Study, University of Michigan, Center for Political Studies, "Party Identification 7-Point Scale (revised in 2008) 1952–2008." See website for question wording.

elect their candidates, and to keep them in the fold as party members. But, in the United States, there is no such thing as formal membership in a political party. The political parties have no master list of members, they do not charge membership dues, and generally they do not offer special benefits to members, as many interest groups do. For all these reasons, political parties are said to have "identifiers" rather than "members."

A Word about the "Tea Party"

After President Barack Obama took office in 2008, he pushed a large health care reform package. This package, officially named the Patient Protection and Affordable Care Act, was approved by Congress (albeit in altered form) in 2010. The reform package was large and ambitious, and I cannot possibly describe it in detail here. For now, it must suffice to say that the legislation has a number of important provisions, including a prohibition on insurance companies dropping people who get sick, a mandate that individuals buy health insurance, a prohibition on insurance companies denying coverage to people with "pre-existing conditions," and an expansion of Medicaid (a government health insurance plan for poor Americans). There is a lot more to the legislation, of course, but these are some of the highlights. After the legislation was passed, some Americans were outraged. They were outraged at what they saw as unprecedented federal government intrusion into the health care market. The passage of the legislation, along with growing federal budget deficits, and a large federal government stimulus plan, led to a backlash against the Obama Administration. In 2010, as the economy continued to flounder and the health care bill was being debated and eventually passed, across the country a number of "Tea Party" group protests took place. These protests were conservative in nature, and featured citizens protesting what they considered federal overreach.

The Tea Party was big news in 2010 (and it remains a force in American politics today, especially within the Republican Party), and that is why I am mentioning it here. It is important to note, however, that the Tea Party is not really a political party or an interest group. Rather, it is what scholars call a "social movement"—an informal, unorganized, collection of people and organizations that work toward a specific political goal. Social movements are amorphous and nebulous, and lack the formal organization of interest groups. They are also different from political parties in that they do not nominate candidates for office. So in the end, while the Tea Party calls itself a party, it is not really a party, as it does not nominate candidates for office. Neither is it an interest group, because it is not formally organized. This said, there are organizations within the Tea Party movement—groups such as the National Tea Party Federation and the Tea Party Express—that *are* interest groups. These groups are organized and they try to affect what the government does (mostly through protests, indirect lobbying, and electoral lobbying). But the Tea Party movement as a whole is neither an interest group nor a political party.

What Do Political Parties Do?

Political parties have existed since the beginning of the republic. Indeed, history books tell us that despite the founders' warnings about the dangers of party politics, they were quick to form them, join them, and attempt to use them for their benefit as soon as America was created as a nation. Of course, entire books have been written about political parties and their activities. But for our purposes, a crash course in political parties will have to suffice. In this section I ask: What do political parties do? After addressing this question I can move on to the more relevant question of what kinds of relationships political parties have with interest groups.

Political Parties Nominate Candidates

First and foremost, political parties nominate candidates for office. Political parties are unique in this respect. No other type of organization in the United States chooses candidates and places them on the ballot for election. In other respects, many interest groups are like political parties. For example, lots of interest groups support candidates by giving them money, advertising on their behalf, endorsing candidates, and doing other things to get candidates elected. But interest groups do not nominate candidates for office.

A person does not necessarily need to be nominated by a political party to get on the ballot. All fifty states allow individual citizens essentially to nominate themselves by filing a petition and putting their name on the ballot. So, for example, if you want to run for the office of governor in your state and you do not like any political party, you can nominate yourself and run as an independent candidate. Each state has different requirements for getting on the ballot. In most cases, all a person has to do is gather a certain number of signatures from voters (the number varies by state and office). Some states make it relatively easy to get on the ballot, while others make it difficult. While a candidate does not have to be nominated by a party to get on the ballot, it certainly helps. In other words, if you want to be elected to office in the United States, it helps a lot to be nominated by a political party. There are a few elected officials sprinkled around the country who do not affiliate with a major political party (the vast majority are either Democrats or Republicans). But in most cases the best way to get on the ballot and the best way to win an election is to "join" a political party.

For the most part, the two major political parties have given the task of choosing their nominees to the party in the electorate. In other words, today, for most offices, parties hold primary elections to choose their candidates for office. This was not always the case (as any political parties textbook will tell you). But today, voters go to polls to choose their party's candidates for most offices.

Political Parties Recruit Candidates

There are over 500,000 elected officials in the United States. Many of them (but not all of them) are elected in partisan elections—that is, elections in which a candidate's name as well as his/her party affiliation appear on the ballot. Most of these candidates run for offices that most people do not think too much about—such as city council member, county commissioner, or clerk of deeds. But they have important jobs, and they have to win elections to get them and keep them. Where do these candidates come from? One answer is that they are recruited by political parties.[4] Party organizations at all levels of government spend some of their time and effort recruiting candidates. In many cases, people have to be asked to run for office—especially if they are going to face an incumbent. Moreover, many elective offices in the United States are quite obscure, including such offices as county supervisor, lieutenant governor, state controller, state insurance commissioner, property assessor, and chancellor. These offices generally do not attract much interest, so people must be recruited to run for them.

Political Parties Help Candidates

Political parties nominate candidates, but they also help candidates once they have nominated them. The type of help they provide varies. Perhaps the most important type of help parties provide candidates is money. The rules vary from place to place, but in states and localities across the country, as well as in federal elections, political parties are allowed to contribute money directly to their candidates. At the federal level, for example, a national political party committee is allowed to give a candidate $5,000 per election, and state, local, and district party committees may give up to $5,000 (combined) per election as well. This is not a whole lot of money if you are running for federal office, but it is better than nothing. For other offices, the amounts that political parties are allowed to provide vary across states.

Political parties also can help candidates monetarily by spending money on their behalf. At the federal level, for example, the parties can spend unlimited amounts of money on independent expenditures. A federal independent expenditure is defined by the Federal Election Commission as a communication of some kind, generally an advertisement, "expressly advocating the election or defeat of a clearly identified candidate that is not made in cooperation, consultation, or concert with, or at the request or suggestion of, a candidate, a candidate's authorized committee, or their agents, or a political party or its agents."[5] Political parties also engage in independent spending at the state and local level, but the rules governing what they can do and how much they can spend on these expenditures vary from place to place. Another way that political parties spend money on behalf of candidates is by making coordinated expenditures. According to the Federal Election Commission, a coordinated expenditure is one that "is made in cooperation, consultation or concert with, or at the request or suggestion of, a candidate, a candidate's authorized committee or their agents, or a political party committee or its agents."[6] At the federal level, coordinated expenditures are considered in-kind contributions, and are limited. States and localities also allow these types of expenditures, but again, how much and what kind are determined by state laws.

Political scientists Matthew Burbank, Ronald Hrebenar, and Robert Benedict state that these days, most candidates for major office "seek the help of specialists and their professional techniques" in their quest to win election.[7]

They go on to state that candidates "now surround themselves with professional managers, statisticians, pollsters, advertising specialists, and lawyers."[8] These types of consultants help candidates formulate campaign strategy, identify messages that resonate with voters, raise money, and design advertisements and mailings and signs. Candidates also use consultants to conduct polls that "identify voter priorities and preferences, assess voter expectations of the officeholder, and measure voter familiarity with the candidates and issues."[9] Candidates who can afford to hire their own personnel tend to do so. But many candidates, especially state and local candidates, rely on party organizations to provide these services for them. State party organizations, for example, do a lot for candidates, including conduct "voter identification programs to determine which voters [are] most likely to support" them, mount "get-out-the-vote drives" for supporters, conduct public opinion polls, and provide "campaign training seminars" that help candidates learn how to win elections.[10]

Political Parties Provide Cues to Voters

One of the most important things that parties do is passive rather than active. By this, I mean it is not something that political parties go out and do as much as it is something that simply happens as a result of their other activities. The passive activity is providing cues to voters. The sad fact of the matter is that most Americans do not pay much attention to politics. Nor do they know much about politics. A party label helps ordinary citizens understand what candidates stand for and what they will do in office. They do this by providing very basic information to voters. For example, when Senator John McCain was running for president against Senator Barack Obama, he ran under the banner of the Republican Party. Thus, on the ballot, accompanying his name, was the word "Republican." This label did not provide voters with information about everything John McCain stood for. But it did tell them that in general, he was conservative. The Republican Party in this country tends to be a right-leaning party, while the Democratic Party tends to be a center-left party. If voters know this very basic information—and most of them do—then the party labels candidates choose for themselves provide valuable information to voters. Voters use this information to decide what the candidates stand for, and ultimately, who they will vote for.

To get an idea of how important parties are in providing cues for voters, consider the following. As I note above, when pollsters ask people about which party they identify with, the vast majority pick one party or the other. In other words, most people have a party identification. This is important because most people *vote* their party identification. For example, in the 2008 presidential election, 89 percent of people who called themselves Democrats voted for Barack Obama (the Democrat), and 90 percent of people who called themselves Republicans voted for John McCain (the Republican).[11]

The Relationships between Political Parties and Interest Groups

Political parties and interest groups are similar in many ways. For one thing, each type of organization is what political scientists call a "linkage institution" —that is, *an entity in society that connects citizens to government*. Political parties often work with interest groups. This is the case, for example, when a conservative interest group such as the Club for Growth works hand in hand with the Republican Party to elect a Republican U.S. Senator to office. Political parties often, however, compete with interest groups. This is the case when, for example, a political party asks a person for a donation in the same week that an interest group does and the person can afford to give to only one of the two. In this section, I examine how political parties work with and against interest groups, and how they push political parties to do and not do things.

Interest Groups Helping Political Parties

In many instances, interest groups have the same goals as political parties. For example, the conservative citizen group Club for Growth shares with the Republican Party the goal of electing conservative Republican candidates to office. Similarly, the AFL-CIO, a liberal coalition of labor unions, shares with the Democratic Party the goal of electing Democrats (who tend to be more favorable to labor unions' interests) to office. So how do interest groups help political parties with which they share goals? There are several ways, including: contributing money to a party's candidates; spending money on behalf of a party's candidate; contributing money to a political party; helping candidates win office; and working with party leaders in government.

The two primary ways that interest groups help political parties are by contributing money to a party's candidates and by spending money on behalf of a party's candidates. Chapter 6 described the ways that interest groups contribute money to candidates and spend money independently on behalf of candidates, so I will not go over these things here. For now, it must suffice to say that any time an interest group contributes money to a candidate or spends independently on behalf of a candidate to try to get him or her elected, the group is helping the candidate's political party (albeit somewhat indirectly) as well.

Another way that interest groups help political parties is by *contributing money* directly to them. FECA allows PACs, and many states allow PACs as well as some other types of interest groups, to contribute money directly to political parties. PACs (at the federal and state levels) and some other types of interest groups (in some states) contribute money to political parties by contributing money to party committees. Currently, for example, the Democrats have three national party committees—the Democratic National Committee, the Democratic Congressional Campaign Committee, and the Democratic Senatorial Campaign Committee; as do the Republicans—the Republican National Committee, the National Republican Congressional Committee, and the National Republican Senatorial Committee. FECA stipulates that a PAC may contribute up to $15,000 per year to any national party committee. The political parties have numerous state, local, and district committees as well.

How much do interest groups contribute to political parties? My perusal of data from the FEC and several states suggests that political party committees, like interest groups and candidates, tend to get most of their money from individual donors. However, interest groups do give large sums of money to political party committees. Just to give you an idea of how much, I created Table 8.2, which lists the contributions given by one PAC—the AT&T Federal PAC (the PAC associated with telecommunications giant AT&T)—to party committees active during the 2009–2010 federal election cycle. This is just one federal PAC, and the table lists only contributions by AT&T's federal PAC to party committees active in national elections. So this table is by no means indicative of the true extent to which PACs provide money to parties. But it is suggestive, as it shows that in only one election cycle the PAC gave money to twenty different party committees. The table also shows something interesting—this PAC, like many other PACs, gave money to both main parties. This fact could not have been too pleasing to either the Republican Party or the Democratic Party, as each would prefer that the PAC give money only to one party (theirs). I will have more to say about this later.

Another way that interest groups help political parties is by *helping their candidates win elections*. Chapter 6 describes the many ways that interest groups help candidates win elections. Helping a party's candidates is another way (again, albeit somewhat indirectly) that interest groups help political parties. Political scientist Michael Heaney, who has studied the relationship between interest groups and political parties, uses the example of a labor group called Working America to show how groups work with parties. The group, which

Table 8.2 AT&T Federal PAC and its Contributions to Party Committees Active in National Elections, 2009–2010 Election Cycle

Recipient	Amount
7th District Republican Committee	$10,000
Arizona State Democratic Central Executive Committee	$1,000
Connecticut Republican State Congressional Committee	$1,000
Democratic Congressional Campaign Committee	$30,000
Democratic Party of Wisconsin	$5,000
Democratic Senatorial Campaign Committee	$30,000
Democratic State Central Committee of Maryland	$1,000
Georgia Republican Party	$10,000
Massachusetts Democratic State Committee	$7,500
Massachusetts Republican State Congressional Committee	$2,500
Michigan Republican Party	$1,000
Missouri Republican State Committee	$5,000
Montana Democratic Party	$2,500
Montana Republican State Central Committee	$2,500
National Republican Senatorial Committee	$30,000
National Republican Congressional Committee	$30,000
Nebraska Republican Party	$2,500
Nevada State Democratic Party	$5,000
Republican National Committee	$30,000
Republican Party of Kentucky	$5,000

Source: Federal Election Commission, "Committee (C00109017) Summary Reports, 2009–2010 Cycle."

was created in 2003 and gets financial support from the AFL-CIO, is a grassroots operation that sends its canvassers door to door to campaign on behalf of liberal Democratic candidates during election season.[12] Officially the group is non-partisan. But in practice it works exclusively on behalf of liberal Democrats.

Another way that interest groups help political parties achieve their goals is by *working with party leaders in government* to make government decisions. Every time a lobbyist works with a member of Congress or a state legislator or a city mayor or a governor to get a piece of legislation passed, that lobbyist is helping him/herself get what his/her group wants, as well as helping the party leader and his/her party get what they want. Some interest groups have very close ties to one political party or the other, and work closely with their aligned party leaders. For example, at the state and national level Republican leaders tend to have close and cordial personal relationships with lobbyists from conservative groups such as the National Right to Life Committee, the National Rifle Association, and the Chamber of Commerce of the United States. Similarly, in many states Democratic leaders have warm and close relationships with lobbyists from the state affiliates of the National Education Association, as well as lobbyists from environmental groups and other labor organizations. Table 8.3 lists several interest groups that have close relationships with political parties.

Michael T. Heaney (whom we encountered above) notes that government decision-makers and lobbyists tend to be "embedded" in the same "elite networks."[13] "Within these networks," he notes, "people exchange information, share resources, build loyalty, and create coalitions."[14] All of this is another way of saying that lobbyists and government decision-makers tend to hang out together, and that lobbyists who are Republicans hang out more with Republican government decision-makers than Democratic decision-makers, and lobbyists who are Democrats hang out more with Democratic government decision-makers. Lobbyists interact directly with government decision-makers all the time (as we learned in Chapter 5), and they contribute money to some government decision-makers (as we learned in Chapter 6). All the things they do during their interactions with government decision-makers help them

Table 8.3   Some Interest Groups with Close Ties to One of the Major Political Parties

Interest group	Political party
American Federation of State, County, and Municipal Employees	Democrats
AFL-CIO	Democrats
Chamber of Commerce of the United States	Republicans
Christian Coalition	Republicans
Club for Growth	Republicans
Emily's List	Democrats
Family Research Council	Republicans
International Brotherhood of Electrical Workers	Democrats
MoveOn.org	Democrats
National Rifle Association	Republicans
National Right to Life Committee	Republicans
Planned Parenthood Federation of America	Democrats
Sierra Club	Democrats
United Auto Workers	Democrats

Source: Based on author's research.

do their job—that is, affect what government does. Heaney notes that some lobbyists and group leaders have such close relationships with government decision-makers of a particular party that they seem to exert substantial impact on the decision-makers' decisions.[15] For example, Grover Norquist, who is the president of an anti-tax citizen group called "Americans for Tax Reform," has such close relationships with Republican leaders in Congress that during Barack Obama's first term in office many gave him credit (or blame) for congressional Republicans' unwillingness to consider any tax increases to help tackle the federal deficit.

Interest Groups Competing with, and Pushing, Political Parties

In many cases, as Michael Heaney points out, "Loyalties to political parties and interest groups . . . reinforce one another."[16] This is the case, for example, for the staunch NRA member and staunch Republican, or the diehard environmentalist and Sierra Club member and staunch Democrat. But what about the case of the Republican voter who is a staunch environmentalist and member of the Natural Resources Defense Council, or the case of the lifelong Democrat who is an evangelical Christian and member of Focus on the Family? In cases like these, a person's party membership contradicts his/her interest group membership. And in cases like these interest groups *compete* with political parties for voter loyalty, effort, and money. Most Americans have limited money, time, and attention, and more time and effort and money given to interest groups may mean less time and money and effort given to political parties. There is little that political parties can do about this other than decry the situation. There was a time in American politics when political parties were kings. Political scientists Allan Cigler and Burdett Loomis note, for example, that until the 1960s political parties were the primary linkage institutions in American politics.[17] Political parties were particularly important during election time, when they ran candidates' campaigns, recruited candidates, and provided important information to voters. Since the 1960s, however, parties have declined, as voters increasingly have turned to the media for information, candidates have begun to run their own campaigns, and more and more candidates decide for themselves they would like to run for office. In addition, the number of interest groups has increased, and interest groups have become more active in electoral politics and in linking voters to government. The most important part of all this for political parties is that some voters care more about their interest group affiliations than their party affiliation.

Still, political parties and interest groups seldom compete for voters' loyalties outright. This is the case because political parties and interest groups are fundamentally different types of organizations. First of all, political parties are most important during election season, while many interest groups are just as active outside of election season as they are in election season. Second, most interest groups focus rather narrowly on one or two or a few issues, while political parties are very broad coalitions that take stands on literally dozens of different issues. Still, in a world in which most citizens devote little time and energy to politics, interest groups are bound to compete for citizens' time and effort and loyalty if party affiliation and interest group memberships do not match up particularly well.

Even when interest groups do not compete outright with political parties for voters' loyalty or money or effort, they may make life difficult for political parties. This is the case when *interest groups pressure political parties* for certain things. The kind of pressure I am talking about here is not the kind of pressure that opponents place upon each other—that is, pressure to cave in, or pressure to give up (as when the AFL-CIO threatens to try to defeat Republican legislators, or when business groups threaten to mobilize voters against a Democratic president). The pressure I am talking about here is the kind that interest groups which tend to be aligned with one or the other party put upon their allied party. And the pressure is designed to make the party "toe the ideological line" supported by the group. An example will illustrate my point. The Club for Growth is a conservative interest group that says it stands for "limited government and economic freedom."[18] Though the group is officially a non-partisan organization, it supports Republican candidates almost exclusively, and pushes for conservative economic policies that are supported more by Republicans than by Democrats. It has helped many Republicans win elections over the past decade, including longtime friend Pat Toomey, the Republican senator from Pennsylvania. The Club's relationship with the Republican Party, however, is not always friendly. In 2005, for example, the group made headlines when it attacked Republican Senator Lincoln Chafee of Rhode Island, saying that he was insufficiently conservative. The group went as far as to support a challenger to Chafee in the Republican primary. Chafee beat the challenger, but went on in the election of 2006 to lose badly to Democrat Sheldon Whitehouse.[19] Many Republicans (including presidential nominee John McCain) were livid with the Club for Growth, arguing that in the long run the group hurt the party rather than helped it. Of course, the Club disagreed, saying that a Republican Party that acted like the Democratic Party was not all that valuable in the first place.

The reason that the Club for Growth pushed for a more conservative alternative to Lincoln Chafee is clear—the group wanted very conservative

Republicans to win office, not moderately conservative Republicans. But it is not just during elections that interest groups put pressure on their allied political parties. Environmental groups consistently have pressured President Obama during his first term to "do the right thing" (as they see it) on environmental issues. And Log Cabin Republicans—a group of Republicans that advocates for "the freedom and equality of gay and lesbian Americans"[20]—has been pressing the Republican Party to embrace gay and lesbian rights since it was founded in 1977. There is some evidence that this sort of thing can work. There is evidence, for example, that starting in the 1960s, Christian evangelical groups, such as the Christian Coalition, Focus on the Family, and the Moral Majority, successfully pushed the Republican Party to become more conservative on moral issues such as abortion, euthanasia, and same-sex marriage.[21] There is also evidence, however, that these sorts of efforts can be futile. For example, Peter Francia notes that for decades the AFL-CIO and other labor groups have worked tirelessly for the Democratic Party. Labor groups have worked to get Democrats elected, and have pushed hard for Democrats to stand up to Republicans on issues of interest to labor (such as taxes on the wealthy and trade agreements). Yet according to Francia, they have received little in return, as Democrats continue to be more liberal than Republicans on issues of interest to labor, but certainly not as liberal as union leaders would like.

Interest groups such as Club for Growth and Log Cabin Republicans work openly and aggressively to change the parties toward which they lean. Other interest groups take a more subtle, bipartisan approach and support and work with *both political parties* to make sure their views are represented before government. Here I am speaking primarily of business interest groups including trade associations and individual business firms. It is a cliché that business groups support the Republican Party and disdain the Democratic Party. Yet while it is probably true that most business groups would prefer Republican government to Democratic government, it is also true that many business groups take a more pragmatic approach, working with and supporting both parties. AT&T, for example, which is the subject of Table 8.2, gives money to both parties (as the table shows), and its lobbyists work closely with leaders of both political parties.

There is probably more bipartisanship in the world of interest groups than most Americans know. AT&T is just one example. This pragmatic bipartisanship was on display during the fight over President Obama's health care reform plan in 2009 and 2010. Consider, for example, the activities of the trade association Pharmaceutical Research and Manufacturers Association of America (PhRMA). At first glance it might appear that the group, which represents the makers of prescription drugs, would be a solidly Republican business organization. But during the fight over health care the group worked closely with Democrats in Congress and the president to craft legislation.[22] The group, which typically espouses "free market" principles, worked closely with Democrats because it had to if it wanted its voice to be heard. Congress at the time was dominated by Democrats, the president was a Democrat, and the party was determined to reform health care one way or another. PhRMA knew that it was better to have a seat at the table and affect the reform than stubbornly to resist reform and risk losing big when reform was adopted. Similarly, Wal-Mart, one of the world's biggest companies and generally a reliable supporter of the type of "free market" economics espoused by the Republican Party, threw its weight behind the health care reform effort early on. In fact, the company went as far as to support an employer mandate—that is, a provision in the law that forces large businesses to provide coverage for its employees.[23] Other businesses that were sure to be affected by health care reform joined the call for reform and worked with Democrats as well.

The types of groups that are most likely to be pragmatic and work with both parties are business firms, professional associations, and trade associations. These types of groups are first and foremost interested in ensuring that business is good. And while they might have a party preference, they know that the key to influence in the long run is maintaining constructive relationships with members of both parties. The dangers of "putting all your eggs in one party basket" are evident in the case of labor unions. For most of our history, the country's major labor unions have been closely aligned with the Democratic Party. To be sure, over the years there have been a few "pro-labor" Republicans. But overall labor unions have tended to side with Democrats. Labor's close ties to the Democratic Party are understandable, as the Democrats are much more likely to support labor's views on issues such as business regulation, health care, taxes, trade, and worker protection. But during periods of Republican rule, labor unions have paid a heavy price for their close alignment with the Democratic Party. For example, in the state of Wisconsin in 2011, Republican Governor Scott Walker and a Republican-controlled state legislature pushed through controversial legislation that hurt unions by eliminating public employee unions' right to bargain collectively.[24] Republican Governor John Kasich and his state legislature did something similar in the state of Ohio. Similarly, when the Republicans took control of the House of Representatives in the 1990s after decades of Democratic rule, labor unions found themselves "on the outs," as many Republican legislators simply refused to listen to them.[25] Labor unions were on the wrong side of many political battles during this period, and their histories suggest that closely aligning with one party may not be a good idea.

Conclusion

Political parties and interest groups are similar types of organizations. Most obviously, both types of organizations have political goals. But parties and interest groups are quite different. The main difference is that political parties try to affect what government does primarily by placing their members in positions of government authority. They do this primarily by recruiting candidates for public office, nominating them to run for office, and then helping them get elected. In contrast, interest groups try to affect government primarily by trying to affect the decisions of people who are in government. Lots of interest groups are active in elections, to be sure, but for most groups electoral activity is just one small part of what they do.

Interest groups have an uneasy relationship with political parties. On the one hand, interest groups work closely with political parties to achieve shared goals. Conservative groups such as the Club for Growth, for example, work to elect Republican candidates to positions of governmental authority. Similarly, the AFL-CIO helps get Democratic candidates elected to office, and also sends its lobbyists to interact with Democratic decision-makers in an attempt to shape government decisions. On the other hand, interest groups compete with political parties. Most Americans do not spend a great deal of time, money, or effort on politics, and thus when interest groups attract any of these things from ordinary citizens, they are almost by definition depriving political parties of them. Moreover, interest groups arguably are an easier "sell" to most people, as they can concentrate on the issue that is most important to their target audience, while political parties are forced to take stands on numerous issues. In addition, there are many instances when interest groups make things difficult for political parties by pressuring them to nominate certain candidates or to take certain positions.

In the end, the relationship between political parties and interest groups is destined to be a close but troubled one. The relationship can be likened to a rocky marriage; the two partners are inextricably bound together, though things are not always cordial between them.

What's Next

Up until now I have assiduously avoided the issue of interest group influence. I have examined what interest groups are, where they come from, and what they do. But I have more or less ignored what impact they have on government decisions. I have done this for a reason—because examining *influence* without understanding the nature, prevalence, and extent of interest group activity is hopeless. I cannot ignore the question of influence any longer. Few issues in American politics are more lasting, controversial, and important than the issue of interest group influence. It is the subject of the next and penultimate chapter.

The Influence of   9
Interest Groups

It is a matter of faith among most Americans that interest groups regularly get their way in Washington and elsewhere. Researchers at the American National Election Studies (ANES) have asked respondents the following question every two years since 1964: "Would you say the government is pretty much run by a few big interests looking out for themselves or that it is run for the benefit of all the people?"[1] As Table 9.1 shows, in 2008, the most recent year for which data are available, 69 percent of respondents said, "run by a few big interests."[2] A majority of respondents have responded "run by a few big interests" in every year of the survey since 1970 except 2002 (in the immediate aftermath of the 9/11 attacks). Are the public's perceptions accurate? *Do* interest groups and their lobbyists dominate American government and politics? Or are accounts of interest group influence mere hyperbole? These questions cut to the very heart of American democracy. After all, a government *for* interest groups and *by* interest groups is exactly what the founders of this country didn't want. In this chapter, I examine what political scientists have learned about interest group influence. I begin with a look at the difficulties inherent in assessing the impact of lobbying on policy outcomes. From here, I examine some theories that purport to explain the role of interest groups in the policymaking process. Finally, I ask: When do interest groups get their way?

Table 9.1 Public Opinion about the Responsiveness of American Government, 1990–2008

Question: *"Would you say the government is pretty much run by a few big interests looking out for themselves or that it is run for the benefit of all the people?"*

	1990	1998	2002	2004	2008
Answer:					
Few big interests	71%	64%	48%	56%	69%
Benefit of all	24%	32%	51%	40%	29%
Don't know/Depends	5%	4%	2%	4%	2%

Source: National Election Study, University of Michigan, Center for Political Studies, "Is the Government Run for the Benefit of All, 1964–2008."

Introduction: The Thorny Question of Interest Group Influence

For most Americans the basic story of interest group influence is simple. An interest group lobbies for something, throws a little money to a government decision-maker, and *presto!*, it gets its way. This is the story, for example, that many gun control advocates tell about the National Rifle Association (NRA). They say that the group passes out lots of money, lobbies government decision-makers, and succeeds in getting the government to pass gun-friendly laws. Unfortunately, this simple story is badly flawed.

In reality, it is very difficult to determine precisely what role interest groups play in affecting government decisions. Why? There are three primary reasons. First, the ultimate government decision to do *anything* generally has numerous causes—not just one. In the end, any government decision you can think of is the result of an exceedingly multifaceted and complex process. Let's return to the case of the NRA for a second. In 2010 in my home state of Tennessee, the group lobbied for and eventually got legislation that allowed handgun carry permit holders to bring their guns into bars. This decision involved literally *thousands* of political actors, each of whom had a different mixture of motives. Among those actively involved were dozens of members of the state legislature, dozens more legislative staffers, and scores of lobbyists. Then there were the thousands of regular citizens who weighed in on the bill, contacting their representatives to express their opinions on the matter. Because there were so many actors involved, it is difficult to determine precisely how much influence each of the actors exerted. A second reason why it is difficult to determine precisely what role interest groups played in the passage of the guns-in-bars bill is that it is very difficult to distinguish influence from agreement. It is not uncommon for government decision-makers to do precisely what interest groups want them to do simply because they agree with them. This is *agreement*. But it looks a lot like *influence*. In cases like this, it is difficult to determine precisely how much influence interest groups exert. Finally, "access" and "activity" do not necessarily mean "influence." In other words, just because an interest group is "there," or has lots of money, or has lots of contacts, does not mean it is influential. While it is tempting to equate presence and activity with influence, it is unwise. Sometimes, interest groups do a lot and get nothing in return.

You can consider this introductory section a caveat—a warning that the question of interest group influence is a thorny one. It is not easy to figure out exactly how much power interest groups exert over government decisions. For one thing, all government decisions have multiple causes, not just one. For another, it's hard to separate agreement from influence. Finally, sometimes smoke does not mean fire. In other words, presence and activity do not automatically add up to influence.

Pluralism: Putting Interest Groups on the Map

Despite James Madison's warnings about the mischiefs of faction, it was not until the middle part of the twentieth century that social scientists began to study interest group influence in earnest. Scholars did not say a whole lot about interest groups until then because they simply did not see them as important players in the political process.[3] For approximately the first 150 years of our history, political analysts focused their attention primarily on governmental actors because they viewed interest groups and other extragovernmental actors as more or less peripheral to the political process.[4]

The Pluralists

At mid-century all of this began to change. As interest groups proliferated in the 1940s and 1950s, political scientists began to take note of their role in politics. One of the first political scientists to address the question of interest group influence was David Truman. In his influential book *The Governmental Process* (1951), Truman found that millions of Americans joined interest groups to further their political goals, and that these interest groups were key players in the political process.[5] In virtually every political battle that Truman investigated, he found the "fingerprints" of interest groups and their lobbyists. In case after case, Washington government decision-makers (Truman did not say too much about state and local politics) interacted extensively with interest groups before reaching their final decisions. Truman stopped short of concluding that interest groups dominated the American political process. But he suggested that government decision-makers of all kinds were quite responsive to the desires of interest groups.

In the 10–15 years after Truman's *Governmental Process*, several scholars weighed in on the question of interest group influence.[6] Most of them agreed with Truman that interest groups were active in most major government decisions. Truman and others who shared this view came to be known as "pluralists."[7] Pluralists differed from most previous scholars of American politics in two respects. First, they recognized that interest groups were deeply immersed in decision-making at all levels of government. Second, pluralists did not view interest groups as threats to American democracy. Unlike Madison and other critics of interest groups, pluralists argued that interest groups were essentially harmless.[8] Pluralists believed that because interest groups represented real people with reasonable political demands, they were legitimate vehicles by which citizens communicated their views to government decision-makers.[9]

Pluralists showed once and for all that interest groups are important players in American politics. This may not seem like a powerful insight to you, but at the time it was very important. Before pluralists began to examine the role of interest groups in American politics, most social scientists viewed policy decisions solely as manifestations of *government* activity.

Subgovernments and Policy Domains

Pluralists showed that interest groups are deeply involved in government decisions at all levels. But the question remained: *How* involved? Do interest groups actually *influence* the decisions of government decision-makers? Or do they merely operate on the fringes of American politics? As interest groups continued to proliferate throughout the 1950s, 1960s, and 1970s, political scientists grappled with these questions in an attempt to discern the true nature and extent of interest group influence.

Subgovernment Theory: Cool but Wrong

At about the same time that pluralists spread the word about interest group involvement in government decision-making, a group of scholars known as "subgovernment theorists" formulated a new theory of interest group influence.[10] After studying how government decisions were made in a number of different issue areas, these theorists concluded that many policy areas had their own *subgovernments*, which consisted of a limited number of interest groups, legislators, and key bureaucrats, who interacted on a stable, ongoing basis to produce government decisions in a particular issue area.[11] At the federal level, on the issue of veterans' affairs, for example, "House and Senate Veterans' Affairs Committees in Congress, the Veterans Administration, and organizations such as the American Legion and the Veterans of Foreign Wars (VFW) work[ed] together in developing policies on education, health care, and housing for veterans."[12] Similarly, on agriculture issues (at the national level) members of the House and Senate Agriculture Committees, interest groups such as the American Farm Bureau Federation and the National Council of Farmer Cooperatives, and bureaucrats from the U.S. Department of Agriculture (U.S.D.A.) interacted regularly to make farm policy.[13]

According to subgovernment theorists, the decisions that came out of subgovernments were self-serving—they "specifically reward[ed] the primary constituencies of the [subgovernment's] participants, often to the detriment of the public at large."[14] The Washington agriculture subgovernment, for example, created farm subsidy programs that benefited farmers (who got cash payments from the national government), members of the House and Senate Agriculture Committees (who curried favor with their constituents by providing them with monetary subsidies), and U.S.D.A. bureaucrats (who got to keep their jobs as long as farm subsidies existed). Similarly, the veterans' affairs subgovernment made policies that guaranteed direct payments to veterans. Veterans groups were happy with the payments, as were bureaucrats from the Veterans' Administration whose jobs depended upon continued government programs, and members of Congress who got to tell their constituents that they were "doing right" by veterans.

Subgovernment theorists seemed to suggest that interest groups were practically equal partners in government decision-making. Across all levels of government, interest groups worked side by side with government decision-makers to make government decisions. This made them *extremely* powerful. Moreover, many, many interest groups were powerful. According to subgovernment theorists, many interest groups had their *own* subgovernments. For example, interest groups representing truckers were part of the transportation subgovernment, interest groups representing health care providers were part of the health care subgovernment, and teachers' unions were part of the education subgovernment. In a process known as "logrolling"—a sort of "you scratch my back and I'll scratch yours" arrangement in which everyone "butts out" of everyone else's subgovernment—America's biggest interest groups exercised power in the issue areas most important to them.[15]

Subgovernment theory had several strengths. First, it was simple and straightforward. Second, it rightly acknowledged that many government decisions are the result of ongoing interactions between interest groups and government decision-makers from lots of different governmental institutions. Third, it recognized that most interest groups had relatively narrow concerns (that is, they deal only with a single issue or two). And finally, subgovernment theory correctly noted that interest groups often work together (with each other as well as with government decision-makers) to get what they want. Unfortunately, subgovernment theory had one fatal flaw: it was *wrong*. First, it ignored the fact that many issue areas are rife with conflict among interest groups (as well as between interest groups and other political actors). For example, contrary to subgovernment theory, lots of interest groups lobby Congress *against* farm subsidies and thus tangle with farm groups. Taxpayers' citizen groups, for example, lobby against subsidies because they lead to higher taxes. Similarly, consumer citizen groups lobby against subsidies because they increase food prices. Second, subgovernment theory falsely portrayed government decision-making as a neat and stable and orderly process. If there is one thing that we know about government decision-making, it is that it is not neat, stable, and orderly. As political scientist William Browne has noted, "There's always been far too much going on in American politics for [subgovernment] theory to be accurate . . . And the goings-on have always been so disorderly, almost chaotic."[16] Finally, subgovernment theory incorrectly suggested that most interest groups got what they wanted from government. This, of course, is not true. The real world of interest group politics comprises both winners and losers. Interest groups don't merely reciprocate with one another and live happily ever after. Sometimes their interests conflict. Seldom does a government decision make *everyone* happy.

A Better Concept: Policy Domains

By the mid-1970s, most political scientists recognized that subgovernment theory was fatally flawed. The search for a better theory was under way. One of the more popular theories went something like this: government decisions are not made in small, exclusive subgovernments, but rather are made in large and permeable, "policy domains"—"well-understood and established policy area[s], or . . . communit[ies] of players."[17] In other words, each issue area has its own policy domain, which comprises the actors who interact to make decisions on the domain issue.

Policy domains were seen as profoundly different from subgovernments. First of all, domains are much larger and more permeable. Domain theorists argued that most policy domains consist not of a handful of actors, but rather of hundreds if not thousands of different political actors.[18] (It is no accident that the concept of a policy domain gained credence during the mid-1970s, when the number of interest groups in America skyrocketed.) Second, policy domains are much more conflictual than subgovernments. Domain theorists argued that because government decisions are made in open and permeable domains (some scholars called them "networks"), interest groups often enter into open conflict with one another as they press competing claims upon government. Finally, policy domains are utterly mutable. Subgovernment theory portrayed relationships among interest groups and between interest groups and other political actors as stable and long-lasting. In contrast, domain theorists maintained that relationships among interest groups and between interest groups and other political actors are anything but stable. In domains, things change constantly as new players move in and out, and issues change and evolve. In the end, no domain looks exactly the same two days in a row. Politics changes too quickly and too unpredictably for that.

The Problem: Policy Domains Don't Teach Us Much about Interest Group Influence

There is absolutely no question that domain theorists did a better job of describing the realities of contemporary government decision-making than subgovernment theorists did. In short, in most cases, government decisions are made in a large, permeable, ever-changing domain. Subgovernments were figments of fertile imaginations. The concept of a policy domain is appealing and accurate because it recognizes that politics is messy and unpredictable. This is a sobering thought for the scholar of interest group influence. It means that *each political battle is unique.* If policy domains are constantly changing, every specific government decision is likely to be the result of a different set of factors and forces. This means that an interest group that succeeds in getting what it wants today may not be successful in getting what it wants tomorrow. It also means that a lobbying technique that works today may not work tomorrow. Most important, it means that life as an interest group is very unpredictable.

It Took a Long Time to Get Here: Interest Group Influence is Situational

So where does all this leave us? In the end, it means the following: interest group influence is situational—that is, it varies, dependent upon the specific set of circumstances. To put it another way, the answer to the question, "How influential are interest groups?" is "It depends." Sometimes interest groups are able to get what they want from government. Sometimes they are not. Sometimes a specific interest group—say, the NRA—gets exactly what it wants. Sometimes it does not. It all depends upon the situation—the unique combination of factors that exists at a given time in a given place.

The Conditions of Interest Group Influence

Every decent study of interest group influence and power ever conducted concludes that sometimes interest groups get what they want, and sometimes they don't. All of this, of course, begs the following question: Under what conditions are interest groups most likely to get what they want? The rest of this chapter is devoted to answering this question.

Before proceeding any further, it is important to note that this question is *probabilistic* in nature. This means that in what follows I do not pretend that I know *with certainty* when interest groups will and will not influence government decisions or precisely how much influence interest groups exert. The process by which government decisions are made is so unpredictable and disordered that definitive statements about interest group influence are impossible to formulate. The best I can do is stipulate several conditions under which interest groups *may* exert substantial influence. Some people may not be satisfied with this approach—they thirst for easy answers to the difficult questions of interest group influence. But because this question is extremely difficult to answer, political scientists approach it from a probabilistic perspective. Now, on to the conditions.

Condition 1: On the Side of the Status Quo

Interest groups are more likely to get what they want when they are on the side of the status quo.[19] In the largest and most thorough examination of interest group influence ever conducted, political scientist Frank Baumgartner and his colleagues find that in any given year, public policy tends not to change. That is, policy change—a situation in which the federal government (Baumgartner and his colleagues look only at the federal government) changes something about an existing policy—is rare. Usually, things stay the same from year to year. This is the case for several reasons, and many of them are quite complicated and difficult to explain. But I will mention a few of them. First, the American political system (especially the federal government) is designed to prevent change. The founders created a federal government in which it is difficult to get things done. For a bill to become a law at the federal level, for example, generally both houses of Congress and the president must agree on it. Anyone who has watched American politics lately knows that this is not easy, especially when Congress and the presidency are controlled by different political parties. State and local governments also have a hard time getting things done, as they too are characterized by some degree of separated powers.

The second reason that policy change is rare is that the attention of government decision-makers—the people who have the ultimate say over what government does—is scarce. Government decision-makers, especially elected officials, are busy people. Baumgartner and his colleagues find that getting them to pay attention to *any* particular issue is difficult; they have lots of things to do! So if an interest group wants to change a standing policy, it first has to draw attention to that policy. And getting government decision-makers to pay attention to your issue instead of someone else's is not always easy. Baumgartner and his colleagues say:

> [interest groups and lobbyists] and their problems will compete for space on an agenda that reflects only a subset of the myriad potential problems that could attract the attention of those in and outside of government. A great number of worthy policy proposals go nowhere not because of active opposition but because agenda gatekeepers and their allies have more urgent concerns.[20]

To prove their point about attention, Baumgartner and his colleagues use the example of advocacy on the issue of racial disparities in the criminal justice system. In 1999 and 2000, several interest groups (including the ACLU) produced good and persuasive research showing that non-whites receive a different kind of justice than whites in this country. The data showed, for example, that non-whites are often the victims of racial profiling by police, and also generally receive harsher sentences for the same crimes than whites. The data were solid and convincing, several interest groups (including the well-heeled ACLU) were lobbying Congress on the issue, and the wealthy Soros Foundation poured money into the lobbying effort. Moreover, the press paid a great deal of attention to the issue, publishing stories about racial profiling and disparities in the criminal justice system. Despite money, lobbyists, public attention, and a seemingly good cause, nothing happened. Nothing happened because federal government decision-makers were too busy dealing with other issues; they just did not have time to take up another issue, no matter how important it was. In short, government decision-makers had other things on their minds and on their desks.

Third, the status quo at any given time exists, presumably, because some government decision-makers and people like it that way. An example can help illustrate this point. The reason marijuana is illegal is that for decades most government decision-makers and Americans have believed that it *should* be illegal.[21] The status quo—the policy that makes smoking, growing, and selling marijuana illegal—is what it is because it is popular. Public opinion polls show that fewer Americans than in the past think marijuana should be illegal.[22] Still, Americans are decidedly ambivalent about changing the policy. Lobbyists for marijuana reform groups such as the National Organization for the Reform of Marijuana Laws (NORML) are battling against a longstanding status quo—a status quo that has had the support of many Americans and many government decision-makers for many, many years. In other words, in many cases, the status quo is the status quo because lots of people like it that way.

Fourth, the status quo is a known commodity. Returning to the marijuana example, lobbyists working for NORML have to convince government decision-makers that changing the laws regarding marijuana sales, possession, and growth would make things better. This is impossible to prove. It is impossible to prove because it has not happened yet. Yes, the NORML lobbyists can show that the current laws do not work very well. They can and do show that the "war on drugs" costs a lot of money, leads to lots of violence, and has not really put a dent in drug use. But it cannot prove to government decision-makers that changes would make any of this better. And this makes it difficult for NORML to win.

In short, if an interest group finds itself on the side of the status quo it is more likely to win than if it finds itself on the side of change. The reasons this is the case are many and varied. But in the end they do not matter much to interest groups. What matters is that if an interest group wants to change something, it faces an uphill battle.

Condition 2: Something to which No One Objects

Interest groups are more likely to get what they want when they ask for something to which no one objects.[23] Believe it or not, interest groups sometimes ask government decision-makers for things to which no one objects. I learned this myself a few years ago when I interviewed land-use lobbyists for a book I wrote called *Total Lobbying*.[24] Several land-use lobbyists told me that on some occasions when they went to local government and asked for permission to do something—for example, build a new shopping center on a vacant piece of land, get a piece of land rezoned for commercial use, or add on to an existing building—no one in the community or in government really cared one way or another. One lobbyist, whom I paraphrase here, told me this:

> When I work for a company that wants the local government to rezone a piece of land from agricultural or residential to commercial or industrial, my chances of winning are very high if no one in the community and no interest group objects. If we ask the local government officials to allow the rezoning and no one shows up at the public meeting to oppose us, or no community or neighborhood organizations oppose us, we will almost certainly win.

In short, in situations in which land-use lobbyists find themselves asking for things that no one opposes, they and the groups they represent (e.g., real estate development firms) have a very high probability of getting what they want.

Land use is not the only arena in which groups ask for things that no one objects to. At the state and federal levels of government business firms often ask government decision-makers for very minor changes in laws and regulations. Because in some cases changes affect no one but the businesses that lobby for them, no one objects. In addition, in many cases a government agency wants to buy something from a private vendor, and there is only one provider. The one provider has a very high probability of getting the government contract if it has no competitors.

Why does lack of opposition correlate with interest group success? One answer is that government decision-makers are in a "no-lose" situation if they go along with interest groups that are asking for things no one objects to. In situations like these they can make interest groups happy by acceding to their demands, and simultaneously avoid upsetting anyone. Any time an interest group or set of interest groups asks for something to which someone objects, its chances of success drop. This implies two things. First, it implies that interest groups exercise little power vis-à-vis other political actors (e.g., legislators, bureaucrats, the chief executive) in situations in which lots of other political actors are involved. In other words, when there are lots of players involved in a government decision, the power of any specific player or set of players tends to decrease. Second, it implies that a *specific* interest group stands a much higher chance of affecting a government decision if no one opposes its demands.

So how often do interest groups ask for things to which no one objects? We do not really know for certain. But we do know that it is not uncommon for interest groups and their lobbyists to face little or no opposition when they ask for things. In a recent study, political scientists Frank Baumgartner and Beth Leech studied interest group activity in Washington and discovered that for many issues, there is not very much interest group competition or involvement.[25] Baumgartner and Leech examined a sample of 137 specific issues, and found that on 32 of these, "only one or two interest groups were involved."[26] Being the only interest group or one of only two interest groups does not necessarily mean that a group will win. But it sure helps. If a group finds itself alone in lobbying, clearly it has no interest group opposition. In addition, Baumgartner and Leech show that on issues on which there is little lobbying, the interest groups involved tend to be business groups or governmental groups that face little or no opposition from labor unions or citizen groups. In short, there are many instances in which groups ask for things to which no one objects. Box 9.1 presents a brief example showing that lack of opposition is good for interest groups.

Box 9.1 The Benefit of Having No Opposition

The federal Lacey Act is a rather obscure law passed in 1900 that was designed to curb international trafficking in endangered wildlife. Over the years, it has been used to stop pet shops and owners from importing to the United States "wildlife, fish, and plants that have been illegally taken, possessed, transported, or sold." In 2008, the law was amended to add illegally harvested foreign wood to the list of things covered by the Act. The 2008 amendments were supported by a host of interest groups including environmental citizen groups such as Friends of the Earth and the World Wildlife Fund, a number of labor unions, and trade groups representing American foresters and manufacturers including the Hardwood Foundation and the American Forest Foundation. The amendments were not particularly controversial, as members of Congress from wood-producing states saw them as a way to protect domestic foresters from cheap, illegal, foreign competition, and environmentally conscious members of Congress saw them as a way to protect endangered ecosystems.

The widespread support for the amendments started to fray in 2010. In 2009, federal agents raided a Gibson guitar making factory in Nashville, Tennessee looking for illegally imported wood from Madagascar. The federal agents alleged that Gibson was using the illegal wood in its guitars. A subsequent raid sought to discover if the company was using wood harvested illegally in India. As of this writing, no charges have been filed against Gibson. But if the company is found to have violated the Lacey Act it faces huge fines and even the possibility of having some of its executives thrown in jail.

After the raids, the Lacey Act and its amendments had a high-profile opponent—the Gibson Guitar Corporation. Gibson is an iconic American company, maker of the famous Gibson Les Paul electric guitar. The Les Paul guitar has been played by some of the most renowned guitarists in the world including Bob Dylan, Eric Clapton, Jimmy Page, and Slash. The company began a high-profile lobbying campaign to change the Lacey Act. And it got lots of other people and interest groups on its side, including legendary country picker Vince Gill, a number of conservative members of Congress (including Kentucky Senator Rand Paul), and dozens of "Tea Party" type conservative citizen groups.

If the amendments adopted in 2008 were considered today, they might not be adopted. Why not? Because some powerful people and interest groups now oppose them. But in 2008 the amendments faced little or no opposition. In sum, the group proponents of the amendments asked for something and they got it—largely because they faced little opposition. Future political battles over the Lacey Act will not be so easily won for its interest group supporters. Now these supporters face opposition, and this decreases their chances of success. Of course, the opponents of the Lacey Act, who are working now to change it, have problems of their own. As I noted earlier in this chapter, the opponents of change (that is, the supporters of the original amendments) are defending the status quo. And this gives them a huge advantage.

Sources: Wisch, "Overview of the Lacey Act (16 U.S.C. SS 3371–3378)"; Mohan, "Wood protection law creates splintering in guitar industry"; Austen, "The U.S. vs. Rock 'n' Roll."

Condition 3: Things about which the Public and the Media Know and Care Little

Interest groups are more likely to get what they want when they lobby on things about which the public and the media know and care little.[27] In many cases, interest groups and lobbyists do their work in relative obscurity. This is to their advantage. Baumgartner and Leech, whom we encountered above, show that some issues "become the object of veritable lobbying extravaganzas."[28] As examples, the authors cite four giant and expensive and important pieces of legislation considered by Congress in 1996 (the year they studied): the Omnibus Consolidated Appropriations Act, the Small Business Protection Act, the Budget Reconciliation Act, and the Department of Defense Appropriations Act. Many other issues, however, have very little group activity. As examples of bills that did not receive much attention from interest groups, Baumgartner and Leech cite one bill that concerned "Safety slides on cargo airplanes," a bill concerning "Federal Home Loan Bank System treatment of derivatives," and "Trade issues related to the New Zealand Dairy Board."[29] These types of issues—mundane, often complex, and never particularly well understood by most people—are good for lobbyists. If you are a lobbyist working, for example, on trade issues related to the New Zealand Dairy Board, you may have the field to yourself (because no one else cares). And if you do, your chances of getting what you want are greater than if the field is occupied by you and 350 other interest groups and their lobbyists. Moreover, if only one or two lobbyists care about an issue, chances are the media and the public do not know or care much about it either. And if a lobbyist is working on an issue on which the media and the public are silent, he/she has an advantage over the lobbyist working on an issue on which the media and public are vocal. The advantage is *lack of competition.*

What types of decisions are likely not to engender media or public attention? One answer is decisions about technical and highly complex matters.[30] And on these matters lobbyists can be very influential. Technical and complex issues are those that few ordinary people (not to mention government decision-makers) understand. Examples of such issues include motor freight regulation, corporate taxation, and banking regulation. Each of these issues is technical and complex. Banking regulation, for example, concerns things such as what services banks can and cannot offer, the differences between banks and savings and loans and credit unions, and the investment opportunities allowed to lending institutions. Bankers and economists—and lobbyists for bankers—may understand these things, but few other people do. On issues such as these, interest groups can be enormously influential, as regular citizens generally are not heard from by government decision-makers. There are two reasons why this is the case. First, the public seldom cares about or understands highly technical and complex issues. This means that interest groups concerned with these issues can go about their business with little attention from either the public or the media (and in many cases, other interest groups). Second, on technical and complex issues government decision-makers are highly dependent upon lobbyists for information. On technical issues on which they lack expertise, government decision-makers often defer to interest groups (because interest groups have information they value).[31] This, of course, has a tendency to improve interest groups' chances of getting what they want. Think of it this way: if a government decision-maker wants information about banking regulation, he/she must go to the people who are most likely to have it—banks and bankers. If the government decision-maker relies solely or primarily upon this information to make his/her decisions, he/she is likely to make decisions that favor the banking industry.

An example here is illustrative. The financial crisis that racked the country in 2008 was partially a result of lobbying. There is evidence that part of the reason the economy took a nosedive into recession in 2008 was that many assets rapidly lost their value. One such asset is the home. At the height of the crisis, many Americans found that their homes were worth much less than they paid for them. Many other Americans found that they were unable to afford their monthly payments. In the end, many Americans found themselves financially insecure, many others were foreclosed upon (that is, kicked out of their houses), and many others saw their net worth drop precipitously. There is some evidence that this situation came to pass partially because of lobbying by mortgage lenders such as Bear Stearns, Bank of America, and Countrywide Financial Corp. These companies, over a period of years, pushed Congress to allow (and not disallow) risky lending—lending that eventually led to a bubble that contributed to the financial meltdown.[32] One of the reasons they were able to get their way was that most Americans do not know or care much about the rules that govern mortgage lending. This is partly because these rules are technical and complex, partly because the media generally do not pay much attention to issues like these (they favor more sensational issues such as gay marriage and abortion), and partly because Americans are busy and simply cannot pay attention to every issue. It is much easier for interest groups to win on technical and complex issues—issues about which no one cares but them— than on simpler, more salient issues.

Condition 4: Matters that are Non-Partisan and Non-Ideological

Interest groups are more likely to get what they want when they lobby on matters that are non-partisan and non-ideological.[33] Some issues—abortion, the death penalty, taxes, and school prayer come to mind—excite ideological and partisan controversy. Both parties have well-defined positions on such issues, and conservatives and liberals have longstanding and consistent differences on them. On issues like these, interest groups are likely to have less influence than on issues that are non-ideological and non-partisan. Instead, factors like party affiliation, ideology, constituent opinion, and pressure from colleagues are likely to determine what government decision-makers do. This is not to say that interest groups that lobby on such issues are completely powerless. But it is to say that interest groups probably "take a back seat" to other factors.

Some issues, however, are neither partisan nor ideological, and do not excite or inflame partisan and ideological differences. On issues like these, interest groups have a high probability of exerting a great deal of influence. Consider, for example, the issue of disability rights. On this issue, the two parties do not have longstanding, easily identifiable differences.[34] In fact, recent history suggests that both parties (at least publicly) support the same types of disability-rights policies and programs.[35] Issues surrounding veterans' benefits are also non-partisan and non-ideological. Neither party wants to take a public position against veterans' benefits, and liberals and conservatives do not have well-defined differences on the issue. Research has found that on issues like disability rights and veterans' affairs, interest groups can exert substantial influence over government decisions.[36] First of all, few government decision-makers have strong views on such issues. Second, government decision-makers often do not have to worry about toeing a "party line." Third, there is no cost in going along with interest groups on such issues. Government decision-makers can safely do what veterans groups and disability groups ask them to do without alienating anybody.

Condition 5: The Chief Executive on their Side

Interest groups are more likely to get what they want when they have the chief executive on their side. In the book *Lobbying and Policy Change*, political scientist Frank Baumgartner and his colleagues find that whether or not interest groups win is profoundly affected by whose side the president is on. In short, if an interest group has the president on its side, it is much more likely to win than if it does not.[37] Similarly if an interest group is on the opposite side to the president, its probability of winning is not very high. The chief executive in local and state politics is powerful as well, and it is reasonable to conclude that getting the governor or the mayor on your side can increase a group's chances of success.[38]

Why is having the chief executive on your side so important? Baumgartner and his colleagues give a very straightforward answer: the chief executive is powerful. In Washington, the president wields a lot of power. Most important, he can veto legislation. Of course, Congress can override a presidential veto, but this is difficult; if the president vetoes something it is usually dead. Gubernatorial powers vary across states, as do mayoral and county executive powers; but in many places these types of executives are powerful as well. Having the chief executive on your side in local and state politics is very helpful.

The health care reform debates of 2009 illustrate the power of the chief executive (at the federal level). In the end, the defenders of the status quo—including lobbying powerhouses America's Health Insurance Plans, the American Petroleum Institute, the Chamber of Commerce of the United States, and many individual insurance companies—lost. There are many reasons why they lost, but at the top of the list is that the president opposed them. The president was determined to get something done and to change the status quo. Even with the status quo advantage noted above, interest groups defending the current system against the president were unsuccessful.

Condition 6: A "Champion" on their Side

Interest groups are more likely to get what they want when they have a "champion" on their side.[39] In political science parlance, a champion is a government decision-maker who commands the attention of other government decision-makers and pushes a particular position on some political matter.[40] Basically, if an interest group has a champion it has a government decision-maker pushing its point of view and working toward its goal. Returning to Baumgartner and his colleagues, they find that in many cases an interest group's chances of winning increase when it enlists the help of "government officials as policy advocates."[41] This is especially true if the group is lobbying for the status quo. Champions are most obviously successful on legislation concerning "pet projects." In Washington and across the country, when it comes time to spend government money, legislators are often more than happy to pass bills that contain money that benefits interest groups. For example, in the state of

Louisiana in 2011, the state legislature approved government grants to a number of interest groups including the YMCA and the Greater Urban League of New Orleans, among others.[42] The groups, of course, call themselves "charities" (which they are). But make no mistake about it, they are interest groups that get money from government partially as a result of their lobbying. Certain legislators champion the grants to such groups, which is one reason why they are provided.

Champions are helpful in other situations as well. One way to think about it is like this—as an interest group, no matter what you want from the government, no matter what government you are lobbying, it is better to have a person "on the inside" pushing your point of view. When it comes to champions in legislatures, no group compares to the NRA. Recently, for example, the House of Representatives passed a bill called the National Right to Carry Reciprocity Act, which allows a person from one state who holds a valid "conceal and carry" permit to carry a concealed weapon in any other state that has a "conceal and carry" law. The bill was co-sponsored by Cliff Stearns, a Republican House member from Florida.[43] Cliff Stearns did not need much arm-twisting by the NRA to introduce the bill. He is a die-hard "gun rights" enthusiast, and he works hard to push laws that loosen controls on guns. The NRA has champions like Cliff Stearns—people who believe strongly in their cause—in state legislatures across the country. Having friends in high places helps the group get what it wants.

Having a champion is especially important if a group is trying to get the government to pay attention to something that it is not currently paying attention to. Recall, getting government decision-makers' attention is not always easy. If a lobbyist represents a group working on an issue that government currently is not paying attention to, the lobbyist needs someone in government to say, "Hey, this issue deserves our attention." Interest groups pushing for campaign finance reform at the national level in the 1990s and 2000s discovered the value of having a champion when John McCain (perhaps unexpectedly, given that he is a Republican) pushed their cause in Congress. There is little question that the issue would not have received much attention from the united Republican government in 2001–2002 had not McCain championed the issue. In the end, pro-reform lobbyists received attention from government decision-makers because McCain believed strongly in reform. The Bipartisan Campaign Reform Act was adopted in 2002.

What About Lobbying?

You may have noticed that many of the conditions that determine whether or not government decision-makers respond to interest groups are out of the interest groups' control. It goes without saying, however, that to capitalize on these conditions, an interest group must *lobby*. In other words, an interest group must *try* to influence government decisions in order to do so. But not all lobbying is created equal. Whatever the conditions are, there are some things that interest groups and their lobbyists can do to increase their chances of getting what they want.

It turns out that some lobbying strategies and tactics are more effective than others. In this section, I ask: Which ones? My approach here is similar to the one I took in the last section—I take a probabilistic approach to examining what interest groups can do to improve their chances of affecting government decisions. Political scientists have discovered that some types of lobbying behavior are more likely to lead to success than others. What have they found?

Strategy 1: Entering into Coalitions with Other Interest Groups

Interest groups can improve their chances of success by entering into coalitions with other interest groups. It is impossible to overestimate the value of coalition-building. In a recent insider look at lobbying, lobbying expert Bertram J. Levine writes, "Forming coalitions has become more than a part of legislative politics . . . it *is* legislative politics."[44] Why are coalitions so beneficial? First, a coalition lends credibility to an interest group's demands. If lots of interest groups want something, chances are it will receive serious consideration from government decision-makers. If, however, only one interest group wants something, government decision-makers may be leery. Second, coalitions dampen conflict. As the last section notes, interest groups stand a much better chance of success when they face little or no opposition from other political actors—including other interest groups. By gathering into coalitions, interest groups can defuse conflict. Third, coalitions allow interest groups to pool their resources to create effective lobbying campaigns. By doing this, each coalition participant spends a bit less than it might have, had it "gone it alone."[45]

Coalitions are so important that interest groups of all kinds now regularly seek out coalition partners before they even begin lobbying government decision-makers. Recent battles over health care reform and campaign finance reform, for example, have featured huge active coalitions on both sides.[46] There were coalitions (formal and informal) all over the place in the battle over President Obama's health care plan in 2008 and 2009, including Health Care for America Now (a liberal coalition of over 1,000 labor unions, coalitions, and citizen groups), the Coalition for Patients' Rights (a coalition of professional associations representing non-physician medical professionals), Stop the HIT (Hidden Insurance Tax; an anti-reform coalition of small for-profit businesses), and many, many others. In the end, the pro-reform side won (though it did not get all that it wanted), partially (again) because President Obama favored reform.

Strategy 2: Seeking "Issue Niches"

Interest groups can improve their chances of success by seeking "issue niches." An issue niche is defined as a narrow, highly specific issue identity that allows an interest group to avoid competition and conflict with other interest groups.[47] Some groups are more or less born into issue niches, while others seek them. Let me explain. First, there are some groups whose issues simply are so narrow that not many people care about them, know about them, or oppose them. Groups like these, in my parlance, are born into issue niches. In his epic article "Organized Interests and their Issue Niches: Search for Pluralism in a Policy Domain," political scientist William Browne found that many agricultural groups, including the Corn Refiners Association, the American Frozen Food Institute, and the National Broiler Council (now called the National Chicken Council), had very narrow issue concerns.[48] All of these trade associations cared only about government decisions affecting their rather specialized businesses. Because they did not care too much about lots of issues, they had the field more or less to themselves (there are not, for example, that many groups that care about chickens). This is in contrast to, for example, groups such as the AFL-CIO, the Chamber of Commerce of the United States, the Club for Growth, or the Sierra Club, which take stands on all sorts of issues and thus attract lots of opponents. Second, there are groups that scale back their demands to avoid conflict. Many anti-abortion citizen groups do this—they scale back their demands in an attempt to get what they want. The National Right to Life Committee (NRLC), for example, would probably prefer a constitutional amendment to ban all abortions in the United States. However, because the group knows that amending the Constitution is difficult, it devotes most of its energy to pushing for other, more incremental changes in abortion policy. Over the years, for example, it has lobbied for state legislation regulating abortion (e.g., legislation that mandates waiting periods for abortions, legislation that requires minors to get parental consent for abortion, and legislation that requires a woman to get an ultrasound before an abortion). The NRLC has not given up on its ultimate goal of banning abortion outright in the United States. But to increase its chances of winning, it has over the years scaled back its immediate demands. In effect, when an interest group seeks a niche it is scaling back its demands until it finds something that it thinks it can get, as opposed to something it probably would not be able to get. This allows an interest group to avoid conflict. In many cases, interest groups would rather go to work on a "sure thing" than enter battles they may lose. Many interest groups choose their battles carefully—avoiding those they think they may lose and entering only those they think they can win. This is the essence of niche-seeking behavior.

Strategy 3: Getting the Public on their Side

Interest groups can improve their chances of success by getting the public on their side.[49] Government decision-makers—especially elected government decision-makers—know that going against the wishes of their constituents is politically risky. This is why some interest groups engage in indirect lobbying in the first place—to convince government decision-makers that the public is "on their side." Studies have shown that indirect lobbying can be extremely effective.[50] If an interest group can convince lots of ordinary citizens to contact government decision-makers—be they legislators, legislative staffers, chief executives, chief executive aides, or executive agency personnel—in support of its position, it stands a pretty good chance of getting what it wants.[51] This is the case because government decision-makers, especially elected government decision-makers, are preoccupied with keeping their jobs. Indirect lobbying campaigns aimed at legislators can be particularly effective. As lobbying expert Bertram Levine points out, the ex-legislators he interviewed consistently told him that members of Congress virtually always consider what their constituents want when they decide what to do.[52] Levine quotes one of his respondents as saying, "If it's right for the district, it's right."[53]

In short, believe it or not, government decision-makers are responsive to citizen pressure. If a group successfully can mobilize people and convince government decision-makers that it has lots of public support, it has a pretty good chance of getting what it wants. However, not all interest groups have the ability to mobilize the public on their behalf. What does it take for a group successfully to lobby the public? First, a group must have *money* to lobby the public. As I pointed out in Chapter 7, lobbying the public is not cheap—things like advertisements, direct mail, and telephone trees cost a lot of money. Second, needless to say, an interest group must have the support of a substantial number of ordinary people. Lobbying the public only works if at least *some* ordinary people are receptive to an interest group's message. Some interest groups *know* that they can mobilize a substantial number of citizens on their behalf. In recent years, for example, the National Rifle Association, the National Education Association, and the AFL-CIO have been very successful at mobilizing members to contact government decision-makers on their behalf. What these organizations have in common is the ability to tap a large membership. Interest groups that have few or no members (such as business firms and government entities and think tanks) do not have a "ready-made" base of ordinary citizens that they can count on for support. They may, however, have a clue as to whether or not the public supports them. They can use public opinion polls, surveys, and media accounts to predict how people will respond if they "lobby the public." Any time an interest group thinks it can successfully mobilize lots of ordinary citizens, it will be tempted to do so.

There is something paradoxical about the effect of public opinion on interest group behavior: sometimes it compels interest groups to go to great lengths *not* to get the public involved. Here's an example. Every year the United States government subsidizes the production of oil. The details of the subsidies are a little complicated (they involve tax deductions for certain things), but in the end they amount to a benefit of approximately $5 billion for oil companies each year.[54] Every year since he became president, President Obama has argued that perhaps the subsidies should be eliminated because they cost the taxpayers a lot of money and they seem a bit silly in light of the oil companies' annual profits of over $30 billion. But Congress has never gone along with this idea, seemingly in the thrall of oil company lobbyists. When this issue comes up, the oil companies and their lobbyists do everything *but* lobby the public. They realize that no matter how good their arguments for the subsidies are (and yes, they have reasonable arguments in support of the subsidies), the public probably would not react positively if they knew about them. So oil company lobbyists lobby government decision-makers (especially friendly members of Congress from places like Texas and Louisiana), but they do not lobby the public.

So how can you tell if an interest group will or will not "lobby the public" in an attempt to get what it wants? Here's a rule of thumb. An interest group that thinks it might *lose* a particular political battle has an incentive to get the public involved. For if the public agrees with the potential loser, this may help "turn the tide" in the organization's favor. In contrast, an interest group that thinks it will *win* a particular political battle has no incentive to get the public involved. If the organization is probably going to win anyway, why run the risk of mobilizing opposition?

Strategy 4: Doing a Lot

Interest groups can improve their chances of success by doing a lot. Scaling back *demands* does not mean scaling back *activity*. Though Chapters 5–7 take a piecemeal approach to the examination of lobbying tactics, lobbyists and interest groups take a more integrated approach, using many lobbying tactics at the same time. In other words, during any given political battle, the typical interest group does a lot.[55] It turns out that all this activity makes sense. One giant study of interest group influence conducted in the 1980s (probably the second most expansive and thorough study of influence after the Baumgartner et al. study I mention above) shows that *the more an interest group does, the more likely it is to get what it wants.*[56] Overall, doing more is better than doing less. This does not mean that interest groups should lobby on lots of different issues, or engage in lots of different political battles. What it means is that when interest groups *do* decide to enter a policy battle, they should do everything they possibly can. "Doing a lot" means different things in different contexts. But in general, no matter what kind of decision an interest group is trying to affect, it means interacting with decision-makers *across* institutions and levels of government. This means lobbying multiple branches (i.e., legislative, judicial, executive) of government, as well as lobbying multiple levels (i.e., state, local, and federal) of government. Second, it means lobbying multiple actors *within* each institution of government. If an interest group lobbies Congress or a state legislature, for example, it should lobby lots of legislators and committees rather than just one or a few.

The value of doing more means that *money* is important to an interest group's success. It is not the case that interest groups with lots of money always win and those without money always lose. In fact, studies of interest group influence consistently show that money is not a determining factor in most political decisions. In other words, in many cases it is not true that the group with the most money wins. This is an important point (partially because no one seems to believe it is true), so it deserves some explication. To begin this explication, I will return for a moment to Baumgartner and his colleagues because they have studied the influence of money on government decisions most thoroughly and extensively. One of the things that their study shows is that though many political battles do not engender conflict between interest groups, many others do. In fact, the majority of issues they studied featured two well-defined sides—that is, one side comprising lots of interest groups lobbying for something, and another side comprising lots of interest groups lobbying against something. If you pay attention to American politics you probably have seen this for yourself. For example, battles over education, gay rights, immigration reform, spending, taxing, and lots of other things feature vocal and well-heeled groups on both sides. In seeking to determine the impact of money on specific political decisions, Baumgartner and his colleagues look not at which *group* has the most money, but at which *side* has the most money. And when they look at dozens of political decisions (some very important, others not so important), they conclude that it is *not* the case that the side with the most money wins. In fact, in lots of the cases they examine, the side with the most money does not win.

In short, Baumgartner and his colleagues conclude that money is not an important predictor of an interest group's success. Why does money not seem to matter much? Baumgartner and his colleagues explain this counterintuitive finding as follows. They say that if one group spends a whole lot of money on one side of an issue the issue is probably pretty important. From here they argue that if an issue is important to one group, it is probably (but not definitely) important to other groups. And some of these groups, they argue, do not agree with the stand of the first group. By the time the battle is really pitched, the first group has attracted allied groups (because the issue is important) *and* opposition groups (because the issue is important). In the end, spending on one side, they find, begets spending on the opposite side. So as spending goes up, so does interest group conflict and opposition. And when there is interest group conflict and opposition, the chances of a specific interest group getting what it wants plummet.

In sum, Baumgartner and his colleagues conclude that money cannot buy political success. By now you might be asking yourself: "Why is he saying money cannot buy success when two pages ago he wrote that money is important to an interest group's success?" The main reason is that I want you to know that money is not all that matters. To prove my point, I will return to the NAMBLA example I used at the beginning of this book. Even if NAMBLA had $10 billion, its "the law should be changed to allow men to have sex with boys" message probably would not go over particularly well. This is an extreme example, of course, but it makes my point—money is not everything. But this does not mean that money does not matter. It does. In a recent study of the Wisconsin state legislature, Nathan Grasse and Brianne Heidbreder show that when two sides compete to affect the passage of a bill, the side that logs the most lobbying hours has a higher probability of winning.[57] More money means more lobbying hours. And doing more, as this study shows, is better than doing less. And it's not just hours that money can buy. The more money an interest group has, the more lobbyists it can hire, the more government decision-makers it can see, and the more levels and institutions of government it can approach. And returning to the main point of this section, more money gives an interest group and its allies the ability to engage in indirect lobbying, which can be very expensive.

I would like to make one final point about money. Virtually all studies of lobbying show that in order to succeed in any given political battle an interest group must *show up*. If a group does not show up, it has little or no voice in the political process and it has ceded the field to other political actors.[58] Showing up costs money. It does not always cost a lot of money, but it does cost money. Returning to another point made earlier, government attention is a scarce commodity. At every level of government there is a limited number of things that government decision-makers are willing to take on. To get government to pay attention to an issue, having an interest group pushing that issue is crucially important. Many issues, it turns out, never make it on to what political scientists call "the governmental agenda" (that is, the list of things the government pays attention to). Numerous studies show that interest groups can be very, very effective at setting the governmental agenda.[59] Interest groups can play a powerful signaling role for government decision-makers. In other words, interest group activity can send a signal to government decision-makers that the public actually cares about an issue. And this signal may be enough to get the government to pay attention to the issue.

In the end, all disclaimers notwithstanding, there is no question that *ceteris paribus*, an interest group with lots of money has a better chance of getting what it wants than an interest group without lots of money. As Baumgartner and his colleagues note:

> [Our] findings do not suggest that it is better in politics to be poor than rich; a large membership, an ample staff, sufficient budget to organize large events, and established linkages with policy makers that come from multiple contacts are the fundamentals of effective lobbying day-in and day-out.[60]

It is good to have money.

Strategy 5: Contributing Money to Government Decision-Makers' Campaigns

Interest groups can improve their chances of success by contributing money to government decision-makers' campaigns. Money does not buy government decision-makers. It can, however, buy *access* to government decision-makers. Government decision-makers pay more attention to interest groups that give them money than they do to interest groups that do not give them money.[61] This does not mean that interest groups that make campaign contributions always get what they want or that interest groups that do not give away money never get what they want. It does mean, however, that if an interest group does not make campaign contributions its ability to interact with government decision-makers is limited. And the ability to interact with government decision-makers—to present them with information—is absolutely crucial to an interest group's success. The value of campaign contributions—like the value of doing a lot—highlights the importance of money in lobbying. The more money an interest group has, the more government decision-makers it can support. And the more government decision-makers it can support, the more doors the group can open for its lobbyists.

There is some debate in the scholarly literature about whether or not money does indeed buy access, and many scholars say that it does not.[62] But my reading of the literature, as well as my conversations with lobbyists, lead me to conclude that money does indeed help buy access. This does not mean that money is all it takes to gain access to a government decision-maker. A hypothetical example will illustrate the role money plays in buying access. Imagine you are an elected official, let's say a state legislator. You go to lunch one day and when you return you find out from your secretary that two people called you and want you to call them back. One of them is a man who gave you $1,000 for your reelection campaign last year. The other is a man who gave you $0 for your reelection campaign last year. Who are you going to call back? And if you decide to call both of them back, who are you going to call back first? I hate to resort to a hypothetical example to make my point. But the point needs to be made, and lots of research backs it up.

In sum, money cannot buy influence. But it can buy other things. Precisely what money can buy is the subject of Box 9.2.

Box 9.2 What Money Can Buy

People who study interest groups have a very hard time showing that money buys influence. In fact, many of the studies cited in this chapter show just the opposite—that money does *not* buy influence. In sum, there just is not very much evidence that lobbyists can get what they want by passing money around. But any lobbyist and any interest group will tell you that it is better to have lots of money than not very much money.

So if money can't buy influence, what can it buy? The research suggests there are several answers. First, money can buy really good lobbyists. Many former high-ranking government decision-makers become lobbyists after they leave government. And not surprisingly, these lobbyists are expensive. Having a lot of money allows a group to hire a well-connected, well-informed lobbyist. Second, money can help a group engage in indirect lobbying. As this chapter points out, indirect lobbying techniques are considered very effective by lobbyists. But they are not cheap. Buying media time, especially on television or in major publications, can be expensive. To reach a lot of people takes money. Third, money allows a group to do more. Studies indicate that, *ceteris paribus*, groups that do more are more successful than groups that do less. Having more money allows a group to hire more lobbyists who can interact with more government decision-makers in more branches of government over longer periods of time. Fourth, money can buy access. Though there is some debate in the scholarly world about this point, interviews with government decision-makers and lobbyists themselves indicate that money (in the form of campaign contributions) does indeed buy access for interest groups. Again, this does not mean that money buys influence. But there is ample evidence that money can help a group gets its lobbyists' "feet in the door." And having more money allows a group to give money to more government decision-makers and thus obtain access to more of these decision-makers.

It simply is not the case that money can buy influence. But there is plenty of evidence that there are things that money can buy for an interest group; and these things can help an interest group get what it wants from government.

Source: Author's research.

Strategy 6: Hiring Good Lobbyists

Interest groups can improve their chances of success by hiring good lobbyists. Finally, there is evidence that interest groups with good lobbyists have more success than interest groups with bad lobbyists. This is an obvious point, but it begs the question: What makes a good lobbyist? If you recall, Chapter 5 addressed this question. I will not recapitulate that answer here. So go back and look at Chapter 5. One thing I will add to that discussion here, however, is that once again, money helps. Not surprisingly, some lobbyists are better than others, and the best tend to be more expensive than the worst. In other words, experienced, seasoned, expert lobbyists cost more to hire than inexperienced, unseasoned, neophyte lobbyists. This is yet one more reason why money matters to interest groups.

Conclusion: How Powerful are Interest Groups?

Public opinion polls and surveys show that overwhelming majorities of Americans believe that "special interests" dominate government decision-making. Are the public's perceptions accurate? *Do* interest groups get what they want from government while the views of ordinary citizens are virtually ignored? My answer to this question represents a bit of an anticlimax. For in the end, I must answer with a resounding: *It depends*.

The primary message of this chapter is this: sometimes interest groups get what they want from government and sometimes they don't. Anyone who tells you that interest groups always win or that ordinary citizens always "get the shaft" is wrong. The real world of politics, as scholars of policy domains have noted, is too messy, contentious, and unpredictable to support broad and sweeping generalizations about the power and influence of interest groups. Each and every government decision is the result of an exceedingly complex and multifaceted process that involves many factors. Interest group lobbying is one of these factors. In some battles—those, for example, where the public is unengaged and uninvolved—interest groups typically exert some (often a great deal of) influence over government decisions. In other battles—those, for example, that involve highly salient, ideologically charged issues or those where the public is heavily involved and highly engaged—interest groups typically exert little or no influence.

In the end, it is clear that interest groups are powerful players in American politics. As pluralists noted fifty years ago, interest groups are left out of very few important political battles. It is just as clear, however, that interest groups do *not* dominate and control American politics. Despite considerable public cynicism, there is plenty of evidence that "when push comes to shove," government decision-makers do what their constituents want them to do—even if this conflicts with the desires of powerful "special interests."

What's Next

The short answer to the question "What's next?" is "Not much." My overview of the world of interest groups is now over. To conclude the book, I will offer a few thoughts about the nature of interest group politics in America. I will also provide an explanation for the paradox of interest groups.

Conclusion: The Role of Interest Groups in American Politics

10

In this book, I have attempted to describe what interest groups are, what they do, and what role they play in American politics. For better or worse, interest groups have been central features of the American political landscape since the founding of the republic. In the end, a full understanding of the American political system requires an understanding of interest group politics. I hope that this book has provided you with the raw material you need to begin making sense of the complex and ever-changing world of interest groups.

In this final chapter, I will do two things. First, I will attempt to explain the paradox of interest groups—that is, the fact that on the one hand, most Americans support interest groups by joining, identifying, or sympathizing with them; yet on the other, most Americans hate interest groups and think they are too powerful. At the heart of my explanation for this paradox is the fact that interest groups do both bad and good, foster both equality and inequality, and ultimately, embody both what is commendable and what is contemptible about American politics. Second, I will ask: Are interest groups good or bad for American democracy? This question has concerned democratic theorists, interest group scholars, and ordinary citizens since the dawn of the republic. As I mentioned in Chapter 1, the father of the Constitution himself —James Madison—grappled with this very question while writing the Constitution. Now it's my turn to weigh in.

Explaining the Paradox

Most Americans have mixed feelings about interest groups. Why? A closer look at the preceding nine chapters can help us answer this question. For starters, let's take a look at the first two chapters. In Chapter 1, I tried to show you that the universe of interest groups in the United States is huge. In Chapter 2, I tried to show you that the universe of interest groups in the United States is diverse. To get an idea of how the combination of size, variety, and diversity fosters ambivalence about interest groups, let's look at a hypothetical situation. Assume for a moment that you have two people in the room with you: Terry, an abortion opponent; and Pat, an abortion rights supporter. We ask Pat and Terry what they think about interest groups. Terry says, "I admire the National Right to Life Committee and the American Life League. They do good work by trying to put an end to the despicable practice of abortion." Pat says, "I admire Planned Parenthood and the NARAL Pro-Choice America. They do good work by trying to put an end to despicable laws that deny women the right to choose." In sum, both Pat and Terry *like* the interest groups that represent the causes they support. But this is not the whole story. After hearing Terry wax positively about anti-abortion interest groups, Pat moderates his/her position on interest groups. Pat says, "I detest the National Right to Life Committee and the American Life League. They actively work against women's interests!" Similarly, after hearing Pat sing the praises of pro-abortion rights organizations, Terry says, "I detest Planned Parenthood and NARAL Pro-Choice America. They actively work to deprive children of the right to life!" The point of this hypothetical example is simple. Most of us are like Pat and Terry—the diversity of the interest group universe means that we can find some interest groups that we like *and* some interest groups that we dislike. Moreover, the size of the interest group universe means that most of us can find more than one interest group that we like and more than one interest group that we dislike. Like accompanied by dislike—this is the definition of ambivalence. And it helps explain the paradox of interest groups.

Chapter 3, which delineates the substantial barriers to interest group formation and survival, also partially explains Americans' ambivalence about interest groups. How? On the one hand, Chapter 3 provides evidence that the substantial barriers to interest group formation and survival can be overcome through hard work, perseverance, and strong leadership. This happy fact helps explain why many people value interest groups and the work they do. It also reinforces the American ideal that people who work hard will be rewarded for this hard work. In the case of interest groups, it means that if people band together and believe in something, they can form an interest group and be heard. On the other hand, Chapter 3 shows that because there are substantial barriers to the formation and survival of interest groups, the distribution of interest groups in the United States does not reflect the distribution of *opinions* in the population as a whole. Moreover, it means that institutions, especially business firms, have a disproportionate presence in the universe of interest groups. All of this helps explain why many people dislike interest groups and the work they do. In the end, what we know about interest group formation and survival is bound to foster ambivalence. While it is nice to know that the barriers to interest group formation and survival can be overcome through hard work, it's disconcerting to know that interest group representation is skewed toward the interests of businesses, and intense and/or well-heeled elites.

In Chapters 4 and 5, we learned about lobbyists and what they do. On the whole, lobbyists deploy a wide variety of techniques, contact a wide array of government decision-makers, and develop as many professional relationships as possible. How do Chapters 4 and 5 help us elucidate the paradox of interest groups? On the one hand, the chapters paint a picture of lobbying that con-tradicts the conventional wisdom. They show that contrary to many of our predispositions, most lobbyists are hard-working professionals who spend a great deal of time monitoring government and providing information to government decision-makers. They also show that the typical lobbyist performs his/her job ethically, responsibly, and honestly. On the other hand, Chapters 4 and 5 contain disquieting information about interest groups and the work they do. For example, Chapter 5 shows that an incredible number of lobbyists spend an incredible amount of time trying to influence government decision-makers. This raises the disturbing possibility that our representatives listen to lobbyists rather than their constituents or consciences. After all, lobbyists spend a lot of time trying to affect government decisions, but do you? In addition, Chapters 4 and 5 suggest that the halls of government are teeming with lobbyists. Everywhere government decisions are made, lobbyists are there. This, of course, is exactly what James Madison warned about in *Federalist #10*. My overall portrait of direct lobbying cannot help but heighten our collective ambivalence about interest groups. While it is comforting to know that most lobbyists are ethical and honest people who rely on facts and figures rather than bribes and lies to make their cases, it is not so comforting to know that despite the wishes of the founders of this country, tens of thousands of lobbyists spend untold sums of money trying to influence government decisions.

At the end of Chapter 5, I tried to show that some forms of lobbying entail contact with government decision-makers outside of formal governmental processes. In a form of lobbying known as informal direct lobbying, lobbyists pressure government decision-makers to do their bidding. What does this discussion add to our explanation of the paradox of interest groups? On the one hand, the section on informal lobbying shows that lobbyists sometimes resort to questionable practices to achieve their goals. Bribery, for example, is not unheard of. Furthermore, the end of Chapter 5 suggests that a number of questionable practices such as gift giving, favor providing, and "schmoozing" remain important weapons in the lobbyist's arsenal. On the other hand, the end of Chapter 5 suggests that informal direct lobbying may not be as bad as you think it is. For one thing, informal direct lobbying is a lot less sleazy than it used to be. Moreover, the evidence suggests that even when lobbyists and government decision-makers do get together informally, their main activity is exchanging information. And finally, the data suggest that most lobbyists are well-educated elite experts rather than unctuous sleazebags. Arguably, my discussion of informal direct lobbying summons more reasons to dislike interest groups than to like them. Ultimately, the problem with informal lobbying is that it may compromise the ability of government decision-makers to make good and fair decisions.

Chapter 6 contains a paradox all its own. While it shows that giving money *directly* to government decision-makers to influence their decisions is against the law, it also details how interest groups use *campaign* money to try to influence elected officials. This paradox is explained by the fact that though direct contributions from most interest groups to elected officials are against federal law, direct contributions from PACs, as well as a number of other techniques of electoral lobbying (including in some places direct contributions), are perfectly legal. Like the chapters that precede it, Chapter 6 helps explain our collective ambivalence about interest groups. On the one hand, it suggests that money can distort government decisions. Though money may not buy elected officials, it certainly buys something—be it access or small favors. Moreover, the importance of money in electoral campaigns means that some candidates—those who are not especially attractive to well-funded interest groups—may be disqualified from running for public office. On the other hand, Chapter 6 suggests that electoral lobbying may not be as bad as you think. First of all, most monetary contributions to candidates are rather small. Furthermore, because most elected officials receive campaign support and help from many interest groups that already share their basic political philosophy, most contributions are more like happy coincidences than bribes. All told, widespread distrust of "moneyed interests" helps to explain antipathy toward interest groups. At the same time, few Americans are comfortable with the idea of outlawing political contributions. In the end, we are left with the uneasy feeling that while electoral lobbying—especially contributing money—may not be particularly good for America, restricting what organizations can do with their money may not be a very good idea either.

In Chapter 7, I tried to show that some lobbying is aimed at ordinary citizens rather than government decision-makers. Indirect lobbying is designed either to influence people's attitudes and opinions or to encourage people to contact government decision-makers. Like Chapters 1–6, Chapter 7 helps explain the paradox of interest groups by providing good reasons to like interest groups and good reasons to dislike interest groups. First, let's look at the good. Chapter 7 clearly shows that indirect lobbying generally entails the provision of information. It is not simple demagoguery and "arm-twisting." In addition, Chapter 7 shows that indirect lobbying may promote true democracy by encouraging citizens to contact their representatives. Now let's look at the bad. One troubling aspect of indirect lobbying is that it is easy to "fake." Though many government decision-makers are able to distinguish real indirect lobbying campaigns from phony ones, slick operators can still fool them. Another potentially disturbing thing about indirect lobbying is that it may exacerbate the problem with intense minority opinions identified in Chapter 3. The effectiveness of indirect lobbying puts a premium on an interest group's ability to produce lots and lots of citizen contact with government decision-makers. This means that government decision-makers often hear not from the majority of American citizens, but from intense minorities of citizens instead. Finally, indirect lobbying is precisely what the founders of this country feared. As I pointed out in Chapter 2, the founders abhorred the idea of direct democracy and built a system that would put the brakes on popular movements driven by temporary passions. Indirect lobbying encourages immediate and passionate citizen responses to serious societal problems. This may make it much more difficult for our representatives to weigh their options, engage in lengthy and serious deliberation, and do the right thing. In short, depending on your perspective, indirect lobbying is either a positive inducement to political participation or yet another underhanded way for interest groups to foil majority opinion and get their way. Most likely, you are like me, and you see both the good and the bad in indirect lobbying.

Chapter 8 explores the relationships that interest groups have with political parties. To be honest, the information in Chapter 8 does not do a whole lot to illuminate or explain the paradox of interest groups. The chapter is designed to give you a basic understanding of how interest groups and political parties compete and interact. Chapter 9, in contrast, provides a great deal of information that illuminates the paradox of interest groups. It begins by noting that large majorities of Americans believe that government decision-makers respond much more to interest groups than they do to ordinary citizens. Are these fears warranted? The answer seems to be *maybe*. Like all of the previous chapters, Chapter 9 provides reasons to worry and reasons not to worry. I will begin with the reasons not to worry. First, Chapter 9 suggests that there is no "power elite" in American politics. The voluminous research on American politics suggests that it simply is not the case that one or a few interest groups dominate politics in the United States. Government decisions are generally made in permeable and large issue domains, most of which are open to competing claims and interest groups. Second, Chapter 9 cites a great deal of research which unequivocally shows that government decision-makers seldom ignore the views of their constituents. The bottom line is this: in cases in which interest groups want one thing and a majority of citizens want another, government decision-makers tend to go with the citizens rather than the interest groups. Third, Chapter 9 shows that there is no sure-fire way for interest groups to get what they want all the time. The real world of politics is messy, unpredictable, and protean. Finally, Chapter 9 suggests that it would be exceptionally difficult for any single interest group to take over American politics. Interest groups are most successful when they keep their demands limited and narrow.

So if the research shows that interest groups do *not* in fact dominate American politics, why should we worry? First of all, Chapter 9 shows that interest groups *do* get what they want from government some of the time. Government decision-makers are indeed responsive to interest groups. In many cases, government decision-makers are not forced to choose between what their constituents and the public want and what interest groups want because lobbyists ask government for things about which most ordinary citizens know and care little. A second cause for worry is that money increases an interest group's chances of getting its way. To put it briefly, though money cannot buy influence, it sure helps. Understandably, this makes many Americans uneasy. In the end, like the chapters before it, Chapter 9 helps to explain our collective ambivalence about interest groups. On the one hand, it shows that government decision-makers do not ignore the views of ordinary Americans. On the other hand, it shows that because most of us are unengaged in politics, government decision-makers often do what interest groups want them to do. In the end, this may lead to government decisions that favor interest groups but are not particularly good for the country as a whole.

So Are Interest Groups Good or Bad?

Here's how I would summarize my explanation for the paradox of interest groups. There's a lot to like about interest groups, but there's a lot to dislike about them too. It's that simple. The preceding section was designed to show you that each and every chapter of this book provides good reasons to value interest groups and the work they do, as well as good reasons to deprecate interest groups and the work they do. But we're not through. One question continues to haunt us—a question that has probably been in the back of your mind since you began reading this book. That question is this: Does the bulk of the information suggest that interest groups in America are good or bad? In other words, are interest groups good for American democracy or bad for American democracy? The answer to this question is that it depends upon who you talk to. In closing this book, I will present two conflicting views of contemporary interest group politics in America. One is that interest groups are good for American politics. The other is that they are bad. Let's take a close look at each point of view.

Interest Groups: Not So Bad and Maybe Even Good

The late interest group expert William P. Browne wrote an ardent defense of interest groups in his book called *Groups, Interests, and U.S. Public Policy*. The book is a little old (it was published in 1998), but its argument still resonates. Because Browne is the most convincing defender of interest groups that I know of, I will spend a little time here exploring his thoughts. In defense of interest groups, Browne argues that they "fit in" well in contemporary American politics, and serve as important linkage institutions between citizens and government decision-makers. In the end, Browne says, interest groups reflect the reality of American politics. He writes that interest group politics "does fairly well fit daily empirical reality. And daily American political reality, throughout society, is dominated by factionalized selfishness and narrow visions."[1] Browne acknowledges that interest groups are selfish in the sense that they want something for themselves. But, he argues, who doesn't? If you are competing for a job with another person and you want that job for yourself, you are by definition hoping to deprive someone else of something they want. This makes you selfish. But does it make you bad? Or evil? No— it makes you human. Interest groups, Browne argues, are like us—they are selfish. They want things that make them and their constituents better off— sometimes at the expense of others. *Selfish*, according to Browne, is not the same as *bad*.

Browne realizes that interest groups have bad reputations mostly because ordinary people believe that they dominate politics and leave the "little people" like you and me powerless. This view, Browne argues, is hogwash. First of all,

Browne points out (and Chapter 3 reiterates) that in America practically any group of people (and any person for that matter) can form an interest group. Ordinary citizens of all kinds can form political organizations and defend their interests before government. While there are barriers to interest group formation and maintenance, Browne notes that "[interest] groups are easily formed, in large part because many Americans have come, or have been led, to believe that political participation is necessary and expected, and produces a social or personal value."[2] In other words, ordinary citizens like you and me are not shut out of the political process. We can be and often are represented by our own interest groups. The interest groups that we support may not always win, but they are often at the table when political decisions are made. In the end, Browne concludes, "Nearly everyone gets represented in America by someone, more or less."[3]

Continuing his defense of interest groups, Browne argues that ordinary citizens are inherently involved in most lobbying campaigns. Ordinary citizens, he notes, are now important targets of lobbying campaigns. Fifteen years after his book was written this is truer than ever. According to Browne, interest groups lose if they ignore or defy ordinary Americans. This is why interest groups try so hard to convince ordinary citizens that they are right. Most Americans, Browne says, are not stupid. They don't just respond *willy-nilly* to the first rich interest group that sends them a letter, calls them, or advertises in the newspaper. To convince people that its way is the right way, an interest group must make a good case. If it fails to do so, Browne argues, it will probably fail in its efforts to influence government decision-makers.

Browne has an interesting take on the types of informal lobbying discussed in Chapter 5. This type of lobbying, Browne writes, may be troubling to you, but in the end usually comprises "an unproductive show, a silly waltz" that produces nothing.[4] "[M]uch personalized political networking," he says, "is indeed wasted time, even as it's sold as so important."[5] In other words, a lot of lobbying produces nothing in the way of results. What does get results, according to Browne, is indirect lobbying that succeeds in mobilizing lots of ordinary people, and forging coalitions with other interest groups. This is good, Browne says, because it means that interest groups are likely to win *only* when they have some reasonable base of support among the general public. Any interest group that "goes it alone" or pushes things that are unpopular with the public will probably fail miserably. No government decision-maker, after all, wants to defy the public.

Finally, there is the question of money. Browne recognizes that the most vehement critics of contemporary interest group politics are most worried about the potential of money to distort democracy, privilege certain interests over others, and generally thwart the will of the public. How does Browne counter critics of big money politics? He argues that money really does not buy very much. (Some of the research cited in Chapter 9 supports this conclusion.) First of all, Browne points out that for many interest groups campaign money is simply "the price of admission" for lobbying. In this sense, money serves no purpose other than to inform government decision-makers that a lobbyist is "around." What money buys in the end, according to Browne, is a little recognition. Second, Browne argues that money does not buy government decision-makers. Some government decision-makers accept money from interest groups, Browne notes, because they, like most of us, are selfish. But this doesn't mean that they are easily bought. There are too many examples of big money contributors losing in the game of politics, Browne argues, for us to conclude that money can purchase political influence.[6]

In the end, Browne paints a fairly benign view of contemporary interest group politics. While he acknowledges that interest groups are selfish, he argues that this hardly is an indictment. Selfish, after all, is not the same as evil. Besides, interest groups in America represent real people. They are important linkage institutions between ordinary citizens and the government. Government decision-makers, he says, do indeed listen to lobbyists and respond to them. But this does not mean that they ignore the wishes of ordinary citizens. In fact, in deciding precisely what they will lobby for, interest groups often consider the views of ordinary citizens. For they recognize that if they ask for too much they will likely lose. In closing his book, Browne notes that though interest groups and their lobbyists have often convinced government decision-makers to do things they otherwise might not have done, "lobbyists haven't sold much that the nation as a whole found either anathema or absolutely wrong at the time."[7]

Interest Groups: Pretty Bad

Browne's rather sanguine view of interest group politics is not shared by everyone. Some political scientists, in fact, believe that the state of contemporary interest group politics is quite distressing. Allan Cigler and Burdett Loomis, for example, two scholars who have studied interest groups for over thirty years, conclude that contemporary interest group politics in the United States may just be bad for democracy.[8] There are two major problems, they argue. First, business is disproportionately represented by interest groups before government. We know this to be the case, they argue, because study after study (some of these studies are cited in Chapter 3) shows that business firms dominate interest representation at all levels of government. In short, when government decisions are made, businesses invariably are there. Second, interest group representation is skewed toward the interests of the upper class. Interest groups that *do* represent individuals rather than institutions—and Cigler and Loomis acknowledge that there are lots of them—tend to represent the interests not of ordinary Americans, but rather represent the interests of a narrow stratum of wealthy and privileged individuals.

Cigler and Loomis are quite guarded in their conclusions, and they do not argue that interest groups per se are bad. Rather, they argue that contemporary interest group politics is dominated by a relatively small number of wealthy, mostly corporate interest groups that have enough money to dominate most political battles. Most political battles, they argue, are not between the haves and the have-nots. Rather, they are between one set of haves and another set of haves. While Cigler and Loomis acknowledge that there are large numbers of not-so-wealthy, non-corporate interest groups out there, they nonetheless are troubled that moneyed corporate interest groups are so prominent at all levels of government.

Cigler and Loomis cannot prove that interest groups representing the wealthiest Americans and institutions have dominated American politics over the past few decades. But there are, they say, troubling signs that this is indeed the case. First, they note that economic inequality has become more pronounced in recent years. They note that the top 1 percent of income earners in the United States now possesses 35 percent of our national wealth.[9] This is compared to 31 percent in 1960, and only 20 percent in 1980. It is hard to argue, they say, that some of this inequality is not the result of government decisions tilted toward the rich and powerful. Second, Cigler and Loomis conclude that "investment banks, corporations, and tax specialists" have fared disproportionately well in recent years due to their incessant lobbying.[10] In light of giant federal government bailouts of Wall Street firms in the late 2000s, it is hard to argue with them on this point. While it is hard to prove that these types of interests win while the rest of us lose, it is not hard to prove either that they seem to be ubiquitous in the halls of government or that they seem to be doing quite well when the rest of America is struggling.

In the end, Cigler and Loomis conclude that though the poor and the middle class are indeed represented by interest groups, they are not as *effectively* represented by interest groups as wealthy people are.[11] Money, as we learned in Chapter 9, can help interest groups buy effective representation. It takes money, for example, to hire good lobbyists. It also takes money to launch effective indirect lobbying campaigns. Again, Cigler and Loomis admit that they cannot prove that interest groups representing the corporate and the wealthy dominate American politics. They point out, however, that the clues supporting this view are everywhere.

Cigler and Loomis echo the sentiments of many Americans who believe that American politics is disproportionately affected by well-heeled interest groups that represent the wealthiest institutions and individuals in the country. Do the rest of us stand a chance when the wealthiest have so much cash to spend on politics and so many groups representing the institutions for which they work and the groups they join? Maybe not. This question is especially trenchant given that political campaigns keep getting more and more expensive.

Contemporary Interest Group Politics: So Where Do You Stand?

Of course, I have really only begun to scratch the surface of these two complex arguments. Using the information you have encountered in this book, think about these issues and reach your own conclusions.

A Final Thought

Ultimately, I have tried to show in this book that interest groups are *us*—they represent the causes we support, as well as the institutions that we work for and buy things from. It is a fact of life that some of us don't like each other's political views very much. And it is clear that some of us are better represented by interest groups than others. It is also clear that some of us are more successful than others at getting what we want from government. As long as these things hold true, our ambivalence about interest groups is likely to remain.

So where does all this leave us? Well, it leaves me satisfied that I have told you a lot of what I know about interest groups; maybe not everything you need to know, but a lot. I hope that all this information leaves you better informed about interest groups and the role they play in American politics. Remember, however, that American politics changes quickly. So keep your eyes and ears open.

Notes

1 Interest Groups in the United States

1 Tom Hamburger and Julia Love, "Gulf Disaster a Boon to Washington Lobbying," *Los Angeles Times* online, July 21, 2010, accessed February 4, 2011, http://articles.latimes.com/2010/jul/21/nation/la-na-oil-lobby-20100722.
2 Anna Palmer, "BP's Influence in Washington Fades," *CNNMoney.com*, June 16, 2010, accessed February 5, 2011, http://money.cnn.com/2010/06/16/news/companies/BP_lobbying_Washington.fortune/index.htm.
3 Hamburger and Love, "Gulf Disaster a Boon to Washington Lobbying."
4 Jeffrey M. Jones, "Lobbyists Debut at Bottom of Honesty and Ethics List: Nurses Again Perceived as Having Highest Honesty and Ethical Standards," *Gallup.com*, December 10, 2007, accessed February 4, 2011, http://www.gallup.com/poll/103123/lobbyists-debut-bottom-honesty-ethics-list.aspx.
5 Gallup Poll, "Major Institutions," *PollingReport.com* online, July 8–11, 2011, accessed February 3, 2011, http://www.pollingreport.com/institut.htm.
6 James Madison, "Federalist #10: The Utility of the Union as a Safeguard Against Domestic Faction and Insurrection (continued)," *Constitution.org*, accessed February 5, 2011, http://www.constitution.org/fed/federa10.htm.
7 U.S. Chamber of Commerce, "About the U.S. Chamber of Commerce," accessed February 11, 2011, http://www.uschamber.com/about.
8 Robert H. Salisbury, "Interest Representation: The Dominance of Institutions," *American Political Science Review* 78 (1984), 64–76.
9 Salisbury, "Interest Representation," 65.
10 This is paraphrased from William H. Riker, *Liberalism Against Populism: A Confrontation Between the Theory of Democracy and the Theory of Social Choice* (San Francisco: W.H. Freeman, 1982), 291.
11 To get an idea of just how many business firms are active in politics, see *National Directory of Corporate Public Affairs, 2011* (Bethesda, MD: Columbia Books, 2011).
12 *National Directory of Corporate Public Affairs.*

13 Richard A. Harris, "Politicized Management: The Changing Face of Business in American Politics," in *Remaking American Politics*, eds. Richard A. Harris and Sidney M. Milkis (Boulder, CO: Westview Press, 1992), 261–88.

14 Secretary of State Debra Bowen, ed., *The Lobbying Directory 2011–2012* (Sacramento, CA: State of California, 2011), accessed June 27, 2011, http://www.sos.ca.gov/prd/Lobbying_Directory.pdf.

15 Texas Ethics Commission, *2011 List of Registered Lobbyists with Employers/Clients (EMP/C), Sorted by Lobbyist Name* (Austin, TX: State of Texas, Texas Ethics Commission 2011), accessed June 23, 2011, http://www.ethics.state.tx.us/tedd/2011_Lobby_List_by_Lobbyists.pdf.

16 The businesses may be non-profit businesses, for-profit businesses, or both. Some trade associations allow individual membership as well.

17 William P. Browne and Allan J. Cigler, eds., *U.S. Agricultural Groups: Institutional Profiles* (Westport, CT: Greenwood Press, 1990).

18 National Education Association, "About NEA," accessed February 14, 2011, http://www.nea.org/home/2580.htm.

19 International Brotherhood of Teamsters, "About Us," accessed April 4, 2011, http://www.teamster.org/content/fast-facts.

20 AFL-CIO, "About Us," accessed January 31, 2012, http://www.aflcio.org/aboutus/.

21 Ricardo Alonso-Zaldivar and Stephen Ohlemacher, "House Republicans Seek IRS Probe of AARP," *WKYC.com*, March 30, 2011, accessed April 4, 2011, http://www.wkyc.com/news/article/183221/16/House-Republicans-seek-IRS-probe-of-AARP-.

22 Jeffrey Sparshott, "House Lawmakers Set Hearing On AARP's Insurance, Advocacy Efforts," *Wall Street Journal* online, March 25, 2011, accessed April 4, 2011, http://online.wsj.com/article/BT-CO-20110325-710474.html.

23 James G. McGann, "Academics to Ideologues: A Brief History of the Public Policy Research Industry," *PS* 25 (1992), 733–40.

24 Check out Citizens for Tax Justice website at http://www.ctj.org/index.php.

25 This definition comes (though marginally amended) from Alan Rosenthal, *The Third House: Lobbyists and Lobbying in the States, 2nd edition* (Washington, DC: CQ Press, 2001), 148.

26 Coalition for Patients' Rights, "About Us," accessed February 14, 2011, http://www.patientsrightscoalition.org/About-Us.aspx.

27 This example comes from Clyde Wilcox, "The Dynamics of Lobbying the Hill," in *The Interest Group Connection: Electioneering, Lobbying, and Policymaking in Washington*, eds. Paul S. Herrnson, Ronald G. Shaiko, and Clyde Wilcox (Chatham, NJ: Chatham House, 1998), 89–99.

28 Check out BALCONY's website at http://www.balconynewyork.com/.

29 Check out the American Coalition for Ethanol's website at http://www.ethanol.org/.

30 North Carolina Coalition for Lobbying Reform, "Coalition Members," accessed June 30, 2011, http://www.nclobbyreform.org/about/members.php.

31 In some cases, however, other types of interest groups may contribute money to candidates for state and local office. This is the case because campaign finance laws vary from place to place.

32 Unaffiliated PACs are also referred to as "non-connected PACs."

33 Federal Election Commission, "PAC Activity Remains Steady in 2009," accessed April 10, 2011, http://www.fec.gov/press/press2010/20100406PAC.shtml.

34 Federal Election Commission, "PAC Activity Remains Steady in 2009."

35 Technically, the AARP is four different organizations—AARP, AARP Foundation, AARP Services Inc., and AARP Global Network.

36 This whole discussion tracks my discussion of government decisions found in my earlier book, Anthony J. Nownes, *Total Lobbying: What Lobbyists Want (and How They Try to Get It)* (New York: Cambridge University Press, 2006), 4.

2 The Evolution of Interest Groups in the United States

1 This is an estimate based on many sources including: *Encyclopedia of Associations: National Organizations of the United States, 50th edition* (Detroit, MI: Gale Cengage Learning, 2011); *Encyclopedia of Associations: Regional, State, and Local Organizations, 22nd edition* (Detroit, MI: Gale Cengage Learning, 2010); Mark P. Petracca, "The Rediscovery of Interest Group Politics," in *The Politics of Interests: Interest Groups Transformed*, ed. Mark P. Petracca (Boulder, CO: Westview Press, 1992), 13–18; *National Directory of Trade and Professional Associations* (Washington, DC: Columbia Books, Inc., various editions); John R. Wright, *Interest Groups and Congress: Lobbying, Contributions, and Influence* (Boston: Allyn and Bacon, 1996), Chapter 5; *Washington Representatives, Spring 2011, 39th edition* (Washington, DC: Columbia Books, 2011).

2 This is an estimate based on my perusal of state and local lobbyist registration lists.

3 Burdett A. Loomis and Allan J. Cigler, "Introduction: The Changing Nature of Interest Group Politics," in *Interest Group Politics, 8th edition*, eds. Allan J. Cigler and Burdett A. Loomis (Washington, DC: CQ Press, 2012), 10–11; Rosenthal, *The Third House, 2nd edition*, 2–6; Jack L. Walker, Jr., *Mobilizing Interest Groups in America: Patrons, Professions, and Social Movements* (Ann Arbor: University of Michigan Press, 1991), 1–3.

4 The U.S. probably ranks No. 1, but we simply cannot be sure. India has lots of interest groups, as does China. No one knows, however, precisely how many interest groups operate in these two countries.

5 John R. Commons, David J. Saposs, Helen L. Sumner, E.B. Mittelman, H.E. Hoagland, John B. Andrews, and Selig Perlman, *History of Labour in the United States* (New York: Macmillan, 1918).

6 Richard Worth, *Teetotalers and Saloon Smashers: The Temperance Movement and Prohibition* (Berkeley Heights, NJ: Enslow, 2009).

7 Richard S. Newman, *The Transformation of American Abolitionism: Fighting Slavery in the Early Republic* (Chapel Hill: University of North Carolina Press, 2002).

8 For an interesting perspective on the activities of interest groups throughout American history, see Daniel J. Tichenor and Richard A. Harris, "Organized Interests and American Political Development," *Political Science Quarterly* 117 (2002/03), 587–612; Daniel J. Tichenor and Richard A. Harris, "The Development of Interest Group Politics in America: Beyond the Conceits of Modern Times," *Annual Review of Political Science* 8 (2005), 251–70.

9 Margaret Susan Thompson, *The "Spider Web": Congress and Lobbying in the Age of Grant* (Ithaca, NY: Cornell University Press, 1985).

10 They probably were always powerful, but not until the 1920s did we have a full appreciation of their power. For an early academic treatment, see Pendleton E. Herring, *Group Representation before Congress* (Baltimore, MD: Johns Hopkins Press, 1929).

11 Tichenor and Harris, "The Development of Interest Group Politics in America."

12 Petracca, "The Rediscovery of Interest Group Politics."

13 Federal Election Commission, "PAC Activity Remains Steady in 2009," accessed April 10, 2011, http://www.fec.gov/press/press2010/20100406PAC.shtml; M. Margaret Conway and Joanne Connor Green, "Political Action Committees and the Political Process in the 1990s," in *Interest Group Politics, 4th edition*, eds. Allan J. Cigler and Burdett A. Loomis (Washington, DC: CQ Press, 1995), 155–74.

14 Jeffrey M. Berry, *Lobbying for the People: The Political Behavior of Public Interest Groups* (Princeton, NJ: Princeton University Press, 1977), 11–17; Ronald G. Shaiko, "Lobbying in Washington: A Contemporary Perspective," in *The Interest Group Connection: Electioneering, Lobbying, and Policymaking in Washington*, eds. Paul S. Herrnson, Ronald G. Shaiko, and Clyde Wilcox (Chatham, NJ: Chatham House, 1998), 3–18.

15 Ronald G. Shaiko, "Making the Connection: Organized Interests, Political Representation, and the Changing Rules of the Game in Washington Politics," in *The Interest Group Connection: Electioneering, Lobbying, and Policymaking in Washington, 2nd edition*, eds. Herrnson et al., 6.

16 Anthony J. Nownes, "The Population Ecology of Interest Group Formation: Mobilizing for Gay and Lesbian Rights in the United States, 1950–98," *British Journal of Political Science* 34 (2004), 49–67.

17 Loomis and Cigler, "Introduction," 1–5; Wright, *Interest Groups and Congress*, 20–30.

18 Thompson, *The Spider Web*.

19 Frank R. Baumgartner and Beth L. Leech, *Basic Interests: The Importance of Groups in Politics and in Political Science* (Princeton, NJ: Princeton University Press, 1998), 102.

20 Baumgartner and Leech, *Basic Interests*, 104.

21 Baumgartner and Leech, *Basic Interests*, 108.

22 Baumgartner and Leech, *Basic Interests*, 108.

23 On citizen groups, see Jeffrey M. Berry, *The New Liberalism: The Rising Power of Citizen Groups* (Washington, DC: Brookings Institution Press, 1999), Chapter 2.

24 See McGann, "Academics to Ideologues"; Andrew Rich, *Think Tanks, Public Policy, and the Politics of Expertise* (New York: Cambridge University Press, 2004); R. Kent Weaver, "The Changing World of Think Tanks," *PS* 3 (1989), 563–78.

25 On the diversity of interest groups in the states, see Virginia Gray and David Lowery, "The Diversity of State Interest Group Systems," *Political Research Quarterly* 46 (1993), 81–97; Virginia Gray and David Lowery, "The Institutionalization of State Communities of Organized Interests," *Political Research Quarterly* 54 (2001), 265–84. On local groups see Jeffrey M. Berry, Kent E. Portney, and Ken Thomson, *The Rebirth of Urban Democracy* (Washington, DC: Brookings Institution, 1993); Barbara Ferman, *Challenging the Growth Machine: Neighborhood Politics in Chicago and Pittsburgh* (Lawrence: University Press of Kansas, 1996).

26 See, for example, Dinissa Duvanova, "Bureaucratic Corruption and Collective Action: Business Associations in the Postcommunist Transition," *Comparative Politics* 39 (2007), 441–61; Conor McGrath, ed., *Interest Groups and Lobbying in Latin America, Africa, the Middle East, and Asia: Essays on Drug Trafficking, Chemical Manufacture, Exchange Rates, and Women's Interests* (Lewiston, NY: Edwin Mellen Press, 2009); Conor McGrath, ed., *Interest Groups and Lobbying in Europe: Essays on Trade, Environment, Legislation, and Economic Development* (Lewiston, NY: Edwin Mellen Press, 2009).

27 The Pew Forum on Religion and Public Life, *U.S. Religious Landscape Survey, Religious Affiliation: Diverse and Dynamic* (Washington, DC: The Pew Forum on Religion and Public Life, 2008).

28 U.S. Census Bureau, "2010 Census Shows America's Diversity," March 24, 2011, accessed April 22, 2011, http://2010.census.gov/news/releases/operations/cb11-cn125.html. The US Census Bureau recognizes only five races—Caucasian, African American, Asian American, American Indian or Alaskan Native, and Native Hawaiian or Pacific Islander. Thus, all Hispanics were asked to place themselves into one of these five racial categories (or to choose "some other race"). This is why these percentages do not add up to 100. Here, I include Hispanics in this discussion to illustrate America's racial and ethnic diversity.

29 U.S. Census Bureau, "2010 Census Shows America's Diversity."

30 The data on food come from FAOSTAT, Food and Agriculture Organization of the United Nations, "Crops," 2011, accessed April 22, 2011, http://faostat.fao.org/site/567/DesktopDefault.aspx?PageID=567#ancor. The data on cars come from Bertel Schmitt, "Top 40 Automobile Manufacturing Countries," *The Truth About Cars.com*, March 22, 2011, accessed April 22, 2011, http://www.thetruthaboutcars.com/2011/03/top-40-automobile-manufacturing-countries-2010/. On copper, see Leia Michele Toovey, "The Top 10 Copper Producing Countries," *International Business Times* online, November 18, 2010, accessed April 25, 2011, http://www.ibtimes.com/articles/83306/20101118/the-top-10-copper-producing-countries.htm. On steel, see World Steel Organization, "World Crude Steel Output Increases by 15% in 2010," accessed April 25, 2011, http://www.worldsteel.org/?action=newsdetail&id=319. On movies, see Saibal Dasgupta, "Chinese Film Industry Races Close to Bollywood," *The Times of India* online, January 10, 2011, accessed April 25, 2011, http://articles.timesofindia.indiatimes.com/2011-01-10/india/28358616_1_film-industry-chinese-film-Chinese-movie.

31 Loomis and Cigler, "Introduction," 5.

32 Loomis and Cigler, "Introduction," 6.

33 George Kateb, "The Value of Association," in *Freedom of Association*, ed. Amy Gutmann (Princeton, NJ: Princeton University Press, 1998), 35.

34 Kateb, "The Value of Association," 35.

35 U.S. Census Bureau, "Census of Governments," accessed May 13, 2011, http://www2.census.gov/govs/cog/2002COGprelim_report.pdf.

36 Loomis and Cigler, "Introduction," 6.

37 David B. Truman, *The Governmental Process: Political Interests and Public Opinion*, 2nd edition (New York: Knopf, 1959 [1951]), Chapters 3 and 4.

38 U.S. Bureau of the Census, *Historical Statistics of the United States, Colonial Times to 1970* (Washington, DC: U.S. Government Printing Office, 1975), 297. Unfortunately, this rising affluence appears to have stalled.

39 See Berry, *The New Liberalism*.

40 Salisbury, "An Exchange Theory of Interest Groups."

41 National Alliance of State and Territorial AIDS Directors, "About NASTAD," accessed April 25, 2011, http://nastad.org/.

42 Loomis and Cigler, "Introduction," 12.

43 Loomis and Cigler, "Introduction," 13.

3 The Formation and Maintenance of Interest Groups

1 Gallup Poll, "Death Penalty," accessed May 23, 2011, http://www.gallup.com/poll/1606/death-penalty.aspx.

2 Gallup Poll, "Death Penalty."

3 Loomis and Cigler, "Introduction," 8.

4 There were a small handful of gay rights groups, but they tended to be small and relatively ineffectual.

5 See *Encyclopedia of Associations: National Organizations of the United States, 50th edition,* various pages.

6 See *Encyclopedia of Associations: National Organizations of the United States, 50th edition,* various pages.

7 Of course, most executions are carried out by state governments, so a look at state interest groups may yield different results. But a perusal of state lobbying rolls also suggests that groups representing death penalty opponents vastly outnumber groups representing death penalty supporters.

8 Mancur Olson, *The Logic of Collective Action: Public Goods and the Theory of Groups* (Cambridge, MA: Harvard University Press, 1965).

9 I am simplifying Olson here. Olson does not use the term "political efficacy problem." He makes the argument that people realize that one person usually does not make a difference, but he does not use the terminology I use here.

10 Loomis and Cigler, "Introduction," 8.

11 Paul E. Johnson, Gary J. Miller, John H. Aldrich, David W. Rohde, and Charles W. Ostrom, Jr., *American Government: People, Institutions, and Politics, 3rd edition* (Boston: Houghton Mifflin, 1994), 406–07.

12 This typology of benefits was originally outlined in Peter B. Clark and James Q. Wilson, "Incentive Systems: A Theory of Organizations," *Administrative Science Quarterly* 6 (1961), 129–66. The typology was further refined in Salisbury, "An Exchange Theory of Interest Groups."

13 James Q. Wilson, *Political Organizations* (Princeton, NJ: Princeton University Press, 1995 [1974]), 45–51.

14 Paul Edward Johnson, "Organized Labor in an Era of Blue-Collar Decline," in *Interest Group Politics, 3rd edition,* eds. Allan J. Cigler and Burdett A. Loomis (Washington, DC: Congressional Quarterly Press, 1991), 36.

15 Johnson, "Organized Labor in an Era of Blue-Collar Decline," 35.

16 American Bar Association, "State and Local Bar Associations," accessed July 24, 2011, http://www.americanbar.org/groups/bar_services/resources/state_local_bar_associations.html.

17 Benjamin Marquez, "Mexican–American Political Organizations and Philanthropy: Bankrolling a Social Movement," *Social Service Review* 77 (2003), 329–46.

18 The Ford Foundation, "Grants Database," accessed June 17, 2011, http://www.fordfoundation.org/grants/search.

19 John D. and Catherine T. MacArthur Foundation, "Human Rights and International Justice: Recent Grants," accessed June 17, 2011, http://www.macfound.org/site/c.lkLXJ8MQKrH/b.938985/k.7091/International_Grantmaking__Human_Rights_and_International_Justice__Recent_Grants.htm.

20 Media Matters for America, "Conservative Transparency: The Money Behind the Movement," accessed June 17, 2011, http://mediamattersaction.org/p/contact_us.

21 Walker, *Mobilizing Interest Groups in America*, 78.

22 Much of this money comes from corporate foundations—private foundations affiliated with companies.

23 Anthony J. Nownes and Allan Cigler, "Corporate Philanthropy in a Political Fishbowl: Perils and Possibilities," in *Interest Group Politics, 5th edition*, eds. Allan J. Cigler and Burdett A. Loomis (Washington, DC: CQ Press, 1998), 63–82.

24 The Sierra Club Foundation, "Partnerships for the Planet: The Sierra Club Foundation Annual Report" (San Francisco: Sierra Club Foundation, 2009). The gifts came from each company's corporate foundation.

25 The Heritage Foundation, "The Heritage Foundation 2010 Annual Report: Solutions for America" (Washington, DC: The Heritage Foundation, 2011).

26 Soros has contributed money personally and through his Open Society Foundations. For details, see georgesoros.com.

27 Jane Mayer, "Covert Operations: The Billionaire Brothers Who Are Waging a War Against Obama," *The New Yorker* online, August 20, 2010, accessed January 25, 2012, http://www.newyorker.com/reporting/2010/08/30/100830fa_fact_mayer?currentPage =all.

28 Robert H. Salisbury, "Interest Representation."

29 Salisbury, "Interest Representation," 74.

30 Glenn Abney and Thomas P. Lauth, "Interest Group Influence in City Policy-Making: The Views of Administrators," *Western Political Quarterly* 38 (1985), 148–61; Gray and Lowery, "The Institutionalization of State Communities of Organized Interests;" Rosenthal, *The Third House, 2nd edition*, 42–49; Paul Schumaker and Russell W. Getter, "Structural Sources of Unequal Responsiveness to Group Demands in American Cities," *Western Political Quarterly* 36 (1983), 7–29.

31 See also E.E. Schattschneider, *The Semisovereign People: A Realist's View of Democracy in America* (New York: Holt, Rinehart and Winston, 1960); Herbert Hyman and Charles Wright, "Trends in Voluntary Association Memberships of American Adults: Replication Based on Secondary Analysis of National Sample Surveys," *American Sociological Review* 36 (1971), 191–206.

32 This means that *income* tends to rise with *level of education*.

33 Salisbury, "An Exchange Theory of Interest Groups."

34 Anthony J. Nownes and Grant Neeley, "Public Interest Group Entrepreneurship and Theories of Group Mobilization," *Political Research Quarterly* 49 (1996), 119–46.

35 Sidney Verba, Kay Lehman Schlozman, and Henry E. Brady, *Voice and Equality: Civic Voluntarism in American Politics* (Cambridge, MA: Harvard University Press, 1995), 190; Hyman and Wright, "Trends in Voluntary Association Memberships of American Adults."

36 Verba, Schlozman, and Brady, *Voice and Equality*, 190.

37 Philip A. Mundo, *Interest Groups: Cases and Characteristics* (Chicago: Nelson-Hall, 1992), 177.

38 Andrew S. McFarland, *Common Cause: Lobbying in the Public Interest* (Chatham, NJ: Chatham House, 1984), 48.

39 R. Kenneth Godwin, "Money, Technology, and Political Interests: The Direct Marketing

of Politics," in *The Politics of Interests: Interest Groups Transformed*, ed. Mark P. Petracca (Boulder, CO: Westview Press, 1992), 308–25.

40 For details, see McFarland, *Common Cause*, 46–52; Nownes and Neeley, "Public Interest Group Entrepreneurship and Theories of Group Formation."

41 The classic is Lester W. Milbrath, *Political Participation: How and Why Do People Get Involved in Politics?* (Chicago: Rand McNally, 1965). See also Verba, Schlozman, and Brady, *Voice and Equality*, Chapter 12.

42 Verba, Schlozman, and Brady, *Voice and Equality*, Chapter 12.

43 See McFarland, *Common Cause*, Chapters 2 and 3; Lawrence S. Rothenberg, "Putting the Puzzle Together: Why People Join Public Interest Groups," *Public Choice* 60 (1989), 241–57.

44 See J. Craig Jenkins, *The Politics of Insurgency: The Farm Worker Movement in the 1960s* (New York: Columbia University Press, 1985).

45 Dennis Chong, *Collective Action and the Civil Rights Movement* (Chicago: The University of Chicago Press, 1991), 232.

46 Chong, *Collective Action and the Civil Rights Movement*, 232.

47 *Encyclopedia of Associations: National Organizations of the United States*, various editions.

4 The Non-Lobbying Activities of Interest Groups

1 Wilson, *Political Organizations*, 10.

2 Jack L. Walker, "The Origins and Maintenance of Interest Groups in America," *American Political Science Review* 77 (1983), 390–406.

3 For basic information, see the Foundation Center's website at http://www.foundationcenter.org/.

4 For information, go to http://foundationcenter.org/getstarted/tutorials/fdoguidedtour/.

5 On what the Foundation Center offers, see The Foundation Center, "Resources and Training," accessed January 30, 2011, http://foundationcenter.org/focus/economy/resources.html.

6 As of this writing, this is available online at General Services Administration, U.S. Government, "Catalogue of Federal Domestic Assistance," accessed February 1, 2012, https://www.cfda.gov/.

7 Kim Klein, *Fundraising for Social Change, 5th edition* (San Francisco: John Wiley and Sons, 2007), Chapter 10; Godwin, "Money, Technology, and Political Interests."

8 Godwin, "Money, Technology, and Political Interests," 310.

9 Gwyneth J. Lister, *Building Your Direct Mail Program* (San Francisco: Jossey-Bass, 2001), 25.

10 Paul E. Johnson, "Interest Group Recruiting: Finding Members and Keeping Them," in *Interest Group Politics, 5th edition*, eds. Allan J. Cigler and Burdett A. Loomis (Washington, DC: CQ Press, 1998), 50.

11 Grant Jordan and William A. Maloney, *Democracy and Interest Groups: Enhancing Participation?* (London: Palgrave Macmillan, 2007), 101.

12 Klein, *Fundraising for Social Change*, 135.

13 Klein, *Fundraising for Social Change*, 150.

14 Klein, *Fundraising for Social Change*, 150.

15 Klein, *Fundraising for Social Change*, 153.

16 Lister, *Building Your Direct Mail Program*, 35–36.

17 Klein, *Fundraising for Social Change*, 156.

18 Lister, *Building Your Direct Mail Program*, 35.

19 Lister, *Building Your Direct Mail Program*, 35.

20 Klein, *Fundraising for Social Change*, 162.

21 Jordan and Maloney, *Democracy and Interest Groups*, 104.

22 See Godwin, "Money Technology, and Political Interests"; Robert Cameron Mitchell, "National Environmental Lobbies and the Apparent Illogic of Collective Action," in *Collective Decision Making: Applications from Rational Choice Theory*, ed. Clifford S. Russell (Baltimore, MD: Johns Hopkins University Press, 1979), 87–123.

23 R. Kenneth Godwin, *One Billion Dollars of Influence: The Direct Marketing of Politics* (Chatham, NJ: Chatham House, 1988), 33.

24 Melissa K. Merry, "Emotional Appeals in Environmental Group Communications," *American Politics Research* 38 (2010), 862–89.

25 Klein, *Fundraising for Social Change*, 150.

26 Klein, *Fundraising for Social Change*, 136; Jordan and Maloney, *Democracy and Interest Groups*, 103; Johnson, "Interest Group Recruiting," 48–51.

27 Klein, *Fundraising for Social Change*, 136.

28 Klein, *Fundraising for Social Change*, 138.

29 Klein, *Fundraising for Social Change*, 138.

30 The study I am talking about is Anthony J. Nownes and Allan J. Cigler, "Big Money Donors to Environmental Groups: What They Give and What They Get," in *Interest Group Politics, 7th edition*, eds. Allan J. Cigler and Burdett A. Loomis (Washington, DC: CQ Press, 2007), 108–29.

31 Klein, *Fundraising for Social Change*, Chapter 7.

32 Bill Connors, *Fundraising with the Raiser's Edge: A Non-Technical Guide* (Hoboken, NJ: John Wiley and Sons, 2010), Chapter 6.

33 Nownes and Cigler, "Big Money Donors to Environmental Groups."

34 Klein, *Fundraising for Social Change*, Chapter 9.

35 Jeff Stanger, "E-Mail and Internet Solicitation," in *Achieving Excellence in Fundraising, 3rd edition*, eds. Eugene R. Tempel, Timothy L. Seiler, and Eva E. Aldrich (San Francisco: Jossey-Bass, 2011), 235–46.

36 Stanger, "E-Mail and Internet Solicitation," 238.

37 Stanger, "E-Mail and Internet Solicitation," 238.

38 Stanger, "E-Mail and Internet Solicitation," 243–44.

39 Klein, *Fundraising for Social Change*, 179–81; Jonathan D. Purvis, "Telephone Solicitation," in *Achieving Excellence in Fundraising, 3rd edition*, eds. Eugene R. Tempel, Timothy L. Seiler, and Eva E. Aldrich (San Francisco: Jossey-Bass, 2011), 256–67.

40 Johnson, "Interest Group Recruiting"; Godwin, "Money, Technology, and Political Interests," 312–13.

41 Jordan and Maloney, *Democracy and Interest Groups*, 96.

42 Jordan and Maloney, *Democracy and Interest Groups*, 96.

43 Jordan and Maloney, *Democracy and Interest Groups*, 96.

44 Jocelyne S. Daw, Carol Cone, with Kristian Darigan Merenda and Anne Erhard, *Breakthrough Nonprofit Branding: Seven Principles to Power Extraordinary Results* (Hoboken, NJ: John Wiley and Sons, 2011), 20.

45 See the Sierra Club Store at http://www.sierraclub.org/store/.

46 Visit the Heritage Foundation bookstore at https://secure.heritage.org/bookstore/.

47 Visit the UFW Store at http://www.ufwstore.com/mm5/merchant.mvc?Screen=SFNT&Store_Code=IS0005.

48 See Chamber of Commerce publications at https://secure.uschamber.com/publications.

49 Robert H. Salisbury, "The Paradox of Interest Groups in Washington—More Groups, Less Clout," in *The New American Political System,* 2nd version, ed. Anthony King (Washington, DC: AEI Press, 1990), 225.

50 Nownes, *Total Lobbying,* 44.

51 Salisbury, "The Paradox of Interest Groups in Washington," 225.

52 Salisbury, "The Paradox of Interest Groups in Washington," 225–26.

53 Richard A. Harris, *Coal Firms Under the New Social Regulation* (Durham, NC: Duke University Press, 1985).

54 Nownes, *Total Lobbying,* 47.

55 Nownes, *Total Lobbying,* 47.

56 Johnson, "Interest Group Recruiting," 43–45.

57 Salisbury, "The Paradox of Interest Groups in Washington," 225–26.

58 Jeffrey M. Berry and Clyde Wilcox, *The Interest Group Society,* 5th edition (New York: Pearson Education, Inc., 2009), 101–03.

59 Anthony J. Nownes, "The Non-Lobbying Activities of Lobbyists: What Lobbyists Do When They are Not Lobbying," Unpublished manuscript available from the author.

60 See ASME, "Advocacy and Government Relations," accessed February 1, 2012, http://www.asme.org/about-asme/advocacy-government-relations.

61 See City of Anaheim, "Welcome to the Government Relations Home Page," accessed January 30, 2012, http://www.anaheim.net/sectionnew.asp?id=185.

62 See National Association of Realtors, "Facebook: National Association of Realtors," accessed January 29, 2011, http://www.facebook.com/nargovernmentaffairs.

63 See United Auto Workers, "Departments Under the International President," accessed February 1, 2012, http://www.uaw.org/node/276.

64 A board may go by other names such as Board of Governors, Board of Visitors, or Executive Board.

65 Johnson et al., *American Government,* 408.

66 See Robert Michels, *Political Parties: A Sociological Study of the Oligarchical Tendencies of Modern Democracy* (New York: Collier Books, 1962 [1915]).

67 See National Education Association, "About NEA," accessed February 14, 2011, http://www.nea.org/home/2580.htm.

68 See Sierra Club, "Board of Directors: 2011 Election," accessed February 1, 2012, http://www.sierraclub.org/bod/2011election/default.aspx.

69 Albert O. Hirschman, *Exit, Voice, and Loyalty: Responses to Decline in Firms, Organizations, and States* (Cambridge, MA: Harvard University Press, 1970).

5 Direct Lobbying

1 The classic treatment is in Wright, *Interest Groups and Congress*, 88.

2 I also use this example in Anthony J. Nownes and Adam Newmark, "Interest Groups in the States," in *Politics in the American States: A Comparative Analysis, 10th edition*, eds. Virginia Gray, Russell L. Hanson, and Thad Kousser (Washington, DC: CQ Press, 2012). I learned about the details of this case from several sources including the following: Daniel B. Wood, "California Set to Ban Plastic Bags," *Christian Science Monitor* online, August 30, 2010, accessed February 24, 2011, http://www.csmonitor.com/Environment/2010/0830/California-set-to-ban-plastic-bags; Nick Taborek, "Brownley Pushes for Statewide Plastic Bag Ban," *SMDP.com*, June 2, 2010, accessed February 24, 2011, http://www.smdp.com/Articles-c-2010-06-02-69726.113116; Ed Joyce, "Calif. Enviro Groups Urge Passage of Plastic Bag Bill," *KPBS.com*, June 1, 2010, accessed February 24, 2011, http://www.kpbs.org/news/2010/jun/01/calif-enviro-groups-urge-passage-plastic-bag-bill/; Thomas Hart, "California Plastic Bag Ban Defeated by Plastic Industry Lobbyists," *Personal Money Store, Personal Money Network Blog*, September 1, 2010, accessed February 23, 2011, http://personalmoneystore.com/moneyblog/2010/09/01/california-plastic-bag-ban/.

3 Frank R. Baumgartner, Jeffrey M. Berry, Marie Hojnackavid, C. Kimball, and Beth L. Leech, *Lobbying and Policy Change: Who Wins, Who Loses, and Why* (Chicago: University of Chicago Press, 2009), Chapter 7. See also Rogan Kersh, "Corporate Lobbyists as Political Actors: A View from the Field," in *Interest Group Politics, 6th edition*, eds. Allan J. Cigler and Burdett A. Loomis (Washington, DC: CQ Press, 2002), 225–48.

4 Baumgartner et al., *Lobbying and Policy Change*, 133.

5 Baumgartner et al., *Lobbying and Policy Change*, 133.

6 Baumgartner et al., *Lobbying and Policy Change*, 133.

7 Unfortunately, we do not know for certain how much attention *local* legislative bodies receive from lobbyists. As I have pointed out before, studies of local interest groups are hard to come by. On state lobbyists, see Anthony J. Nownes and Krissy Walker DeAlejandro, "Lobbying in the New Millennium: Evidence of Continuity and Change in Three States," *State Politics and Policy Quarterly* 9 (2009), 429–55; Anthony J. Nownes and Patricia Freeman, "Interest Group Activity in the States," *Journal of Politics* 60 (1998), 86–112; on Washington lobbyists, see; Heinz et al., *The Hollow Core*.

8 R. Eric Petersen, Parker H. Reynolds, and Amber Hope Wilhelm, *House of Representatives and Senate Staff Levels in Member, Committee, Leadership, and Other Offices, 1977–2010* (Washington, DC: Congressional Research Service, 2010).

9 Donny Shaw, "The Vast Majority of Bills Go Nowhere," *Opencongress.org*, August 25, 2009, accessed August 30, 2011, http://www.opencongress.org/articles/view/1180-The-Vast-Majority-of-Bills-Go-Nowhere.

10 Shaw, "The Vast Majority of Bills Go Nowhere."

11 Wright, *Interest Groups and Congress*, 40–43.

12 Wright, *Interest Groups and Congress*, 41.

13 This chapter contains tables about state and Washington lobbyists' use of lobbying techniques. I did not include a table on the activities of local lobbyists because there simply are not usable studies showing how often local lobbyists use the techniques I talk about in this chapter.

14 Baumgartner et al., *Lobbying and Policy Change*, Chapter 8; Nownes and DeAlejandro, "Lobbying in the New Millennium," 441.

15 Richard L. Hall and Alan Deardorff, "Lobbying as Legislative Subsidy," *American Political Science Review* 100 (2006), 69–84.

16 Some local governments have chief executives as well, while some do not.

17 Baumgartner et al., *Lobbying and Policy Change*, 151.

18 Paul Light, *The President's Agenda: Domestic Policy Choice from Kennedy to Clinton*, 3rd edition (Baltimore, MD: Johns Hopkins University Press), 228; Joseph A. Pika, "The White House Office of Public Liaison," *Presidential Studies Quarterly* 39 (2009), 549–73.

19 Pika, "The White House Office of Public Liaison."

20 See Jeffrey M. Berry and Kent E. Portney, "Centralizing Regulatory Control and Interest Group Access: The Quayle Council on Competitiveness," in *Interest Group Politics*, 4th edition, eds. Allan J. Cigler and Burdett A. Loomis (Washington, DC: CQ Press, 1995), 319–47.

21 State of Pennsylvania, Tom Corbett, Governor, "Offices and Commissions," accessed September 1, 2012, http://www.portal.state.pa.us/portal/server.pt/community/offices_and_commissions/2996.

22 Arizona Governor Jan Brewer, "Offices and Appointments," accessed September 1, 2011, http://azgovernor.gov/GOA.asp.

23 Nownes and Freeman, "Interest Group Activity in the States," 97.

24 U.S. Office of Personnel Management, "Total Government Employment Since 1962," accessed September 1, 2011, http://www.opm.gov/feddata/HistoricalTables/TotalGovernmentSince1962.asp.

25 For details, see James William Fesler and Donald F. Kettl, *The Politics of the Administrative Process* (Chatham, NJ: Chatham House, 1991); Charles T. Goodsell, *The Case for Bureaucracy: A Public Administration Polemic*, 2nd edition (Chatham, NJ: Chatham House Publishers, 1985).

26 50 CFR 21.24 - Taxidermist permits.

27 50 CFR 21.24 - Taxidermist permits.

28 Of course, this is a simplification of the actual rule-making process. Moreover, the rule-making process varies across states, so this is an approximation.

29 Nownes and DeAlejandro, "Lobbying in the New Millennium," 441.

30 Not all regulations, however, require a public comment period. Federal law contains many exceptions to the rule that proposed regulations be publicized and interested parties be allowed to comment.

31 See, for example, Keith Naughton, Celeste Schmid, Susan Webb Yackee, and Xueyong Zhan, "Understanding Commenter Influence During Agency Rule Development," *Journal of Policy Analysis and Management* 28 (2009), 258–77; Jason Webb Yackee and Susan Webb Yackee, "A Bias Towards Business? Assessing Interest Group Influence on the U.S. Bureaucracy," *Journal of Politics* 68 (2006), 128–39.

32 For additional data on levels of lobbyist participation in rulemaking, see Cornelius M. Kerwin, *Rulemaking: How Government Agencies Write Law and Make Policy*, 3rd edition (Washington, DC: CQ Press, 2003), Chapter 5.

33 See A. Lee Fritschler, *Smoking and Politics: Policy Making and the Federal Bureaucracy*, 4th edition (Englewood Cliffs, NJ: Prentice-Hall, 1989).

34 Wright, *Interest Groups and Congress*, 52.

35 Thomas E. Mann, *The Negative Impact of the Use of Filibusters and Holds* (Washington, DC: Brookings Institution Press, 2010).

36 Mann, "The Negative Impact of the Use of Filibusters and Holds." See also Judith E. Michaels, *The President's Call: Executive Leadership from FDR to George Bush* (Pittsburgh, PA: University of Pittsburgh Press, 1997). These are studies of federal bureaucrats, though I think it is safe to assume that appointed bureaucrats at other levels of government also are approved at a very high rate.

37 Kay Lehman Schlozman and John T. Tierney, "More of the Same—Washington Pressure Group Activity in a Decade of Change," *Journal of Politics* 45 (1983), 357.

38 Cornelius Kerwin, "Interest Group Participation in Rule-Making: A Decade of Change," *Journal of Public Administration Research and Theory* 15 (2005), 353–70; Scott R. Furlong, "Exploring Interest Group Participation in Executive Policymaking," in *The Interest Group Connection: Electioneering, Lobbying, and Policymaking in Washington, 2nd edition*, eds. Paul S. Herrnson, Ronald G. Shaiko, and Clyde Wilcox (Chatham, NJ: Chatham House, 1998), 286. Unfortunately I do not have the time or space to discuss which agencies do and do not hold public hearings, when, and why.

39 The reality is a little more complicated than this. *Brown* was actually a consolidation of five different cases.

40 See Lee Epstein and C.K. Rowland, "Interest Groups in the Courts: Do Groups Fare Better?," in *Interest Group Politics, 2nd edition*, eds. Allan J. Cigler and Burdett A. Loomis (Washington, DC: Congressional Quarterly Press, 1986), 275–88.

41 For details on standing, see Karen Orren, "Standing to Sue: Interest Group Conflict in the Federal Courts," *American Political Science Review* 70 (1976), 723–41.

42 Jane Mayer and Jill Abramson, *Strange Justice: The Selling of Clarence Thomas* (Boston: Houghton Mifflin, 1994), 225–33.

43 G. Calvin Mackenzie and Robert Shogan, *Obstacle Course: The Report of the Twentieth Century Fund Task Force on the Presidential Appointment Process with Background Papers* (New York: Twentieth Century Fund Press, 1996), 133.

44 Christine DeGregorio and Jack E. Rossotti, "Campaigning for the Court: Interest Group Participation in the Bork and Thomas Confirmation Processes," in *Interest Group Politics, 4th edition*, eds. Allan J. Cigler and Burdett A. Loomis (Washington, DC: CQ Press, 1995), 215–38.

45 Larry Sabato and Glenn R. Simpson, *Dirty Little Secrets: The Persistence of Corruption in American Politics* (New York: Times Books, 1996), 10.

46 For the full story of Albert Fall, see David H. Stratton, *Tempest over Teapot Dome: The Story of Albert B. Fall* (Norman: University of Oklahoma Press, 1998).

47 For a look at this scandal, see Logan Douglas Trent, *The Credit Mobilier* (New York: Arno Press, 1981).

48 On this and other salacious scandals, see Paul Slansky, *The Little Quiz Book of Big Political Sex Scandals* (New York: Simon and Schuster, 2009).

49 Alan Rosenthal, *The Third House* (Washington, DC: CQ Press, 1993), 105.

50 Rosenthal, *The Third House, 2nd edition*, 108.

51 Rosenthal, *The Third House, 2nd edition*, 108.

52 Rosenthal, *The Third House, 2nd edition*, 108.

53 Schlozman and Tierney, "More of the Same—Washington Pressure Group Activity in a Decade of Change," 357.

54 Rosenthal, *The Third House, 2nd edition*, 112–13.

55 Office of the Clerk, U.S. House of Representatives, "Lobbying Disclosure Act Guidance," December 15, 2011, accessed October 28, 2011, http://lobbyingdisclosure.house.gov/amended_lda_guide.html.

56 Office of the Clerk, U.S. House of Representatives, "Lobbying Disclosure Act Guidance."

57 Ronald G. Shaiko, "Lobbying in Washington: A Contemporary Perspective," in *The Interest Group Connection: Electioneering, Lobbying and Policymaking in Washington*, eds. Paul S. Herrnson, Ronald G. Shaiko, and Clyde Wilcox (Chatham, NJ: Chatham House, 1998), 14.

58 Shaiko, "Lobbying in Washington," 14.

59 Shaiko, "Lobbying in Washington," 14.

60 Thomas M. Susman, "Honest Leadership and Open Government Act of 2007—Changes to Lobbying Disclosure Act (LDA)," http://www.alldc.org/publicresources/documents/susman_S_1_handout.pdf.

61 C. Randall Nuckolls, "Compliance and Disclosure Under the Honest Leadership and Open Government Act of 2007," July 14, 2008, accessed November 1, 2011, http://government.fiu.edu/docs/FIU_Lobbying_Disclosure_Workshop_-_July_14_2008.pdf.

62 Keenan Steiner, "Fundraisers as Elemental as Breakfast," *Party Time*, January 10, 2011, accessed November 1, 2011, http://blog.politicalpartytime.org/2011/01/10/fundraisers-as-elemental-as-breakfast/.

63 National Institute on Money in State Politics, "Home > Texas 2010 > Lobbyists," accessed January 25, 2012, http://www.followthemoney.org/database/StateGlance/state_lobbyists.phtml?s=TX&y=2010.

64 National Institute on Money in State Politics, "Home > Montana 2010 > Lobbyists," accessed April 25, 2011, http://www.followthemoney.org/database/StateGlance/state_lobbyists.phtml?s=MT&y=2010.

65 National Institute on Money in State Politics, "Home > Iowa 2010 > Lobbyists," accessed April 26, 2011, http://www.followthemoney.org/database/StateGlance/state_lobbyists.phtml?s=IA&y=2010.

66 Rosenthal, *The Third House, 2nd edition*, 18.

67 Lester W. Milbrath, *The Washington Lobbyists* (Chicago: Rand McNally, 1963).

68 Anthony J. Nownes and Patricia K. Freeman, "Female Lobbyists: Women in the World of 'Good ol' Boys'," *Journal of Politics* 60 (1998), 1181–201.

69 Nownes and Freeman, "Female Lobbyists."

70 "How to Become a Lobbyist," *Degreefinders.com*, accessed March 26, 2011, http://www.degreefinders.com/education-articles/careers/how-to-become-a-lobbyist.html.

71 Jeanne Cummings, "The Gilded Capital: Lobbying to Riches," *Politico.com*, June 26, 2007, accessed February 1, 2012, http://www.politico.com/news/stories/0607/4652.html; "Check it Out: Big Salaries for Washington Lobbyists," *Washington Post* online, April 2, 2010, accessed January 25, 2012, http://voices.washingtonpost.com/reliable-source/2010/04/check_it_out_big_salaries_for.html.

72 Rosenthal, *The Third House, 2nd edition*, 30.

73 Rosenthal, *The Third House, 2nd edition*, 30.

74 Kim Eisler, "Hired Guns: The City's 50 Top Lobbyists," *The Washingtonian Magazine* online, June 1, 2007, accessed January 30, 2012, http://www.washingtonian.com/articles/mediapolitics/4264.html; Rosenthal, *The Third House, 2nd edition*, 26–33.

75 T.W. Farnam, "Revolving Door of Employment Between Congress, Lobbying Firms, Study Shows," *The Washington Post* online, September 13, 2011, accessed January 3, 2012, http://www.washingtonpost.com/politics/study-shows-revolving-door-of-employment-between-congress-lobbying-firms/2011/09/12/gIQAxPYROK_story.html.

76 Farnam, "Revolving Door of Employment Between Congress, Lobbying Firms, Study Shows."

77 David DeGraw, "Political Bribery Watch: 79% of Former Members of Congress Have Become Lobbyists," *Daviddegraw.org*, online, July 25, 2011, accessed February 8, 2012, http://daviddegraw.org/2011/07/political-bribery-watch-79-of-former-members-of-congress-have-become-lobbyists/.

78 Ryan J. Reilly, "Shadow Congress: Nearly 200 Ex-Lawmakers Work for Lobbying Shops," *Talkingpointsmemo.com*, June 14, 2011, accessed February 1, 2012, http://tpmmuckraker.talkingpointsmemo.com/2011/06/shadow_congress_nearly_200_ex-lawmakers_work_for_lobbying_shops.php.

79 Pat Choate, *Agents of Influence: How Japan Manipulates America's Political and Economic System* (New York: A.A. Knopf, 1990).

80 Baumgartner et al., *Lobbying and Policy Change*.

81 Conor McGrath, "The Ideal Lobbyist: Personal Characteristics of Effective Lobbyists," *Journal of Communication Management* 10 (2006), 67–79.

82 McGrath, "The Ideal Lobbyist," 75.

83 McGrath, "The Ideal Lobbyist," 75.

84 Baumgartner et al., *Lobbying and Policy Change*, Chapter 7.

85 Baumgartner et al., *Lobbying and Policy Change*, 184–87.

86 John P. Heinz, Edward O. Laumann, Robert L. Nelson, and Robert H. Salisbury, *The Hollow Core: Private Interests in National Policy Making* (Cambridge, MA: Harvard University Press, 1993), Chapter 11.

87 Nownes and Freeman, "Interest Group Activity in the States," 104.

6 Electoral Lobbying

1 Federal Election Commission, "2008 Presidential Campaign Finance, Contributions to All Candidates," accessed February 3, 2012, http://www.fec.gov/disclosurep/pnational.do;jsessionid=F46FB44FEB006545EC904E92A6731C2D.worker1.

2 Center for Responsive Politics, "The Money Behind the Elections," accessed September 9, 2011, http://www.opensecrets.org/bigpicture/index.php.

3 Center for Responsive Politics, "Price of Admission," accessed September 9, 2011, http://www.opensecrets.org/bigpicture/stats.php?cycle=2010.

4 Center for Responsive Politics, "Election Stats, 2010," accessed September 9, 2011, http://www.opensecrets.org/bigpicture/elec_stats.php?cycle=2010.

5 "The World's Billionaires: #23 Michael Bloomberg," *Forbes*, online, accessed September 9, 2011, http://www.forbes.com/lists/2010/10/billionaires-2010_Michael-Bloomberg_C610.html.

6 Jack Chang, "Meg Whitman's Campaign Spending Totals $178.5 million," *McClatchy.com*, January 2, 2011, accessed September 9, 2011, http://www.mcclatchydc.com/2011/02/01/107827/meg-whitmans-campaign-spending.html.

7 National Institute on Money in State Politics, "Home > Iowa 2010 > Lobbyists," accessed April 26, 2011, http://www.followthemoney.org/database/StateGlance/state_lobbyists.phtml?s=IA&y=2010.

8 Mike Stucka, "Reichert, Paris Had Expensive Winning Campaigns," *Macon.com*, August

26, 2011, accessed September 9, 2011, http://www.macon.com/2011/08/26/1678375/reichert-paris-had-expensive-winning.html.

9   Larry Makinson, *The Big Picture: Money Follows Power Shift on Capitol Hill* (Washington, DC: Center for Responsive Politics, 1997), 6.

10 Shanto Iyengar, *Media Politics: A Citizen's Guide, 2nd edition* (New York: W.W. Norton, 2011), Chapter 6.

11 I base my estimate on several sources including: Brian E. Adams, *Campaign Finance in Local Elections: Buying the Grassroots* (Boulder, CO: First Forum Press, 2010); Larry M. Bartels, *Unequal Democracy: The Political Economy of the New Gilded Age* (New York: Princeton University Press, 2008); Lawrence Grey, *How to Win a Local Election: A Complete Step-by-Step Guide, 3rd edition* (Lanham, MD: National Book Network, 2007); Travis N. Ridout and Michael M. Franz, *The Persuasive Power of Campaign Advertising* (Philadelphia, PA: Temple University Press, 2011); James A. Thurber, Candice J. Nelson, and David A. Dulio, *Crowded Airwaves: Campaign Advertising in Elections* (Washington, DC: Brookings Institution Press, 2000).

12 Center for Responsive Politics, "Barack Obama," accessed January 25, 2012, http://www.opensecrets.org/pres08/summary.php?cycle=2008&cid=N00009638.

13 Center for Responsive Politics, "John McCain," accessed January 12, 2012, http://www.opensecrets.org/pres08/summary.php?cycle=2008&cid=N00006424.

14 On congressional campaigns, see, for example, Kathleen Ronayne, "OpenSecrets.org Unveils 2010 'Big Picture' Analysis," July 26, 2011, accessed January 4, 2012, http://www.opensecrets.org/news/2011/07/2010-election-big-picture.html.

15 Frank J. Sorauf, *Inside Campaign Finance: Myths and Realities* (New Haven, CT: Yale University Press, 1992), 2–7.

16 Sorauf, *Inside Campaign Finance*, 2–3.

17 Sorauf, *Inside Campaign Finance*, 4.

18 424 U.S. 1 (1976).

19 I say "some" here because some types of business firms—for example, sole proprietorships that contract with the federal government—are not allowed under federal law to form PACs. Likewise, some citizen groups and coalitions—and it really comes down to how the groups organize themselves for tax purposes—are not allowed to form PACs.

20 Wright, *Interest Groups and Congress*, 120.

21 Federal Election Commission, "Contribution Limits 2011–12," accessed December 5, 2011, http://www.fec.gov/pages/brochures/contriblimits.shtml. The combined limit for state, district, and local party committees is $5,000 per year. The national party committee limit is shared by the national party committee and the Senate campaign committee.

22 This is a little-known aspect of federal campaign finance law.

23 James D. King and Helenan S. Robin, "Political Action Committees in State Elections," *American Review of Politics* 16 (1995), 61–77.

24 Clive S. Thomas and Ronald J. Hrebenar, "Political Action Committees in the States: Some Preliminary Findings" (Paper presented at the annual meeting of the American Political Science Association, Washington DC, September, 1991).

25 Nevada Secretary of State, Ross Miller, "Political Action Committee Registration List," accessed October 31, 2011, http://nvsos.gov/PacReport/.

26 Maryland State Board of Elections, "Maryland PACs List," accessed October 13, 2011, http://www.elections.state.md.us/campaign_finance/pac_list.html.

27 Texans for Public Justice, "Texas PACs: 2010 Election Cycle Spending," accessed October 18, 2011, http://info.tpj.org/reports/pdf/PACs2010.pdf.

28 Center for Responsive Politics, "Recipients: Every Republican is Crucial PAC Contributions to Federal Candidates," accessed December 5, 2011, http://www.opensecrets.org/pacs/pacgot.php?cycle=2010&cmte=C00384701.

29 Federal Election Commission, "PAC Count, 1974–present," accessed February 1, 2012, http://www.fec.gov/press/summaries/2011/2011paccount.shtml.

30 Federal Election Commission, "Growth in PAC Financial Activity Slows," accessed January 21, 2012, http://www.fec.gov/press/press2009/20090415PAC/20090424PAC.shtml.

31 Federal Election Commission, "PAC Activity Increases in First Six Months of 2011," accessed February 3, 2012, http://www.fec.gov/press/Press2011/20110909_6mthPAC.shtml.

32 Federal Election Commission, "2008 Presidential Campaign Finance, Contributions to All Candidates."

33 Ronayne, "OpenSecrets.org Unveils 2010 'Big Picture' Analysis."

34 "PAC Spending at Record High in Massachusetts Politics," *The Patriot Ledger* online, September 23, 2011, accessed October 18, 2012, http://www.patriotledger.com/answerbook/hull/x372774989/PAC-spending-at-record-high-in-Massachusetts-politics.

35 Texans for Public Justice, "Texas PACs."

36 National Conference of State Legislatures, "State Limits on Contributions to Candidates, 2011–2012 Election Cycle," accessed December 6, 2012, http://www.ncsl.org/Portals/1/documents/legismgt/Limits_to_Candidates_2011–2012.pdf.

37 Sorauf, *Inside Campaign Finance*, 180.

38 Federal Election Commission, "Summary of PAC Activity, 1990–2010," 2011, accessed January 25, 2012, http://www.fec.gov/press/bkgnd/cf_summary_info/2010pac_fullsum/4sumhistory2010.pdf.

39 Frank J. Sorauf, "Adaptation and Innovation in Political Action Committees," in *Interest Group Politics, 4th edition*, eds. Allan J. Cigler and Burdett A. Loomis (Washington, DC: CQ Press, 1995), 178.

40 Emily's List, "Ways to Give," accessed January 25, 2012, http://emilyslist.org/action/ways_to_give/; See also Sorauf, "Adaptation and Innovation in Political Action Committees," 178.

41 Sorauf, "Adaptation and Innovation in Political Action Committees," 181.

42 It does have to disclose this to the FEC, however.

43 For more information on Super PACs, see Center for Responsive Politics, "Super PACs," accessed December 6, 2011, http://www.opensecrets.org/pacs/superpacs.php?cycle=2012.

44 Christian Coalition of America, "Voter Guide—Christian Coalition of America," accessed December 5, 2011, www.cc.org/files/3/2008_Presidential_voter_guide_.pdf.

45 "The NRA's Electoral Influence," *Washington Post* online, December 15, 2010, accessed December 5, 2011, http://www.washingtonpost.com/wp-srv/special/nation/guns/nra-endorsements-campaign-spending/.

46 Matthew J. Burbank, Ronald J. Hrebenar, and Robert C. Benedict, *Parties, Interest Groups, and Political Campaigns, 2nd edition* (Boulder, CO: Paradigm Publishers, 2012), 79–81.

47 David C. Kimball, "Interest Groups in the 2008 Presidential Election: The Barking Dog That Didn't Bite," *The Forum* 6 (2008), Article 2.

48 See Nownes and Freeman, "Interest Group Activity in the States," 92.

49 Brooks Jackson, *Honest Graft: Big Money and the American Political Process* (New York: Knopf, 1988), 295.

50 See Stephen Ansolabehere, James M. Snyder, Jr., and Micky Tripathi, "Are PAC Contributions and Lobbying Linked? New Evidence from the 1995 Lobby Disclosure Act," *Business and Politics* 4 (2002), 131–55; Janet Grenzke, "Shopping in the Congressional Supermarket: The Currency is Complex," *American Journal of Political Science* 33 (1989), 1–24; Gregory Wawro, "A Panel Probit Analysis of Campaign Contributions and Roll-Call Votes," *American Journal of Political Science* 45 (2001), 563–79; John R. Wright, "Contributions, Lobbying, and Committee Voting in the U.S. House of Representatives," *American Political Science Review* 84 (1990), 417–38. There are, of course, those who believe that campaign money *does* substantially alter government decision-makers' behavior. See, for example, John P. Frendreis and Richard W. Waterman, "PAC Contributions and Legislative Behavior: Senate Voting on Trucking Deregulation," *Social Science Quarterly* 66 (1985), 401–12; Stephen Moore, Sidney M. Wolfe, Deborah Lindes, and Clifford Douglas, "Epidemiology of Failed Tobacco Control Legislation," *Journal of the American Medical Association* 272 (1994), 1171–73; Douglas D. Roscoe and Shannon Jenkins, "A Meta-Analysis of Campaign Contributions' Impact on Roll Call Voting," *Social Science Quarterly* 86 (2005), 52–68; Thomas Stratmann, "Can Special Interests Buy Congressional Votes? Evidence from Financial Services Legislation," *Journal of Law and Economics* 45 (2002), 345–73.

51 Stephen Ansolabehere, John M. de Figueiredo, and James M. Snyder, Jr., "Why is There so Little Money in U.S. Politics?," *The Journal of Economic Perspectives* 17 (2003), 105–30.

52 Scott Ainsworth, "Regulating Lobbyists and Interest Group Influence," *Journal of Politics* 55 (1993), 41–56; Ansolabehere, de Figueiredo, and Snyder, "Why is There so Little Money in U.S. Politics?"; Grenzke, "Shopping in the Congressional Supermarket"; Laura I. Langbein, "Money and Access: Some Empirical Evidence," *Journal of Politics* 48 (1986), 1052–62.

53 Bertram J. Levine, *The Art of Lobbying: Building Trust and Selling Policy* (Washington, DC: CQ Press, 2009), 74–75.

54 Rosenthal, *The Third House*, 139.

55 Rosenthal, *The Third House*, 139.

56 Rosenthal, *The Third House*, 136.

57 See Gary C. Jacobson, *The Politics of Congressional Elections*, 8th edition (Upper Saddle River, NJ: Pearson, 2012).

58 See Richard L. Hall and Frank W. Wayman, "Buying Time: Moneyed Interests and the Mobilization of Bias in Congressional Committees," *American Political Science Review* 84 (1990), 797–820; Wright, "Contributions, Lobbying, and Committee Voting in the U.S. House of Representatives."

59 Federal Election Commission, "Summary of PAC Financial Activity," accessed December 8, 2011, http://www.fec.gov/press/press2010/20100406Pary_Files/1pac 2009.pdf.

60 Hall and Wayman, "Buying Time."

61 Sabato and Simpson, *Dirty Little Secrets*.

62 Massie Ritsch and Courtney Mabeus, "Casting Off Jack Abramoff," *Opensecrets*, April 7, 2006, accessed December 8, 2011, http://www.opensecrets.org/news/2006/04/casting-off-abramoff.html.

63 George Will, "Too Much Ado About Campaign Spending," *Billings Gazette* online, October 19, 2010, accessed January 3, 2012, http://billingsgazette.com/news/opinion/editorial/columnists/george_will/article_06e69f86-db26-11df-a862-001cc4c03286.html#ixzz1iQF8ZkNt.

64 Federal Election Commission, "Table 6: PACs Grouped by Total Spent, 2009–2010," accessed January 3, 2012, http://www.fec.gov/press/bkgnd/cf_summary_info/2010pac_fullsum/6groupbyspending2010.pdf.

65 In fact, the Supreme Court more or less sanctioned this view when it declared campaign spending a form of speech in its famous *Buckley v. Valeo* (1976) decision.

7 Indirect Lobbying

1 See John W. Kingdon, *Congressmen's Voting Decisions, 2nd edition* (New York: Harper and Row, 1981).

2 Initiative and Referendum Institute at the University of Southern California, "What are Ballot Propositions, Initiatives, and Referendums?," accessed December 14, 2011, http://www.iandrinstitute.org/Quick%20Fact%20-%20What%20is%20I&R.htm#Initiatives. There are different types of initiatives, and to learn more about them see the source above.

3 Initiative and Referendum Institute at the University of Southern California, "State-by-State List of Initiative and Referendum Provisions," accessed December 4, 2011, http://www.iandrinstitute.org/statewide_i&r.htm.

4 Initiative and Referendum Institute at the University of Southern California, "State-by-State List of Initiative and Referendum Provisions."

5 Initiative and Referendum Institute at the University of Southern California, "State-by-State List of Initiative and Referendum Provisions."

6 Initiative and Referendum Institute at the University of Southern California, "Information on the Initiative and Referendum Process at the Local Level," accessed December 4, 2011, http://www.iandrinstitute.org/Local%20I&R.htm.

7 Initiative and Referendum Institute at the University of Southern California, "Initiative Use," accessed December 4, 2011, http://www.iandrinstitute.org/IRI%20Initiative%20Use%20(2010-1).

8 Initiative and Referendum Institute at the University of Southern California, "Initiative Use."

9 This phrase was coined by interest group expert Jeffrey Berry. For details, see Berry and Wilcox, *The Interest Group Society, 5th edition*, 128–29.

10 See, for example, Morris P. Fiorina, *Retrospective Voting in American National Elections* (New Haven, CT: Yale University Press, 1981); D. Roderick Kiewiet, *Macroeconomics and Micropolitics: The Electoral Effects of Economic Issues* (Chicago: University of Chicago Press, 1983). The classic is Verba, Schlozman, and Brady, *Voice and Equality*.

11 Exxon Mobil, "An Amazing Resource for Americans. A Responsible Way to Produce It," *Washington Post* online, May 23, 2011, accessed December 14, 2011, http://www.washingtonpost.com/rw/WashingtonPost/Content/Epaper/2011-05-23/Ax7.pdf.

12 Burdett A. Loomis and Eric Sexton, "Choosing to Advertise: How Interests Decide," in *Interest Group Politics, 4th edition*, eds. Allan J. Cigler and Burdett A. Loomis (Washington, DC: CQ Press, 1995), 193–214.

13 Rex Briggs and Greg Stuart, *What Sticks: Why Most Advertising Fails and How to Guarantee Yours Succeeds* (Chicago: Kaplan Publishing, 2006); Raj Sethuraman, Gerard J. Tellis and Richard. A. Briesch, "How Well Does Advertising Work? Generalizations from Meta-Analysis of Brand Advertising Elasticities," *Journal of Marketing Research* 48 (2011), 457–71; Bryce Corrigan and Ted Brader, "Campaign Advertising: Reassessing the Impact of Campaign Ads on Political Behavior," in *New Directions in Campaigns and Elections*, ed. Stephen K. Medvic (New York: Routledge, 2011), 79–97.

14 Stephen Ansolabehere and Shanto Iyengar, *Going Negative: How Attack Advertisements Shrink and Polarize the Electorate* (New York: Free Press, 1995); Edwin Diamond and Stephen Bates, *The Spot: The Rise of Political Advertising on Television, 3rd edition* (Cambridge, MA: MIT Press, 1992); Karen M. Kaufmann, John R. Petrocik, and Daron R. Shaw, *Unconventional Wisdom: Facts and Myths About American Voters* (New York: Oxford University Press, 2008); Richard R. Lau, Lee Sigelman, Caroline Heldman, and Paul Babbitt, "The Effects of Negative Political Advertisements: A Meta-Analytic Assessment," *American Political Science Review* 93 (1999), 851–75.

15 Christopher A. Cooper and Anthony J. Nownes, "Money Well Spent? An Experimental Investigation of the Effects of Advertorials on Citizen Opinion," *American Politics Research* 32 (2004), 546–69.

16 Wilcox, "The Dynamics of Lobbying the Hill," 96.

17 Wilcox, "The Dynamics of Lobbying the Hill," 96–98.

18 Richard L. Hall and Richard Anderson, "Issue Advertising and Legislative Advocacy in Health Politics," in *Interest Group Politics, 8th edition*, eds. Allan J. Cigler and Burdett A. Loomis (Washington, DC: CQ Press, 2012), 223.

19 Hall and Anderson, "Issue Advertising and Legislative Advocacy in Health Politics," 223.

20 Hall and Anderson, "Issue Advertising and Legislative Advocacy in Health Politics," 223.

21 Paul R. Abramson and William Claggett, "Recruitment and Political Participation," *Political Research Quarterly* 54 (2001), 905–16; Henry E. Brady, Kay Lehman Schlozman, and Sidney Verba, "Prospecting for Participants: Rational Expectations and the Recruitment of Political Activists," *American Political Science Review* 93 (1999), 153–68; Michael W. Giles and Marilyn K. Dantico, "Political Participation and Neighborhood Social Context Revisited," *American Journal of Political Science* 26 (1982), 144–50; Verba, Schlozman, and Brady, *Voice and Equality*, Chapter 5; Alan S. Zuckerman and Darrell M. West, "The Political Bases of Citizen Contacting: A Cross-National Analysis," *American Political Science Review* 79 (1985), 117–31. The classic work is Steven J. Rosenstone and John Mark Hansen, *Mobilization, Participation, and Democracy in America* (New York: Macmillan, 1993).

22 Allan J. Cigler and Burdett A. Loomis, "Contemporary Interest Group Politics: More Than 'More of the Same,'" in *Interest Group Politics, 4th edition*, eds. Allan J. Cigler and Burdett A. Loomis (Washington, DC: CQ Press, 1995), 402.

23 Cigler and Loomis, "Contemporary Interest Group Politics," 395.

24 Burbank, Hrebenar, and Benedict, *Parties, Interest Groups, and Political Campaigns, 2nd edition*, 193.

25 Rose-An Jessica Dioquino, "Children Ask US Govt to Stop Deporting Undocumented Immigrants," *GMA News* online, December 13, 2011, accessed January 2, 2012, http://www.gmanetwork.com/news/story/241537/pinoyabroad/children-ask-us-govt-to-stop-deporting-undocumented-immigrants.

26 Brad Fitch and Kathy Goldschmidt, with Ellen Fulton and Nicole Griffin,

"Communicating with Congress: How Capitol Hill is Coping with the Surge in Citizen Advocacy," accessed December 15, 2011, http://www.congressfoundation.org/index. php?option=com_content&view=article&id=67&Itemid=.

27 Lori Johnston, "Q: How Many Letters Does the President Receive Daily?," *Atlanta Journal Constitution* online, December 30, 2009, accessed December 15, 2011. http://www.ajc.com/news/q-how-many-letters-262394.html.

28 William P. Browne, *Cultivating Congress: Constituents, Issues, and Interests in Agricultural Policymaking* (Lawrence: University Press of Kansas, 1995).

29 Donald E. deKieffer, *The Citizen's Guide to Lobbying Congress* (Chicago: Chicago Review Press, 2007), Chapter 11; Wilcox, "The Dynamics of Lobbying the Hill," 97.

30 Laura R. Woliver, "Abortion Interests: From the Usual Suspects to Expanded Coalitions," in *Interest Group Politics*, 5th edition, eds. Allan J. Cigler and Burdett A. Loomis (Washington, DC: CQ Press, 1998), 327–42.

31 Jim Galloway, "The Myth of the 15,000," *Atlanta Journal Constitution* online, April 27, 2009, accessed January 5, 2012, http://blogs.ajc.com/political-insider-jim-galloway/.

32 "ABC News Was Misquoted on Crowd Size," *ABC News* online, September 13, 2009, accessed December 15, 2011, http://abcnews.go.com/Politics/protest-crowd-size-estimate-falsely-attributed-abc-news/story?id=8558055.

33 "Madison Protests Hit Largest Numbers on Saturday," *Huffington Post*, February 19, 2009, accessed December 15, 2011, http://www.huffingtonpost.com/2011/02/19/madison-protests_n_825616.html.

34 "Occupy Wall Street: A Protest Timeline," *The Week*, November 21, 2011, accessed December 15, 2011, http://theweek.com/article/index/220100/occupy-wall-street-a-protest-timeline.

35 Marjorie Randon Hershey, "Direct Action and the Abortion Issue: The Political Participation of Single-issue Groups," in *Interest Group Politics*, 2nd edition, eds. Allan J. Cigler, and Burdett A. Loomis (Washington, DC: CQ Press, 1986), 27–45.

36 You can see some of the group's images and learn more about the group at its website, which is http://www.abortionno.org/. I must warn you, however, that what you will see is quite graphic and may be disturbing.

37 You can see these and other disturbing signs at http://www.godhatesfags.com/.

38 Daniel Human, "Postal Service: $3M in Cuts for Kokomo," *Insurancenews.net*, November 29, 2011, accessed December 16, 2011, http://insurancenewsnet.com/article.aspx?id=304395.

39 Wright says that the best way to think of indirect lobbying campaigns are as "field experiments in electoral mobilization." See Wright, *Interest Groups and Congress*, 90.

40 See Schattschneider, *The Semisovereign People*.

41 Christopher H. Foreman, Jr., "Grassroots Victim Organizations: Mobilizing for Personal and Public Health," in *Interest Group Politics*, 4th edition, eds. Allan J. Cigler and Burdett A. Loomis (Washington, DC: CQ Press, 1995), 40–47.

42 Truman, *The Governmental Process*, 213.

43 Truman, *The Governmental Process*, 213.

44 Truman, *The Governmental Process*, 389.

45 Some interesting early studies of indirect lobbying include: L.E. Gleeck, "96 Congressmen Make Up Their Minds," *Public Opinion Quarterly* 4 (1940), 3–24; Rowena Wyant, "Voting Via the Senate Mailbag," *Public Opinion Quarterly* 5 (1941), 359–82.

46 Chong, *Collective Action and the Civil Rights Movement*.

47 Lindsay William-Ross, "Rap or Run: Going Door to Door for Greenpeace in LA," *laist* online, September 3, 2007, accessed December 15, 2011, http://laist.com/2007/09/03/rap_or_run_goin.php.

48 This quotation comes from "The Voluntary Way is the American Way" (Chicago: American Medical Association National Education Campaign, 1949). The brochure is described in detail in Truman, *The Governmental Process*, 231.

49 Enter "death panels" into the Google search engine and you will find the websites of numerous interest groups that use the term to deride President Obama's health care bill.

50 To see these publications, see PETA's website at http://www.petacatalog.com/catalog/Literature-39-1.html.

51 In 1949, for example, a trade association of privately owned power companies placed an advertisement in a number of national magazines. The advertisement stated that private power companies were overregulated and should be left alone by the federal government (which was threatening to adopt further regulations). See Truman, *The Governmental Process*, 232.

52 This advertisement appeared in the *New York Times* on September 21, 1993, A11.

53 Conservatives for Patients' Rights, "An Open Letter to President Obama," accessed December 15, 2011, http://wonkroom.thinkprogress.org/wp-content/uploads/2009/03/cprad1.JPG.

54 You can see some of these advertisements for yourself at Eric M. Appleman, "Print Advertising in the Health Care Reform Debate," *P2012*.com, April 4, 2010, http://www.p2012.org/2010/hcprint.html.

55 Appleman, "Print Advertising in the Health Care Reform Debate."

56 Godwin, "Money, Technology, and Political Interests."

57 Godwin, "Money, Technology, and Political Interests," 311.

58 Godwin, "Money, Technology, and Political Interests," 310.

59 Darrell M. West, Diane Heith, and Chris Goodwin, "Harry and Louise Go to Washington: Political Advertising and Health Care Reform," *Journal of Health Politics, Policy, and Law* 21 (1996), 35–68.

60 Vanessa Fuhrmans, "Harry and Louise are Back. Again," *WSJ Blogs* online, July 16, 2009, accessed December 16, 2011, http://blogs.wsj.com/health/2009/07/16/harry-and-louise-are-back-again/.

61 You can see both advertisements here: http://www.time.com/time/specials/packages/article/0,28804,1917490_1917489_1917466,00.html, accessed on December 16, 2011.

62 Dan Eggen, "The Influence Industry: Coming Soon to a Screen Near You—A Lobbying Campaign," *The Washington Post* online, July 13, 2011, accessed December 16, 2011, http://www.washingtonpost.com/politics/the-influence-industry-coming-soon-to-a-screen-near-you—a-lobbying-campaign/2011/07/13/gIQAFyK9CI_story.html.

63 Eric Alterman, *Sound and Fury: The Washington Punditocracy and the Collapse of American Politics* (New York: HarperCollins, 1992).

64 For a study of who gets on the air, see A. Trevor Thrall, "The Myth of the Outside Strategy: Mass Media News Coverage of Interest Groups," *Political Communication* 23 (2006), 407–20.

65 http://www.cc.org, accessed on December 16, 2011.

66 U.S. Chamber of Commerce, "Untitled Wall Post," accessed December 21, 2011, http://www.facebook.com/uschamber?sk=wall.

67 Visit the Heritage Foundation bookstore at https://secure.heritage.org/bookstore/.

68 Cigler and Loomis, "Contemporary Interest Group Politics," 394–98.

69 Cigler and Loomis, "Contemporary Interest Group Politics," 394–98.

70 You can go check out the company at www.americandirections.com.

71 Cigler and Loomis, "Contemporary Interest Group Politics," 396.

72 Wilcox, "The Dynamics of Lobbying the Hill," 98.

73 Daniel Schulman, "Bonner's Latest Astroturf Admission (Plus More Fake Letters)," *Mother Jones* online, Aug. 18, 2009, accessed December 21, 2011, http://motherjones.com/mojo/2009/08/bonners-latest-astroturf-admission.

74 Schulman, "Bonner's Latest Astroturf Admission (Plus More Fake Letters)."

8 Interest Groups and Political Parties

1 Marjorie Randon Hershey, *Party Politics in America*, 12th edition (New York: Pearson Longman, 2007), 6.

2 Hershey, *Party Politics in America*, 7.

3 Hershey, *Party Politics in America*, 7–8.

4 John F. Bibby and Brian F. Schaffner, *Politics, Parties, and Elections in America*, 6th edition (Boston: Thomson/Wadsworth, 2008); Kira Sanbonmatsu, "Political Parties and the Recruitment of Women to State Legislatures," *Journal of Politics* 64 (2002), 791–809; Kira Sanbonmatsu, "The Legislative Party and Candidate Recruitment in the American States," *Party Politics* 12 (2006), 233–56.

5 Federal Election Commission, "Coordinated Communications and Independent Expenditures," accessed January 9, 2012, http://www.fec.gov/pages/brochures/indexp.shtml#Who_IE.

6 Federal Election Commission, "Coordinated Communications and Independent Expenditures."

7 Burbank, Hrebenar, and Benedict, *Parties, Interest Groups, and Political Campaigns*, 2nd edition, 134.

8 Burbank, Hrebenar, and Benedict, *Parties, Interest Groups, and Political Campaigns*, 2nd edition, 134.

9 Burbank, Hrebenar, and Benedict, *Parties, Interest Groups, and Political Campaigns*, 2nd edition, 135.

10 Hershey, *Party Politics in America*, 61.

11 "Exit Polls," *CNN.com*, 2008. Accessed January 10, 2012, http://www.cnn.com/ELECTION/2008/results/polls/#USP00p1.

12 Michael T. Heaney, "Bridging the Gap between Political Parties and Interest Groups," in *Interest Group Politics*, 8th edition, eds. Allan J. Cigler and Burdett A. Loomis (Washington, DC: CQ Press, 2012), 194–218.

13 Heaney, "Bridging the Gap between Political Parties and Interest Groups," 204.

14 Heaney, "Bridging the Gap between Political Parties and Interest Groups," 204.

15 Heaney, "Bridging the Gap between Political Parties and Interest Groups," 204–07.

16 Heaney, "Bridging the Gap between Political Parties and Interest Groups," 196.

17 Loomis and Cigler, "Introduction," 18–21.

18 These are the group's own words. See clubforgrowth.org.

19 Aaron Astor, "Knee-Capping: Why the Club for Growth Does it (And Why It Will Never Work)," *The Moderate Voice*, April 28, 2009, accessed January 21, 2012, http://the moderatevoice.com/30329/knee-capping-why-the-club-for-growth-does-it-and-why-it-will-never-work/.

20 These are the group's own words. See http://www.logcabin.org/site/c.nsKSL7PML pF/b.5468093/k.BE4C/Home.htm.

21 See, for example, Ruth Murray Brown, *For a "Christian America": A History of the Religious Right* (Amherst, NY: Prometheus Books, 2002); Michael Sean Winters, *God's Right Hand: How Jerry Falwell Made God a Republican and Baptized the American Right* (New York: HarperOne, 2012).

22 "Pharmaceutical Companies Offer $80 Billion Toward Health Care Reform," *PBSNewsHour* online, June 22, 2009, accessed January 24, 2012, www.pbs.oeg/ newshour/updates/health/jan-june09/pharma_06-22.html.

23 Allison Linn, "Big Employers Dip Into Health Care Debate: Hoping to Rein In Costs, Some are Taking a Stand on Health Care Reform," *MSNBC.com*, August 25, 2009, accessed January 24, 2012, www.msnbc.msn.com/id/32513127/ns/business-us_ business/t/big-employers-dip-health-cre-debate/#.Tx7JEJJ-L9k.

24 Whitford David, "How Scott Walker Ignited a Labor Renaissance," *CNNMoney*, March 7, 2011, accessed January 24, 2012, http://management.fortune.cnn.com/2011/03/07/ how-scott-walker-ignited-a-labor-renaissance/.

25 Herbert B. Asher, Eric S. Heberlig, Randall B. Ripley, and Karen Snyder, *American Labor Unions in the Electoral Arena* (Lanham, MD: Rowman and Littlefield, 2001), Chapter 8.

9 The Influence of Interest Groups

1 National Election Study, University of Michigan, Center for Political Studies, "Is the Government Run for the Benefit of All, 1964–2008," accessed January 12, 2012, http://electionstudies.org/nesguide/toptable/tab5a_2.htm.

2 National Election Study, University of Michigan, Center for Political Studies, "Is the Government Run for the Benefit of All, 1964–2008."

3 Some scholars were "ahead of the curve." Two of the earliest works to examine the role of interest groups in American politics are Herring, *Group Representation before Congress*, and Peter H. Odegard, *Pressure Politics: The Story of the Anti-Saloon League* (New York: Columbia University Press, 1928).

4 See, for example, Frank Johnson Goodnow, *Politics and Administration: A Study in Government* (New York: Macmillan, 1900); W.A. Schaper, "What Do Students Know About American Government, Before Taking College Courses in Political Science? A Report to the Section on Instruction in Political Science," *Proceedings of the American Political Science Association* 2 (1905), 207–28. Woodrow Wilson, *Congressional Government: A Study in American Politics* (Boston: Houghton Mifflin, 1885).

5 Truman, *The Governmental Process*.

6 One of the best known is Robert A. Dahl, *Who Governs? Democracy and Power in an American City* (New Haven, CT: Yale University Press, 1961).

7 Other pluralist works include Arthur Fisher Bentley, *The Process of Government: A Study of Social Pressures* (Chicago: University of Chicago Press, 1908); Earl Latham, *The Group*

Basis of Politics: A Study in Basing-Point Legislative (Ithaca, NY: Cornell University Press, 1952); Robert T. Golembiewski, "'The Group Basis of Politics': Notes on Analysis and Development," *American Political Science Review* 54 (1960), 962–71.

8 Not all early scholars of interest groups shared pluralists' optimism. Political sociologist C. Wright Mills, for example, argued that government decision-makers listened solely to the demands of a very narrow stratum of interest groups that represented rich and powerful people—people Mills called "the power elite." Because the "power elite" were better represented than ordinary citizens, Mills argued, government decisions were skewed toward the interests of the rich and famous. See C. Wright Mills, *The Power Elite* (New York: Oxford University Press, 1956). See also Peter Bachrach and Morton S. Baratz, "Two Faces of Power," *American Political Science Review* 56 (1962), 947–52. For a more recent study, see John Gaventa, *Power and Powerlessness: Quiescence and Rebellion in an Appalachian Valley* (Urbana: University of Illinois Press, 1980).

9 Some early studies that portrayed lobbyists as benevolent transmitters of information from citizens to government decision-makers include: Raymond A. Bauer, Ithiel de Sola Pool, and Lewis A. Dexter, *American Business and Public Policy: The Politics of Foreign Trade* (New York: Atherton Press, 1963); Lester W. Milbrath, *Political Participation: How and Why Do People Get Involved in Politics?* (Chicago: Rand McNally, 1965); Andrew M. Scott and Margaret A. Hunt, *Congress and Lobbies: Image and Reality* (Chapel Hill: University of North Carolina Press, 1966).

10 Works utilizing the subgovernment concept include Douglas Cater, *Power in Washington: A Critical Look at Today's Struggle to Govern in the Nation's Capital* (New York: Vintage Books, 1964); J. Leiper Freeman, *The Political Process: Executive Bureau–Legislative Committee Relations* (Garden City, NY: Doubleday, 1955); Ernest S. Griffith, *Impasse of Democracy: A Study of the Modern Government in Action* (New York: Harrison-Hilton Books, 1939).

11 Jeffrey M. Berry, "Subgovernments, Issue Networks, and Political Conflict," in *Remaking American Politics*, eds. Richard A. Harris and Sidney M. Milkis (Boulder, CO: Westview Press, 1989), 239–60.

12 Wright, *Interest Groups and Congress*, 168–69.

13 Because the shape of a subgovernment resembles that of a triangle, some subgovernment theorists called subgovernments "iron triangles."

14 William P. Browne, "Policy and Interests: Instability and Change in a Classic Issue Subsystem," in *Interest Group Politics, 2nd edition*, eds. Allan Cigler and Burdett A. Loomis (Washington, DC: CQ Press, 1986), 185.

15 Subgovernment theorists were highly critical of the policy outcomes produced by subgovernments. The problem with subgovernment policymaking was this: the opinions of ordinary citizens were more or less ignored by government decision-makers. Because (as we learned in Chapter 3) some interests were not represented by interest groups, they were ignored by government decision-makers.

16 William P. Browne, *Groups, Interests, and U.S. Public Policy* (Washington, DC: Georgetown University Press, 1998), 213.

17 Browne, *Groups, Interests, and U.S. Public Policy*, 216.

18 See Hugh Heclo, "Issue Networks and the Executive Establishment," in *The New American Political System*, ed. Anthony King (Washington, DC: American Enterprise Institute, 1978), 102. Heclo uses the term "issue network" instead of policy domain. But the concepts are similar.

19 On how much easier it is for opponents of something than proponents, see Amy McKay, "Negative Lobbying and Policy Outcomes," *American Politics Research* 20 (2012), 116–46.

20 Baumgartner et al., *Lobbying and Policy Change*, 114.

21 Gallup Poll, "New High of 46% of Americans Support Legalizing Marijuana," *Gallup Politics*, October 28, 2010, accessed February 1, 2012, http://www.gallup.com/poll/144086/new-high-americans-support-legalizing-marijuana.aspx.

22 Gallup Poll, "New High of 46% of Americans Support Legalizing Marijuana."

23 See, for example, William P. Browne, "Organized Interests and Their Issue Niches: A Search for Pluralism in a Policy Domain," *Journal of Politics* 52 (1990), 477–509; Nownes, *Total Lobbying*, 95.

24 Nownes, *Total Lobbying*, Chapter 5.

25 Frank R. Baumgartner and Beth L. Leech, "Interest Niches and Policy Bandwagons: Patterns of Interest Group Involvement in National Politics," *Journal of Politics* 63 (2001), 1191–213.

26 Baumgartner and Leech, "Interest Niches and Policy Bandwagons," 1204.

27 This is the basic theme of Schattschneider's *The Semi-Sovereign People*. Empirical studies of interest group influence have reached the same conclusion. See, for example: John E. Chubb, *Interest Groups and the Bureaucracy: The Politics of Energy* (Stanford, CA: Stanford University Press, 1983); M. Margaret Conway, "PACS in the Political Process," in *Interest Group Politics, 3rd edition*, eds. Allan J. Cigler and Burdett A. Loomis (Washington, DC: CQ Press, 1991), 199–216; Nathan Grasse and Brianne Heidbreder, "The Influence of Lobbying Activity in State Legislatures: Evidence from Wisconsin," *Legislative Studies Quarterly* 36 (2011), 567–89; Richard A. Harris, "Politicized Management: The Changing Face of Business in American Politics," in *Remaking American Politics,* eds. Richard A. Harris and Sidney M. Milkis (Boulder, CO: Westview Press, 1989), 261–86; Woodrow Jones Jr. and K. Robert Keiser, "Issue Visibility and the Effects of PAC Money," *Social Science Quarterly* 68 (1987), 170–76; Trevor Rubenzer, "Campaign Contributions and U.S. Foreign Policy Outcomes: An Analysis of Cuban American Interests," *American Journal of Political Science* 55 (2011), 105–16. For details on the public's lack of interest in politics, see Michael X. Delli Carpini and Scott Keeter, *What Americans Know About Politics and Why It Matters* (New Haven, CT: Yale University Press, 1996); W. Russell Neuman, *The Paradox of Mass Politics: Knowledge and Opinion in the American Electorate* (Cambridge, MA: Harvard University Press, 1986).

28 Baumgartner and Leech, "Interest Niches and Policy Bandwagons," 1200.

29 Baumgartner and Leech, "Interest Niches and Policy Bandwagons," 1210 (Appendix A).

30 On groups getting what they want when they lobby on small, technical things, see: Browne, "Organized Interests and Their Issue Niches"; Chubb, *Interest Groups and the Bureaucracy*; Rubenzer, "Campaign Contributions and U.S. Foreign Policy Outcomes;" W.P. Welch, "Campaign Contributions and Legislative Voting: Milk Money and Dairy Price Supports," *Western Political Quarterly* 35 (1982), 478–95; Wright, "Contributions, Lobbying, and Committee Voting in the U.S. House of Representatives."

31 This is one of the themes of John Mark Hansen, *Gaining Access: Congress and the Farm Lobby, 1919–1981* (Chicago: University of Chicago Press, 1991).

32 Deniz Igan, Prachi Mishra, and Thierry Tressel, *A Fistful of Dollars: Lobbying and the Financial Crisis* (Washington, DC: International Monetary Fund, 2009).

33 See Rosenthal, *The Third House, 2nd edition*, 212–18; Richard K. Scotch, *From Good Will*

to Civil Rights: Transforming Federal Disability Policy (Philadelphia: Temple University Press, 1984).

34 Nonetheless, a small number of conservatives continue to complain that granting the disabled "special rights" is too costly.

35 This is the reason why the Americans with Disabilities Act (1991) was passed overwhelmingly by a Democratic Congress and then signed by a Republican president (George H.W. Bush).

36 On disability rights issues, see Scotch, *From Good Will to Civil Rights*. I heard this veterans' affairs example at a conference many years ago from interest group scholar Robert Salisbury.

37 Baumgartner et al., *Lobbying and Policy Change*, 233–34. See also Levine, *The Art of Lobbying*, 104–07.

38 Thad Kousser and Justin H. Phillips, "The Roots of Executive Power," Working paper, 2010, accessed January 12, 2012, www.columbia.edu/~jhp2121/workingpapers/RootsOfExecutivePower.pd.

39 See especially Baumgartner et al., *Lobbying and Policy Change*, Chapter 11. At the local level, this innovative study shows that in land-use disputes it is very important to have the planning commission on your side: Arnold Fleischmann and Carol A. Pierannunzi, "Citizens, Development Interests, and Local Land-Use Regulation," *Journal of Politics* 52 (1990), 838–53.

40 This is a very bastardized version of a definition found in Christine A. DeGregorio, *Networks of Champions: Leadership, Access, and Advocacy in the U.S. House of Representatives* (Ann Arbor: University of Michigan Press, 1997), 1.

41 Baumgartner et al., *Lobbying and Policy Change*, 234.

42 Jim Beam, "Pet Projects Never Really Disappear," *The Hayride.com*, May 5, 2011, accessed January 19, 2012, http://thehayride.com/2011/05/pet-projects-never-really-disappear/.

43 Amy Bingham and John Parkinson, "Houses Passes Bill Making Concealed Carry Permits Valid Across State Lines," *AbcNews* online, November 16, 2011, accessed January 12, 2012, http://abcnews.go.com/blogs/politics/2011/11/houses-passes-bill-making-concealed-carry-permits-valid-across-state-lines/.

44 Levine, *The Art of Lobbying*, 199. Italics in original.

45 The preeminent work on the value of coalitions is Kevin W. Hula, *Lobbying Together: Interest Group Coalitions in Legislative Politics* (Washington, DC: Georgetown University Press, 1999).

46 Allan J. Cigler and Burdett A. Loomis, "From Big Bird to Bill Gates: Organized Interests and the Emergence of Hyperpolitics," in *Interest Group Politics, 5th edition*, eds. Allan J. Cigler and Burdett A. Loomis (Washington, DC: CQ Press, 1998), 389–403.

47 This definition is based on Browne, "Organized Interests and Their Issue Niches."

48 Browne, "Organized Interests and Their Issue Niches," 486.

49 One of the best studies to show this is Daniel E. Bergan, "Does Grassroots Lobbying Work? A Field Experiment Measuring the Effects of an e-Mail Lobbying Campaign on Legislative Behavior," *American Politics Research* 37 (2009), 327–52.

50 See, for example, Kenneth M. Goldstein, *Interest Groups, Lobbying, and Participation in America* (New York: Cambridge University Press, 1999); Ken Kollman, *Outside Lobbying: Public Opinion and Interest Group Strategies* (Princeton, NJ: Princeton University Press, 1998).

51 James G. Gimpel, "Grassroots Organizations and Equilibrium Cycles in Group

Mobilization and Access," in *The Interest Group Connection: Electioneering, Lobbying, and Policymaking in Washington*, ed. Paul S. Herrnson, Ronald G. Shaiko, and Clyde Wilcox (Chatham, NJ: Chatham House, 1998), 100–15.

52 Levine, *The Art of Lobbying*, 87–90.

53 Levine, The Art of Lobbying, 87.

54 Richard Posner, "The U.S. Tax Subsidies for Oil Companies—Posner," *The Becker–Posner blog*, May 15, 2011, accessed January 27, 2012, http://www.becker-posner-blog.com/2011/05/the-us-tax-subsidies-for-oil-companiesposner.html.

55 See especially Schlozman and Tierney, "More of the Same: Washington Pressure Group Activity in a Decade of Change"; Nownes and DeAlejandro, "Lobbying in the New Millennium"; Nownes and Freeman, "Interest Group Activity in the States."

56 Heinz et al., *The Hollow Core*, Chapter 11. See also Grasse and Heidbreder, "The Influence of Lobbying Activity in State Legislatures."

57 Grasse and Heidbreder, "The Influence of Lobbying Activity in State Legislatures."

58 This is one of the points of this exceptional and insightful recent paper: Nancy Scherer, Brandon L. Bartels, and Amy Steigerwalt, "Sounding the Fire Alarm: The Role of Interest Groups in the Lower Federal Court Confirmation Process," *Journal of Politics* 70 (2008), 1026–39.

59 See, for example: Frank R. Baumgartner and Bryan D. Jones, *Agendas and Instability in American Politics* (Chicago: University of Chicago Press, 1993), Chapter 9; Thomas A. Birkland, *An Introduction to the Policy Process: Theories, Concepts, and Models of Public Policy Making, 3rd edition* (Armonk, NY: M.E. Sharpe, 2011), Chapter 5; Christopher J. Bosso, "Rethinking the Concept of Membership in Nature Advocacy Organizations," *Policy Studies Journal* 31 (2003), 397–411; Gregory A. Caldeira and John R. Wright, "Organized Interests and Agenda Setting in the U.S. Supreme Court," *American Political Science Review* 82 (1988), 1109–27; Elise A. Sochart, "Agenda Setting, the Role of Groups and the Legislative Process: The Prohibition of Female Circumcision in Britain," *Parliamentary Affairs* 41 (1988), 508–26.

60 Baumgartner et al., *Lobbying and Policy Change*, 212.

61 Stephen Ansolabehere, James M. Snyder, Jr., and Micky Tripathi, "Are PAC Contributions and Lobbying Linked? New Evidence from the 1995 Lobby Disclosure Act," *Business and Politics* 4 (2002), 131–55; Dorie Apollonio, Bruce E. Cain, and Lee Drutman, "Access and Lobbying: Looking Beyond the Corruption Paradigm," *Hastings Constitutional Law Quarterly* 36 (2008), 13–50; Marie Hojnacki and David C. Kimball, "PAC Contributions and Lobbying Contacts in Congressional Committees," *Political Research Quarterly* 54 (2001), 161–80; Jill Nicholson-Crotty and Sean Nicholson-Crotty, "Industry Strength and Immigrant Policy in the American States," *Political Research Quarterly* 64 (2011), 612–24; Rosenthal, *The Third House, 2nd edition*, 136–44; Richard A. Smith, "Interest Group Influence in the U.S. Congress," *Legislative Studies Quarterly* 20 (1995), 89–139; Christopher Witko, "PACs, Issue Context, and Congressional Decision-making," *Political Research Quarterly* 59 (2006), 283–95.

62 See, for example, Michelle L. Chin, "Constituents Versus Fat Cats: Testing Assumptions about Congressional Access Decisions," *American Politics Research* 33 (2005), 751–86.

10 Conclusion: The Role of Interest Groups in American Politics

1 Browne, *Groups, Interests, and U.S. Public Policy*, 231.
2 Browne, *Groups, Interests, and U.S. Public Policy*, 26.
3 Browne, *Groups, Interests, and U.S. Public Policy*, 167.
4 Browne, *Groups, Interests, and U.S. Public Policy*, 136.
5 Browne, *Groups, Interests, and U.S. Public Policy*, 136.
6 Browne, *Groups, Interests, and U.S. Public Policy*, 236–37.
7 Browne, *Groups, Interests, and U.S. Public Policy*, 231.
8 Allan J. Cigler and Burdett A. Loomis, "Stalemate Meets Uncertainty: Organized Interests in a Partisan Era," in *Interest Group Politics, 8th edition*, eds. Allan J. Cigler and Burdett A. Loomis (Washington, DC: CQ Press, 2012) 386–87.
9 Cigler and Loomis, "Stalemate Meets Uncertainty," 386.
10 Cigler and Loomis, "Stalemate Meets Uncertainty," 386.
11 Cigler and Loomis, "Stalemate Meets Uncertainty," 386.

Bibliography

AARP. "Member Benefits." Accessed May 23, 2011, http://www.aarp.org/benefits-discounts/financial-services/.

"ABC News Was Misquoted on Crowd Size." *ABC News* online, September 13, 2009. Accessed December 15, 2011, http://abcnews.go.com/Politics/protest-crowd-size-estimate-falsely-attributed-abc-news/story?id=8558055.

Abney, Glenn and Thomas P. Lauth. "Interest Group Influence in City Policy-Making: The Views of Administrators." *Western Political Quarterly* 38 (1985): 148–61.

Abramson, Paul R. and William Claggett. "Recruitment and Political Participation." *Political Research Quarterly* 54 (2001): 905–16.

Adams, Brian E. *Campaign Finance in Local Elections: Buying the Grassroots.* Boulder, CO: First Forum Press, 2010.

AFL-CIO. "About Us." Accessed January 31, 2012, http://www.aflcio.org/aboutus/.

Ainsworth, Scott. "Regulating Lobbyists and Interest Group Influence." *Journal of Politics* 55 (1993): 41–56.

Alonso-Zaldivar, Ricardo and Stephen Ohlemacher. "House Republicans Seek IRS Probe of AARP." *WKYC.com,* March 30, 2011. Accessed April 4, 2011, http://www.wkyc.com/news/article/183221/16/House-Republicans-seek-IRS-probe-of-AARP-.

Alterman, Eric. *Sound and Fury: The Washington Punditocracy and the Collapse of American Politics.* New York: HarperCollins, 1992.

American Bar Association. "State and Local Bar Associations." Accessed July 24, 2011, http://www.americanbar.org/groups/bar_services/resources/state_local_bar_associations.html.

"America's Most Hated Family." *BBC News* online, March 30, 2007. Accessed February 1, 2012, http://news.bbc.co.uk/2/hi/6507971.stm.

Ansolabehere, Stephen and Shanto Iyengar. *Going Negative: How Attack Advertisements Shrink and Polarize the Electorate.* New York: Free Press, 1995.

Ansolabehere, Stephen, James M. Snyder, Jr., and Micky Tripathi. "Are PAC Contributions and Lobbying Linked? New Evidence from the 1995 Lobby Disclosure Act." *Business and Politics* 4 (2002): 131–55.

Ansolabehere, Stephen, John M. de Figueiredo, and James M. Snyder, Jr. "Why is There so Little Money in U.S. Politics?" *The Journal of Economic Perspectives* 17 (2003): 105–30.

Apollonio, Dorie, Bruce E. Cain, and Lee Drutman. "Access and Lobbying: Looking Beyond the Corruption Paradigm." *Hastings Constitutional Law Quarterly* 36 (2008): 13–50.

Appleman, Eric M. "Print Advertising in the Health Care Reform Debate." *P2012.com*, April 4, 2010. http://www.p2012.org/2010/hcprint.html.

Arizona Governor Jan Brewer. "Offices and Appointments." Accessed September 1, 2011, http://azgovernor.gov/GOA.asp.

Asher, Herbert B., Eric S. Heberlig, Randall B. Ripley, and Karen Snyder. *American Labor Unions in the Electoral Arena.* Lanham, MD: Rowman and Littlefield, 2001.

ASME. "Advocacy and Government Relations." Accessed February 1, 2012, http://www.asme.org/about-asme/advocacy-government-relations.

Astor, Aaron. "Knee-Capping: Why the Club for Growth Does it (And Why It Will Never Work)." *The Moderate Voice*, April 28, 2009. Accessed January 21, 2012, http://themoderatevoice.com/30329/knee-capping-why-the-club-for-growth-does-it-and-why-it-will-never-work/.

Austen, Ben. "The U.S. vs. Rock 'n' Roll." *Bloomberg BusinessWeek* online. Accessed January 25, 2012, http://www.businessweek.com/magazine/the-us-vs-rock-n- roll-01192012, html on January 25, 2012,

Bachrach, Peter and Morton S. Baratz. "Two Faces of Power." *American Political Science Review* 56 (1962): 947–52.

Bartels, Larry R. *Unequal Democracy: The Political Economy of the New Gilded Age.* New York: Princeton University Press, 2008.

Bauer, Raymond A., Ithiel de Sola Pool, and Lewis A. Dexter. *American Business and Public Policy: The Politics of Foreign Trade.* New York: Atherton Press, 1963.

Baumgartner, Frank R. and Bryan D. Jones. *Agendas and Instability in American Politics.* Chicago: University of Chicago Press, 1993.

Baumgartner, Frank R. and Beth L. Leech. *Basic Interests: The Importance of Groups in Politics and in Political Science.* Princeton, NJ: Princeton University Press, 1998.

Baumgartner, Frank R. and Beth L. Leech. "Interest Niches and Policy Bandwagons: Patterns of Interest Group Involvement in National Politics." *Journal of Politics* 63 (2001): 1191–213.

Baumgartner, Frank R., Jeffrey M. Berry, Marie Hojnacki, David C. Kimball, and Beth L. Leech. *Lobbying and Policy Change: Who Wins, Who Loses and Why.* Chicago: University of Chicago Press, 2009.

Beam, Jim. "Pet Projects Never Really Disappear." *The Hayride.com*, May 5, 2011. Accessed January 19, 2012, http://thehayride.com/2011/05/pet-projects-never-really-disappear/.

Beck, Paul Allen. *Party Politics in America, 8th edition.* New York: Longman, 1997.

Bentley, Arthur Fisher. *The Process of Government: A Study of Social Pressures.* Chicago: University of Chicago Press, 1908.

Bergan, Daniel E. "Does Grassroots Lobbying Work? A Field Experiment Measuring the Effects of an e-Mail Lobbying Campaign on Legislative Behavior." *American Politics Research* 37 (2009): 327–52.

Berry, Jeffrey M. *Lobbying for the People: The Political Behavior of Public Interest Groups.* Princeton, NJ: Princeton University Press, 1977.

Berry, Jeffrey M. "Subgovernments, Issue Networks and Political Conflict." In *Remaking American Politics,* edited by Richard A. Harris and Sidney M. Milkis, 239–60. Boulder, CO: Westview Press, 1989.

Berry, Jeffrey M. *The New Liberalism: The Rising Power of Citizen Groups.* Washington, DC: Brookings Institution, 1999.

Berry, Jeffrey M. and Kent E. Portney. "Centralizing Regulatory Control and Interest Group Access: The Quayle Council on Competitiveness." In *Interest Group Politics, 4th edition,* edited by Allan J. Cigler and Burdett A. Loomis, 319–47. Washington, DC: CQ Press, 1995.

Berry, Jeffrey M. and Clyde Wilcox. *The Interest Group Society, 5th edition.* New York: Pearson Education, 2009.

Berry, Jeffrey M., Kent E. Portney, and Ken Thomson. *The Rebirth of Urban Democracy.* Washington, DC: Brookings Institution, 1993.

Bibby, John F. and Brian F. Schaffner. *Politics, Parties and Elections in America, 6th edition.* Boston: Thomson/Wadsworth, 2008.

Bingham, Amy and John Parkinson. "Houses Passes Bill Making Concealed Carry Permits Valid Across State Lines." *AbcNews* online, November 16, 2011. Accessed January 12, 2012, http://abcnews.go.com/blogs/politics/2011/11/houses-passes-bill-making-concealed-carry-permits-valid-across-state-lines/.

Birkland, Thomas A. *An Introduction to the Policy Process: Theories, Concepts and Models of Public Policy Making, 3rd edition.* Armonk, NY: M.E. Sharpe, 2011.

Bosso, Christopher J. "Rethinking the Concept of Membership in Nature Advocacy Organizations." *Policy Studies Journal* 31 (2003): 397–411.

Bowen, Debra, Secretary of State, ed. *The Lobbying Directory 2011–2012,* Sacramento: State of California, 2011.

Brady, Henry E., Kay Lehman Schlozman, and Sidney Verba. "Prospecting for Participants: Rational Expectations and the Recruitment of Political Activists." *American Political Science Review* 93 (1999): 153–68.

Briggs, Rex and Greg Stuart. *What Sticks: Why Most Advertising Fails and How to Guarantee Yours Succeeds.* Chicago: Kaplan Publishing, 2006.

Brown, Ruth Murray. *For a "Christian America": A History of the Religious Right.* Amherst, NY: Prometheus Books, 2002.

Browne, William P. "Policy and Interests: Instability and Change in a Classic Issue Subsystem." In *Interest Group Politics, 2nd edition,* edited by Allan Cigler and Burdett A. Loomis, 183–201. Washington, DC: CQ Press, 1986.

Browne, William P. "Organized Interests and Their Issue Niches: A Search for Pluralism in a Policy Domain." *Journal of Politics* 52 (1990): 477–509.

Browne, William P. *Cultivating Congress: Constituents, Issues and Interests in Agricultural Policymaking.* Lawrence: University Press of Kansas, 1995.

Browne, William P. and Allan J. Cigler, eds. *U.S. Agricultural Groups: Institutional Profiles.* Westport, CT: Greenwood Press, 1990.

Burbank, Matthew J., Ronald J. Hrebenar, and Robert C. Benedict. *Parties, Interest Groups and Political Campaigns, 2nd edition.* Boulder, CO: Paradigm, 2012.

Caldeira, Gregory A. and John R. Wright. "Organized Interests and Agenda Setting in the U.S. Supreme Court." *American Political Science Review* 82 (1988): 1109–127.

Cater, Douglas. *Power in Washington: A Critical Look at Today's Struggle to Govern in the Nation's Capital.* New York: Vintage Books, 1964.

Center for Responsive Politics. "Barack Obama." Accessed January 25, 2012, http://www.opensecrets.org/pres08/summary.php?cycle=2008&cid=N00009638.

Center for Responsive Politics. "Election Stats, 2010." Accessed September 9, 2011, http://www.opensecrets.org/bigpicture/elec_stats.php?cycle=2010.

Center for Responsive Politics. "John McCain." Accessed January 12, 2012, http://www.opensecrets.org/pres08/summary.php?cycle=2008&cid=N00006424.

Center for Responsive Politics. "Lobbying Database." Accessed March 3, 2012, http://www.opensecrets.org/lobby/.

Center for Responsive Politics. "Price of Admission." Accessed September 9, 2011, http://www.opensecrets.org/bigpicture/stats.php?cycle=2010.

Center for Responsive Politics. "Recipients: Every Republican is Crucial PAC Contributions to Federal Candidates." Accessed December 5, 2011, http://www.opensecrets.org/pacs/pacgot.php?cycle=2010&cmte=C00384701.

Center for Responsive Politics. "Revolving Door: Former Members of the 111th Congress." Accessed March 23, 2012, http://www.opensecrets.org/revolving/departing.php.

Center for Responsive Politics. "Super PACs." Accessed December 6, 2011, http://www.opensecrets.org/pacs/superpacs.php?cycle=2012,

Center for Responsive Politics. "The Money Behind the Elections." Accessed September 9, 2011, http://www.opensecrets.org/bigpicture/index.php.

Center for Responsive Politics. "Top Spenders, 2011." Accessed March 24, 2012, http://www.opensecrets.org/lobby/top.php?showYear=2011&indexType=s.

Chang, Jack. "Meg Whitman's Campaign Spending Totals $178.5 Million." *McClatchy.com*, January 2, 2011. Accessed September 9, 2011, http://www.mcclatchydc.com/2011/02/01/107827/meg-whitmans-campaign-spending.html.

"Check it Out: Big Salaries for Washington Lobbyists." *Washington Post* online, April 2, 2010. Accessed January 25, 2012, http://voices.washingtonpost.com/reliable-source/2010/04/check_it_out_big_salaries_for.html.

Chin, Michelle L. "Constituents Versus Fat Cats: Testing Assumptions about Congressional Access Decisions." *American Politics Research* 33 (2005): 751–86.

Choate, Pat. *Agents of Influence: How Japan Manipulates America's Political and Economic System.* New York: A.A. Knopf, 1990.

Chong, Dennis. *Collective Action and the Civil Rights Movement.* Chicago: University of Chicago Press, 1991.

Christian Coalition of America. "Voter Guide—Christian Coalition of America." Accessed December 5, 2011, www.cc.org/files/3/2008_Presidential_voter_guide_.pdf.

Chubb, John E. *Interest Groups and the Bureaucracy: The Politics of Energy.* Stanford, CA: Stanford University Press, 1983.

Cigler, Allan J. and Burdett A. Loomis. "Contemporary Interest Group Politics: More Than 'More of the Same.'" In *Interest Group Politics, 4th edition*, edited by Allan J. Cigler and Burdett A. Loomis, 393–406. Washington, DC: CQ Press, 1995.

Cigler, Allan J. and Burdett A. Loomis. "From Big Bird to Bill Gates: Organized Interests and the Emergence of Hyperpolitics." In *Interest Group Politics, 5th edition*, edited by Allan J. Cigler and Burdett A. Loomis, 389–403. Washington, DC: CQ Press, 1998.

Cigler, Allan J. and Burdett A. Loomis. "Stalemate Meets Uncertainty: Organized Interests in a Partisan Era." In *Interest Group Politics, 8th edition*, edited by Allan J. Cigler and Burdett A. Loomis, 377–89. Washington, DC: CQ Press, 2012.

City of Anaheim. "Welcome to the Government Relations Home Page." Accessed January 30, 2012, http://www.anaheim.net/sectionnew.asp?id=185.

Clark, Peter B. and James Q. Wilson. "Incentive Systems: A Theory of Organizations." *Administrative Science Quarterly* 6 (1961): 129–66.

Coalition for Patients' Rights. "About Us." Accessed February 14, 2011, http://www.patientsrightscoalition.org/About-Us.aspx.

Commons, John R., David J. Saposs, Helen L. Sumner, E.B. Mittelman, H.E. Hoagland, John B. Andrews, and Selig Perlman. *History of Labour in the United States*. New York: Macmillan, 1918.

Connors, Bill. *Fundraising with the Raiser's Edge: A Non-Technical Guide*. Hoboken, NJ: John Wiley and Sons, 2010.

Conservatives for Patients' Rights. "An Open Letter to President Obama." Accessed December 15, 2011, http://wonkroom.thinkprogress.org/wp-content/uploads/2009/03/cprad1.JPG.

Conway, M. Margaret. "PACs in the Political Process." In *Interest Group Politics, 3rd edition*, edited by Allan J. Cigler and Burdett A. Loomis, 199–216. Washington, DC: CQ Press, 1991.

Conway, M. Margaret and Joanne Connor Green. "Political Action Committees and the Political Process in the 1990s." In *Interest Group Politics, 4th edition*, edited by Allan J. Cigler and Burdett A. Loomis, 155–73. Washington, DC: CQ Press, 1995.

Cooper, Christopher A. and Anthony J. Nownes. "Money Well Spent? An Experimental Investigation of the Effects of Advertorials on Citizen Opinion." *American Politics Research* 32 (2004): 546–69.

Corrigan, Bryce and Ted Brader. "Campaign Advertising: Reassessing the Impact of Campaign Ads on Political Behavior." In *New Directions in Campaigns and Elections*, edited by Stephen K. Medvic, 79–97. New York: Routledge, 2011.

Cummings, Jeanne. "The Gilded Capital: Lobbying to Riches." *Politico.com*, June 26, 2007. Accessed February 1, 2012, http://www.politico.com/news/stories/0607/4652.html.

Dahl, Robert A. *Who Governs? Democracy and Power in an American City*. New Haven, CT: Yale University Press, 1961.

Dasgupta, Saibal. "Chinese Film Industry Races Close to Bollywood." *The Times of India* online, January 10, 2011. Accessed April 25, 2011, http://articles.timesofindia.indiatimes.com/2011-01-10/india/28358616_1_film-industry-chinese-film-chinese-movie.

David, Whitford. "How Scott Walker Ignited a Labor Renaissance." *CNNMoney*, March 7, 2011. Accessed January 24, 2012, http://management.fortune.cnn.com/2011/03/07/how-scott-walker-ignited-a-labor-renaissance/.

Davidson, Roger H., Walter J. Oleszek, and Frances Lee. *Congress and Its Members, 13th edition*. Washington, DC: CQ Press, 2012.

Daw, Jocelyne S. and Carol Cone, with Kristian Darigan Merenda and Anne Erhard. *Breakthrough Nonprofit Branding: Seven Principles to Power Extraordinary Results*. Hoboken, NJ: John Wiley and Sons, 2011.

DeGraw, David. "Political Bribery Watch: 79% of Former Members of Congress Have Become Lobbyists." *Daviddegraw.org*, July 25, 2011. Accessed September 15, 2011, http://daviddegraw.org/2011/07/political-bribery-watch-79-of-former-members-of-congress-have-become-lobbyists/.

DeGregorio, Christine A. *Networks of Champions: Leadership, Access and Advocacy in the U.S. House of Representatives*. Ann Arbor: University of Michigan Press, 1997.

DeGregorio, Christine and Jack E. Rossotti. "Campaigning for the Court: Interest Group Participation in the Bork and Thomas Confirmation Processes." In *Interest Group Politics, 4th edition*, edited by Allan J. Cigler and Burdett A. Loomis, 215–38. Washington, DC: CQ Press, 1995.

deKieffer, Donald E. *The Citizen's Guide to Lobbying Congress.* Chicago: Chicago Review Press, 2007.

Delli Carpini, Michael X. and Scott Keeter. *What Americans Know About Politics and Why It Matters.* New Haven, CT: Yale University Press, 1996.

Diamond, Edwin and Stephen Bates. *The Spot: The Rise of Political Advertising on Television,* 3rd edition. Cambridge, MA: MIT Press, 1992.

Dioquino, Rose-An Jessica. "Children Ask US Govt to Stop Deporting Undocumented Immigrants." *GMA News* online, December 13, 2011. Accessed January 2, 2012, http://www.gmanetwork.com/news/story/241537/pinoyabroad/children-ask-us-govt-to-stop-deporting-undocumented-immigrants.

Doan, Alesha E. *Opposition and Intimidation: The Abortion Wars and Strategies of Political Harassment.* Ann Arbor: University of Michigan Press, 2007.

Duvanova, Dinissa. "Bureaucratic Corruption and Collective Action: Business Associations in the Postcommunist Transition." *Comparative Politics* 39 (2007): 441–61.

Edwards, David V. and Alessandra Lippucci. *Practicing American Politics: An Introduction to Government.* New York: Worth Publishers, 1998.

Eggen, Dan. "The Influence Industry: Coming Soon to a Screen Near You—A Lobbying Campaign." *The Washington Post* online, July 13, 2011. Accessed December 16, 2011, http://www.washingtonpost.com/politics/the-influence-industry-coming-soon-to-a-screen-near-you—a-lobbying-campaign/2011/07/13/gIQAFyK9CI_story.html.

Eisler, Kim. "Hired Guns: The City's 50 Top Lobbyists." *The Washingtonian Magazine* online, June 1, 2007. Accessed January 30, 2012, http://www.washingtonian.com/articles/mediapolitics/4264.html.

Emily's List. "Ways to Give." Accessed January 25, 2012, http://emilyslist.org/action/ways_to_give/.

Encyclopedia of Associations: National Organizations of the United States, 50th edition. Detroit, MI: Gale Cengage Learning, 2011.

Encyclopedia of Associations: Regional, State and Local Organizations, 22nd edition. Detroit, MI: Gale Cengage Learning Gale, 2010.

Epstein, Lee and C.K. Rowland. "Interest Groups in the Courts: Do Groups Fare Better?" In *Interest Group Politics, 2nd edition,* edited by Allan J. Cigler and Burdett A. Loomis, 275–88. Washington, DC: Congressional Quarterly Press, 1986.

"Exit Polls." *CNN.com,* 2008. Accessed January 10, 2012, http://www.cnn.com/ELECTION/2008/results/polls/#USP00p1.

Exxon Mobil. "An Amazing Resource for Americans. A Responsible Way to Produce It." *Washington Post* online, May 23, 2011. Accessed December 14, 2011, http://www.washingtonpost.com/rw/WashingtonPost/Content/Epaper/2011-05-23/Ax7.pdf.

FAOSTAT, Food and Agriculture Organization of the United Nations. "Crops." Accessed April 22, 2011, http://faostat.fao.org/site/567/DesktopDefault.aspx?PageID=567#ancor.

Farnam, T.W. "Revolving Door of Employment Between Congress, Lobbying Firms, Study Shows." *The Washington Post* online, September 13, 2011. Accessed January 3, 2012, http://www.washingtonpost.com/politics/study-shows-revolving-door-of-employment-between-congress-lobbying-firms/2011/09/12/gIQAxPYROK_story.html.

Federal Election Commission. "2008 Presidential Campaign Finance, Contributions to All Candidates." Accessed February 3, 2012, http://www.fec.gov/disclosurep/pnational.do;jsessionid=F46FB44FEB006545EC904E92A6731C2D.worker1.

Federal Election Commission. "Committee (C00109017) Summary Reports, 2009–2010 Cycle." Accessed January 9, 2012, http://query.nictusa.com/cgi-bin/cancomsrs/?_10+ C00109017.

Federal Election Commission. "Contribution Limits 2011–12." Accessed December 5, 2011, http://www.fec.gov/pages/brochures/contriblimits.shtml.

Federal Election Commission. "Coordinated Communications and Independent Expenditures." Accessed January 9, 2012, http://www.fec.gov/pages/brochures/ indexp.shtml#Who_IE.

Federal Election Commission. "Coordinated Communications and Independent Expenditures." Accessed January 9, 2012, http://www.fec.gov/pages/brochures/ indexp.shtml#Who_IE.

Federal Election Commission. "Growth in PAC Financial Activity Slows." Accessed January 21, 2012, http://www.fec.gov/press/press2009/20090415PAC/20090424PAC.shtml.

Federal Election Commission. "PAC Activity Increases in First Six Months of 2011." Accessed February 3, 2012, http://www.fec.gov/press/Press2011/20110909_6mthPAC. shtml.

Federal Election Commission. "PAC Activity Remains Steady in 2009." Accessed April 10, 2011, http://www.fec.gov/press/press2010/20100406PAC.shtml.

Federal Election Commission. "PAC Count, 1974—present." Accessed February 1, 2012, http://www.fec.gov/press/summaries/2011/2011paccount.shtml.

Federal Election Commission. "PAC Count, 1974 to Present." Accessed April 1, 2012, http://www.fec.gov/press/summaries/2011/2011paccount.shtml.

Federal Election Commission. "Pacronyms." Accessed January 25, 2012, http://www.fec. gov/pubrec/pacronyms/pacronyms.shtml.

Federal Election Commission. "Summary of PAC Activity, 1990–2010." Accessed January 25, 2012, http://www.fec.gov/press/bkgnd/cf_summary_info/2010pac_fullsum/ 4sumhistory2010.pdf.

Federal Election Commission. "Summary of PAC Financial Activity." Accessed December 8, 2011, http://www.fec.gov/press/press2010/20100406Pary_Files/1pac2009.pdf.

Federal Election Commission. "Table 6: PACs Grouped by Total Spent, 2009–2010." Accessed January 3, 2012, http://www.fec.gov/press/bkgnd/cf_summary_info/ 2010pac_fullsum/6groupbyspending2010.pdf.

Federal Election Commission. "Table 9, Top 50 PACs By Disbursements January 1, 2009–December 31, 2010." Accessed January 25, 2011, http://www.fec.gov/press/ bkgnd/cf_summary_info/2010pac_fullsum/9top50pacdisbursements2010.pdf.

Ferman, Barbara. *Challenging the Growth Machine: Neighborhood Politics in Chicago and Pittsburgh*. Lawrence: University Press of Kansas, 1996.

Fesler, James William and Donald F. Kettl. *The Politics of the Administrative Process*. Chatham, NJ: Chatham House, 1991.

Fiorina, Morris P. *Retrospective Voting in American National Elections*. New Haven, CT: Yale University Press, 1981.

Fitch, Brad and Kathy Goldschmidt, with Ellen Fulton and Nicole Griffin. "Communicating with Congress: How Capitol Hill is Coping with the Surge in Citizen Advocacy." Accessed December 15, 2011, http://www.congressfoundation.org/index.php?option =com_content&view=article&id=67&Itemid= .

Fleischmann, Arnold and Carol A. Pierannunzi. "Citizens, Development Interests and Local Land-Use Regulation." *Journal of Politics* 52 (1990): 838–53.

The Ford Foundation. "Grants Database." Accessed June 17, 2011, http://www.ford foundation.org/grants/search.

Foreman, Jr., Christopher H. "Grassroots Victim Organizations: Mobilizing for Personal and Public Health." In *Interest Group Politics, 4th edition,* edited by Allan J. Cigler and Burdett A. Loomis, 33–53. Washington, DC: CQ Press, 1995.

The Foundation Center. "Resources and Training." Accessed January 30, 2011, http://foundationcenter.org/focus/economy/resources.html.

Freeman, J. Leiper. *The Political Process: Executive Bureau–Legislative Committee Relations.* Garden City, NY: Doubleday, 1955.

Frendreis, John P. and Richard W. Waterman. "PAC Contributions and Legislative Behavior: Senate Voting on Trucking Deregulation." *Social Science Quarterly* 66 (1985): 401–12.

Fritschler, A. Lee. *Smoking and Politics: Policy Making and the Federal Bureaucracy, 4th edition.* Englewood Cliffs, NJ: Prentice Hall, 1989.

Fuhrmans, Vanessa. "Harry and Louise are Back. Again." *WSJ Blogs* online, July 16, 2009. Accessed December 16, 2011, http://blogs.wsj.com/health/2009/07/16/harry-and-louise-are-back-again/.

Furlong, Scott R. "Exploring Interest Group Participation in Executive Policymaking." In *The Interest Group Connection: Electioneering, Lobbying and Policymaking in Washington, 2nd edition,* edited by Paul S. Herrnson, Ronald G. Shaiko, and Clyde Wilcox, 282–97. Chatham, NJ: Chatham House, 1998.

Galloway, Jim. "The Myth of the 15,000." *Atlanta Journal Constitution* online, April 27, 2009. Accessed January 5, 2012, http://blogs.ajc.com/political-insider-jim-galloway/.

Gallup Poll. "Abortion." Accessed December 16, 2011, http://www.gallup.com/poll/1576/abortion.aspx.

Gallup Poll. "Death Penalty." Accessed May 23, 2011, http://www.gallup.com/poll/1606/death-penalty.aspx.

Gallup Poll. "Major Institutions." Accessed February 3, 2011, http://www.pollingreport.com/institut.htm.

Gaventa, John. *Power and Powerlessness: Quiescence and Rebellion in an Appalachian Valley.* Urbana: University of Illinois Press, 1980.

Geer, John and Richard R. Lau. "Filling in the Blanks: A New Method for Estimating Campaign Effects." *British Journal of Political Science* 36 (2006): 269–90.

General Services Administration, U.S. Government. "Catalogue of Federal Domestic Assistance." Accessed February 1, 2012, https://www.cfda.gov/.

Giles, Michael W. and Marilyn K. Dantico. "Political Participation and Neighborhood Social Context Revisited." *American Journal of Political Science* 26 (1982): 144–50.

Gimpel, James G. "Grassroots Organizations and Equilibrium Cycles in Group Mobilization and Access." In *The Interest Group Connection: Electioneering, Lobbying and Policymaking in Washington,* edited by Paul S. Herrnson, Ronald G. Shaiko, and Clyde Wilcox, 100–15. Chatham, NJ: Chatham House, 1998.

Gleeck, L.E. "96 Congressmen Make Up Their Minds." *Public Opinion Quarterly* 4 (1940): 3–24.

Godwin, R. Kenneth. *One Billion Dollars of Influence: The Direct Marketing of Politics.* Chatham, NJ: Chatham House, 1988.

Godwin, R. Kenneth. "Money, Technology and Political Interests: The Direct Marketing of Politics." In *The Politics of Interests: Interest Groups Transformed,* edited by Mark P. Petracca, 308–25. Boulder, CO: Westview Press, 1992.

Goldstein, Kenneth M. *Interest Groups, Lobbying and Participation in America*. New York: Cambridge University Press, 1999.

Golembiewski, Robert T. "'The Group Basis of Politics': Notes on Analysis and Development." *American Political Science Review* 54 (1960): 962–71.

Goodnow, Frank Johnson. *Politics and Administration: A Study in Government*. New York: Macmillan, 1900.

Goodsell, Charles T. *The Case for Bureaucracy: A Public Administration Polemic, 2nd edition*. Chatham, NJ: Chatham House, 1985.

Grasse, Nathan and Brianne Heidbreder. "The Influence of Lobbying Activity in State Legislatures: Evidence from Wisconsin." *Legislative Studies Quarterly* 36 (2011): 567–89.

Gray, Virginia and David Lowery. "The Diversity of State Interest Group Systems." *Political Research Quarterly* 46 (1993): 81–97.

Gray, Virginia and David Lowery. "The Institutionalization of State Communities of Organized Interests." *Political Research Quarterly* 54 (2001): 265–84.

Grenzke, Janet. "Shopping in the Congressional Supermarket: The Currency is Complex." *American Journal of Political Science* 33 (1989): 1–24

Grey, Lawrence. *How to Win a Local Election: A Complete Step-by-Step Guide, 3rd edition*. Lanham, MD: National Book Network, 2007.

Griffith, Ernest S. *Impasse of Democracy: A Study of the Modern Government in Action*. New York: Harrison-Hilton Books, 1939.

Groppe, Maureen. "House Votes to Block Funds to Planned Parenthood." *AzCentral.com*, February 18, 2011. Accessed February 21, 2011, http://www.azcentral.com/news/articles/2011/02/18/20110218house-blocks-planned-parenthood-money18-ON.html.

Hall, Richard L. and Richard Anderson. "Issue Advertising and Legislative Advocacy in Health Politics." In *Interest Group Politics, 8th edition*, edited by Allan J. Cigler and Burdett A. Loomis, 221–42. Washington, DC: CQ Press, 2012.

Hall, Richard L. and Alan Deardorff. "Lobbying as Legislative Subsidy." *American Political Science Review* 100 (2006): 69–84.

Hall, Richard L. and Frank W. Wayman. "Buying Time: Moneyed Interests and the Mobilization of Bias in Congressional Committees." *American Political Science Review* 84 (1990): 797–820.

Hamburger, Tom and Julia Love. "Gulf Disaster a Boon to Washington Lobbying." *Los Angeles Times* online, July 21, 2010. Accessed February 4, 2011, http://articles.latimes.com/2010/jul/21/nation/la-na-oil-lobby-20100722.

Hansen, John Mark. *Gaining Access: Congress and the Farm Lobby, 1919–1981*. Chicago: University of Chicago Press, 1991.

Harris, Richard A. *Coal Firms Under the New Social Regulation*. Durham, NC: Duke University Press, 1985.

Harris, Richard A. "Politicized Management: The Changing Face of Business in American Politics." In *Remaking American Politics*, edited by Richard A. Harris and Sidney M. Milkis, 261–86. Boulder, CO: Westview Press, 1989.

Hart, Thomas. "California Plastic Bag Ban Defeated by Plastic Industry Lobbyists." *Personal Money Store, Personal Money Network Blog*, September 1, 2010. Accessed February 23, 2011, http://personalmoneystore.com/moneyblog/2010/09/01/california-plastic-bag-ban/.

Heaney, Michael T. "Bridging the Gap between Political Parties and Interest Groups." In *Interest Group Politics, 8th edition*, edited by Allan J. Cigler and Burdett A. Loomis, 194–218. Washington, DC: CQ Press, 2012.

Heclo, Hugh. "Issue Networks and the Executive Establishment." In *The New American Political System*, edited by Anthony King, 87–124. Washington, DC: American Enterprise Institute, 1978.

Heinz, John P., Edward O. Laumann, Robert L. Nelson, and Robert H. Salisbury. *The Hollow Core: Private Interests in National Policy Making.* Cambridge, MA: Harvard University Press, 1993.

The Heritage Foundation. "The Heritage Foundation 2010 Annual Report: Solutions for America." Washington, DC: The Heritage Foundation, 2011.

Herring, Pendleton E. *Group Representation before Congress.* Baltimore, MD: Johns Hopkins Press, 1929.

Hershey, Marjorie Randon. "Direct Action and the Abortion Issue: The Political Participation of Single-issue Groups." In *Interest Group Politics, 2nd edition*, edited by Allan J. Cigler and Burdett A. Loomis, 27–45. Washington, DC: CQ Press, 1986.

Hershey, Marjorie Randon. *Party Politics in America, 12th edition.* New York: Pearson Longman, 2007.

Hirschman, Albert O. *Exit, Voice and Loyalty: Responses to Decline in Firms, Organizations and States.* Cambridge, MA: Harvard University Press, 1970.

Hojnacki, Marie and David C. Kimball. "PAC Contributions and Lobbying Contacts in Congressional Committees." *Political Research Quarterly* 54 (2001): 161–80.

"How to Become a Lobbyist." *Degreefinders.com.* Accessed March 26, 2011, http://www.degreefinders.com/education-articles/careers/how-to-become-a-lobbyist.html.

Hula, Kevin. *Lobbying Together: Interest Group Coalitions in Legislative Politics.* Washington, DC: Georgetown University Press, 1999.

Human, Daniel. "Postal Service: $3M in Cuts for Kokomo." *Insurancenews.net*, November 29, 2011. Accessed December 16, 2011, http://insurancenewsnet.com/article.aspx?id=304395.

Hyman, Herbert and Charles Wright. "Trends in Voluntary Association Memberships of American Adults: Replication Based on Secondary Analysis of National Sample Surveys." *American Sociological Review* 36 (1971): 191–206.

Igan, Deniz, Prachi Mishra, and Thierry Tressel. *A Fistful of Dollars: Lobbying and the Financial Crisis.* Washington, DC: International Monetary Fund, 2009.

Initiative and Referendum Institute at University of Southern California. "Information on the Initiative and Referendum Process at the Local Level." Accessed December 4, 2011, http://www.iandrinstitute.org/Local%20I&R.htm.

Initiative and Referendum Institute at University of Southern California. "Initiative Use." Accessed December 4, 2011, http://www.iandrinstitute.org/IRI%20Initiative%20Use%20(2010-1).

Initiative and Referendum Institute at University of Southern California. "State-by-State List of Initiative and Referendum Provisions." Accessed December 4, 2011, http://www.iandrinstitute.org/statewide_i&r.htm.

Initiative and Referendum Institute at University of Southern California. "What are Ballot Propositions, Initiatives and Referendums?" Accessed December 14, 2011, http://www.iandrinstitute.org/Quick%20Fact%20-%20What%20is%20I&R.htm#Initiatives.

International Brotherhood of Teamsters. "About us." Accessed April 4, 2011, http://www.teamster.org/content/fast-facts.

Iyengar, Shanto. *Media Politics: A Citizen's Guide, 2nd edition.* New York: W.W. Norton, 2011.

Jacobson, Gary C. *The Politics of Congressional Elections, 8th edition.* Upper Saddle River, NJ: Pearson, 2012.

Jenkins, J. Craig. *The Politics of Insurgency: The Farm Worker Movement in the 1960s*. New York: Columbia University Press, 1985.

John D. and Catherine T. MacArthur Foundation. "Human Rights and International Justice: Recent Grants." Accessed June 17, 2011, http://www.macfound.org/site/c.lkLXJ8MQ KrH/b.938985/k.7091/International_Grantmaking__Human_Rights_and_International _Justice__Recent_Grants.htm.

Johnson, Paul E. "Interest Group Recruiting: Finding Members and Keeping Them." In *Interest Group Politics, 5th edition*, edited by Allan J. Cigler and Burdett A. Loomis, 35–62. Washington, DC: CQ Press, 1998.

Johnson, Paul E., Gary J. Miller, John H. Aldrich, David W. Rohde, and Charles W. Ostrom, Jr. *American Government: People, Institutions and Politics, 3rd edition*. Boston: Houghton Mifflin, 1994.

Johnson, Paul Edward. "Organized Labor in an Era of Blue-Collar Decline." In *Interest Group Politics, 3rd edition*, edited by Allan J. Cigler and Burdett A. Loomis, 33–61. Washington, DC: CQ Press, 1991.

Johnston, Lori. "Q: How Many Letters Does the President Receive Daily?" *Atlanta Journal Constitution* online, December 30, 2009. Accessed December 15, 2011, http://www. ajc.com/news/q-how-many-letters-262394.html.

Jones, Jeffrey M. "Lobbyists Debut at Bottom of Honesty and Ethics List: Nurses Again Perceived as Having Highest Honesty and Ethical Standards." Accessed February 4, 2011, http://www.gallup.com/poll/103123/lobbyists-debut-bottom-honesty-ethics-list.aspx.

Jones Jr., Woodrow and K. Robert Keiser. "Issue Visibility and the Effects of PAC Money." *Social Science Quarterly* 68 (1987): 170–76.

Jordan, Grant and William A. Maloney. *Democracy and Interest Groups: Enhancing Participation?* London: Palgrave Macmillan, 2007.

Joyce, Ed. "Calif. Enviro Groups Urge Passage of Plastic Bag Bill." *KPBS.com*, June 1, 2010. Accessed February 24, 2011, http://www.kpbs.org/news/2010/jun/01/calif-enviro-groups-urge-passage-plastic-bag-bill/.

Kateb, George. "The Value of Association." In *Freedom of Association*, edited by Amy Gutmann, 35–63. Princeton, NJ: Princeton University Press, 1998.

Kaufmann, Karen M., John R. Petrocik, and Daron R. Shaw. *Unconventional Wisdom: Facts and Myths About American Voters*. New York: Oxford University Press, 2008.

Keefe, William J. *Parties, Politics and Public Policy in America, 7th edition*. Washington, DC: CQ Press, 1994.

Kersh, Rogan. "Corporate Lobbyists as Political Actors: A View from the Field." In *Interest Group Politics, 6th edition*, edited by Allan J. Cigler and Burdett A. Loomis, 225–48. Washington, DC: CQ Press, 2002.

Kerwin, Cornelius M. *Rulemaking: How Government Agencies Write Law and Make Policy, 3rd edition*. Washington, DC: CQ Press, 2003.

Kerwin, Cornelius M. "Interest Group Participation in Rule-Making: A Decade of Change," *Journal of Public Administration Research and Theory* 15 (2005): 353–70.

Kiewiet, D. Roderick. *Macroeconomics and Micropolitics: The Electoral Effects of Economic Issues*. Chicago: University of Chicago Press, 1983.

Kimball, David C. "Interest Groups in the 2008 Presidential Election: The Barking Dog That Didn't Bite." *The Forum* 6 (2008): Article 2.

King, James D. and Helenan S. Robin. "Political Action Committees in State Elections." *American Review of Politics* 16 (1995): 61–77.

Kingdon, John W. *Congressmen's Voting Decisions, 2nd edition*. New York: Harper and Row, 1981.

Klein, Kim. *Fundraising for Social Change, 5th edition, revised and expanded*. San Francisco: John Wiley and Sons, 2007.

Kilff, Sarah. "Mike Pence's War on Planned Parenthood." *Politico.com*, February 16, 2011. Accessed July 12, 2011, http://www.politico.com/news/stories/0211/49609.html

Kollman, Ken. *Outside Lobbying: Public Opinion and Interest Group Strategies*. Princeton, NJ: Princeton University Press, 1998.

Kousser, Thad and Justin H. Phillips. "The Roots of Executive Power." Working paper, 2010. Accessed January 12, 2012, www.columbia.edu/~jhp2121/workingpapers/RootsOfExecutivePower.pdf.

Langbein, Laura I. "Money and Access: Some Empirical Evidence." *Journal of Politics* 48 (1986): 1052–62.

Latham, Earl. *The Group Basis of Politics: A Study in Basing-Point Legislation*. Ithaca, NY: Cornell University Press, 1952.

Lau, Richard R., Lee Sigelman, Caroline Heldman, and Paul Babbitt. "The Effects of Negative Political Advertisements: A Meta-Analytic Assessment." *American Political Science Review* 93 (1999): 851–75.

Levine, Bertram J. *The Art of Lobbying: Building Trust and Selling Policy*. Washington, DC: CQ Press, 2009.

Light, Paul. *The President's Agenda: Domestic Policy Choice from Kennedy to Clinton, 3rd edition*. Baltimore, MD: Johns Hopkins University Press, 1999.

Linn, Allison. "Big Employers Dip Into Health Care Debate: Hoping to Rein in Costs, Some are Taking a Stand on Health Care Reform." *MSNBC.com*, August 25, 2009. Accessed January 24, 2012, www.msnbc.msn.com/id/32513127/ns/business-us_business/t/big-employers-dip-health-cre-debate/#.Tx7JEJJ-L9k.

Lister, Gwyneth J. *Building Your Direct Mail Program*. San Francisco: Jossey-Bass, 2001.

The Lobbying Directory 2011–2012, Sacramento: State of California, 2011.

Loomis, Burdett A. and Allan J. Cigler. "Introduction: The Changing Nature of Interest Group Politics." In *Interest Group Politics, 8th edition*, edited by Allan J. Cigler and Burdett A. Loomis, 1–34. Washington, DC: CQ Press, 2012.

Loomis, Burdett A. and Eric Sexton. "Choosing to Advertise: How Interests Decide." In *Interest Group Politics, 4th edition*, edited by Allan J. Cigler and Burdett A. Loomis, 193–214. Washington, DC: CQ Press, 1995.

McDonald, Michael. "2008 General Election Turnout Rates." Accessed March 22, 2012, http://elections.gmu.edu/Turnout_2008G.html.

McFarland, Andrew S. *Common Cause: Lobbying in the Public Interest*. Chatham, NJ: Chatham House, 1984.

McGann, James G. "Academics to Ideologues: A Brief History of the Public Policy Research Industry." *PS* 25 (1992): 733–40.

McGrath, Conor, ed. *Interest Groups and Lobbying in Latin America, Africa, the Middle East and Asia: Essays on Drug Trafficking, Chemical Manufacture, Exchange Rates and Women's Interests*. Lewiston, NY: Edwin Mellen Press, 2009.

McGrath, Conor, ed. *Interest Groups and Lobbying in Europe: Essays on Trade, Environment, Legislation and Economic Development*. Lewiston, NY: Edwin Mellen Press, 2009.

McGrath, Conor. "The Ideal Lobbyist: Personal Characteristics of Effective Lobbyists." *Journal of Communication Management* 10 (2006): 67–79.

McKay, Amy. "Negative Lobbying and Policy Outcomes." *American Politics Research* 40 (2012): 116–46.

Mackenzie, G. Calvin and Robert Shogan. *Obstacle Course: The Report of the Twentieth Century Fund Task Force on the Presidential Appointment Process with Background Papers.* New York: Twentieth Century Fund Press, 1996.

Madison, James. "Federalist #10: The Utility of the Union as a Safeguard Against Domestic Faction and Insurrection (continued)." *Constitution.org.* Accessed February 5, 2011, http://www.constitution.org/fed/federa10.htm.

"Madison Protests Hit Largest Numbers on Saturday." *Huffington Post*, February 19, 2009. Accessed December 15, 2011, http://www.huffingtonpost.com/2011/02/19/madison-protests_n_825616.html.

Mann, Thomas E. *The Negative Impact of the Use of Filibusters and Holds.* Washington, DC: Brookings Institution Press, 2010.

Marquez, Benjamin. "Mexican–American Political Organizations and Philanthropy: Bankrolling a Social Movement." *Social Service Review* 77 (2003): 329–46.

Maryland State Board of Elections. "Maryland PACs List." Accessed October 13, 2011, http://www.elections.state.md.us/campaign_finance/pac_list.html.

Maxwell, Carol J.C. *Pro-Life Activists in America: Meaning, Motivation and Direct Action.* New York: Cambridge University Press, 2002.

Mayer, Jane and Jill Abramson. *Strange Justice: The Selling of Clarence Thomas.* Boston: Houghton Mifflin, 1994.

Mayer, Jane. "Covert Operations: The Billionaire Brothers Who Are Waging a War Against Obama." *The New Yorker* online, August 20, 2010. Accessed January 25, 2012, http://www.newyorker.com/reporting/2010/08/30/100830fa_fact_mayer?currentPage=all.

Mayhew, David R. *Congress: The Electoral Connection.* New Haven, CT: Yale University Press, 1974.

Media Matters for America. "Conservative Transparency: The Money Behind the Movement." Accessed June 17, 2011, http://mediamattersaction.org/p/contact_us.

Merry, Melissa K. "Emotional Appeals in Environmental Group Communications." *American Politics Research* 38 (2010): 862–89.

Michaels, Judith E. *The President's Call: Executive Leadership from FDR to George Bush.* Pittsburgh, PA: University of Pittsburgh Press, 1997.

Michels, Robert. *Political Parties: A Sociological Study of the Oligarchical Tendencies of Modern Democracy.* New York: Collier Books, 1962.

Milbrath, Lester W. *The Washington Lobbyists.* Chicago: Rand McNally, 1963.

Milbrath, Lester W. *Political Participation: How and Why Do People Get Involved in Politics?* Chicago: Rand McNally, 1965.

Mills, C. Wright. *The Power Elite.* New York: Oxford University Press, 1956.

Mitchell, Robert Cameron. "National Environmental Lobbies and the Apparent Illogic of Collective Action." In *Collective Decision Making: Applications from Rational Choice Theory,* edited by Clifford S. Russell, 87–123. Baltimore, MD: Johns Hopkins University Press, 1979.

Mohan, Geoffrey. "Wood protection law creates splintering in guitar industry." *Bangor News* online, January 25, 2012. Accessed January 25, 2012, http://bangordailynews.com2012/01/25/business/wood-protection-law-creates-splintering-in-guitar-industry/.

Moore, Stephen, Sidney M. Wolfe, Deborah Lindes, and Clifford Douglas. "Epidemiology of Failed Tobacco Control Legislation." *Journal of the American Medical Association* 272 (1994): 1171–73.

Mundo, Philip A. *Interest Groups: Cases and Characteristics.* Chicago: Nelson-Hall Publishers, 1992.

National Alliance of State and Territorial AIDS Directors. "About NASTAD." Accessed April 25, 2011, http://nastad.org/.

National Association of Realtors. "Facebook: National Association of Realtors, Government Affairs Division." Accessed January 29, 2011, http://www.facebook.com/nargovernmentaffairs.

National Conference of State Legislatures. "State Limits on Contributions to Candidates, 2011–2012 Election Cycle." Accessed December 6, 2012, http://www.ncsl.org/Portals/1/documents/legismgt/Limits_to_Candidates_2011-2012,pdf.

National Directory of Corporate Public Affairs, 2011. Bethesda, MD: Columbia Books, 2011.

National Education Association. "About NEA." Accessed February 14, 2011, http://www.nea.org/home/2580.htm.

National Education Association. "Our Leaders." Accessed February 1, 2012, http://www.nea.org/home/609.htm.

National Election Study, University of Michigan, Center for Political Studies. "Is the Government Run for the Benefit of All, 1964–2008." Accessed January 12, 2012, http://electionstudies.org/nesguide/toptable/tab5a_2.htm.

National Election Study, University of Michigan, Center for Political Studies. "Party Identification 7-Point Scale (revised in 2008) 1952–2008." Accessed January 12, 2012, http://www.electionstudies.org/nesguide/toptable/tab2a_1.htm.

National Institute on Money in State Politics. "Home > Iowa 2010 > Lobbyists." Accessed April 26, 2011, http://www.followthemoney.org/database/StateGlance/state_lobbyists.phtml?s=IA&y=2010.

National Institute on Money in State Politics. "Home > Montana 2010 > Lobbyists." Accessed April 25, 2011, http://www.followthemoney.org/database/StateGlance/state_lobbyists.phtml?s=MT&y=2010.

National Institute on Money in State Politics. "Home > Texas 2010 > Lobbyists." Accessed January 25, 2012, http://www.followthemoney.org/database/StateGlance/state_lobbyists.phtml?s=TX&y=2010.

National Institute on Money in State Politics. "Lobbyist Map 2009, Total Lobbyists for 2009." Accessed April 27, 2011, www.followthemoney.org/database/graphs/lobbyistlink/lobbymap.phtml?p=0&y=2009&l=0.

National Directory of Trade and Professional Associations of the United States, 2011, 46th edition. Bethesda, MD: Columbia Books, 2011.

Naughton, Keith, Celeste Schmid, Susan Webb Yackee, and Xueyong Zhan. "Understanding Commenter Influence During Agency Rule Development." *Journal of Policy Analysis and Management* 28 (2009): 258–77.

Neuman, W. Russell. *The Paradox of Mass Politics: Knowledge and Opinion in the American Electorate.* Cambridge, MA: Harvard University Press, 1986.

Nevada Secretary of State, Ross Miller. "Political Action Committee Registration List." Accessed October 31, 2011, http://nvsos.gov/PacReport/.

"New High of 46% of Americans Support Legalizing Marijuana." *Gallup Politics*, October 28, 2010. Accessed February 1, 2012, http://www.gallup.com/poll/144086/new-high-americans-support-legalizing-marijuana.aspx.

Newman, Richard S. *The Transformation of American Abolitionism: Fighting Slavery in the Early Republic*. Chapel Hill: University of North Carolina Press, 2002.

Nicholson-Crotty, Jill and Sean Nicholson-Crotty. "Industry Strength and Immigrant Policy in the American States." *Political Research Quarterly* 64 (2011): 612–24.

North Carolina Coalition for Lobbying Reform. "Coalition Members." Accessed June 30, 2011, http://www.nclobbyreform.org/about/members.php.

Nownes, Anthony J. "The Population Ecology of Interest Group Formation: Mobilizing for Gay and Lesbian Rights in the United States, 1950–98." *British Journal of Political Science* 34 (2004): 49–67.

Nownes, Anthony J. *Total Lobbying: What Lobbyists Want (and How They Try to Get It)*. New York: Cambridge University Press, 2006.

Nownes, Anthony J. and Allan J. Cigler. "Corporate Philanthropy in a Political Fishbowl: Perils and Possibilities." In *Interest Group Politics, 5th edition*, edited by Allan J. Cigler and Burdett A. Loomis, 63–82. Washington, DC: CQ Press, 1998.

Nownes, Anthony J. and Allan J. Cigler. "Big Money Donors to Environmental Groups: What They Give and What They Get." In *Interest Group Politics, 7th edition*, edited by Allan J. Cigler and Burdett A. Loomis, 108–29. Washington, DC: CQ Press, 2007.

Nownes, Anthony J. and Patricia Freeman. "Interest Group Activity in the States." *Journal of Politics* 60 (1998): 86–112.

Nownes, Anthony J. and Patricia K. Freeman. "Female Lobbyists: Women in the World of 'Good ol' Boys'." *Journal of Politics* 60 (1998): 1181–201.

Nownes, Anthony J. and Adam Newmark. "Interest Groups in the States." In *Politics in the American States: A Comparative Analysis, 10th edition*, edited by Virginia Gray, Russell L. Hanson, and Thad Kousser. Washington, DC: CQ Press, 2012.

Nownes, Anthony J. and Grant Neeley. "Public Interest Group Entrepreneurship and Theories of Group Mobilization." *Political Research Quarterly* 49 (1996): 119–46.

Nownes, Anthony J. and Krissy Walker DeAlejandro. "Lobbying in the New Millennium: Evidence of Continuity and Change in Three States." *State Politics and Policy Quarterly* 9 (2009): 429–55.

"The NRA's Electoral Influence." *Washington Post* online, December 15, 2010. Accessed December 5, 2011, http://www.washingtonpost.com/wp-srv/special/nation/guns/nra-endorsements-campaign-spending/.

Nuckolls, C. Randall. "Compliance and Disclosure Under the Honest Leadership and Open Government Act of 2007." July 14, 2008. Accessed November 1, 2011, http://government.fiu.edu/docs/FIU_Lobbying_Disclosure_Workshop_-_July_14__2008.pdf.

"Occupy Wall Street: A Protest Timeline." *The Week*, November 21, 2011, Accessed December 15, 2011, http://theweek.com/article/index/220100/occupy-wall-street-a-protest-timeline.

Odegard, Peter H. *Pressure Politics: The Story of the Anti-Saloon League*. New York: Columbia University Press, 1928.

Office of the Clerk, House of Representatives. "Lobbying Disclosure Act Guidance." Accessed October 28, 2011, http://lobbyingdisclosure.house.gov/amended_lda_guide.html.

Office of Management and Budget, Executive Office of the President of the United States. "Fiscal Year 2012, Historical Tables, Budget of the U.S. Government." Accessed January 3, 2012, http://www.gpoaccess.gov/usbudget/fy12/hist.html.

Olson, Mancur. *The Logic of Collective Action: Public Goods and the Theory of Groups*. Cambridge, MA: Harvard University Press, 1965.

Orren, Karen. "Standing to Sue: Interest Group Conflict in the Federal Courts." *American Political Science Review* 70 (1976): 723–41.

"PAC Spending at Record High in Massachusetts Politics." *The Patriot Ledger* online, September 23, 2011. Accessed October 18, 2011, http://www.patriotledger.com/answerbook/hull/x372774989/PAC-spending-at-record-high-in-Massachusetts-politics.

Palmer, Anna. "BP's Influence in Washington Fades." *CNNMoney.com*, June 16, 2010. Accessed February 5, 2011, http://money.cnn.com/2010/06/16/news/companies/BP_lobbying_Washington.fortune/index.htm.

Petersen, R. Eric, Parker H. Reynolds, and Amber Hope Wilhelm. *House of Representatives and Senate Staff Levels in Member, Committee, Leadership and Other Offices, 1977–2010*. Washington, DC: Congressional Research Service, 2010.

Petracca, Mark P. "The Rediscovery of Interest Group Politics." In *The Politics of Interests: Interest Groups Transformed*, edited by Mark P. Petracca, 3–31. Boulder, CO: Westview Press, 1992.

The Pew Forum on Religion and Public Life. *U.S. Religious Landscape Survey, Religious Affiliation: Diverse and Dynamic*. Washington, DC: The Pew Forum on Religion and Public Life, 2008.

"Pharmaceutical Companies Offer $80 Billion Toward Health Care Reform." *PBSNewsHour* online, June 22, 2009. Accessed January 24, 2012, www.pbs.oeg/newshour/updates/health/jan-june09/pharma_06-22.html.

Pika, Joseph A. "The White House Office of Public Liaison." *Presidential Studies Quarterly* 39 (2009): 549–73.

"Political Campaign Media Spend to Reach All-Time High of $4.5 Billion in '08." *Marketing Charts.com*, December 6, 2007. Accessed January 30, 2012, http://www.marketingcharts.com/television/political-campaign-media-spend-to-reach-all-time-high-of-45-billion-in-08-2643/.

Posner, Richard. "The U.S. Tax Subsidies for Oil Companies—Posner." *The Becker–Posner blog*, May 15, 2011. Accessed January 27, 2012, http://www.becker-posner-blog.com/2011/05/the-us-tax-subsidies-for-oil-companiesposner.html.

Postman, Neil. *Amusing Ourselves to Death: Public Discourse in the Age of Show Business*. New York: Viking Penguin Books, 1985.

Purvis, Jonathan D. "Telephone Solicitation." In *Achieving Excellence in Fundraising, 3rd edition*, edited by Eugene R. Tempel, Timothy L. Seiler, and Eva E. Aldrich, 256–67. San Francisco: Jossey-Bass, 2011.

Reilly, Ryan J. "Shadow Congress: Nearly 200 Ex-Lawmakers Work for Lobbying Shops." *Talkingpointsmemo.com*, June 14, 2011. Accessed February 1, 2012, http://tpmmuckraker.talkingpointsmemo.com/2011/06/shadow_congress_nearly_200_ex-lawmakers_work_for_lobbying_shops.php.

Rich, Andrew. *Think Tanks, Public Policy and the Politics of Expertise*. New York: Cambridge University Press, 2004.

Ridout, Travis N. and Michael M. Franz. *The Persuasive Power of Campaign Advertising*. Philadelphia, PA: Temple University Press, 2011.

Riker, William H. *Liberalism Against Populism: A Confrontation Between the Theory of Democracy and the Theory of Social Choice*. San Francisco: W.H. Freeman, 1982.

Ritsch, Massie and Courtney Mabeus. "Casting Off Jack Abramoff." Accessed December 8, 2011, http://www.opensecrets.org/news/2006/04/casting-off-abramoff.html.

Ronayn, Kathleen. "OpenSecrets.org Unveils 2010 'Big Picture' Analysis." Accessed January 4, 2012, http://www.opensecrets.org/news/2011/07/2010-election-big-picture.html.

Roscoe, Douglas D. and Shannon Jenkins. "A Meta-Analysis of Campaign Contributions' Impact on Roll Call Voting." *Social Science Quarterly* 86 (2005): 52–68.

Rose, Melody. *Safe, Legal and Unavailable? Abortion Politics in the United States*. Washington, DC: CQ Press, 2007.

Rosenstone, Steven J. and John Mark Hansen. *Mobilization, Participation and Democracy in America*. New York: Macmillan, 1993.

Rosenthal, Alan. *The Third House: Lobbyists and Lobbying in the States*. Washington, DC: CQ Press, 1993.

Rosenthal, Alan. *The Third House: Lobbyists and Lobbying in the States, 2nd edition*. Washington, DC: CQ Press, 2001.

Rothenberg, Lawrence S. "Putting the Puzzle Together: Why People Join Public Interest Groups." *Public Choice* 60 (1989): 241–57.

Rothenberg, Lawrence S. *Linking Citizens to Government: Interest Group Politics at Common Cause*. New York: Cambridge University Press, 1992.

Rubenzer, Trevor. "Campaign Contributions and U.S. Foreign Policy Outcomes: An Analysis of Cuban American Interests." *American Journal of Political Science* 55 (2011): 105–16.

Sabato, Larry and Glenn R. Simpson. *Dirty Little Secrets: The Persistence of Corruption in American Politics*. New York: Times Books, 1996.

Sailer, Steve. "The Five Billion Dollar Election." *UPI.com*, November 6, 2000. Accessed January 26, 2012, http://www.isteve.com/2000_Five_Billion_Dollar_Election.htm.

Salisbury, Robert H. "An Exchange Theory of Interest Groups." *Midwest Journal of Political Science* 13 (1969): 1–32.

Salisbury, Robert H. "Interest Representation: The Dominance of Institutions." *American Political Science Review* 78 (1984): 64–76.

Salisbury, Robert H. "The Paradox of Interest Groups in Washington: More Groups, Less Clout." In *The New American Political System*, 2nd version, edited by Anthony King, 203–29. Washington, DC: AEI Press, 1990.

Sanbonmatsu, Kira. "Political Parties and the Recruitment of Women to State Legislatures." *Journal of Politics* 64 (2002): 791–809.

Sanbonmatsu, Kira. "The Legislative Party and Candidate Recruitment in the American States." *Party Politics* 12 (2006): 233–56.

Schaper, W.A. "What Do Students Know About American Government, Before Taking College Courses in Political Science?: A Report to the Section on Instruction in Political Science." *Proceedings of the American Political Science Association* 2 (1905): 207–28.

Schattschneider, E.E. *The Semisovereign People: A Realist's View of Democracy in America*. New York: Holt, Rinehart and Winston, 1960.

Scherer, Nancy, Brandon L. Bartels, and Amy Steigerwalt. "Sounding the Fire Alarm: The Role of Interest Groups in the Lower Federal Court Confirmation Process." *Journal of Politics* 70 (2008): 1026–39.

Schlozman, Kay Lehman and John T. Tierney. "More of the Same: Washington Pressure Group Activity in a Decade of Change." *Journal of Politics* 45 (1983): 351–77.

Schmitt, Bertel. "Top 40 Automobile Manufacturing Countries, 2010." *The Truth About Cars.com*, March 22, 2011. Accessed April 22, 2011, http://www.thetruthaboutcars.com/2011/03/top-40-automobile-manufacturing-countries-2010/.

Schulman, Daniel. "Bonner's Latest Astroturf Admission (Plus More Fake Letters)." *Mother Jones* online, Aug. 18, 2009. Accessed December 21, 2011, http://motherjones.com/mojo/2009/08/bonners-latest-astroturf-admission.

Schumaker, Paul and Russell W. Getter. "Structural Sources of Unequal Responsiveness to Group Demands in American Cities." *Western Political Quarterly* 36 (1983): 7–29.

Scotch, Richard K. *From Good Will to Civil Rights: Transforming Federal Disability Policy.* Philadelphia, PA: Temple University Press, 1984.

Scott, Andrew M. and Margaret A. Hunt. *Congress and Lobbies: Image and Reality.* Chapel Hill: University of North Carolina Press, 1966.

Sethuraman, Raj, Gerard J. Tellis, and Richard. A. Briesch. "How Well Does Advertising Work? Generalizations from Meta-Analysis of Brand Advertising Elasticities." *Journal of Marketing Research* 48 (2011): 457–71.

Shaiko, Ronald G. "Lobbying in Washington: A Contemporary Perspective." In *The Interest Group Connection: Electioneering, Lobbying and Policymaking in Washington*, edited by Paul S. Herrnson, Ronald G. Shaiko, and Clyde Wilcox, 3–18. Chatham, NJ: Chatham House, 1998.

Shaiko, Ronald G. "Making the Connection: Organized Interests, Political Representation and the Changing Rules of the Game in Washington Politics." In *The Interest Group Connection: Electioneering, Lobbying and Policymaking in Washington, 2nd edition*, edited by Paul S. Herrnson, Ronald G. Shaiko, and Clyde Wilcox, 1–24. Chatham, NJ: Chatham House, 1998.

Shaw, Donny. "The Vast Majority of Bills Go Nowhere." Accessed August 30, 2011, http://www.opencongress.org/articles/view/1180-The-Vast-Majority-of-Bills-Go-Nowhere.

Shelley, Fred M., J. Clark Archer, Fiona M. Davidson, and Stanley D. Brunn. *Political Geography of the United States.* New York: Guilford Press, 1996.

Sierra Club. "Board of Directors: 2011 Election." Accessed February 1, 2012, http://www.sierraclub.org/bod/2011election/default.aspx.

Sierra Club Foundation. "Partnerships for the Planet: The Sierra Club Foundation Annual Report." San Francisco: Sierra Club Foundation, 2009.

Slansky, Paul. *The Little Quiz Book of Big Political Sex Scandals.* New York: Simon and Schuster, 2009.

Smith, Aaron, Kay Lehman Schlozman, Sidney Verba, and Henry Brady. *The Internet and Civic Engagement.* Washington, DC: Pew Research Center, 2010.

Smith, Richard A. "Interest Group Influence in the U.S. Congress." *Legislative Studies Quarterly* 20 (1995): 89–139

Sochart, Elise A. "Agenda Setting, the Role of Groups and the Legislative Process: The Prohibition of Female Circumcision in Britain." *Parliamentary Affairs* 41 (1988): 508–26.

Sorauf, Frank J. *Inside Campaign Finance: Myths and Realities.* New Haven, CT: Yale University Press, 1992.

Sorauf, Frank J. "Adaptation and Innovation in Political Action Committees." In *Interest Group Politics, 4th edition*, edited by Allan J. Cigler and Burdett A. Loomis, 175–92. Washington, DC: CQ Press, 1995.

Sparshott, Jeffrey. "House Lawmakers Set Hearing on AARP's Insurance, Advocacy Efforts." *Wall Street Journal* online, March 25, 2011. Accessed April 4, 2011, http://online.wsj.com/article/BT-CO-20110325-710474.html.

Stanger, Jeff. "E-Mail and Internet Solicitation." In *Achieving Excellence in Fundraising, 3rd edition*, edited by Eugene R. Tempel, Timothy L. Seiler, and Eva E. Aldrich, 308–25. San Francisco: Jossey-Bass, 2011.

State of Pennsylvania, Tom Corbett, Governor. "Offices and Commissions." Accessed September 1, 2012, http://www.portal.state.pa.us/portal/server.pt/community/offices_and_commissions/2996.

Steiner, Keenan. "Fundraisers as Elemental as Breakfast." *Party Time*, January 10, 2011. Accessed November 1, 2011, http://blog.politicalpartytime.org/2011/01/10/fundraisers-as-elemental-as-breakfast/.

Stratmann, Thomas. "Can Special Interests Buy Congressional Votes? Evidence from Financial Services Legislation." *Journal of Law and Economics* 45 (2002): 345–73.

Stratton, David H. *Tempest over Teapot Dome: The Story of Albert B. Fall*. Norman: University of Oklahoma Press, 1998.

Stucka, Mike. "Reichert, Paris Had Expensive Winning Campaigns." *Macon.com*, August 26, 2011. Accessed September 9, 2011, http://www.macon.com/2011/08/26/1678375/reichert-paris-had-expensive-winning.html.

Susman, Thomas M. "Honest Leadership and Open Government Act of 2007: Changes to Lobbying Disclosure Act (LDA)." Presentation, September 27, 2007. http://www.alldc.org/publicresources/documents/susman_S_1_handout.pdf.

Taborek, Nick. "Brownley Pushes for Statewide Plastic Bag Ban." *SMDP.com*, June 2, 2010. Accessed February 24, 2011, http://www.smdp.com/Articles-c-2010-06-02-69726.113116.

Texans for Public Justice. "Texas PACs: 2010 Election Cycle Spending." Accessed October 18, 2011, http://info.tpj.org/reports/pdf/PACs2010.pdf.

Texas Ethics Commission. *2011 List of Registered Lobbyists with Employers/Clients (EMP/C), Sorted by Lobbyist Name*. Austin: State of Texas, Texas Ethics Commission 2011. Accessed June 23, 2011, http://www.ethics.state.tx.us/tedd/2011_Lobby_List_by_Lobbyists.pdf.

Thompson, Margaret Susan. *The "Spider Web": Congress and Lobbying in the Age of Grant*. Ithaca, NY: Cornell University Press, 1985.

Thrall, A. Trevor. "The Myth of the Outside Strategy: Mass Media News Coverage of Interest Groups." *Political Communication* 23 (2006): 407–20.

Thurber, James A., Candice J. Nelson, and David A. Dulio. *Crowded Airwaves: Campaign Advertising in Elections*. Washington, DC: Brookings Institution, 2000.

Tichenor, Daniel J. and Richard A. Harris. "Organized Interests and American Political Development." *Political Science Quarterly* 117 (2002/03): 587–612.

Tichenor, Daniel J. and Richard A. Harris. "The Development of Interest Group Politics in America: Beyond the Conceits of Modern Times." *Annual Review of Political Science* 8 (2005): 251–70.

Toovey, Leia Michele. "The Top 10 Copper Producing Countries." *International Business Times* online, November 18, 2010. Accessed April 25, 2011, http://www.ibtimes.com/articles/83306/20101118/the-top-10-copper-producing-countries.htm.

Trent, Logan Douglas. *The Credit Mobilier*. New York: Arno Press, 1981.

Truman, David Bicknell. *The Governmental Process: Political Interests and Public Opinion, 2nd edition*. New York: Knopf, 1971.

U.S. Bureau of the Census. *Historical Statistics of the United States, Colonial Times to 1970*. Washington, DC: Government Printing Office, 1976.

U.S. Census Bureau. "2010 Census Shows America's Diversity." Accessed April 22, 2011, http://2010.census.gov/news/releases/operations/cb11-cn125.html.

U.S. Census Bureau. "Census of Governments." Accessed May 13, 2011, http://www2.census.gov/govs/cog/2002COGprelim_report.pdf.

U.S. Chamber of Commerce. "About the U.S. Chamber of Commerce." Accessed February 11, 2011, http://www.uschamber.com/about.

U.S. Chamber of Commerce. "Facebook: Untitled Wall Post." Accessed December 21, 2011, http://www.facebook.com/uschamber?sk=wall.

U.S. Chamber of Commerce. "Untitled Wall Post." Accessed December 21, 2011, http://www.facebook.com/uschamber?sk=wall.

U.S. Office of Personnel Management. "Total Government Employment Since 1962." Accessed September 1, 2011, http://www.opm.gov/feddata/HistoricalTables/Total GovernmentSince1962.asp.

United Auto Workers. "Departments Under the International President." Accessed February 1, 2012, http://www.uaw.org/node/276.

Verba, Sidney, Kay Lehman Schlozman, and Henry E. Brady. *Voice and Equality: Civic Voluntarism in American Politics.* Cambridge, MA: Harvard University Press, 1995.

"The Voluntary Way is the American Way." Chicago: American Medical Association National Education Campaign, 1949.

Walker, Jack L. "The Origins and Maintenance of Interest Groups in America." *American Political Science Review* 77 (1983): 390–406.

Walker, Jack L., Jr. *Mobilizing Interest Groups in America: Patrons, Professions and Social Movements.* Ann Arbor: University of Michigan Press, 1991.

Washington Representatives, Spring 2011, 39th edition. Washington, DC: Columbia Books, 2011.

Wawro, Gregory. "A Panel Probit Analysis of Campaign Contributions and Roll-Call Votes." *American Journal of Political Science* 45 (2001): 563–79.

Weaver, R. Kent. "The Changing World of Think Tanks." *PS* 3 (1989): 563–78.

Welch, W.P. "Campaign Contributions and Legislative Voting: Milk Money and Dairy Price Supports." *Western Political Quarterly* 35 (1982): 478–95.

West, Darrell M., Diane Heith, and Chris Goodwin. "Harry and Louise Go to Washington: Political Advertising and Health Care Reform." *Journal of Health Politics, Policy and Law* 21 (1996): 35–68.

Westboro Baptist Church. "God Hates Fags." Accessed February 1, 2012, http://www.godhatesfags.com.

Wilcox, Clyde. "The Dynamics of Lobbying the Hill." In *The Interest Group Connection: Electioneering, Lobbying and Policymaking in Washington,* edited by Paul S. Herrnson, Ronald G. Shaiko, and Clyde Wilcox, 89–99. Chatham, NJ: Chatham House, 1998.

Will, George. "Too Much Ado About Campaign Spending." *Billings Gazette* online, October 19, 2010. Accessed January 3, 2012, http://billingsgazette.com/news/opinion/editorial/columnists/george_will/article_06e69f86-db26-11df-a862-001cc4c03286.html#ixzz1iQF8ZkNt.

William-Ross, Lindsay. "Rap or Run: Going Door to Door for Greenpeace in LA." *Laist,* September 3, 2007. Accessed December 15, 2011, http://laist.com/2007/09/03/rap_or_run_goin.php.

Wilson, James Q. *Political Organizations.* Princeton, NJ: Princeton University Press, 1995 [1974].

Wilson, Woodrow. *Congressional Government: A Study in American Politics.* Boston: Houghton Mifflin, 1885.

Winters, Michael Sean. *God's Right Hand: How Jerry Falwell Made God a Republican and Baptized the American Right*. New York: HarperOne, 2012.

Wisch, Rebecca F. "Overview of the Lacey Act (16 U.S.C. SS 3371–3378)." American Legal and Historical Center, Michigan State University School of Law. Accessed January 25, 2012, http://www.animallaw.info/articles/ovuslaceyact.htm.

Witko, Christopher. "PACs, Issue Context and Congressional Decision-making." *Political Research Quarterly* 59 (2006): 283–95.

Woliver, Laura R. "Abortion Interests: From the Usual Suspects to Expanded Coalitions." In *Interest Group Politics, 5th edition*, edited by Allan J. Cigler and Burdett A. Loomis, 327–42. Washington, DC: CQ Press, 1998.

Wood, Daniel B. "California Set to Ban Plastic Bags." *Christian Science Monitor* online, August 30, 2010. Accessed February 24, 2011, http://www.csmonitor.com/Environment/2010/0830/California-set-to-ban-plastic-bags.

"The World's Billionaires: #23 Michael Bloomberg." *Forbes* online. Accessed September 9, 2011, http://www.forbes.com/lists/2010/10/billionaires-2010_Michael-Bloomberg_C610.html.

World Steel Organization. "World Crude Steel Output Increases by 15% in 2010." Accessed April 25, 2011, http://www.worldsteel.org/?action=newsdetail&id=319.

Worth, Richard. *Teetotalers and Saloon Smashers: The Temperance Movement and Prohibition*. Berkeley Heights, NJ: Enslow, 2009.

Wright, John R. "Contributions, Lobbying and Committee Voting in the U.S. House of Representatives." *American Political Science Review* 84 (1990): 417–38.

Wright, John R. *Interest Groups and Congress: Lobbying, Contributions and Influence*. Boston: Allyn and Bacon, 1996.

Wyant, Rowena. "Voting Via the Senate Mailbag." *Public Opinion Quarterly* 5 (1941): 359–82.

Yackee, Jason Webb and Susan Webb Yackee. "A Bias Towards Business? Assessing Interest Group Influence on the U.S. Bureaucracy." *Journal of Politics* 68 (2006): 128–39.

Zuckerman, Alan S. and Darrell M. West. "The Political Bases of Citizen Contacting: A Cross-National Analysis." *American Political Science Review* 79 (1985): 117–31.

Index